To

John Hadley,

All the best,

from

Steve Harle

CRIMINAL SENTENCES

CRIMINAL SENTENCES

true crime in fiction and drama

STEVE HASTE

cygnus arts

PUBLISHED IN THE UNITED KINGDOM BY
Cygnus Arts, a division of Golden Cockerel Press
16 Barter Street
London
WC1A 2AH

First published 1997

ISBN 1 900541 25 4

BRITISH LIBRARY CATALOGUING-IN-PUBLICATION DATA

Haste, Steve
  Criminal Sentences : true crime in fiction and drama
  1.Crime in literature 2.Crime writing
  I.Title
  809.9'3355

ISBN 1900541254

PRINTED BY BOOKCRAFT (BATH) LIMITED IN THE UNITED KINGDOM

CONTENTS

ACKNOWLEDGEMENTS

As this is the first full-length study of fiction and drama based on true crimes and criminals, I had to devise a short, snappy name for the genre. After due consideration, I settled for 'crime faction', knowing full well that some readers will object to my use of a term that carries a more specific connotation. In the introduction that follows, I give my reasons for using this term, and offer guidelines that I intend to follow in including and excluding specific publications.

Regarding acknowledgements, I must state that this book is a tribute, not only to the literary genre it investigates, but to the British library service in general, and the one corner of it in particular where I work—Birmingham Libraries. From the stock of Birmingham Central Library's reference collection, I have found most of the background material on the crimes, criminals, authors and texts covered in this study. What little Birmingham itself didn't hold was obtained for me by the Library's Inter-Lending section. The inter-library loan facility, whereby a library can obtain a published work from any other library nationally (or even internationally) for a modest sum, is one of the unsung benefits of the public library service. My eternal thanks to the staff of Inter-Lending for all their efforts.

I have received nothing but encouragement from the staff of both reference departments that I worked in while I was researching this book—the Arts, Languages and Literature section and (my present 'home') the Social Sciences section of the Central Library. You couldn't hope to meet a more supportive bunch of colleagues. Many thanks to them, and to my fellow-workers in other parts of Birmingham Libraries.

Crime writer Paul Woods read the book in its original form, and was kind enough to suggest improvements and to indicate several cases and works that I had overlooked. My thanks to him.

Several booksellers have helped me build my own collection of crime faction. Anyone interested in crime, factual or fictional, cannot but applaud the existence of Murder One bookshop in Charing Cross Road, London. They have been a useful source for books-in-print on crime faction. Several second-hand and antiquarian booksellers have assisted me in tracking down out-of-print items. Chief among these have been Ralph Spurrier of Post-Mortem Books, Don Ireland of A1 Crime Fiction and R. Andrews of The Barn (their addresses can be found in *Sheppard's Book Dealers in the British Isles*). In America, Grant and Maureen Thiessen of Pandora Books in Neche, North Dakota have been instrumental in obtaining a number of US imprints that would otherwise have passed me by.

I would like to thank the following for permission to reproduce copyright material from the works identified here: Oxford University Press for *The Oxford English Dictionary* and A. N. Wilson's *Laird of Abbotsford*; Routledge for Frank McLynn's *Crime and Punishment in Eighteenth-Century England*; Addison Wesley Longman Ltd. for Gary Kelly's *English Fiction of the*

Romantic Period; Keith Heller and Headline for Heller's *Man's Loving Family*; and the estate of Julian Symons for Symons's *Bloody Murder*.

My special thanks are reserved for my immediate family who have all been tremendously supportive over the past few years—and beyond. Particularly, my father and mother who, over the last couple of weeks while I've been using my father's word processor, must have thought I'd moved back home for good! My love and gratitude to them as always.

CRIMINAL SENTENCES

INTRODUCTION: CRIME FACTION – THE GENRE

I will begin with a definition of the term which will be used for the genre to be discussed—'crime faction'—and its scope in the present work. 'Faction' is defined by the *Oxford English Dictionary* as 'a literary genre in which fictional narrative is developed from a basis of real events or characters'; or as 'documentary fiction'. The word originated, according to the *OED*, back in the mid-sixties; a surprisingly recent term for a genre which, as I will illustrate, has been around for centuries. Crime faction is therefore, by extension, a fictional narrative based on criminal events and characters. For the purposes of the present study, I have taken the liberty of including drama within the scope of 'fictional narrative'; after all, what is a play but an adaptation of words and deeds to the false (or fictional) environment of the stage? A play makes no pretence to be fact, no matter what basis it has in reality, and can therefore logically be included in the field.

As for the scope of the genre, the first reaction might be to view crime faction as merely a sub-genre of the crime fiction field. A glance through the crime faction works listed in this book will show that to be an over-simplification. True, crime fiction is represented, but so too are historical fiction, social fiction, melodrama, farce, even science fiction. The crime element, important though it is, can often be subverted in favour of historical content, humour, romance, character delineation, or a hundred other facets of the plot, according to the author's whim. So the scope of the field is dictated to a certain extent by the degree of importance that the author places on the crime. The less vital to the plot the crime becomes, the more diverse can be the genres of fiction covered. It could be argued that crime faction must by necessity rely heavily on the facts that form its basis. But the original *OED* definition gives no such limitation to the field—as long as the basis is there, one might interpret the chosen genre as broadly or as narrowly as desired.

This degree of faithfulness to facts within crime faction results in discernible sub-divisions of the field. Firstly, there is a group of crime faction authors who go to great pains to situate their work in reality. Recent or historical events will be related meticulously, names and details retained intact, dates and locations strictly adhered to. The fictional element in these publications is minimal. Perhaps the only invention in the plot is the author's attempts to penetrate a character's feelings or thoughts. The domestic tragedies which form the origins of the genre (see the history of crime faction that follows) are cases in point. Often the division between fact and fiction is so blurred that we have only the author's word that a work is not non-fiction. Should, for example, Truman Capote's 'non-fiction novel', *In Cold Blood*, be included in the present survey?[1]

There is a second category of works which most readers would readily

---

1. For the purpose of discussing the fine line between crime faction and non-fiction crime writing, I have included Capote's 'novel'.

admit as crime faction. These are writings still heavily indebted to the facts—names, locations and period will remain unchanged, unusual features will still be retained. The writer, however, will take greater licence than in the first category. Facts may be considered from one character's perspective to give a keenly subjective interpretation of the action. The author may introduce a fictional character or two to provide a fresh stance, a new or unusual motive, an unforeseen impetus to events, or merely to comment on the action. The main point is that the author is accepting greater freedom to provide a vision of the crime—or even a solution to a factually unsolved crime—that would appear speculative in the extreme in a non-fiction work. Examples of this second group are the factional works of Philip Lindsay and John Cashman (see the index), and many of the fictional reworkings of the Jack the Ripper case.

The third category of crime faction deals with works in which the names of genuine characters have been altered, in which locations may be changed, in which even the time of events may not match those of the original case. This decision usually stems from the author's desire to distance the work from its basis, perhaps to allow freedom of experiment without earning a frown from the knowing reader. It can also be essential, particularly with contemporary crimes, if the author wishes to avoid a libel action. The reader cannot always take at face value an author's disclaimer that a book has any basis in truth. F. Tennyson Jesse's denial of a factual source for her novel, *A Pin to See the Peepshow* (1934), is a case in point. Ms. Jesse had to bear in mind that the relatives of Edith Thompson and Frederick Bywaters—whose murder trial formed the background of her plot—were very much alive at the time of its publication.

The fourth group encompasses works where the plot is merely 'suggested' by a criminal case or character. Here fiction will predominate over fact, liberties will be taken with the source, maybe only one facet of a crime will be presented in a totally imaginary tale. It is often difficult to identify these works, particularly if the writer declines to acknowledge a basis in truth. The reader can only rely on observant reviewers.

For the purposes of the present investigation, I have taken the liberty of including several borderline publications that have been inspired by genuine crimes or criminals but have little in common with their source. This is a different category from the previous ones, where the basis—whether implicit or overt—can still be ascertained by the reader. In this latter category we *must* rely on the author's admission of a plot's genesis. Take, for example, the inspiration that Thomas Hardy drew from attending the hanging of Elizabeth Martha Brown in 1856. The sights and sounds of that day and that event stayed with the author throughout his life, and he relived them, as he readily admitted himself, when he created the character of Tess Durbeyfield later in his literary career.[2] Like Tess, Elizabeth had murdered a

---

2. See Robert Gittings's *Young Thomas Hardy* (London: William Heinemann, 1975), pp. 32–34.

man, but there the similarity ends. And yet it is doubtful whether Hardy would have published *Tess of the D'Urbervilles* in 1891—or have made her pathetic story so engaging—had he not experienced the execution of Elizabeth Brown all those years before. Similarly, Aldous Huxley wrote his short story, 'The Gioconda Smile' (1922), after reading the dissimilar case of Harold Greenwood. Poison and adultery are the only common factors between the tale and its source (in fact, one author assumed that Huxley drew his inspiration from the Armstrong poisoning case of 1922—see the entry for the latter crime in the main body of this book). Had the author not acknowledged the influence of the Greenwood trial on his 'thrice-told tale', no-one would have been any the wiser.[3] And yet once again the work might not have existed had Huxley not read the facts of the genuine case.

Just as varied as the categories of crime faction are the reasons why an author is writing the work; why, in effect, he is using factual details of a true crime at all. In the first category examined above, where details, names, etc. are retained religiously, it could be said that the writer is merely introducing the facts to a new audience. This was particularly the case with the domestic tragedies mentioned above. The plays were intended, to a certain extent, as moral edification for the 'groundlings', the lower-middle and working-classes that made up the basic audiences of the early theatre; it was assumed that these people weren't in the position to read the facts in current broadsheets or pamphlets.

Other authors might turn to a case with the purpose of discovering *why* such a crime was committed. To quote Keith Heller: 'History is necessary—it is where we start from—but it is never the same as story. It can tell us what happened, but it can only rarely tell us why'.[4] Looking at one of the classics of the genre, Meyer Levin's 1956 novel, *Compulsion*, we see that the author's prime concern is to attempt an understanding of what drove two students to commit such a horrifying crime as that perpetrated by Leopold and Loeb in 1920s Chicago. The author uses contemporary psychoanalytical theories to accomplish this, investigating the murder within a Freudian framework.

This is definitely a useful *modus operandi* for viewing crimes where the culprits are known. However, just as Levin attempted to provide a reason for the crime he was investigating—a 'whydunit', if you like—so other authors will use the genre to give a solution to an unsolved crime, without the strictures of non-fiction writing—a 'whodunit'. A glance through the main entries of this book will show that two of the most popular sources for crime faction are the cases of Jack the Ripper and William Wallace—both technically unsolved. Crime faction provides the writer with the flexibility to posit a variety of solutions to factual mysteries. However strong the author's factual basis, because he or she is defining the work as fiction, the scope of speculation allowed is broader—and is acceptable as such.

3. 'Mr Huxley Discusses his Thrice-Told Tale', *New York Times* (1 October 1950).
4. See the Preface to Keith Heller's *Man's Loving Family* (London: Collins, 1986).

This demonstrates a noticeable link between the field of crime faction and detective fiction. Here, I am following Julian Symons's distinction between 'detective fiction' and 'crime fiction' as outlined in his book, *Bloody Murder* (1972). Briefly, Symons sees detective fiction as based heavily on a puzzle element (a 'deception' as he calls it), whereas crime fiction relies on the psychology of characters. As we have seen above, crime faction can fall into either category. The solution of unsolved factual crimes, however, is more akin to the works of Agatha Christie and Dorothy L. Sayers than that of Meyer Levin. The prime ingredient in these works is the unmasking of the criminal, rather than the reasoning behind the crime.

Reviewing the crime factions of Walter Scott and Charles Dickens, one can see that, important as the crime element is in their work, there are other factors that take precedence. Crime is used here to spice the fiction, to make it more accessible to the reader, to retain the interest and whet the appetite. This is particularly true of works in the field which one might regard as historical fiction. It is almost as if the author is using the contemporary reader's interest in crime to show a link between past and present. Another example of this trend is the practice of transposing a historical crime to an alternative period, such as Josephine Tey did with the Elizabeth Canning case, or Francis King with that of Constance Kent. *Plus ça change*, the author is saying in effect, *plus c'est la même chose*.

And so the degree of reliance upon the facts alter, as do the genres covered by crime faction. We have moved on considerably from a view of crime faction as merely a sub-field of crime fiction itself. Its scope is as broad as the intentions of the writers themselves. And why should the reader be amazed? If crime is universal and complex in structure, we should not be surprised if its fictional—or factional—counterpart is likewise many-faceted.

CRIME FACTION – THE GUIDELINES

The scope of crime faction as outlined above will be that of the present book. However, with so large a field, it has been necessary to decide on specific guidelines for the inclusion or exclusion of material. I have concerned myself with three forms of literature: novels, plays and short stories. Foreign works have been included if they have at some time been translated into English (the translation noted is not necessarily the first, but rather an acceptable one). I have rejected cases where I have been unable to discover sufficient details about the original crime or criminal to provide a source. Therefore, for example, the murder committed by Fortunée Auphante in 1861 in France that formed the basis for Emile Zola's novel and play, *Thérèse Raquin* (novel published in 1887) has had to be—reluctantly—excluded; as has the French crime that A. E. W. Mason used as the inspiration for his detective thriller, *At The Villa Rose* (1910).

I have included cases which are no longer regarded as criminal, although they were at the time. Isobel Walker, whose fate formed the basis of Sir Walter Scott's *The Heart of the Midlothian* (1818), would not appear in court nowadays, but her story appears in this study. Libel cases have been included on the basis that, at one time, libel was a criminal offence (today it is dealt with in the civil courts). This has enabled me to outline interesting cases such as the Leon Uris libel trial, which would otherwise have been omitted.

Likewise, I have included many cases which purists would not expect to see within this work. Surely the Archer-Shee case was not a criminal one? True—but it did concern the guilt or innocence of a boy accused of theft. How can Starr Faithfull be included, when it is still debated whether her death was murder or suicide? My reply is that the case is still on the books of the New York Police Department as unsolved. If I have erred in my judgement, it has been on the basis of inclusion (and possible argument) rather than exclusion.

As for the works that have been excluded, I have omitted several broad categories of crime due to limitations of space. Thus, factional works covering gangsters, organised crime, Western outlaws and Australian bush rangers have had to be overlooked. Similarly, the modern cult of serial killer faction—which began in earnest when Robert Bloch used the Ed Gein case of 1957 for his classic 1959 novel, *Psycho*—will not be considered in the present volume. I hope to return to these areas in a subsequent book.

Regicides, political assassinations and (most) state trials have been left out; the field of historical fiction is strewn with the bodies of beheaded kings, mortally-wounded presidents and political and religious martyrs. Some particular types of publication have been rejected as well. Victorian penny dreadfuls are out, as are most items in periodical fiction (short stories or other short works are included because of their publication in book form, either independently or in a collection). The one or two exceptions to this rule have been included on the basis of literary merit, or mention in an important work of criminology.

In dealing with the Jack the Ripper factions—a field that has received separate coverage elsewhere[5]—I have followed one guideline. Unlike Alexander Kelly who, in his Ripper bibliography, included modern murders based on the Ripper's 'style', I have dealt only with works featuring an historical Jack, or Victorian murderers in fiction who are obvious representations of this infamous, anonymous character. This has still enabled me to include a few science fiction entries with time-travelling Victorian Rippers that are regarded as classics in the genre, such as Robert Bloch's short story on the subject (see index).

Entries in the main body of the text are arranged in alphabetical order by the name of the criminal in most cases, followed by the date of the criminal's

---

5. Alexander Kelly: *Jack the Ripper: a bibliography and review of the literature* (London: Association of Assistant Librarians, 1973).

trail, or, failing that, of the crime itself. Where a trial has resulted in no conviction, the entry is distinguished by the word 'case' after the name of the individual tried (e.g. 'Lizzie Borden Case', 'William H. Wallace Case'). In homicides where no one was brought to trial, the entry is distinguished by the word 'murder' after the name of the victim (e.g. 'Rosemary Nitribitt Murder'). If the case is better known under another name ('Black Dahlia' rather than 'Elizabeth Short'), preference is given to that popular denomination.

In each entry, the basic facts of the case are outlined. These are followed by a discussion of the fictional works based on those facts. The bibliographic details of the fictional works are listed after the entry itself. I have indicated playscripts with a (**p**). This listing is followed by a reference to a non-fictional work giving a more complete account of the crime or criminal concerned, for those who wish to pursue the facts further. As readers will notice, I have not automatically chosen the latest publication on a case. Where there are several choices for such as work—the Jack the Ripper and Crippen cases are obvious examples—I have chosen a source that I consider to present a comprehensive and balanced view of events. This will of necessity be a subjective decision.

Many of the crime faction works featured in this survey have been filmed. Also, in a few cases, a film script that takes a fictional look at a crime or criminal has been novelised. In addition, one or two film scripts that fall into the genre of crime faction have been published—Dylan Thomas's *The Doctor and the Devils*, for example. At the end of relevant entries, I have listed film versions of those works mentioned within the entry itself. If the title of a film differs from its source, this has been indicated. An asterisk following the filmographic listing indicates that there have been several film adaptations. In this event, I have indicated the film generally considered by critics to be the best. It may not be the film most faithful to the source, but neither is it so drastically altered as to make its inclusion in this survey pointless. Once again, in some cases this has had to be a subjective decision.

Although this is the first book dedicated to crime faction, the field has been investigated briefly by other authors, and I have included a short bibliography of works that have helped me in compiling this study. Any readers interested in the field will find useful background information in these sources.

My original intention was for this book to be a comprehensive study of the field. However, comprehensiveness in such a broad and all-pervading genre is an elusive goal. I am aware that some crime faction works will have escaped my attention, and I hope that I may be able to retrieve some of the older items in the future, as well as adding new ones to my collection as they appear.

CRIME FACTION – A BRIEF HISTORY

The reporting of crime has a long (and not always honourable) tradition predating that of its fictional counterpart—predating even the growth of the tabloids that rely so heavily on it today. Returning to the chronicles of Shakespeare's time, to the works of John Stow and Raphael Holinshed, we see that these popular annals of English history drew as much on the brutal deaths of commoners as they did on the births of princes. These books were social history in its truest sense, and they did not flinch from presenting the gruesome facts concerning the lowest of crimes. They relied for their sources on the money-grubbing pamphleteers of the period and, on a higher plane, on contemporary court records.

Since crime denotes the infringement of laws, legal documents themselves give us another form of crime reportage. Court records take the literary historian further back through time to medieval society—to a period before printing itself was widespread in England. Taking the broader view, we need not limit ourselves to English legal records. Return to the days of Cicero; in that great lawyer's eloquent pleas for the defence and prosecution are found succinct descriptions of the criminal mind at work in ancient Rome. Return to the recorded speeches of Demosthenes in the courts of Athens for a fascinating view of a Greece peopled by forgers, embezzlers, fraudsters, hooligans and corrupt politicians, worthy of any American TV soap. Thus, the origins of crime reporting go far back in the history of humankind.

As for the origins of crime faction? One could follow the historians of *detective* fiction—since crime reportage relies principally on the detection of crime for the full facts of a case, this would seem a useful fictional simile—and search for its beginnings there. There is Gilbert Thomas, who viewed the story of Bel and the Dragon from the ancient Jewish Apocrypha as 'a tale of pure detection of the highest order'.[1] Or the French critic Regis Messac, who returned to the writings of Voltaire—specifically the deductions of the eponymous Zadig.[2] Or A. E. Murch, who examined the English novels of the eighteenth century—in particular, Henry Fielding's *Jonathan Wild the Great* (1743).[3] Or Julian Symons, who plumps for 1794, the date of publication of William Godwin's novel, *Caleb Williams*.[4]

Actually, it is in the dramatic works of the Elizabethan theatre that is found the mother lode from which the sub-genre of crime faction springs. Modern English drama—and Elizabethan drama itself—grew out of the religious theatre of medieval times. The performance of fictional and quasi-factual tales

---

1. Gilbert Thomas, *How to Enjoy Detective Fiction* (London: Rockliff, 1947).
2. Regis Messac, *Le 'Detective Novel' et l'Influence de la Pensée Scientifique* (Paris: Librarie Ancienne Honore Champion, 1929).
3. A. E. Murch, *The Development of the Detective Novel* (London: Peter Owen, 1958).
4. Julian Symons, *Bloody Murder* (London: Faber & Faber, 1972).

for a paying audience was originally grudgingly accepted by a repressive establishment because of drama's close links with the church. The medieval Cycles of plays based on Biblical themes, and the fictional morality plays that followed, were regarded by the all-powerful clergy as the best form of propaganda, accessible to all levels of society, whether literate or not. With the Reformation and the removal of the church's monopoly on education, early English drama left its protective religious refuge and proceeded—via schools, colleges, country houses and inn courtyards—to establish itself physically within the playhouses and theatres that still house it.

This break from religious ties resulted in a search for secular sources of inspiration for drama. Many learned playwrights returned to the literature of ancient Greece and Rome for inspiration. There was a corresponding return to the classical concept of tragedy; the downfall of a person of nobility through some flaw in his or her character. This movement resulted in the mature and enduring works of Shakespeare and his contemporaries. In an age of self-doubt and uncertainty, the characters of Hamlet, Othello and Lear, of Tamberlaine and Faustus, of Vittoria Corombona and the Duchess of Malfi—following a set pattern of rules and principles laid down in ancient drama—appealed to the free-thinking nobility and upper-middle classes of Elizabethan England. Apart from the latter two characters (see entries for 'Vittoria Accoramboni' and the 'Duchess of Amalfi Murder'), most of these nobles fall outside the scope of our study.

But while the upper classes of Shakespeare's time responded enthusiastically to the kings, princes, officials and courtiers in his works, the lower-middle and working classes who made up the 'groundlings' in the theatre found their enjoyment in the antics of the Bardolphs and Nims, the gravediggers and porters, the nurses and servants that populate his plays. All comic characters; Shakespeare provided little in the way of tragic figures among his lower-class *dramatis personae*.

Some authors, however, turned their attention to the masses, and produced plays in which ordinary people featured as principal heroes and villains of sorts. Thomas Heywood's *A Woman Killed with Kindness* (1605) is a good example of this genre—a Yorkshireman catches his wife in the arms of a friend and banishes her from his house; she, remorseful and guilt-ridden, dies of a broken heart.[5] Heywood took his inspiration from a fictional source. Other playwrights employed factual tragedies, using details of recent criminal trials (usually murder trials). There was no shortage of material available: the aforementioned works of Stow and Holinshed, or the many pamphleteers of the time, provided the facts; the playwrights provided the dramatic licence. This usually came in the form of a strong moral tone. Murderers and their accomplices would suffer pangs of conscience leading up to the crime, and probably accept retribution with pious satisfaction. In this respect, domestic tragedies—as these works were called—

---

5. All dates quoted after titles of plays are dates of publication, not performance.

formed a noticeable link between the high-flown Elizabethan and Jacobean tragedies, and the morality plays that preceded them. There was often a contrast between piety and the depiction of cold-blooded crimes shown on stage—many of these dramas would have passed muster in the French Grand Guignol theatre of the nineteenth century—but the writers were merely reflecting the tone of their sources (and, in effect, anticipating the tone of modern tabloids[6]).

The *factional* domestic tragedy cycle began in 1592 with its most famous representation, the anonymously-scripted *Arden of Faversham*. It is this work that provides us with our first source of crime faction. Within ten years, at least five plays were published in this genre that were based on true crimes.[7] These were followed by three comedies based on criminals of the period, and two plays by Webster on the aforementioned Accoramboni and Amalfi cases.[8]

Then for almost a century, there was a hiatus in the genre before the next published work. This period saw the nadir of English drama—the Cromwell protectorate during which actors were effectively driven from the stage—and its zenith—the powerful royal patronage afforded to dramatists during the Restoration. Perhaps as a reaction to the solemnity of Cromwell's persecution of drama, the theatre of Charles II tended towards comedy. What tragedies there were reverted to the highbrow, high society rhetoric of Shakespeare and the Jacobean dramatists rather than domestic drama. When the theatre of crime faction reared its head again, it was once more in response to contemporary crime.

The post-Civil War period saw many of the troops who fought for the King without a cause or career. The easy option for such men was a life of crime, and so that romantic breed of criminal, the highwayman, came into being. The likes of Claude Duval in the seventeenth century and Dick Turpin in the eighteenth captured the public imagination, and would eventually find their way into drama and fiction. Also, at the beginning of the eighteenth century, a criminal of amazing dexterity and ingenuity in the art of jail-breaking became the toast of England: the legendary Jack Sheppard.

Though his crimes were mundane in themselves, Sheppard's frequent escapes from London prisons (including his final breakout from Newgate, where he had been heavily manacled) guaranteed him star status among

6. Keith Sturgess, ed., *Three Elizabethan Domestic Tragedies* (Harmond-sworth: Penguin, 1969), pp. 9–10.
7. *Arden of Faversham* (1592), *A Warning for Faire Women* (1599) and *A Yorkshire Tragedy* (1601)—all anonymous—Robert Yarington's *Two Lamentable Tragedies* (1601) and George Wilkins's *Miseries of Inforst Marriage* (1607). Yarington's play is excluded from this study due to lack of sufficient source material on the crime itself. In its own crude way, the play is the most spectacular of the five: the victim's body is cut up and then re-assembled for identification purposes *on stage!*
8. The comedies were Middleton's and Dekker's *The Roaring Girle* (1611), Field's *Amends for Ladies* (1618) and Massinger's *A New Way to Pay Old Debts* (1633).

contemporary crooks. From 1724 (the year of his final arrest and execution) to 1728, many plays were produced on the English stage celebrating Sheppard's real and imagined exploits. Few survive in print; of these John Gay's *The Beggar's Opera* (1728) is the most celebrated.

This new wave of crime faction heralded a lenient response to the criminal. Admittedly, in the case of Jack Sheppard, we are discussing a robber rather than a murderer; but the salient point is that the strong moral tone of Elizabethan and Jacobean times had become muted. The reason for this was that crime was seen increasingly as a reaction to, and a reflection of, the corruption in British government. In his novel, *Jonathan Wild the Great* (1743) Henry Fielding drew a fictional comparison between arch-villain Jonathan Wild and prime minister Robert Walpole. Fielding's work, incidentally, was the second novel in the history of crime faction, the first being Daniel Defoe's *Moll Flanders* (1722), which was itself based on the career of a character familiar to Wild. Jonathan Wild's notoriety may be seen to partially explain Jack Sheppard's popularity. Wild, the thief-taker general, working closely with the authorities, was seen as the guardian of a corrupt social system. Sheppard was the 'little man' against that system. As Frank McLynn put it, 'In time, he [Sheppard] came to represent to the English public the forces of light ranged against Wild's prince of darkness'.[9] Even crime faction engendered its own murky heroes.

In such a criminal society, crime began to gain significance as a subject for discussion, and contemporary novelists and playwrights responded accordingly. Gay's *The Beggar's Opera* and Lillo's *The London Merchant* (1731) stand among eighteenth-century plays, as does Defoe's *Moll Flanders* (1722) in fiction. This thirst for criminal sensationalism would eventually give way to sensationalism of a more ethereal nature with the gothic novels and plays of the late eighteenth and early nineteenth century. But the eighteenth century contribution is meagre compared to that of the centuries that preceded and succeeded it. The flood-gates opened with a vengeance during the eighteen-hundreds.

The nineteenth century saw the novel taking over from the play as the principal vehicle for crime faction. Appropriately, it was the first best-selling novelist, Sir Walter Scott, who made the running. Britain had already produced a sizeable crop of important authors such as Defoe, Fielding, Jane Austen and Maria Edgeworth. But Scott was the first to make a national— and international—career from his writings. Like his contemporary, Byron, his works echoed the Romanticism that pervaded art and society at the beginning of the century.

Unlike Byron, however, Scott was acutely conscious of his place in the commercial world of literature: he 'adopted an attitude at once slightly self-mocking yet at the same time aware of the reality of literature as part of the

---

9. Frank McLynn, *Crime and Punishment in Eighteenth-Century England* (London: Routledge, 1989), p.26.

market economy'.[10] Scott's popularity in the field of fiction was based on his ability to mix well-researched historical plots and backgrounds with a range of interesting and believable characters from all walks of life. He had an affinity with the public taste for spectacle, drama—and sensationalism.

Two of his novels were based on genuine criminal cases of the past, and like many of his fictional works formed the bases themselves of several theatrical adaptations. His style had a profound influence on both the fiction and drama of the nineteenth century—sometimes to their detriment; one has only to read a novel such as Emma Robinson's *Whitefriars* (1844—see entry on 'Edmund Godfrey Murder') to realise that Scott's disciples were rarely on a par with Scott himself.

While Scott looked to the past for his inspiration, other authors turned to contemporary events for theirs. The beginning of the century saw a plethora of criminal cases that attract attention to this day. This was the time of the murder of Maria Marten, the trial of Abraham Thornton, and the Thurtell and Hunt case, to name but three. Public interest in crime was aroused as never before since the days of Sheppard and Wild.

Dramatists and novelists responded to this enthusiasm accordingly; many of the cases of the day found their way into fiction and drama eventually. Even American literature took a local crime to its heart with the so-called 'Kentucky Tragedy' of 1825, involving Jeroboam O. Beauchamp. Apart from the later Lizzie Borden case, the Kentucky Tragedy is the most 'factionalised' American crime. Most of the authors adapting these contemporary crimes to fiction and drama were well below the level of literary talent of a Walter Scott.

However, Scott's influence sparked the imaginations of a group of writers who were even more willing to emphasise the sensationalism inherent in their sources. The two prominent disciples were Edward Bulwer Lytton and William Harrison Ainsworth. Bulwer Lytton used past and present cases for his crime faction, covering the eighteenth-century case of Eugene Aram as well as the contemporary cases of Thurtell, Wainewright and Fauntleroy. Ainsworth relied on historical villains, creating definitive fictional portraits of both Jack Sheppard and Dick Turpin. Their predilection for criminals whose exploits appeared in the *Newgate Calendar* led to their works being described as 'Newgate novels'.[11]

The Newgate novels, frequently centring as they did on the lives of lower-class crooks, were often accused in the Tory press of glamorising and even condoning criminal life. Fuel was added to the controversy at the trial of the murderer Courvoisier, who confessed to having killed his master, Lord William Russell, after reading Ainsworth's *Jack Sheppard* and seeing a stage

---

10. Gary Kelly, *English Fiction of the Romantic Period 1789–1830* (London: Longmans, 1989), p. 139.
11. First published around 1723, the definitive version of *The Newgate Calendar* was produced by Knapp and Baldwin in the 1820s. See Keith Hollingsworth's *The Newgate Novel 1830–1847* (Detroit: Wayne State University Press, 1963).

adaptation of it. The fact that quality authors such as Dickens used features of the genre to highlight social injustices didn't help the cause of the Tory press.

Thackeray entered the conflict with his own intended satire of the form, *Catherine* (1840), based on the Catherine Hayes case of 1725. He fell into the trap of showing sympathy for his murderess, and the squib backfired. He later produced a more successful parody in *Punch* magazine of Bulwer Lytton's style that effectively sounded the death-knell of the Newgate school. Moreover, times were changing; Victoria had recently succeeded to the throne, and the Tory star was in the ascendancy.

Although they fall outside the scope of the present survey, mention should be made of the prolific 'penny dreadfuls'—serialised literature sold in penny parts—that were produced in the mid-nineteenth century. Aimed at the literate lower-middle and working classes, they often took their inspiration, like the Newgate novels, from past criminal cases. Dick Turpin, Jack Sheppard, Jonathan Wild and Claude Duval all found their way into this genre of fiction. Also, like the Newgate novels, the 'dreadfuls' would sensationalise the careers of their genuine protagonists, often placing them alongside lurid, eccentric fictional characters (Turpin found himself allied to the, literally, colourful Blue Dwarf in the book of that title).[12]

While Newgate fiction passed away through lack of public interest and the general political and moral climate, the demise of Newgate drama was helped along by positive action from the censors. Dramatisations of recent crimes had incensed the moral majority. *Maria Martin; or, The Murder in the Red Barn* played in various forms throughout the country. In 1824, *The Gamblers*, a drama based on the Thurtell and Hunt crime, was performed in London, with the coach and horse used by Thurtell supposedly appearing on stage. As the trial was still in progress, the play was suppressed by the censors.

With the publication of Ainsworth's *Jack Sheppard* (1839), dramatists rushed to put on stage adaptations of varying fidelity to the novel. The sensationalism evident in Ainsworth's work was seized upon with relish, much to the disgust of the Lord Chamberlain's office. When Courvoisier's confession suggested a link between Newgate literature and current crime, the officers pounced. Further plays based on the character of Sheppard were rigorously discouraged and refused a licence. The censorship spread to other Newgate-influenced plots, such as dramatisations of Dickens's *Oliver Twist*, and remained active until the late eighteen-sixties.

Even after this period, playwrights hedged their bets by disguising the criminal characters in their plays. Thus, in 1873, when Ben Webster decided to stage J.B. Buckstone's 1839 adaptation of Ainsworth's novel, and met with a frosty reception from the Lord Chamberlain's office, he altered the names of the principal characters. Jack Sheppard became Robert Chance and Wild

12. Michael Anglo, *Penny Dreadfuls and Other Victorian Horrors* (London: Jupiter Books, 1977) provides an entertaining and well-illustrated overview of the genre, and its reliance on true crime.

was Sampson Savage; and the much-altered text was re-christened *The Stone Jug*. Public opinion had altered, however; the play was roundly condemned in the press and the audiences failed to materialise.[13]

During the 1840s—a popular time for crime faction in America (no less than four adaptations of the aforementioned Kentucky Tragedy were written during the decade[14])—a minor American poet began a series of short stories concerning the art of analytical deduction, or 'ratiocination' as the author called it. In 1841, Edgar Allan Poe produced the first of these tales, 'The Murders in the Rue Morgue', and the figure of the amateur detective was established in fiction.

Appropriately, it was Poe who developed the crime faction detective short story with his second tale of ratiocination, 'The Mystery of Marie Roget' (1842). Before Poe, fictional counterparts of genuine criminals were caught by chance, or while committing a crime, or through confession, or as a result of obvious clues (such as the traces of Arden's blood found in his house in the first crime faction play mentioned above). Poe's detective, Chevalier C. Auguste Dupin, discovers the murderer of Marie Roget (the fictional Mary Rogers) through the reading of newspaper reports, without personally visiting the scene of the crime.

Later exponents of detective fiction were to employ similar methods to Poe's in providing solutions to other unsolved cases. In England, after the spate of crime faction associated with Newgate literature, there was meagre production in the genre until the 1860s, when it found new strength through the inception of another school of literature. The high moral tone initiated by early Victorian society was destined to produce a reaction in the arts. In fiction, the response came through the so-called 'sensation novels'. 'Drawing on elements of the Gothic novel of the late eighteenth and early nineteenth centuries, the fiction of Poe and Victor Hugo, and the Newgate novels of the 1830s, Wilkie Collins, Charles Reade, M. E. Braddon, and Mrs Henry Wood produced novels which sold in great numbers, and which were widely considered by reviewers to be not only innovatory but also subversive'.[15] Several of these works were based on true crimes, in particular, three of Collins's novels. *The Moonstone* (1868) received particular attention in literary history due to T. S. Eliot's claim that it was 'the first and greatest of English detective novels'.[16] It is without doubt the first crime faction detective novel, taking many features from the Constance Kent case of 1865.

Just as the success of Newgate fiction saw a corresponding leap on the

13. For an overview of Newgate drama and its censorship problems, see 'The Opposition to Newgate Drama', chapter 4 of J. R. Stephens's *The Censorship of English Drama, 1824–1901* (Cambridge: Cambridge University Press, 1980).

14. One of these, Poe's *The Politian*, remained unpublished in book format until 1923.

15. Michael Wheeler, *English Fiction of the Victorian Period, 1830–1890* (London: Longmans, 1985), p. 92.

16. T. S. Eliot, 'Wilkie Collins and Dickens', *Selected Essays 1917–1932* (London: Faber & Faber, [1932]).

band-wagon from dramatists, so too did playwrights follow the success of the sensation novel with stage adaptations. Collins himself, for example, was to dramatise several of his own novels, although primarily in an effort to protect his dramatic rights. Principally, however, Victorian theatre followed the success (and censorship) of Newgate drama by turning to what—with improved stage mechanisation—it could provide best: spectacle.

The 1840s and 1850s was the period of J. R. Planché's elaborate burlesques and extravaganzas. With sensation novelists reaping the rewards of a renewed interest in crime, dramatists saw a new vein of material to be tapped. These melodramas of the late nineteenth century were, in one sense, merely a return to the heady drama of the pre-Victorian stage, just as the sensation novel was a continuation of Newgate fiction. The sole difference was that, taking a leaf from Planché's book, playwrights such as Dion de Boucicault and Ben Webster were able and willing to provide sumptuous sets, elaborate stage effects and (occasionally) actors of the quality of Henry Irving.

Like Scott's fiction at the beginning of the century, melodrama now drew its inspiration from historical rather than contemporary events. Webster's adaptation of *The Courier of Lyons* (1897) was based on a robbery in Napoleonic France (see entry for 'Lyons Mail Robbery'); Boucicault's *The Colleen Bawn* (1865) was inspired by a fifty-year-old Irish crime (see 'John Scanlan'). One interesting aspect of nineteenth-century crime faction is the lack of political, social or psychological commitment; unlike the eighteenth-century writers who saw crime as a reflection of the turpitude of their society. Only Dickens in the nineteenth century seemed engaged with social concerns; or rather, employed elements of crime faction to enhance a tale concentrating on social evils—as in *Bleak House* (1853).

For the most part, however, Victorian authors used criminal fact to beef up fictional plots. The motives of criminals were easily identifiable, even mundane—greed being the most obvious. Despite the fact that nineteenth-century England produced two crimes of unparalleled horror and psychological mystery—namely, the Ratcliffe Highway murders of 1811 and those of Jack the Ripper in 1888—authors showed little interest in the complex motivations that drove criminals of this sort. Insanity, sexual frustration, pressures of the industrial environment—motives such as these would have to wait until the next century, and familiarity with the work of Freud, before finding a place in crime faction.[17]

At first, the genre saw little change in the twentieth century. An interest in historical cases still held sway (the lack of interest in identifiable contemporary cases was probably indicative of the stronger libel laws prevailing). Novels and short stories continued to be the popular vehicle for crime faction; true crime was still used as a piquant sauce for jaded appetites. 1913,

---

17. In Germany, playwright Georg Büchner had stolen a march on twentieth-century writers in this respect with his dramatic treatment of the murderer Johann Woyzeck, written around 1837 (see relevant entry).

however, saw the first classic in the genre this century: Marie Belloc Lowndes's *The Lodger*. The first and possibly best-known novel adaptation of the Jack the Ripper case, the book seems light by today's standards. At the time, however, it was an innovative investigation of a mass-murderer's psychological make-up. The motive of religious mania suggested here is one that few Victorian authors would have dared employ. Lowndes prepared the ground that future authors such as Meyer Levin and Julian Symons would tread in their investigation of the criminal mind.

The 1920s and 1930s saw a peak in crime faction writing. During the latter decade alone, over sixty works were published; more than were produced in the first two hundred and fifty years of the genre's history. There were several reasons for this. Generally speaking, the fifty years since the 1870 Education Act had seen a dramatic rise in the level of adult literacy. The reduction in book prices and the evolution of a cheap fiction market helped satisfy the demand for literature, especially fiction.[18] The growth of the national library system, and of circulating libraries attached to shops, also played a part.

It was no coincidence that the twenties and thirties also marked the Golden Age of detective fiction: detection and crime were popular subjects for novel-readers. This interest added to the popularity of crime faction. The period also coincided with the growth of a strong socialist and realist sentiment in American fiction. The American labour movement had witnessed an upsurge in support after the First World War, and the Wall Street Crash of 1929 and subsequent depression added fuel to popular resentment against a failing capitalist system.

The cracks could be seen in the legal system as well. The execution in 1927 of anarchists Sacco and Vanzetti for murder—after a seven-year legal battle—shocked the world and inspired many American authors to rise in literary protest. Novelist Theodore Dreiser saw in the Chester Gillette case of 1907 an indictment of the American way of life. Ward Greene's *Death in the Deep South* (1936) highlighted the gulf of racial and political bigotry that existed between the Northern and Southern states.

All the above factors, coupled with a continuing interest in distant historical cases, resulted in a multitude of novels, stories and plays in the crime faction field, the like of which has not been seen since. Some of the masterpieces of the genre appeared during this period—Theodore Dreiser's novel, *An American Tragedy* (1925), based on the aforementioned Gillette case; F. Tennyson Jesse's examination of the Thompson and Bywaters murder trial, *A Pin to See the Peepshow* (1922); Francis Iles's masterly *Malice Aforethought* (1931), a reconstruction of the Herbert Rowse Armstrong story; Lillian Hellman's modern re-telling of the 1810 Scottish Drumsheugh case in her play, *The Children's Hour* (1934). All these works have remained as pertinent as in the time they were written.

---

18. See chapter 11 of Douglas Hewitt, *English Fiction of the Modern Period, 1890–1940* (London: Longmans, 1988).

The 1930s saw the debut of the most prolific writer in the crime faction genre. Joseph Shearing was the pseudonym of Margaret Gabrielle Long, who also wrote under the names of Marjorie Bowen and George R. Preedy. Her forte was historical fiction; her crime faction works, under the Shearing nom de plume, were reconstructions of historical, mostly Victorian, crimes. From 1932 (with the publication of *Forget-Me-Not*) through to 1951 (the year of *To Bed at Noon*), a series of novels appeared from Shearing covering such cases as that of Florence Maybrick, the Bravo poisoning, the murder of the Duchess de Praslin and that of Harriet Buswell.

Although the choice of cases was interesting, the novels themselves were unfortunately weighed down with often overbearing symbolism and the purple prose that marred Long's other fictional works. The author did, however, display a perceptive insight into the female criminal psyche and the pressures on women of the strict Victorian moral values.

Detective fiction adaptations of true crime continued to predominate in the genre through the forties. In Britain, established detection writers such as Julian Symons, Josephine Tey and John Rhode turned their attentions to crime faction in this decade, as did Lillian de la Torre in the States. The forties also saw the continuation of a sense of realism in the genre: the influence of American socialist writers of the previous decades. America still led the running here; Richard Wright opened the decade with his masterpiece, *Native Son* (see 'Robert Nixon').

This realism was to continue through the fifties, keeping pace with the similar trend in general fiction. The Post-War period opened the way for plainer speaking in literature, freer expression of thought and feeling. Authors and publishers challenged the bounds of 'good taste' laid down by the establishment and the law. The flurry of literary obscenity trials in the sixties—the Lady Chatterley case of 1961 was the most famous—resulted in the collapse of more barriers for the writer. The resulting freedom of expression especially in matters of sex and violence, has made its presence felt in all literary fields.

In crime faction, the line between fact and fiction had been, for the most part, well defined. Authors disguised cases by changing the names of principal characters, gave their own broad interpretation of events and added a proportion of fictional elements to true crimes—distancing themselves one way or another, in effect, from the facts that formed the basis of their fiction. In 1965, Truman Capote opened the debate on what constitutes faction and what constitutes fact, with the publication of his 'non-fiction novel', *In Cold Blood* (see 'Hickock and Smith'). Capote was accused in some quarters of pretentiousness, of publishing a non-fiction work under another guise, of falsely claiming to have invented a new literary form. Whatever the author's claim, the book has remained the principal source for any factual study of the Hickock and Smith case on which it was based.

Crime faction of the past two decades has proven to be more of the same recipe. Historical reconstructions seem to predominate, combined with a greater freedom of sexual expression. Old cases, especially Victorian ones, have been re-interpreted in the light of new perspectives on sexual tension, jealousy and even perversion. The hypocritical moral code of the Victorians in all its aspects has been investigated and deconstructed in well-known cases of the period. The spate of Jack the Ripper factions continues apace—even to the extent of pitting the world's greatest fictional detective, Sherlock Holmes, against England's best-known mass-murderer.

Realism in relation to crime has reached its peak—one only has to read James Ellroy's brutal thriller, *The Black Dahlia* (1987), to realise that little more can be achieved in this area. Fictional solutions to such unsolved cases are still in vogue, with the Wallace case of 1931 continuing to attract particular attention (five novels in the past three decades). One innovation during this twenty-year period has been the genre known as the 'book-of-the-film', in which scripts of popular films have been converted into novels. Admittedly, there have been scattered examples of this genre previously, but in the seventies and eighties publishers and film-makers realised the full potential of such a field. Several interesting items have been added to the survey with this new area of literature.

Before concluding, it would be appropriate to point out the spate of novels and plays that transfer old cases to modern settings. Josephine Tey and Francis King have been two pioneers in this, and I see no reason for such examples not to continue being produced in the future.

So what of the future for the genre? Will crime faction continue to retain its position in the affections of the fiction-reading and play-going public? Surely, after surviving and blossoming over three centuries, the answer to that particular question must be in the affirmative. The genre will continue as long as our fascination with crime continues. Interest in crime stems from a desire for self-knowledge, a need to understand—and possibly control—the forces and passions that affect us as humans. Only by coming to terms with criminal behaviour can we combat it, contain it and hope to eradicate it. And while this interest abounds, one of its more curious offshoots, crime faction, will flourish. Julian Symons, in his history of crime fiction, *Bloody Murder*, provided a fitting epilogue to that genre, which applies also to the genre of crime faction: 'What the modern crime story can do, in short, is to say something of interest about our own time. The fine art of murder, as de Quincey called it, can tell us something about the world we live in, and about the best way of living in it'.[19]

19. Julian Symons, *Bloody Murder* (London: Viking, 1985), p. 239.

CRIMINAL SENTENCES
AN A-Z OF CRIME FACTION

VITTORIA ACCORAMBONI MURDER ITALY 1585

The story of Vittoria Accoramboni, prototype for the female catalyst of John Webster's play, *The White Devil* (1612), is one of intrigue, murder and vengeance in equal (and ample) proportions. Vittoria was born in Gubbio, Northern Italy, in 1557 and married one Francesco Peretti in 1573. Vittoria's brother, Marcello, worked as chamberlain to Paolo Giordano Orsini, Duke of Bracciano, and within eight years of her marriage, it is certain that Vittoria had met and fallen in love with Bracciano. In 1581, Peretti was lured from his house on a false pretext and murdered in the streets of Rome. Within a fortnight, Vittoria and Bracciano were secretly married (the duke's wife had died under equally suspicious circumstances five years earlier). The marriage was not recognised by the Pope, and Vittoria remained Bracciano's mistress.

In 1583, a second marriage ceremony was performed—in fact, the couple had to wed a third time before the union was accepted. When Bracciano himself died in 1585, rumours of poisoning flew around Italy. Lodovico Orsini, a relative of Bracciano—and himself a murderer of three years past— was hoping for a portion of the duke's estate, but Vittoria's lawyers established her right to all her husband's property. Within five weeks of Bracciano's death, Lodovico and his followers caught her at her prayers and stabbed her and her younger brother to death. The murderers were soon caught and executed.

It is not known where John Webster discovered the facts of the case, but his adaptation of the tale is interesting. In *The White Devil*, Vittoria Corombona's brother, Flamineo intrigues to marry his sister to Bracciano, being directly involved in the murders of her husband and his previous wife. Vittoria is tried for the murder, but is rescued by her lover, who takes her to Padua to be married. The Duke of Florence—brother of Bracciano's poisoned wife—follows the lovers to Padua and, with the help of one Lodovico, who secretly loves Vittoria (Webster was either unaware of Lodovico's relationship to Bracciano or chose to ignore it), poisons her new husband. Flamineo plans to blackmail his now-wealthy sister, but they are both murdered at the instigation of the Duke of Florence.

French author Robert Merle gave a new twist to the story in his novel *L'Idole* (1987), translated as *The Idol* in 1989. He sets his tale against a background of court and Vatican intrigue. Vittoria, Peretti and Paolo Orsini are seen as pawns rather than protagonists, in a greater game played by the Medicis and the Orsinis, the Pope and his cardinals. Paolo and Vittoria are guiltless of Peretti's death—Ludovico has had Peretti murdered, knowing that suspicion would fall on the two lovers. He is jealous of Paolo's wealth and, in trying to save the Orsini fortune for Paolo's first son, Virginio, hopes to obtain money that he desperately needs from his new master.

The story is told in statements by the characters involved: the murderous, Machiavellian Marcello, whose love for his sister is almost incestuous; the scheming but pious Cardinal Montalto, who becomes Pope Sixtus IV; and the lascivious Caterina Acquaviva, Vittoria's flighty and worldly-wise maid. Vittoria's only sin is her haughty pride; Merle sees her as a honest and brave woman—totally at odds with Webster's portrait of a murdering vixen.

FACTIONAL WORKS:

John Webster, *The White Divel* (London: N.O. for Thomas Archer, 1612). (P)

Robert Merle, *The Idol* (London: Collins Harvill, 1989). First published in French as *L'Idole*, 1987.

FURTHER READING:

Gunnar Boklund, *The Sources of the White Devil* (Cambridge, Mass.: Harvard University Press, 1957).

JAMES ACHEW GB 1930

James Achew was a Native American who lived in Bayswater, London, with his common-law wife Sybil da Costa and her daughter, under the name of Starr. Among the residents in their boarding house was William Plomer, an editor, novelist and poet recently returned from South Africa. James Achew was intensely jealous of his wife, apparently without cause, and had beaten her on several occasions. She, however, was deeply in love with him and would not leave him. Achew suspected a relationship between Sybil and Plomer.

One Sunday evening in November 1929, a boarder, Mrs Blackwell, woke to the sound of a struggle in the room below—the room occupied by the Starrs. She looked down the staircase and saw Sybil Starr coming out of the room, covered in blood from a throat wound. The police were called and discovered Achew with a similar injury, trying to gas himself in the kitchen oven. Sybil died before medical assistance could be called, and Achew, who recovered from his suicide attempt, was arrested for murder.

In January 1930, he stood trial at the Old Bailey. His defence was one of insanity; the medical officer of Brixton prison, who had studied Achew, stated that he was suffering from melancholia. Despite this evidence, the jury found Achew guilty of murder, and he was sentenced to death. An appeal was lodged, in which his lawyer suggested that the verdict had been reached against the strong medical evidence. The appeal was refused, but after the Home Secretary saw Achew's medical record, he was reprieved and sent to Broadmoor.

William Plomer had returned to his flat to discover the aftermath of the tragedy and had helped to clear up the traces of the crime. This did not prevent him, however, from holding a party at the house, where he invited his literary acquaintances, including Leonard and Virginia Woolf. Two years after Achew's trial, the Woolfs's Hogarth Press published Plomer's novel, *The Case is Altered*, based on the murder. Achew is Paul Fernandez, who is married to Beryl. Plomer's emphasis is less on the crime itself (which is seen as inevitable, given Fernandez's mental state) than on the assortment of characters who live in the boarding house. There is the haughty Mrs

Gambitt, who has provided the capital for the establishment; Miss Bixworth, a timid, genteel lady who acts as confidante to her neighbour, the eccentric Miss Haymer, keeping her abreast of events in the house; Eric Alston, the young greengrocer's assistant who is in love with a local shop girl, and who is the unwitting object of Fernandez's misplaced jealousy. Alston appears to be Plomer's fictional alter-ego, the catalyst in the tragedy that will overtake the occupants of the house. The murder itself is horrifying because of its very intrusion into the characters' humdrum lives. The title of the book acts as a recurring and ironic comment on the changes within their circumstances.

FACTIONAL WORKS:
William Plomer, *The Case is Altered* (London: Leonard & Virginia Woolf [Hogarth Press], 1932).

FURTHER READING:
Robert Curzon, ed., *The Crime Annual, 1931* (London: F. V. White & Co. Ltd., [1931]).

DUCHESS OF AMALFI MURDER ITALY 1513

Giovanna was the daughter of Enrico of Aragon, step-brother of the King of Naples. Her brothers were Ludovico, Cardinal of Aragon, and Carlo, Marquis of Gerace. In 1490, Giovanna married Alphonso Piccolimini, who succeeded to the dukedom of Amalfi in 1493. They had a son, Alphonso, born in 1499, just after his father's death. Giovanna became regent of Amalfi during young Alphonso's minority. However, she had fallen in love with Antonio Bologna, a courtier who had served the King of Naples. Giovanna and Antonio married secretly (her maid the only witness); however, rumours circulated.

Following the birth of her second child by Antonio, Giovanna confessed to the marriage and promised to give up her regency of Amalfi and retire into obscurity. Her brothers were scandalised. After a third child was born to the couple, Giovanna and her husband fled to Sienna, but Ludovico used his influence and had them expelled. On their way to Venice, her brothers' troops overtook them. The Duchess, convinced that her brothers would not harm her, persuaded Antonio to escape with their eldest son. She and her children were taken back to Amalfi and killed; Antonio was subsequently murdered.

Dramatist John Webster came across the story of Giovanna in a highly fictionalised account by the French writer Francesco de Belleforest. In the French version, the Duchess is characterised as a victim of her own lust and sinfulness—a moralistic view far removed from Webster's sympathetic portrayal. In his play, *The Duchess of Malfi* (1623), Webster views the brothers' anger regarding the secret marriage as jealousy of their social rank, and their violent actions as a way of protecting their claim on her estates. Webster also portrays Ferdinand, the Duke of Calabria, Giovanna's twin brother in the play, as suffering from an incestuous longing for his sister.

Webster introduces a protagonist in the person of Bosola, an escaped slave who is employed by the brothers to spy on the couple. He is the one who informs the brothers first of the secret marriage, and then of the birth of the child. After Giovanna is killed and Ferdinand has gone mad from guilt, Bosola, learning of the cardinal's intent to kill him, throws in his lot with Antonio and plans to murder the two brothers. In the final scenes, after accidentally murdering Antonio, Bosola takes the lives of the scheming cardinal and marquis, before receiving his own death-wound from Ferdinand. Thus, Webster's moral ending is at odds with Belleforest's interpretation; it is the brothers who are finally brought to judgement for their crimes, not the Duchess.

FACTIONAL WORKS:

John Webster, *The Tragedy of the Dutchess of Malfy* (London: Nicholas Okes, 1623). (**P**)

FURTHER READING:

Gunnar Boklund, *The Duchess of Malfi: Sources, Themes, Characters* (Cambridge, Mass.: Harvard University Press, 1962).

EUGENE ARAM GB 1759

Aram, an eminent scholar of Greek and Latin, was an impoverished teacher who lived in Knaresborough. In 1745, a local shoemaker, David Clark, disappeared from his home. Shortly afterwards, Aram settled his debts in the village and left. He was subsequently traced to King's Lynn, where he earned a living as an usher and by taking in private pupils. In 1758, a skeleton was unearthed in Knaresborough which was mistakenly identified as the missing David Clark, by then believed to have been murdered.

Suspicion fell on William Houseman, a local weaver. Under interrogation, Houseman admitted to involvement in the murder of Clark, but named Aram as the person who committed the deed. He described the spot where Clark was murdered, and sure enough, the true remains of David Clark were discovered nearby. A warrant was issued for Aram's arrest.

At the trial that followed, it transpired that Aram had led a double life, supplementing his teacher's income with petty theft and fencing stolen goods. Clark had been murdered for the money he was carrying. Despite a spirited defence by the accused, he was found guilty and hanged outside York. Houseman, because of his role as informer, was released.

In 1832, Edward Bulwer Lytton painted a reasonably sympathetic portrayal of the Knaresborough schoolmaster in his 'Newgate novel' *Eugene Aram*. Aram had actually served as tutor to the children of Bulwer Lytton's grandfather. In the novel, Aram is portrayed as a scholar rather than schoolmaster. His Byronic melancholia and temperament attracts the attention of young Madeline Lester from the village of Grassdale. Aram and Lester marry, and Madeline's cousin Walter, who has hidden his love for her, leaves the village in search of his long-lost father. At Knaresborough, he meets

Houseman and learns that his father, a cynical lecher, was murdered by Aram. Houseman's confession provides the sole evidence against Aram. Bulwer Lytton's trial scenes follow the original account more closely than the rest of novel's plot. Aram is hanged for a murder for which he was, in Bulwer Lytton's version, only morally—not physically—responsible.

The novel proved a popular success, leading to a spate of stage adaptations. Of these, only W. T. Moncrieff's *Eugene Aram; or, St. Robert's Cave* appears to have been published (in the same year as Bulwer Lytton's novel). The play was performed at the Surrey Theatre in February 1832. Following the novel closely, Moncrieff's dramatisation ends with Aram's bride-to-be visiting him in the death cell and dying in his arms. Aram cheats the gallows by taking poison.

FACTIONAL WORKS:
Edward Bulwer Lytton, *Eugene Aram* (London: Henry Colburn & Richard Bentley, 1832).
William T. Moncrieff, *Eugene Aram; or, St. Robert's Cave* (London: T. Richardson, [1832]). (P)

FURTHER READING:
Rayner Heppenstall, *Reflections on the Newgate Calendar* (London: W. H. Allen, 1975).

GEORGE ARCHER-SHEE CASE GB 1910

In 1908, a young cadet named George Archer-Shee, who was studying at the Royal Naval College, Osborne, found himself accused of stealing a postal order from a fellow cadet's locker. He was ordered to leave the college. The principal piece of evidence against Archer-Shee was a signature on the postal order identified by handwriting experts as his. George's father was convinced of his son's innocence and contacted Edward Carson, one of the most eminent lawyers of his time. After a three-hour interview with George, Carson agreed to take the case.

The matter proved difficult to bring to trial, however. At a subsequent Admiralty enquiry, the accused cadet was not allowed legal representation, and the authorities upheld the original verdict. The only course open to Carson was to apply for a Petition of Right, by which a subject entering into a contract with the Crown and being accused of breach of such a contract, could bring action in the courts. The case was finally heard in 1910. Carson managed to discredit the prosecution's handwriting expert and to cast doubt on the evidence of the postmistress who identified Archer-Shee as the boy who cashed the forged cheque.

Finally, the Solicitor-General informed the court that the Admiralty were satisfied the boy's innocence had been proved. The Admiralty refused to reinstate George, but his father won compensation of £7120, including costs. Tragically, George Archer-Shee was killed seven years later at the Battle of Ypres.

Terence Rattigan employed the facts of the Archer-Shee case for his drawing-room drama, *The Winslow Boy* (staged and published in 1946). Ronnie

Winslow is the fictional George, Arthur Winslow the infirm father who fritters away the family's wealth to prove his son's innocence. Apart from Ronnie's harrowing preliminary interview with Sir Robert Morton (the play's fictional Carson), the drama of the trial takes place offstage. Rattigan's interest lies in the effect of the case on the family: Kate Winslow, Ronnie's suffragette sister, who sacrifices her forthcoming marriage for her belief in Ronnie's right to a fair trial; Dickie, Ronnie's frivolous brother, who loses his place at university, and is reduced to working as a clerk at a bank; Arthur's wife, Grace, who is unable to accept her husband's reasons for pursuing the case, putting it down to his 'pride and self-importance and sheer brute stubbornness'.

There is a hint of comic-romantic play between Kate, the feminist and political ideologist, and Sir Robert, a reactionary whose reasons for accepting the case she questions. 'No one party has a monopoly of concern for individual liberty,' Sir Robert informs her at the end of the play, 'on that issue all parties are united'. To which Kate replies, 'Not all parties. Only some people from all parties'.

When Rattigan later adapted his play for the cinema (it was filmed in 1948), he extended the action to include courtroom scenes based closely on the Archer-Shee case. His screen adaptation is therefore more faithful to the original story than the play itself.

FACTIONAL WORKS:
Terence Rattigan, *The Winslow Boy* (London: Hamish Hamilton, [1946]).

FURTHER READING:
R. M. Bennett, *The Archer-Shees against the Admiralty* (London: Robert Hale, 1973).

FILM ADAPTATIONS:
The Winslow Boy, d. Anthony Asquith. GB: British Lion, 1948. Screenplay by Terence Rattigan, based on his play.

ALICE ARDEN GB 1551

In February 1551, the body of Thomas Arden, controller of customs in Faversham, Kent, was discovered in a field close to his house. His head had been crushed by a great weight, his throat had been cut and there were other knife marks on his body which had been made after death. Following a trail back to Arden's house, investigators found traces of blood and tufts of hair inside. They also came across a cloth apparently used to mop up the blood and a knife which could have produced the stab wounds. Under interrogation, Thomas's wife, Alice, readily confessed to having planned her husband's death.

It transpired that Alice had a lover named Mosby. Although Thomas knew of the relationship and turned a blind eye, Alice wished to rid herself of her husband. She and Mosby, together with several ruffians—Black Will, Shakebag and a couple of Arden's servants—made a series of attempts on Arden's life. Alice tried to poison him, but Thomas recovered; Black Will and Shake-bag attempted to ambush him, but he escaped. After further botched opportunities, Arden was finally attacked in his own house while playing a game of cards with Mosby.

He was held from behind with a scarf, while Mosby brained him with a pressing iron. His throat was then cut, and to make completely certain, Alice stabbed him several times. The poor concealment of the body and Alice's ready confession resulted in the eventual capture and execution of all the conspirators. Mosby himself was hanged in London, and Alice burnt alive in Canterbury.

The story, related in Holinshed's *Chronicles* (1577), was dramatised as *The Lamentable and True Tragedie of M. Arden of Feversham in Kent* (published in 1592, and commonly called *Arden of Faversham*). The play has been ascribed to Shakespeare in the past, although the style of domestic tragedy is unlike any of the author's known work. A close adaptation of Holinshed's account of the murder, *Arden of Faversham* adds superstition to the facts— Arden's wounds bleed as his wife is forced to look on his mangled body. Apart from this, however, the realism inherent in such a close approxima-tion of the facts is a reflection of other domestic tragedies of the period. One interesting addition to the plot is the introduction of the fictional Franklin, Arden's confidant, who acts as go-between for Arden and the audience, allowing Arden to express his concerns without resorting to soliloquy. An ironic juxtaposition is also provided between the comic courting of Susan, Alice Arden's maid (wooed both by Arden's servant, Michael, and a painter called Clarke) and the sinister love-making of her mistress and Mosby.

George Lillo, the eighteenth-century dramatist, turned his attention to the case in a play that he never finished. In 1759, twenty years after his death, Lillo's *Arden of Feversham* was staged at Drury Lane, revised and completed by J. Hoadly; the text was published three years later. Lillo presents a psychological study of the murder. It is not good fortune that saves Arden from the early attempts on his life, but the plotter's sense of guilt, particulary Alice's (or Alicia, as she is called in the play). Time after time, Alicia fails in her part of the scheme, as she becomes aware that her husband is preferable to her manipulative lover, Mosby. At the end, when Arden has been murdered and the assassins are caught, Alicia readily accepts her punish-ment with a penitent heart.

FACTIONAL WORKS:
Anon., *The Lamentable and True Tragedie of M. Arden of Feversham in Kent* (London: for Edward White, 1592). (**P**)
George Lillo, *Arden of Feversham* (London: printed for T. Davies, 1762). (**P**)

FURTHER READING:
M. L. Wine, ed., *The Tragedy of Master Arden of Faversham* (London: Methuen & Co., 1973). Contains the Holinshed version of the murder, together with another account from the manuscript Wardmote Book of Faversham.

HERBERT ROWSE ARMSTRONG GB 1922

One of the most 'Crippenesque' of murderers, Armstrong—like Crippen before him—was married to an overbearing wife who drove him finally to murder. Unlike Crippen, Armstrong didn't flee from the law, but was brought to justice after a second murder attempt. Armstrong and his wife, Katherine, lived in Hay-on-Wye, where Herbert had a solicitor's practice. Katherine was a dominant woman who forced her temperance on her husband at home, and frequently rebuked him in public. Despite such behaviour, it was generally believed that the couple were devoted to each other.

In 1920, Mrs Armstrong had a nervous breakdown and was taken to a private asylum. The next year, Armstrong was pressing for his wife's return home. Shortly after her arrival back in Hay-on-Wye, she was taken ill, apparently after catching a chill. With her husband supervising her meals and administering her medicines, she lingered in great agony for over a week. Her eventual death was attributed to heart disease. Freed from his wife's oppressive regime, Armstrong indulged in all the vices of which she disapproved—smoking, drinking and womanising (even during her stay in the asylum, he had managed to contract syphilis). But Armstrong finally invited suspicion after pursuing a grievance against a rival in the village, solicitor Oswald Martin.

In October 1921, he invited Martin to tea. Returning home from the meal, Martin was violently ill. His doctor, puzzled by the symptoms, sent a sample of his urine for analysis—traces of arsenic were detected. The police were contacted and Armstrong was placed under surveillance. In December, he was arrested for attempted murder. Small sachets of arsenic were found in his pockets and his desk. His wife's body was exhumed and found to contain a massive quantity of the poison. Armstrong was tried in April 1922 for the murder of Katherine. The significance of the sachets of arsenic did not go unquestioned. Armstrong claimed that he had prepared them to treat dandelions individually. The jury, however, found him guilty and he was hanged in Gloucester the following month.

Francis Iles's masterly novel, *Malice Aforethought* (1931), recasts Armstrong as a doctor, Edmund Bickleigh—a philandering weakling, married to the overbearing Julia, whom he poisons (here with an overdose of morphia). With Julia out of the way, Bickleigh pursues his relationship with young Ivy Ridgeway, who is unfortunately engaged to a young solicitor, William Chatford. After her marriage, Ivy informs Bickleigh that due to local gossip, Chatford has become suspicious of Julia's death and is approaching Scotland Yard. In the meantime, another of Bickleigh's old flames, Madeleine Bourne, has also married.

The doctor decides to kill both Chatford and Bourne. He invites them to tea, during which he serves sandwiches smeared with bacillus botulinus. They are both violently ill and—like Armstrong and Oswald Martin—Bickleigh goes in pursuit of Chatford to deliver the coup de grace. The authorities keep watch on Bickleigh and eventually arrest him on a charge of attempted murder. After the exhumation of Julia's body, the charge is altered to one of murder. The jury bring in a verdict of not guilty, and Bickleigh believes himself safe. However. . .

It would be a crime in itself to disclose the ending of the novel, one of the most dramatic twists in crime fiction. In fact, both the ending and the beginning of the work are masterful. We are left in no doubt from the outset that Bickleigh is a murderer; the novel starts with this amazing revelation: 'It was not until several weeks after he had decided to murder his wife that Dr Bickleigh took any active steps in the matter. Murder is a serious matter. The slightest slip might be disastrous. Dr Bickleigh had no intention of risking disaster'. How Bickleigh *does* risk disaster is the subject of one of the key works in modern crime faction.

Laurie York Erskine published his short story, 'Tea for Two', in *Collier's* magazine in 1936; it was reprinted in *Ellery Queen's Mystery Magazine* in 1946 with further comments from the author and journal editor identifying the basis of the tale. Erskine's plot takes as its principal character the curious 'Madame X', one of Armstrong's mistresses whose identity was hidden and who was exonerated from any connection with the murders by the trial judge. The tale's principal (false) premise is that Aldous Huxley based his short story, 'The Giaconda Smile', on the Armstrong murder (see HAROLD GREENWOOD CASE for the genuine source) and that Huxley identified 'Madame X' as the murderer. Erskine envisages author Alden Buxtree invited to tea with Mrs Enderby, who is—unbeknown to him—the unnamed lady in the Armitage murder trial which he has fictionalised in his novel, *The Strangefleet Case*. After explaining that he has proof, alluded to in the novel, that 'Madame X' was the real murderer of Mrs Armitage (for whose death her husband went to the gallows), Buxtree leaves, but is later striken with stomach pains which prove terminal. Despite the flaw in Erskine's ascription of Huxley's source, the story is sardonically enjoyable.

Catherine Meadows's *Friday Market* (1938) is more faithful to the details of the Armstrong case than Francis Iles's novel. Bealby, her Armstrong, a solicitor living in the fictional village of Clench, is portrayed as egotistic and self-obsessed—as was Bickleigh and, presumably, Armstrong himself. But Meadows shows greater sympathy for the wife. Mrs Bealby is a staid, sad, at times implacable spouse, undeserving of such an extreme end.

One additional well-known and well-received novel that uses a feature of the Armstrong case is C. S. Forester's *Payment Deferred* (1926). Armstrong's defence implied that Katherine had learned of her husband's affairs and had committed suicide while the balance of her mind was affected. Forester uses the same argument, with a twist, for his first novel: William Marble, a destitute bank clerk, murders his rich nephew to pay his debts. While enjoying his new-found wealth, Marble has an affair with a French girl. His wife, learning of this, swallows potassium cyanide from her husband's photography kit. Marble is tried and executed for her murder.

The novel was written four years after Armstrong's trial, which presumably gave the author his inspiration for the denouement of his thriller. Jeffrey Dell's dramatisation of the novel (1934) retains this denouement. The play proved a great success for actor Charles Laughton on the London stage.

FACTIONAL WORKS:
C. S. Forester, *Payment Deferred* (London: John Lane, [1926]).
Francis Iles, *Malice Aforethought* (London: Victor Gollancz, 1931).
Jeffrey Dell, *Payment Deferred* (London: Samuel French Ltd., 1934). (**P**)
Laurie York Erskine, 'Tea for Two', in *Collier's Magazine*, 1936
Catherine Meadows, *Friday Market* (London: Victor Gollancz, 1938).

FURTHER READING:
Robin Odell, *Exhumation of a Murder* (London: Harrap, 1975).

FILM ADAPTATIONS:
Payment Deferred, d. Lothar Mendes. US: MGM, 1932. Screenplay by Ernest Vajda and Claudine West, based on the play by Jeffrey Dell.

BACCARAT SCANDAL GB 1891

In September 1890, Arthur Wilson and his guests at Tranby Croft in Yorkshire settled down to a game of baccarat. The guests included Edward Albert, the Prince of Wales, and Sir William Gordon Cumming, a lieutenant-colonel of the Scots Guards. During the game, two players suspected that Gordon Cumming was cheating by adding money to his stake when he won a hand. They reported this to others who watched the next night; they too became convinced that Gordon Cumming was cheating. The guests were more concerned with avoiding a scandal that might affect the Prince of Wales than in recouping their losses.

Gordon Cumming was confronted with the charge, which he denied vehemently. He was forced to sign a prepared document declaring that he would never play cards for money again, or the incident would be announced in society circles. Gordon Cumming, realising the social stigma that would follow such a proclamation, had no option but to sign. If he had believed that it was the end of the affair, he was sadly mistaken. Despite the promise that his secret would be safe, rumours flew round the racecourses and drawing-rooms of the country.

In December, an anonymous letter informed him that the incident was the talk of fashionable Paris. He contacted his solicitors and a writ of slander was issued against several of the guests. The case was tried in June 1891. Gordon Cumming was on uncertain footing from the start, having signed the document which the lawyers for the guests claimed was an admission of guilt. He had been seen cheating, so there could be no suggestion of slander, the defence argued. Gordon Cumming gave evidence himself, protesting his innocence and declaring that he had signed the document merely to avoid a scandal. The Prince of Wales himself was called as a witness for the guests.

Despite a brilliant closing speech by Gordon Cumming's lawyer, Sir Charles Russell, the judge (the Lord Chief Justice, John Coleridge) found the defendants not guilty, and Gordon Cumming had to pay costs. He returned to his estates in Scotland, married the woman who had stood by him throughout the trial, and was subsequently shunned by society. Ironically, the only other person to be affected adversely by the trial was the Prince of Wales himself—his popularity slumped in the wake of a scandal that had been brought about by a bungled effort to protect him.

Mary Borden's *Action for Slander* (1936) gives us the Baccarat Scandal without the royal connection. Major Daviot has been accused of cheating at cards during a weekend house party. Although an agreement not to mention the incident has been obtained from the other guests, rumours about Daviot's offence cause him to pursue an action for slander. The plot is related in flashback from the court-room where the action is taking place. It transpires that there are several motives for the slander: one of the accusers is a fellow-officer with a grudge against Daviot, the accused is a womaniser who is having an affair with one of the guests' wives. A suggestion in the court-room to re-stage the card game leads to a solution to the mystery, and a different ending from that of the historical case.

Royce Ryton's play, *The Royal Baccarat Scandal* was staged in London in 1989. The story is told in flashback: in the course of a discussion with her father, Sir William Gordon Cumming, Mrs Gibbs hears the story of the scandal that ruined the family's position in society. Ryton follows the suggestion put forward in Sir Michael Havers's book on the case (listed below) that Gordon Cumming was the victim of a jealous guest, Lycett Green, whose wife he had attempted to seduce. Lycett Green, not above using his wife's charms to gain him favour with the Prince of Wales, is outraged at the lieutenant-colonel's attentions. When the other guests suspect Gordon Cumming of cheating, they are willing to give him a restrained admonishment, but Lycett Green insists on the harshly-worded document. It is also Lycett Green who begins the rumours that lead to the slander suit. Ryton leaves Gordon Cumming's guilt or innocence unresolved—his daughter is given an ambiguous answer to the question at the end of the play.

FACTIONAL WORKS:
Mary Borden, *Action for Slander* (London: William Heinemann, 1936).
Royce Ryton, *The Royal Baccarat Scandal* (London: Samuel French Ltd., 1990). (**P**)

FURTHER READING:
Sir Michael Havers, Edward Grayson and Peter Shankland, *The Royal Baccarat Scandal* (London: Kimber, 1977).

FILM ADAPTATIONS:
Action for Slander, d. Tim Whelan. GB: London Films, 1937. Screenplay by Ian Dalrymple and Miles Malleson, based on the novel by Mary Borden.

GEORGE BARRINGTON GB 1790

Barrington was born near Dublin, possibly the son of a silversmith named Waldron. His criminal career began at the age of sixteen when he stabbed a fellow schoolboy. After being flogged for the offence, he ran away to join a troupe of travelling players. It was then he learned the art of picking pockets. He practised his trade in Dublin and London, and was eventually arrested and deported to America in 1773. He soon returned to England, however, and attained legendary status in the underworld for his upper-class posturing and his criminal dexterity. He served a sentence of hard labour on the Woolwich hulks, but on his release he continued his career as a gentleman pickpocket.

In 1790, caught stealing a gold watch at Enfield racecourse, he was sentenced at the Old Bailey to transportation for seven years. Within a year of his arrival in Australia, he had achieved a conditional pardon (made absolute in 1796). He was appointed chief constable of Parramatta and settled to a life of hard work and reasonable luxury. Eventually, however, he became insane and died in 1804.

Barrington's first appearance in fiction can be found in a short story by John Lang entitled 'An Illustrious British Exile'. Originally published in Charles Dickens's magazine, *Household Words*, the tale found its way into a collection of Lang's stories, *Botany Bay* (1859). The fictional plot features Barrington, a ticket-of-leave man in Australia, practising his 'art' on a major's wife (to convince himself that his powers have not deserted him), and—more honestly—restoring a diamond necklace to its rightful owner.

A more substantial, and slightly more factual account is Ernest Dudley's novel *Picaroon* (1952). Dudley admits in a sub-title that his story is 'freely based on the scandalous career of George Barrington'. Opening with Barrington in Newgate Prison, awaiting his transportation to Australia, the novel looks back over the pickpocket's career in England, from his beginnings as a starving child thieving to survive, through his (fictional) encounters with the likes of Boswell and Johnson, Cagliostro and Emma Hamilton. The plot ends with his arrest by a worthy adversary created by the author, the Bow Street runner, Townsend.

FACTIONAL WORKS:
John Lang, 'An Illustrious British Exile', in *Botany Bay* (London: William Tegg, 1859).
Ernest Dudley, *Picaroon* (London: Robert Hale, 1952).

FURTHER READING:
Richard Lambert, *The Prince of Pickpockets* (London: Faber & Faber, 1930).

Mrs Bartlett was born into a French family in 1856. She married Edwin Bartlett, a grocer who was ten years her senior, and they settled down in Pimlico. The Bartletts had a friend, the Rev. George Dyson, who would spend many evenings chatting to Edwin. Dyson and Adelaide were having an affair, with (according to their later testimony) Bartlett's full approval—Edwin had unusual views on the sanctity of marriage. Late in 1885, Edwin fell ill. His doctor concluded that he was suffering from gastritis. He died on New Year's Day, 1886.

An autopsy resulted in the discovery of a massive dose of chloroform in Bartlett's stomach, although there were no traces of the substance in his mouth or throat. Adelaide was tried for murder, the prosecution presenting evidence that she had purchased chloroform from a chemist shortly before her husband's death. Adelaide insisted that it was intended as an anaesthetic for Edwin, implying that he had committed suicide. As there was insufficient proof of the administration of chloroform, she was acquitted by the jury. One eminent medical practitioner voiced the universal opinion that, 'in the interest of science', Adelaide should tell the world how she committed the murder.

Novelists were late in coming to the Pimlico poisoning case for inspiration. Elbur Ford's *Poison in Pimlico* (1950) started the ball rolling. As is the case with all four of Ford's novels, the attention is focussed on the characters themselves rather than the crime. Ford investigates the effect of the twisted relationships on the three principals, but comes to no definite conclusion about Edwin's death.

Freda M. Long's *Ever-Loving Adelaide* (1980), on the other hand, has no qualms in accusing Mrs Bartlett of the murder. Beginning in 1873, when Adelaide was still at a convent in France, to 1886, when she purchases a ticket for her voyage to America after the trial, Long gives a picture of a determined and self-obsessed woman. Adelaide commits the murder (Long doesn't delve into the intricacies of the poisoning), salving her conscience by deluding herself that Edwin knew what she was doing to him and approved.

The most successful factional treatment of this case was Julian Symons's *Sweet Adelaide* (1980), a novel of fascinating period detail and psychological insight. Symons's portrait of Adelaide spans from her first childhood memories to a few years prior to her death in America. Several chapters take the form of Adelaide's journal. Symons provides an ingenious and believable solution to the mystery of how Adelaide could have administered a corrosive poison to her husband without leaving traces in his throat and mouth.

FACTIONAL WORKS:
Elbur Ford, *Poison in Pimlico* (London: Werner Laurie, [1950]).
Freda M. Long, *Ever-loving Adelaide* (London: Robert Hale, 1980).
Julian Symons, *Sweet Adelaide* (London: Collins, 1980).

FURTHER READING:
Yseult Bridges, *Poison and Adelaide Bartlett* (London: Hutchinson & Co., 1962).

ERZSÉBET BATHORY HUNGARY 1610

The future Countess Bathory was born in 1561. She exhibited sadistic tendencies and sexual precocity from an early age. When Count Ferencz Nadasy took her as his wife, he little realised the sort of woman he was marrying. She would cheerfully inflict all manner of cruelty on her servant girls. When she reached the conclusion that bathing in virgin blood was the best cure for ageing skin, local women began to disappear around the Bathory estates in Csejthe.

During their marriage, her husband was frequently abroad fighting for his country; after his death in 1604 any possible rein on her murderous activities was removed. Her courtiers were compliant in her whims, procuring females for her cruel purposes. When she turned her attention to high-born women, the authorities were forced to act. Her castle was raided, and the horrified soldiers caught the Countess literally in the middle of a bloodbath. Erzsébet denied her involvement in the murders, placing the blame on her servants. As a member of Hungarian nobility and the widow of a noble and heroic lord, she probably regarded herself as safe from prosecution. King Matthias, however, faced with overwhelming proof of her guilt, decided otherwise. She was walled up in a small room of her castle, where she was kept alive for three years. The Bloody Countess died on 21st August 1614.

In 1971, Hammer Films pounced upon the horrific elements of the story (and the geographical location close to Transylvania), and produced a film entitled *Countess Dracula*. The script by Jeremy Paul was novelised by Michel Parry in 1971 (Parry had himself been working on a film script based on the Bathory case, but that had fallen through). The facts were used as a peg on which to hang a *She*-like fantasy story in which a wizened old woman is kept youthful-looking, not by fire as in Rider Haggard's novel, but by blood.

The Countess sets her sights on a handsome young hussar and poses as her own daughter to ward off suspicion concerning her unusual beauty treatment. At the altar, her features disintegrate into hideous old age. In a scene reminiscent of Greek tragedy, the Countess attempts to murder her real daughter to restore her beauty, but kills her husband-to-be instead.

FACTIONAL WORKS:
Michel Parry, *Countess Dracula* (London: Sphere Books, 1971).

FURTHER READING:
Valentine Penrose, *The Bloody Countess* (London: Calder & Boyars, 1970).

FILM ADAPTATIONS:
Countess Dracula, d. Peter Sasdy. GB: Rank/Hammer, 1971. Screenplay by Jeremy Paul, novelised by Michel Parry.

JEROBOAM O. BEAUCHAMP USA 1826

Beauchamp was a successful lawyer of twenty-one, the archetypal 'Southern gentleman', when he married Ann Cook, who was seventeen years older than him. Ann had previously had an affair with the former attorney-general of Kentucky, Colonel Solomon P. Sharp, who had abandoned her in pregnancy; the child died in infancy. Beauchamp claimed in his later confession that one of Ann's conditions for their marriage was that he should avenge her honour. Beauchamp had challenged Sharp to a duel, but his opponent had refused, spreading malicious rumours about Ann and her dead child.

Early in 1826, Beauchamp, dressed in a cloak and hood, called at Sharp's house and stabbed him to death on his porch. Despite his crude disguise, Beauchamp was recognised as he fled the scene, and was promptly arrested. After he was sentenced to death, his wife proposed that they commit suicide together. On the eve of his execution, Ann visited him in his cell. They drank the poison she had smuggled in with her, but it had no effect. They then proceeded to stab one another. By the time the horrified guards discovered what was happening, Ann was dead. They dragged Beauchamp, still bleeding, to the gallows, where he was hanged on 7th July 1826.

The 'Kentucky Tragedy', as the case was known—with its ingredients of revenge, honour and suicide—was a godsend to novelists and playwrights; it still ranks as the second most popular American crime to be factionalised (following the story of Lizzie Borden). The case particularly appealed to Southern writers—its emphasis on family pride and 'gentlemanly' conduct struck a chord.

Edgar Allan Poe adopted the plot as the basis for his only attempt at drama, *The Politian*. Written before 1835, five scenes of the play were published in the *Southern Literary Messenger* between 1835-6, but the full manuscript didn't find its way into print until 1923. Almost a century after it was written, the play was finally staged in 1933.

Charles Fenno Hoffmann, an author who himself produced a fictional account of the Kentucky Tragedy, had written that the facts seemed 'as belonging to a bygone age'. Poe, who was closely associated with Hoffmann, may have taken his cue from these words. He transferred the events to medieval Rome, where the Politian (Beauchamp) is none other than the travelling Earl of Leicester, in love with a local beauty, Lalage. She has been seduced by Castiglione (the name but not the character is taken from the historical Italian courtier). Castiglione intends to marry his cousin, Alessandra, and Lalage urges the Politian to avenge her shame by murdering her seducer.

The Hamlet-like Politian wrestles with his conscience. He challenges Castiglione to a duel, but when the wretched man refuses to fight and offers himself up to be murdered in cold blood, Politian cannot perform the deed.

The final extant scene is set in a coliseum, where Castiglione and Alessandra are to be wed. Lalage and Politian enter, the latter finally resolved to kill his lover's seducer, and then to join her in suicide. The play ends before the murder is committed.

Poe, in reviewing Hoffmann's subsequent novel *Greyslaer*, which was based on the case, said that 'the incidents might be better woven into a tragedy'. By that time, however, he had already demonstrated that he was not the man to do it, having lost interest in the play before it was finished. Despite the work's Shakespearian iambic pentameter and its references to Hamlet, it is well below par for Poe, certainly not as impressive or dramatic as his prose and poetry. There is little dramatic tension or development, and the characters are melodramatic. Had he recast the plot into a short story, complete with his usual macabre touches, it might have been another classic of the genre.

Thomas Holly Chivers, later to become a friend of Poe's, also turned to the case in his 1834 play, *Conrad and Eudora*. Like Poe's effort, Chivers's work was written in blank verse reminiscent of Renaissance drama (around this time, Shakespeare was in vogue in America, with actors such as Edwin Forrest and Junius Brutus Booth popularising his plays; this influence was not always beneficial to the output of American playwrights). Chivers returned the story to its Kentucky setting, where Conrad (Beauchamp), Eudora (Ann) and Alonzo (Sharp) go through the motions of the tragedy. The play begins with Eudora's seduction and follows the facts reasonably closely (more so than in Poe's version), casting Eudora in the Lady Macbeth role of vengeful instigator. Unsatisfied with his work, Chivers revised the play as *Leoni; or, The Orphan of Venice*. This version was published in serial form in *The Georgia Citizen* in 1851; it was not published in book form until the appearance of Chivers's *Complete Works* in 1957.

Like Poe, Charlotte Barnes transfers the action of her Beauchamp tragedy, *Octavia Bragaldi*, to Italy—in this case, fifteenth-century Milan. The Count Castelli goes through a false marriage ceremony with Octavia. When he leaves her and she believes he is dead, she marries Bragaldi. The count, meanwhile, has married a wealthy, respectable lady and begins spreading malicious rumours about Octavia. She persuades her husband to avenge her honour, and Bragaldi kills his wife's slanderer. Having confessed his guilt, he stabs himself and his wife takes poison. *Octavia Bragaldi* was staged in New York in 1837 and was eventually published in 1848.

Charles Fenno Hoffmann's Beauchamp factional work appeared in 1840. The novel, *Greyslaer*, moves the facts back in time to Revolutionary America. In the Mohawk Valley, a young lawyer named Max Greyslaer finds himself imprisoned for his radical actions. He escapes and flees to the home of his guardian. When a band of Mohawks working for the British attack the house, Greyslaer and his guardian's daughter Alida are the only survivors. They are taken prisoner, but manage to break loose from their captors.

When Greyslaer proposes to Alida, she tells him she was coerced into a secret marriage with a sinister individual named Bradshawe; even when evidence comes to light that the marriage was illegal, Alida still refuses Greyslaer's hand. Greyslaer leaves for the American army, where Alida's brother Derrick is serving. When Derrick is killed, Alida takes responsibility for his son, but malicious rumours circulate claiming he is Alida's child. Greyslaer meets up with Bradshawe in Albany and fights with him. When Bradshawe subsequently disappears, Greyslaer is arrested and tried for his murder. Evidence is produced to prove his innocence and the parentage of the child. Greyslaer and Alida are finally united in marriage.

Whereas Hoffmann adapted the case to suit the needs of his fictional tale, W. G. Simms gives a close reading of the facts in his novel, *Beauchampe*. The work was first published in 1842, and a revised, two-volume edition appeared fourteen years later, as *Charlemont* and *Beauchampe*. According to his biographer, Simms gives 'a detailed and often salacious account' of the true case.

The first section of the tale tells how Warham Sharpe, a young lawyer masquerading as a theology student, seduces Margaret Cooper. He refuses to abide by his promise of marriage and leaves her. She gives birth to a child who dies, and vows revenge on her seducer. The second half of the plot takes up the story five years later, Margaret now known by the name of Anna Cooke. Beauchampe, a young attorney, proposes marriage and is accepted, on condition that he avenge his wife's seduction. Sharpe visits Beauchampe, an old friend of his, and attempts to seduce Margaret once more. At this stage, Beauchampe is unaware of the true identity of his wife's seducer. When he discovers that Sharpe is the man, he stabs him. He is tried and condemned to death. As in the real case, he and his wife attempt suicide; she succeeds and he is taken to his execution.

In 1944, Katherine Anne Porter gave fellow writer Robert Penn Warren 'an old pamphlet, the trial of Beauchamp for killing Colonel Sharpe'; 'I read it in five minutes. But I was six years making the book'. The 'book' was Warren's 1950 novel, *World Enough and Time*, a mammoth blockbuster that gave a new slant to the Beauchamp case. The plot takes the form of a contemporary historian perusing and commenting on the journal of Jeremiah Beaumont, a young lawyer of the early nineteenth century. Beaumont marries Rachel Jordan on the strict understanding that he kill her seducer, Colonel Fort. As the story progresses, the narrator gives his own insights into the case, and investigates the thoughts and feelings of Beaumont and the other protagonists.

Beaumont is a self-deluding young man, a knight in shining armour at odds with the frontier life around him. Even when Rachel withdraws her condition, he insists on completing his part of the contract. After his trial and sentencing, the plot veers markedly from the original. Beaumont and Rachel escape from the prison where he awaits execution, and hole up in an outlaws' colony. Here, Beaumont's honourable pretensions are thrown into stark relief against the law of the criminals around him. Rachel, ridden with guilt and remorse, takes her own life, while her husband is slain for the reward on his head, just as pitilessly as he killed Fort.

The only British factional novel based on the Beauchamp case was Joseph Shearing's *To Bed At Noon*, published in 1951. Marcus Dallam, a lawyer, is sent by his friend, Kain Bowman, to survey the land in Hazel, Kentucky that Bowman has acquired by grant from Congress. Under an assumed name, Dallam comes to know the eccentric Allen family and is seduced by the tomboyish Challis Allen. Although he has an agreement with Bowman's sister, he proposes to Challis, but a bout of fever keeps him from the church, and Challis, believing herself jilted, vows revenge.

Changing her name to Jessamine Rowan, she travels to Frankfort, where Dallam, having married Bowman's sister, is now Attorney General of the state. She meets and marries Bowman, extracting a promise from him that he will force a duel with 'Orlando Fineall', Dallam's assumed persona. When Dallam learns of the threat, and Bowman and his wife discover the identity of Fineall, the Attorney General quits his post and prepares to leave Frankfort, rather than duel with his friend. Bowman takes Dallam to a deserted spot and murders him. After his trial and conviction, he takes poison and Challis stabs herself. Shearing's novel begins promisingly, with a faithful reproduction of life and manners in the American South, but the author allows the melodrama to eventually overbalance the plot. Heavy symbolism works against the overall effect of the novel: the book's title is taken from the alternative name for the convulvulus plant, 'go to bed at noon', which presages early death; also, Kain slays his 'brother', like his Biblical counterpart.

FACTIONAL WORKS:

[Thomas Holley Chivers], *Conrad and Eudora; or, The Death of Alonzo* (Philadelphia: [Thomas Holley Chivers], 1834). (**P**)

[Charles Fenno Hoffmann], *Greyslaer* (New York: Harper & Bros., 1840).

W. G. Simms, *Beauchampe* (Philadelphia: Lea & Blanchard, 1842).

Charlotte Barnes, *Octavia Bragaldi* (Philadelphia: E. H. Butler, 1848). (**P**)

W. G. Simms, *Charlemont* (New York: RedWeld, 1856). Revised first part of the 1842 novel.

W. G. Simms, *Beauchampe* (New York: RedWeld, [1856]). Revised second part of the 1842 novel.

Edgar Allan Poe, *The Politian. An Unfinished Tragedy* (Richmond: Edgar Allan Poe Shrine, 1923). (**P**)

Robert Penn Warren, *World Enough and Time* (New York: Random House, 1950).

Joseph Shearing, *To Bed at Noon* (London: William Heinemann, 1951).

Thomas Holley Chivers, *Leoni; or, The Orphan of Venice*, in *Complete Works* (Providence, RI: Brown University press, 1957).

FURTHER READING:

Jules Zanger, ed., *The Beauchamp Tragedy* (Philadelphia: Lippincott, [1963]).

BECK AND FERNANDEZ USA 1949

Raymond Fernandez, a balding Spanish-American, and Martha Beck, an overweight nurse, met through a Lonely Hearts club in 1947. Fernandez was a natural charmer of women, and the two decided to put his charm to good use, contacting single, divorced or widowed ladies through the Lonely Hearts agencies and swindling them. Beck posed as Fernandez's sister, but her jealousy of the attachments he had to form with other women eventually led to a further development in the plot. Soon they were murdering the women as well as stealing from them.

In all, they are believed to have killed over twenty ladies, although they were only charged with the murders of three. In 1949, the couple were living in Michigan at the home of Mrs Delphine Dowling, a widow. Mrs Dowling, and her daughter, Ranielle, eventually disappeared. Police called at the house, where they discovered a wet patch of cement in the cellar. Underneath they found the bodies of Delphine and Ranielle Dowling. Beck and Fernandez were arrested and freely confessed to these murders and a host of others. They were transferred from Michigan to New York, where they were accused of another murder—and where, unlike Michigan, the death penalty still applied. The two were found guilty and executed two years later in 1951.

In 1969, an American film version of the case was produced under the title *The Honeymoon Killers.* The script was turned into a novel of the same title by author Paul Buck, who utilised more facts from the original case. Buck's novel became a best-seller in France, where it was published in the prestigious Série Noire edition of crime fiction. The author concentrates specifically on Martha Beck, whose life teeters between a Mills-and-Boon-like view of the world and her murderous, jealous hold over the street-wise Ray. It is a brutal portrait of two amoral characters trapped in a largely sexual relationship, trying to make a success of their tawdry lives—and using any means to do so.

FACTIONAL WORKS:
Paul Buck, *The Honeymoon Killers* (London: Sphere Books, 1970).

FURTHER READING:
Wenzell Brown, *Introduction to Murder* (London: Andrew Davies, 1953).

FILM ADAPTATIONS:
The Honeymoon Killers, d. Leonard Kastle. US: AIP, 1969. Screenplay by Leonard Kastle, novelised by Paul Buck.

MENDEL BEILISS CASE RUSSIA 1913

In March 1911, the body of thirteen-year-old Andrei Yushchinsky was discovered in a cave near the city of Kiev. He had been viciously stabbed to death. At his funeral, leaflets were distributed accusing the local Jewish population of ritual murder—of killing a Christian to obtain blood for ritual purposes. Despite the 'blood accusation' (a slander that was first employed, in the Middle Ages against the Jews), suspicion fell strongly upon a local Christian family who were well known as thieves and fences. Several pieces of evidence pointed to their involvement in the crime.

However, the local judiciary (with the full backing of the Russian central government—even the Tsar expressed an interest in the case) charged a Jewish workman, Mendel Beiliss, with the murder. For over two years, Beiliss was confined in appalling conditions while a case against him was constructed. The intention seemed to be two-fold: to use the eventual trial as a precedent to establish ritual murder in the law-books, and to instigate a new pogrom against the Jews in Russia. For this reason, the prosecution was not so much concerned with Beiliss's guilt as with clearing the names of the suspected Christian family, and proving the blood accusation. Facts were suppressed, anti-Semitic 'expert' witnesses were called to give an historical perspective to the idea of ritual murder, and important witnesses for the defence were spirited away.

At the end of Beiliss's trial, two questions were put to the jury: whether they believed the murder to have been ritual, and whether they considered Beiliss to be guilty. The judge worded the first question so ambiguously that, although the jury answered in the affirmative, it was still debatable whether they accepted the principle of ritual murder (anti-Semites claimed a victory, of course). The defence had presented their case so well, however, that Beiliss was acquitted. In the long run, the trial failed in both its objectives, merely presenting the Russian legal system and government in a poor light internationally. Beiliss left Russia shortly after his acquittal, eventually settling in America where he died twenty-one years later.

In 1966 Bernard Malamud's novel, *The Fixer*, was published in New York; it subsequently won its author both the Pulitzer prize and the National Book Award. The 'fixer' of the title is Yakov Bok, an odd-job man and Russian Jew living incognito in the gentile community of Kiev and trying to pass for a Christian. Like Beiliss, Bok is accused of the ritual murder of a young Christian boy. The anti-Semitic feeling aroused by the case is further inflamed by his living in an area of the city forbidden to the Jews. The central government get involved in the case, as they most certainly did in the Beiliss trial. Some critics have suggested that the title also refers to the Tsar himself, in his attempts to fix the result of the trial.

Malamud's novel, however, doesn't dwell specifically on the case; it ends before it comes to court. The author's subject is Bok's term in prison, the effects of his physical and mental torment and torture and his eventual redemption in his own eyes as a Jew and as a figurehead for his people. Bok, through his suffering, is reborn into his abandoned faith. At least one critic has pointed out the dual definition of Bok's surname: in his own language, 'Bok' can mean 'goat' (i.e. a scapegoat) and also 'a piece of iron'. Yakov Bok stands as firm as iron in his newly-found self-identity and in his position as a symbol of the plight of Jews throughout Russia.

FACTIONAL WORKS:
Bernard Malamud, *The Fixer* (New York: Farrar, Straus & Giroux Inc., 1966).

FURTHER READING:
Samuel Maurice, *Blood Accusation* (Philadelphia: Jewish Publication Society of America, 1966).

FILM ADAPTATIONS:
The Fixer, d. John Frankenheimer. US: MGM, 1968. Screenplay by Dalton Trumbo, based on the novel by Bernard Malamud.

BENDER FAMILY USA 1870s

The Benders—mother, father, son and daughter—lived in a remote district of Labetta County, Kansas. In 1873, a Dr York disappeared in the area after visiting his brother. A search party was organised, with Mr Bender and his son assisting. Colonel York grew suspicious of the Benders and called at their home later with a posse, only to find that the family had fled. A search of the area uncovered the bodies of twelve people, including that of Dr York, who had been bludgeoned to death.

The motive appeared to be robbery in each case. It seems that visitors were invited to sit down to a meal and then clubbed from behind by one of the family hiding behind a curtain. The Benders were never found, and rumours circulated for some time as to their supposed whereabouts. Some even believed that they had been discovered by a posse and given a summary execution.

In 1943, Anthony Boucher wrote a short horror story, 'They Bite', which presented a supernatural extension to the Benders's murderous careers following their massacre by a posse. It was another twenty-seven years before a substantial and more factual account was produced about the family.

Robert Adleman's novel, *The Bloody Benders*, tells the story through the eyes of the fictional Bradley Fisher, a confidant of the Benders and Kate Bender's lover. The discovery of bodies at the Benders's farm causes Bradley to review his dealings with them, and the signs of their murderous activities that he chose at the time to ignore. Adleman presents a picture of an apparently civilised community corrupted and diseased by the malignant family within its boundaries.

FACTIONAL WORKS:
Anthony Boucher: 'They Bite', in *The Compleat Weerewolf* (New York: Curtis Brown, 1943).
Robert Adleman, *The Bloody Benders* (New York: Stein & Day, [1970]).

FURTHER READING:
Richard Glyn Jones, ed., *The Mammoth Book of Killer Women* (London: Robinson, 1993).

HERBERT JOHN BENNETT GB 1901

Bennett was a small-time crook who indulged in petty confidence tricks with the aid of his wife, Mary. He was often unfaithful to her, and at the turn of the century was involved in an affair with a parlourmaid. About this time, Mary Bennett moved into lodgings in Great Yarmouth, giving a false home address and claiming to be a widow. In September 1900, her body was discovered on Yarmouth beach; she had been strangled with a bootlace and sexually assaulted.

The police caught up with Bennett in London. Among his belongings, they discovered a gold chain similar to one belonging to his wife; her landlady claimed that she had worn this on the night of her death. Also witnesses had claimed to have seen Bennett in Yarmouth at the time of the murder. His trial opened in February 1901, with Edward Marshall Hall appearing for the defence. One witness was called to give evidence of Bennett presence in London on the day of his wife's death, but the prosecution threw doubt on the witness' reliability. Bennett himself declined to enter the witness box. The jury found him guilty and he was hanged in March 1901. Marshall Hall remained convinced of Bennett's innocence, claiming that the murder had been committed by an unknown sex-maniac. This theory was reinforced when, eleven years later, another body was discovered on Yarmouth beach in similar circumstances.

American author Hilary Waugh transferred the Bennett case to the States in his novel, *The Missing Man* (1964). Police Chief Fred C. Fellowes investigates the murder of an unknown girl whose body is found on the beach of a Connecticut resort. The case becomes known as the 'Little Bohemia' murder, and Waugh's police procedural plot follows the chief as he pursues several dead-end enquiries and fruitless leads before discovering the murderer's identity. The 'Little Bohemia' murderer, like Bennett, lives under an alias, has a record of theft, and murders his wife to marry someone else. As with the Bennett case, his wife lives as a widow in the resort town, and her murderer-husband is finally trapped with the aid of jewellery removed from the body.

FACTIONAL WORKS:
Hilary Waugh, *The Missing* Man (New York: Doubleday, 1964).

FURTHER READING:
Julian Symons, *A Reasonable Doubt* (London: Cresset Press, 1960).

HARRY BENSON AND WILLIAM KURR GB 1877

Benson and Kurr were two accomplished con-artists whose gang operated principally in France in the latter half of the nineteenth century, specialising in horseracing swindles. They also had connections with detective officers at Scotland Yard, who received bribes to keep them from pressing charges and to warn the con-artists of impending investigations into their affairs on home turf. Among these was Chief Inspector John Mieklejohn, who introduced other officers into the bribery network, including Nathaniel Druskovich, responsible for investigating foreign frauds. At one time, Druskovich had to warn Benson that he was travelling to Scotland to arrest him. Benson, who had already moved some of his funds from the Bank of England to the Clydesdale Bank (the Scottish bank, unlike the Bank of England, used unmarked and therefore untraceable notes), was able to escape with £13,000.

Despite the crooked detectives' efforts, however, Scotland Yard was closing in on the gang. Benson was arrested at Rotterdam, and Druskovich arranged for a telegram to be sent from 'Scotland Yard' telling the Dutch police that they had arrested the wrong man. Fortunately, the Dutch waited for a letter of authority from the Yard before releasing their man. When none was forthcoming, Druskovich himself was sent to bring Benson back. He could do little for his criminal colleague, since he was now also under suspicion.

In the meantime, Kurr had also been arrested and the two masterminds of the fraud ring stood trial in 1877. Found guilty, they were sent to Milbank Prison, where they informed the authorities of their spy network. Four detectives, including Meiklejohn and Druskovich, were arrested and tried. One of them, Chief Inspector Clarke, was released due to insufficient evidence, and was retired on a pension. The others received two years hard labour each. When Benson and Kurr were released they returned to their criminal activities, covering Europe and America. Caught and held in New York's Tombs Prison after one failed scam, Harry Benson committed suicide by throwing himself from a balcony.

Donald Thomas, who had already written an atmospheric novel concerning the Victorian poisoner Thomas Neill Cream, put his series detective Inspector Swain on the Benson and Kurr case in the 1993 novel, *The Arrest of Scotland Yard*. Swain is hired by the sinister Lerici family to investigate the murder in Greece of John Posthumous Lerici, supposedly the illegitimate son of Lord Byron. While he pursues his enquiries among Heinrich Schliemann's excavations of Mycenae, a Major Hugh Montgomery, alias Harry Benson, is executing another swindle in France with his colleague, William Kurr. Returning to England, Swain uncovers Lerici's criminal dealings with Benson and Kurr. At the same time, he is aware of odd occurrences at Scotland Yard, and reveals a network of bribery and fraud to his superiors. He himself is under suspicion, and must clear his name, bring the real police spies to justice and solve the mystery of Lerici's death. The self-educated Swain, reading Browning's translation of Agamemnon to pass the weary hours of travelling, is struck by the similarity between Aeschylus's tale of murder, corruption and incest and the criminal web that he has to untangle. Once again, Thomas twists the facts of the original case, but nevertheless presents a convincing period feel and manages to blend two crimes— factual and fictional—with exceptional skill.

FACTIONAL WORKS:
Donald Thomas, *The Arrest of Scotland Yard* (London: Macmillan, 1993).

FURTHER READING:
Colin Wilson and Donald Seaman, *An Encyclopedia of Scandal* (London: Weidenfeld & Nicholson, 1986).

ALAN BERG MURDER USA 1984

Alan Berg was one of the new breed of confrontational radio show hosts that swept through America in the 1980s. Outspoken and opinionated, he provoked emotional extremes in his listeners. A Jewish ex-lawyer, Berg was particularly unpopular with redneck right-wing extremists. On 18th June 1984, 'the man you love to hate' (as he was called on station KAO in Denver, Colorado, where he worked) was gunned down as he climbed out of his car. Police followed several leads, and various suggestions were put forward by the media, ranging from an execution instigated by Colonel Gadafi of Libya to a murder carried out by the Ku Klux Klan. In an unrelated incident in October of that year, FBI agents raided a house in Sandpoint, Idaho, where an arsenal of rifles, pistols and explosives was uncovered. The house was believed to be a base for a neo-Nazi group called the Bruders Schweigen (the Silent Brotherhood), and amongst the arms was a MAC-10, the gun used to kill Berg. Eleven members of the group were arrested following a shoot-out in which their leader, Robert Jay Matthews, was killed.

Their trial opened in Seattle in September 1985. The Brotherhood were known to target blacks, liberals, homosexuals and Jews. Berg's name was discovered on a hit list produced by them. The accused men received a range of sentences, but following a failed attempt at plea-bargaining, the murder charge concerning Berg was dropped. Two members of the group, David Lane and Bruce Pierce, were convicted of Berg's murder in a later trial in 1987.

Barry Champlain, the cynical, abrasive talk-show host of Eric Bogosian's one-man show *Talk Radio*, was loosely based on the character of Berg, and shows the hostile, defiant style of radio broadcasting that led to Berg's death. Champlain is portrayed as a morally bankrupt, misanthropic person, manipulating and exploiting his listeners. After putting down an anti-Semite with a (false) tale of a visit to a concentration camp, he inflames a black caller's wrath against his Jewish landlord. He has no scruples, no beliefs, no values. His only concern is that his ratings must be high, totally oblivious to the moral and psychological cost to both himself or his audience.

Originally staged in 1985 (and published three years later), Bogosian's play was filmed in its year of publication by Oliver Stone. The script by Bogosian and Stone opened up the play, and emphasised the basis in Berg's career, showing Champlain's eventual murder in a parking lot after being threatened over the radio. As in the stage play, Bogosian played Champlain to maximum effect, winning the viewers' sympathy for his self-loathing and turmoil, while horrifying with his vitriolic radio style.

FACTIONAL WORKS:
Eric Bogosian, *Talk Radio* (New York: Random House, 1988). (P)

FURTHER READING:
Stephen Singular, *Talked to Death* (New York: Beech Tree Books, 1987).

FILM ADAPTATIONS:
Talk Radio, d. Oliver Stone. US: Fox, 1988. Screenplay by Eric Bogosian, based on his play.

ANTOINE BERTHET FRANCE 1827

Berthet was born in 1802 in Brangues near Grenobles. His father was a shoe-maker, but Antoine set his sights on an ecclesiastical vocation. However, in 1822, he fell seriously ill and had to find a gentler occupation. Monsieur Michoud de la Tour gave him employment as private tutor to his children. At his later trial, Berthet claimed that he and Mme. Michoud became lovers, and upon the discovery of the relationship, his master dismissed him. Michoud himself claimed that Berthet had made advances to his wife which she rejected.

Whatever the truth of the matter, Berthet left the house and entered a seminary for two years. The shoemaker's son once more applied himself to theology, but when he was informed that he was unsuitable for the priest-hood, he began writing threatening letters to the Michoud family, blaming them for his failure. To prevent a scandal, M. Michoud obtained him a post with another family. Shortly after his appointment, Berthet was dismissed. Once more he laid the blame for his rejection upon the Michoud family, and Mme. Michoud in particular.

Berthet continued to write insulting letters to the Michouds, and on 22nd July 1827, he attended high mass in Brangues. When Mme. Michoud entered the church and knelt in prayer, Berthet pulled out a concealed pistol and shot her in the back. With another pistol, he fired at his own throat. Mme. Michoud survived the attempt on her life, as did Berthet himself—temporarily. He was tried at Grenobles and sentenced to death. His execu-tion took place in February 1828.

Henri Marie Beyle, who wrote under the pseudonym of Stendhal, was a native of Grenobles and had read the reports of the trial in the *Gazette des Tribunaux*. Three years after Berthet's execution, Stendhal's novel, *Le Rouge et le Noir*, appeared in print (translated variously as *The Red and The Black*, or *Scarlet and Black*). In the character of the self-deluding hypocrite, Julien Sorel, Stendhal presents a close portrait of Berthet. Reaching manhood after the glories of Napoleon's reign, Sorel turns his back on a career in the Army (*le rouge* of the title) and seeks advancement through the church (*le noir*). He obtains a post as tutor in the house of the mayor of Verrieres, M. de Rênal. Obsessed by the mayor's beautiful wife, Sorel presents himself with the chal-lenge of seducing her—and succeeds. Rumours abound concerning the handsome tutor and Mme. de Rênal; to safeguard his career, Sorel leaves the house and enters a seminary at Besancon.

From here he obtains a position with the Marquis de la Mole, and falls for the Marquis' young daughter. History repeats itself—Sorel seduces the lady of the house. The Marquis is forced to arrange a marriage between the two lovers, first providing Sorel with a commission in the Army. At this juncture, Sorel's hopes are dashed when Mme. de Rênal writes to the Marquis, denouncing his future son-in-law as an opportunist. Sorel buys a pistol and shoots Mme. de Rênal in church (unlike his historical prototype, Sorel does not attempt suicide; Stendhal's hypocrite would not go to such lengths). He accepts his sentence of death with stoicism, and Mme. de Rênal, recovered from the attempt on her life, dies of a broken heart.

FACTIONAL WORKS:

Stendhal, *The Scarlet and Black* (Harmondsworth: Penguin, 1953). First published in French as *Le Rouge et Le Noir*, 1831.

FURTHER READING:

Rayner Heppenstall, *French Crime of the Romantic Age* (London: Hamish Hamilton, 1970).

BLACK DAHLIA MURDER USA 1947

Elizabeth Short was born in Boston, Massachusetts in 1924. In her late teens she worked in Miami and Santa Barbara as a waitress in army camps. In 1943, she was caught in a police raid on a cafe suspected of selling drink to juveniles. She was sent back to her parents, but returned to waitress work soon after. She had a few brief relationships with servicemen, including one airforce major whom she later claimed to have married (he died during the war). After the war, Elizabeth moved to California, hoping to get a job in films, but she was reduced to prostitution. Because of her jet-black hair and clothes to match, she became known as the Black Dahlia.

In January 1947, her naked and dismembered body was discovered on waste ground near Los Angeles. She was identified from fingerprints taken in the police raid in 1943. Due to her activities as a call-girl, the police found themselves with more suspects than they wanted. The search was narrowed down to a tall, red-haired man last seen talking to Elizabeth. Several suspects were questioned but the police lacked any serious evidence to construct a viable case. They were also inundated with cranks confessing to the murder. They did receive a parcel containing some of the Dahlia's belongings and promising 'a letter to follow', but no further correspondence from this source appeared. The case remains officially unsolved.

The gruesome details of the Black Dahlia case seem to have repelled faction writers for over thirty years. In 1977, however, American novelist John Gregory Dunne tackled the subject in *True Confessions*. Tom Spellacy, a Los Angeles policeman, investigates the murder of a woman, Lois Fazzenda, whose body has been found cut in two. She is a small-time actress who has appeared in stag films. Meanwhile, Tom's brother, Des, a pastor working for the powerful Cardinal Danahar, is informed that he is to be recommended for a bishopric.

Tom's investigations into the Fazzenda case uncover local political corruption that would reflect badly on the church, and would also implicate his brother. Although not a devoted cop, Tom is determined to pin the murder on the crooked contractor Jack Amsterdam, whom he believes is the real killer. Tom realises that Amsterdam will reveal Des's connection, albeit tenuous, with the murdered woman, and will thus ruin the clergyman's career. Dunne uses the Short case merely as a starting point from which to develop the intricate plot.

James Ellroy's *The Black Dahlia* (1987) is firmly structured around the factual murder. Ellroy's fictional detectives, Bucky Reichart and Lee Blanchard—two ex-boxers turned cops—are assigned to investigate the Elizabeth Short case. Each of them, in their own way, falls under the posthumous spell of the Black Dahlia as they pursue dead-end enquiries and tantalising clues around a Chandleresque Los Angeles. The final solution again involves corrupt business and political double-crossing, along with psychopathic insanity. All the characters are portrayed as sexually, psychologically or morally corrupt, giving the novel an aura of intense pessimism. This does not make the story any less believable, but it is definitely not the type of novel to read for enjoyment.

FACTIONAL WORKS:
John Gregory Dunne, *True Confessions* (New York: Dutton, [1977]).
James Ellroy, *The Black Dahlia* (New York: Mysterious Press, 1987).

FURTHER READING:
Richard and Mollie Whittington-Egan, *The Bedside Book of Murder* (London: David & Charles, 1988).

FILM ADAPTATIONS:
True Confessions, d. Ulu Grosbard. US: United Artists, 1981. Screenplay by Joan Didion and John Gregory Dunne, based on his novel.

MARY BLANDY GB 1752

Mary Blandy lived with her parents at Henley-on-Thames. In 1746, she made the acquaintance of a Scottish aristocrat, William Henry Cranstoun, who stayed with the Blandy family for six months. Mary fell in love with Cranstoun and a marriage was expected. However, it transpired that Cranstoun was already married and Mr Blandy threw him out of his house. Cranstoun, desperately impoverished despite his noble connections, continued to correspond with Mary.

According to Mary's later statement at her trial, Cranstoun persuaded her to administer a 'love powder' to her father, which would persuade him to look favourably on her lover. Evidently, Cranstoun sent the powder through the post to Mary. When she gave her father the concoction, he fell sick and eventually died in agony. The powder was analysed and found to contain arsenic. Mary was tried for murder, and her story of the 'love powder' was rejected by the jury. She was sentenced to death and hanged; as for Cranstoun, he fled abroad and died in poverty.

The Blandy case inspired three fine post-war novels, all similar in style and content, but each enjoyable in its own fashion. Joan Morgan's *The*

Hanging Wood (1950) follows Mary from her first meeting with Cranstoun to the day of her execution. The bibliography and author's note at the beginning of the book readily identify the source of the novel. Morgan gives a sympathetic portrayal of Mary as a naive, innocent dupe blinded by love and trust. The 'hanging wood' of the title is the ironically-named local woodland in which Mary spends many of her dreamy leisure hours.

Philip Lindsay's *In Her Looking Glass* (1956) presents the Blandy story from the viewpoint of Ned Hearne, who in reality was Mr Blandy's clerk. Hearne, in Lindsay's narrative, is deeply in love with Mary himself, and willingly plays Iago to Mr Blandy's Othello, seeking to remove Cranstoun from Mary's favour. Hearne acts as confidant not only to Mary and Mr Blandy, but also to Mary's maid who is in love with Hearne, thus providing a reason for her to testify against Mary. As the link between these characters, Hearne is in a suitable position to present the facts of the case thoroughly. He believes Mary to have been Cranstoun's dupe in the murder.

Jean Stubbs, in her novel, *My Grand Enemy* (1967), sees Mary as a willing accomplice to Cranstoun, reading the intent behind his tale of love philtres. Her narrative begins with Mary's birth, traces her courtship with Cranstoun, her trial and execution, and ends with the appearance of her ghost at Cranstoun's death-bed in 1752.

FACTIONAL WORKS:
Joan Morgan, *The Hanging Wood* (London: Macdonald, 1950).
Philip Lindsay, *In Her Looking Glass* (London: Hutchinson & Co., 1956).
Jean Stubbs, *My Grand Enemy* (London: Macmillan, 1967).

FURTHER READING:
Rayner Heppenstall, *Reflections on the Newgate Calendar* (London: W. H. Allen, 1975).

BOORN BROTHERS CASE USA 1819

In 1812, Russell Colvin vanished from his house in the town of Manchester, Vermont. Seven years later, Amos Boorn, the uncle of Colvin's wife, claimed to have had a dream in which Colvin told him that he had been murdered, and that his killers were Amos's nephews, Stephen and Jesse Boorn. Two knives and a button were found at the Boorn's barn, which were all identified as Colvin's. Bones were also discovered, although they were later claimed to be animal remains, not human. By that time, the two Boorns had already confessed to the murder—committed after an altercation with their brother-in-law.

However, by the time of their trial in 1819, the brothers had withdrawn their confessions. They were still found guilty and sentenced to death, although Jesse's sentence was later commuted to life imprisonment. Their lawyer, in a last attempt to clear them, advertised for information concerning Colvin's disappearance. The advertisement appeared in a New

York paper, where it was seen by a reader whose brother-in-law had a workman fitting Colvin's description. The man was taken to Manchester where he was identified as the supposed murder victim. The Boorns were released and petitioned the state for compensation. This was refused on the grounds that they had confessed freely to the killing. Nevertheless, the Boorn case is frequently cited by anti-capital punishment campaigners in America.

Wilkie Collins published his short story 'John Jago's Ghost' in the *Home Journal* between December 1873 and February 1874 (it appeared almost simultaneously in the *New York Fireside Companion* under the title 'The Dead Alive'). Collins had written the story during a reading tour of America in 1873, when he must have come across details of the Boorn case. In his tale, an overworked English barrister, Philip Lefrank, is persuaded to take a holiday with hi s distant relative, Isaac Meadowcroft, in America. At Morwick Farm, Lefrank meets Meadowcroft's sons Silas and Ambrose, his puritanical daughter, his surly farmhand John Jago, and his niece Naomi Colebrook. Naomi is in love with Ambrose, although Jago has set his sights on her. There is no love lost between the brothers and Jago; he has already stabbed Silas during an argument.

After a final row culminating in Jago's disappearance, bones are discovered that are assumed to be the remains of the farmhand. The brothers, fearful of a death sentence, plead guilty at their trial for murder, hoping for clemency. Naomi persuades Lefrank to advertise for Jago, although the Englishman is convinced that Jago is dead. However, Jago returns to meet with Naomi—knowing full well the results his disappearance has had on the brothers—and is arrested by Lefrank. The brothers are released and Naomi, disappointed with Ambrose's weakness in confessing to the murder, marries Lefrank.

FACTIONAL WORKS:

Wilkie Collins, 'John Jago's Ghost', in *The Frozen Deep and Other Tales* (London: Bentley, 1874).

FURTHER READING:

Carl Sifakis, *The Encyclopedia of American Crime* (New York: Facts on File Inc., 1982).

LIZZIE BORDEN CASE USA 1893

The Borden case in America has elicited as much interest and speculation as the Wallace case in England, and for the same reasons: it remains an officially unsolved crime which might possibly have been the 'perfect murder'—if we assume that the tried suspects were indeed guilty. The scene of the Borden crime was the town of Fall River, Massachusetts, where Lizzie, who was 32 at the time, lived with her father, step-mother, sister and a maid. On 4th August 1892, Andrew Borden was discovered in the sitting-room of his house hacked to death. Further investigation resulted in the discovery of his wife Abbey's corpse in her bedroom with similar injuries. At the supposed time of death, the house had been empty, apart from the maid, Bridget Sullivan, who claimed to have been washing windows, and Lizzie, who said she had been in the barn.

It was well known that Lizzie and her sister disliked their step-mother intensely. Subsequently, Lizzie was arrested for murder. One fact which was brought against her was that she had tried to buy prussic acid the day before the killings. The maid also gave several detrimental statements at the trial. However, the crowning point in Lizzie's favour was that, although the murderer would have been soaked in blood, Lizzie and her clothes were spotless immediately after the event. Borden was acquitted of the double murder, and lived out her life in Fall Rivers for thirty-four more years.

Such a *cause célèbre* was ideal for adaptation to fiction and drama. As Lizzie herself lived until 1927, no identifiable factional work could be written prior to that date. Edmund Pearson mentions that Mary Wilkins's 1895 novella, 'The Long Arm', was frequently cited as a fictional version of the story, although as Pearson admits 'it really contains hardly as much of the case as an analytical chemist would call a trace'. Wilkins's novella centres on Sarah Fairbanks, whose father is bludgeoned to death with a gun-butt. Like Lizzie Borden, Sarah is suspected of the murder, but in this instance the case is resolved by detection (Sarah's own) and a confession. The most interesting part of the story—and one which shows similarities with later suggested solutions to the Borden killings—is an early instance in fiction of suppressed lesbian desire as a motive for murder.

Pearson also states that 'a few sentences' of Lily Dougall's novel, *The Summit House Mystery* (1905; published a year earlier in Britain as *The Earthly Purgatory*), show more affinity to the Borden mystery than Wilkins's story. In this gripping thriller, Neil Durgan comes to the Appalachian Mountains to work as a miner, and makes the acquaintance of the reclusive Smith sisters, Hermie and Bertha. It transpires that their name is in fact Claxton, and that Hermione Claxton had been tried and acquitted of the brutal axe-murder of her father and the shooting of her step-mother years before. Although young Bertha believes her sister actually did commit the murders, she feels obliged to protect her.

When a black acquaintance of the Claxtons is murdered in their home, Bertha believes her sister is responsible. Durgan, however, thinks that Hermie is protecting someone else. At the end of an eventful plot, we learn that Mr Claxton had not been killed all those years before. In an argument with a rival, Beardsley, Claxton had accidentally shot his wife. In a rage, he had bludgeoned Beardsley to death with an axe, and ran off. The disfigured Beardsley had been mistaken for the father and the brave Hermie, aware of what had happened, had covered for her father at the risk of her own life.

Nine Pine Street, the 1934 play by John Colton and Carlton Miles, tells of Effie Holden, who murders her father and mother (although a flat-iron and walking stick are the weapons, rather than an axe). Her position in her home town, particularly in the religious community, leads to her acquittal. She lives out the rest of her life in her parents' home, to the continued puzzlement of her neighbours. Evidently, the play inspired Edmund Pearson to write a famous essay, 'Legends of Lizzie', about the case.

In Edward Hale Bierstadt's novel, *Satan was a Man* (1935), Carroll Lindsay, a writer oppressed by his drunken mother, finds himself reliving the trial of Lizzie Borden in a dream. When he wakes, he finds he has actually killed his mother's canary! In later chapters, his dreams of Jack the Ripper and Dr Crippen have more damaging results: the deaths of his mother and wife (see relevant entries).

In 1937, British authors Edward Percy and Reginald Denham transferred the murders to England, and approached them obliquely. In their play, *Suspect*, a criminologist becomes concerned about the forthcoming marriage of his goddaughter when he suspects that her fiance's mother is a murderess. Like Lizzie, Mrs Smith is suspected of the slaughter of her father and mother with an axe. The play did not prove as successful as the authors' later factional drama, *Ladies in Retirement* (see 'Euphrasie Mercier').

Who would have expected to find Miss Borden in one of the most successful comedy plays of the thirties? And yet she makes an appearance in *The Man Who Came to Dinner* by George S. Kaufman and Moss Hart, which was staged in New York in 1939 and published the same year. The plot concerns irascible theatre critic Sheridan Whiteside, who imposes himself on the Stanley family when he injures himself falling on the pavement outside their house. The quirky celebrity turns the Stanley's home into a veritable circus and drives them to desperation. When Mr Stanley threatens to throw Whiteside out at an inopportune moment, the critic resorts to blackmail. He has recognised Stanley's sister, Miss Harriet—a timid old woman obsessed with the past—as the infamous murderess Harriet Sedley, who hacked her parents to death with an axe years earlier. He promises to inform the local community of Mr Stanley's secret if he goes ahead with his threat. The verse that Whiteside quotes—'Harriet Sedley took an axe/ And gave her mother forty whacks'—is a paraphrase of a contemporary children's song concerning Lizzie Borden.

That indefatigable faction writer, Marie Belloc Lowndes, turned her attentions to Lizzie Borden in her 1939 novel of the same name. Sub-titled *A Study in Conjecture*, the book accepts Lizzie's guilt from the outset, setting out to discover why the seemingly dutiful daughter turned against her parents in such an horrific manner. Lowndes's solution is based on Edmund Pearson's theory of the case, suggesting that Lizzie was involved in a passionate love affair that affected her actions towards her parents. The fictional centre of the book is sandwiched between factual details of the case.

Lillian de la Torre, who has concentrated on eighteenth-century crime with her series of detective pastiches featuring Dr Johnson, wrote a short play about the Borden murder. *Goodbye, Miss Lizzie Borden* was first published in James Sandoe's collection, *Murder Plain and Fanciful* (1948). De la Torre comes up with an unusual solution to the outstanding question of what happened in Fall Rivers on 4th August 1892. She concludes that Lizzie was covering for her sister who was the real murderer.

Another Borden stage adaptation appeared in 1957. James Reach's *Murder Takes The Stage* concerns 'Miss Liz', acquitted of a double axe-murder fifty years before the action of the play, and now suspected of involvement in a recent killing. Reach does not disguise the fact that Lizzie Borden is the model for Miss Liz—once again, a verse similar to the famous 'Lizzie Borden took an axe' is quoted.

There is no doubt of the factual basis for the following works. All the principal characters are assigned their real names and are placed in their correct period and location. Sharon Pollock's 1981 drama, *Blood Relations*, is the most ambitious, setting a play-within-a-play to recreate the actions of 1892. The play proper takes place in 1902, when Lizzie Borden is visited by her actress-lover who is as fascinated by the case as everyone else. They re-stage those fatal days of ten years earlier, with the actress in the role of Lizzie, and Lizzie herself—when not commenting on the action—as the maid, Bridget. The emphasis is on Lizzie's claustrophobic existence, caught between her domineering step-mother, her step-mother's grasping brother, and her weak father and sister. The pressures and passions that led to the killings are re-enacted, until the two women are brought back to 1902 and into a confrontation with Lizzie's sister, Emma.

Evan Hunter's thriller, *Lizzie* (1983) follows two threads of the story. From brief references at her trial, Hunter reconstructs a trip taken by Lizzie to Europe in 1890, where events occur that will have a direct bearing on the homicide itself. The second thread deals with the events of 1892-3, the murder and the trial. Once more, a lesbian relationship plays an important part in the story—is, in fact, directly responsible for the killings.

Walter Satterthwait's 1989 novel, *Miss Lizzie*, presents a fictional story in which the events in Fall River play their part. It is 1921 in a Massachusetts seaside town, and thirteen-year-old Amanda Burton is making the acquaintance of her elderly spinster neighbour, Lizzie Borden. When Amanda's step-father is murdered with an axe, suspicion naturally falls on Miss Lizzie. To her aid comes a tough Pinkerton agent and a local lawyer—as well as Amanda herself, who cannot believe her new-found friend guilty of such a deed. In addition to helping solve the current case, Miss Lizzie rakes over the ashes of thirty years ago, giving Satterthwait the opportunity of presenting his own theory on the Fall River Murders of 1892.

Elizabeth Engstrom gives a new slant to the case in her 1991 novel, *Lizzie Borden*. Engstrom portrays a young woman who has managed to subdue her disappointments and anger over forced self-denial and lost independence under a serene, controlled exterior. Her weak father relies on her continued presence in the house, her embittered sister tries to turn her against her step-mother, who is herself intent on claiming some of the Borden estate for her natural family. Having created such a realistic setting with believable period detail, Engstrom plumps for a supernatural solution to the murders completely at odds with the treatment of the crime in other works.

FACTIONAL WORKS:
Mary Wilkins, *The Long Arm* (London: Chapman & Hall, 1895).

Lily Dougall, *The Earthly Paradise* (London: Hutchinson & Co., 1904). US title: *The Summit House Mystery*.

John Colton and Carlton Miles, *Nine Pine Street* (New York: Samuel French Ltd., [1934]). (**P**)

Edward Hale Bierstadt, *Satan Was a Man* (New York: Doubleday, 1935).

Edward Percy and Reginald Denham, *Suspect* (London: Secker & Warburg, 1937). (**P**)

George S. Kaufman and Moss Hart, *The Man Who Came To Dinner* (New York: Random House, [1939]). (**P**)

Marie Belloc Lowndes, *Lizzie Borden* (New York: Longmans, 1939).

Lillian de la Torre, 'Goodbye, Miss Lizzie Borden' in James Sandoe, ed., *Murder Plain and Fanciful* (New York: Sheridan House, [1948]). (**P**)

James Reach, *Murder Takes the Stage* (New York: Samuel French Ltd., [1957]). (**P**)

Sharon Pollock, *Blood Relations* (Edmonton: NeWest Press, 1981). (**P**)

Evan Hunter, *Lizzie* (New York: Arbor House, 1983).

Walter Satterthwait, *Miss Lizzie* (New York: Thomas Dunne Books, 1989).

Elizabeth Engstrom, *Lizzie Borden* (New York: Tor, 1991).

FURTHER READING:
Frank Spiering, *Lizzie* (New York: Random House, 1984).

FILM ADAPTATIONS:
The Man Who Came to Dinner, d. William Keighley. US: Warner, 1941. Screenplay by Julius J. and Philip G. Epstein, based on the play by George S. Kaufman and Moss Hart.

ANDREW ROBINSON BOWES GB 1787

Andrew Robinson Stoney was born in County Durham, Ireland, in 1745. He married Hannah Newton, a wealthy heiress, whom he continually mistreated throughout their short life together. After her death, he became interested in a rich widow, Mary Eleanor, Lady Strathmore, who at the time had another suitor. Following a duel of honour in which he was seriously wounded, Stoney finally won the hand of Lady Strathmore and took her maiden name, Bowes, as his surname.

It did not take his wife long to realise what kind of man she had married. He subjected her to every type of mental and physical cruelty, until, eight years after the marriage in 1785, she took him to court for ill-treatment. It transpired that she had executed a deed of trust prior to the marriage, thus placing her husband on very uncertain financial ground. His response to this was to kidnap his wife and attempt to force her to return to him. Following eleven days of physical and psychological torture, she was rescued and Bowes found himself under arrest. He was sentenced to three years imprisonment, but was retained in prison for debt until his death in 1810.

In 1841, novelist William Makepeace Thackeray was staying with his friend

John Bowes in County Durham, when he happened upon a book in Bowes's library about his notorious ancestor. Thackeray recorded that he had discovered 'material (rather a character) for a story'; three years later, *The Luck of Barry Lyndon* began to make its serial appearance in *Fraser's* magazine. In 1856, it appeared in a revised form in the third volume of *Thackeray's Miscellanies: Prose and Verse* under the title, *The Memoirs of Barry Lyndon, Esq.* The novel, Thackeray's first great work of fiction (if one discounts the shorter *Catherine*—see the listing for 'Catherine Hayes), is written in the form of an autobiography.

Redmond Barry leads a dissolute life and is finally forced to flee Ireland, after believing he has killed a rival in a duel. He enlists in the army during the Thirty Years' War, changing sides periodically. After the war, he establishes a reputation as a gambler, and marries the Countess of Lyndon, adopting her name. He treats her and his stepson cruelly, while squandering her fortune. He has a son by the countess, whom he dotes upon and spoils shamelessly. When his son dies after a fall from a horse, the countess breaks from her husband with the help of her son from her first marriage. Lyndon flees abroad, but the countess dies, and he is left destitute. He dies in Fleet Prison.

FACTIONAL WORKS:

William Makepeace Thackeray, *The Memoirs of Barry Lyndon, Esq.* (London: Bradbury & Evans, 1856).

FURTHER READING:

Gordon N. Ray, *Thackeray: The Uses of Adversity, 1811-1844* (London: Oxford University Press, 1955).

FILM ADAPTATIONS:

Barry Lyndon, d. Stanley Kubrick. GB: Warner, 1975. Screenplay by Stanley Kubrick, based on the novel *The Memoirs of Barry Lyndon, Esq.* by William Makepeace Thackeray.

JIMMY BOYLE GB 1967

Born and raised in the Gorbals area of Glasgow, Jimmy Boyle turned to a life of petty crime. At the age of thirteen, he was sent to a remand home for stealing money from a fruit gum machine. From there, he moved between remand, borstal and prison with brief periods outside. In July 1967, Boyle and another ex-con called Babs Rooney got into a fight at Rooney's house. When Rooney was found dead the following morning, a friend of Boyle's was arrested and charged with the murder; Boyle escaped to London.

He was arrested in London, and taken back to Glasgow, where he stood trial for the murder in November 1967. Found guilty and sentenced to life, he was taken to Inverness Prison. Here, he was placed in solitary confinement and subjected to various kinds of brutality by the wardens. He responded in kind. There seemed no way out of this vicious circle, until in 1973 a Special Unit was opened at Barlinnie Prison for Scotland's most dangerous criminals.

Boyle was transferred there and his rehabilitation began in earnest. He took up art, particularly sculpture, and began writing. His autobiography (see below) was published in 1977, by which time he was in the third year of a psychology degree. He was released from prison in 1982, and has since been involved in rehabilitation work and prison reform.

Apart from his autobiography, 1977 also saw the staging and publication of Boyle's play, *The Hard Man*, which was co-written with Tom McGrath and based on his experiences. Johnny Byrne, the fictional Jimmy Boyle, relates his story of growing up in Glasgow and becoming a major figure in the gang wars directly to the audience. The audience sees his past reconstructed in a series of scenes played out as ritual drama, concentrating on his violent lifestyle. Imprisoned for murder, Byrne fights the brutality and discipline in the only way he knows, trying to retain his identity as a hard street fighter. Forced for days on end to squat in a minuscule steel cage, he manages to transcend the squalor and degradation of his prison existence by concentrating on his mental state (see also 'Ed Morrell').

FACTIONAL WORKS:
Tom McGrath and Jimmy Boyle, *The Hard Man* (Edinburgh: Canongate, 1977). (P)

FURTHER READING:
Jimmy Boyle, *A Sense of Freedom* (Edinburgh: Canongate, 1977).

JONATHAN BRADFORD GB 1736

Only the most basic facts are available concerning the murder which provided the inspiration for one of the most popular Victorian melodramas. Jonathan Bradford was the owner of an inn on the Oxford-London road. One evening a gentleman by the name of Hayes arrived with his manservant and was assigned a room. That night, the sound of groans awoke two other guests, who looked into Hayes's room. They saw Bradford stooping over the body of Hayes with a knife in his hand. Bradford was arrested, convicted of murder and hanged at Oxford.

Years later, Hayes's manservant—or Bradford's ostler, depending on which version one reads—confessed to the murder on his death-bed. It appears that he had robbed and murdered Hayes, and afterwards hidden the money. Later that night, Bradford was apprehended just as he was about to do the same. The story was well enough known at the beginning of the next century for John Thurtell (see entry) to mention it at his trial as a classic case of a miscarriage of justice due to circumstantial evidence—a point that failed to impress his jury.

In 1833, *Jonathan Bradford; or, The Murder at the Roadside Inn* was staged at the Surrey Theatre in London; the text, by Edward Fitzball, was published around the same time in the *Duncombe British Theatre* series. Fitzball's melodrama was innovative as it was one of the first to be staged on a multi-based set, so that the action in various rooms—in this case, two bedrooms, the parlour and the bar of the inn—could be viewed simultaneously.

In Fitzball's text, Bradford, owner of the George Inn, is innocent of any attempt on the life of Hayes. The real villain is one Dan Macraisy, also known as Gentleman O'Connor or Ratcatching Jack. He appears on stage as Bradford is due to be executed and, with his dying breath, confesses to the murder. Bradford is released to general applause—including, presumably, the audience's, since the play was successful enough to run for 264 nights.

Fitzball was happy to adapt a past crime for the stage, but he had his scruples. When the manager of the Surrey tried to persuade him to write up the recent Thurtell and Hunt case in play form, Fitzball recoiled from the project. Nonplussed, the manager assigned the project to another playwright (see entry on 'Thurtell and Hunt').

FACTIONAL WORKS:
Edward Fitzball, *Jonathan Bradford; or, The Murder at the Roadside Inn* (London: J. Duncombe, [1833]). (P)

FURTHER READING:
Richard D. Altick, *Victorian Studies in Scarlet* (New York: W. W. Norton & Co., 1970).

THOMAS BRAM USA 1896

On July 3rd 1896, the *Herbert Fuller* sailed for Argentina, carrying a cargo of lumber. Under Captain Charles Nash and his new first mate Thomas Bram were a crew of eight; also travelling were the captain's wife, Laura and one passenger, Lester Monks, a Harvard student taking the voyage for his health. At around midnight on July 14th, Monks was awakened by a woman's scream. Upon investigation, he found the bodies of both the captain and his wife; they had been hacked to death as if by an axe.

He discovered Bram walking the deck, acting suspiciously. Bram told Monks that he feared a mutiny was in progress. The two men continued their search, now joined by the ship's steward. They found the second mate's body in his cabin; he too had been hacked to death. Bram came across an axe covered in blood, although when he first pointed it out to the steward and Monks, neither man could see it. He promptly threw it overboard, suggesting that they should eventually deny its existence to the authorities.

By this time, the other members of the crew had appeared. Bram was hysterical, proposing wild theories for the murders. The ship finally reached Halifax after six anxious days for the crew and passengers. The crew were taken to Boston, where Bram was indicted for murder. One of the crew stated that he had seen Bram commit the murders, and the steward gave evidence of Bram's vindictiveness towards the captain and his wife.

Evidence of incitement to murder and mutiny on other ships he had served on was also presented, and he was found guilty and sentenced to death. He appealed on technicalities, but in the retrial in 1898, he was again found guilty. This time the sentence was life imprisonment.

Sixteen years later, Mary Roberts Rinehart, who had already established a reputation as a crime writer of some merit with her first novel, *The Spiral Staircase* (1908), came upon the facts of the Bram trial. After a little research, she produced a novel entitled *The After House* (1914), in which she presents a case for Bram's innocence, claiming that another crew member was responsible for the crime. It has been suggested that Rinehart's novel persuaded ex-President Theodore Roosevelt to lobby the authorities for Bram's release. Whatever the reason, President Wilson signed a pardon for Bram in 1919, possibly making this the only time that a factional novel has affected the case on which it was based.

FACTIONAL WORKS:
Mary Roberts Rinehart, *The After House* (Boston: Houghton Miffin Co., 1914).

FURTHER READING:
Jay Robert Nash, *Murder, America* (New York: Simon & Schuster, 1980).

BRAVO CASE GB 1876

In December 1875, Florence Ricardo, the widow of a captain of guards, married Charles Bravo, a young barrister. Before the marriage, Florence had had an affair with a well-known doctor, James Gully, who was almost forty years her senior. She had promised her new husband upon their marriage that this relationship was over. Bravo and Florence set up house at the Priory, Balham, with Florence's companion, Mrs Jane Cox. The first month of the marriage seemed pleasant enough, despite Florence's heavy drinking and Charles's niggardly way with money (although it was mostly his wife's).

On April 18th 1876, after a dinner during which Charles had drunk burgundy and Florence and Mrs Cox sherry, they retired to their separate rooms. At about 10 p.m. Mrs Cox was roused by Charles's cries for hot water. He was vomiting and in great pain. Doctors were summoned but could not ascertain what Charles had taken to cause this illness; he himself would only confess to having rubbed his gums with laudanum (a cure for toothache). After three days of agony, Charles died. A post-mortem discovered signs of antimony, an irritant poison, in Charles's system. At the subsequent inquest, an open verdict was returned, but due to continuing speculation, the verdict was quashed and a second inquest opened.

The second inquest developed the theory that Florence Bravo was involved in her husband's murder. The details of her affair with Gully were brought to light (including strong evidence of a possible abortion performed on Florence by Gully). Mrs Cox gave evidence that Charles had frequently beaten his wife. The jury eventually returned a verdict of wilful murder, but with 'insufficient evidence to fix the guilt upon any person or persons'. The case remains officially unsolved.

Obviously such a great unresolved *cause célèbre* cried out for fictional treatment. Fifty years after the events, the criminologist and crime fiction writer Marie Belloc Lowndes (who was to adapt many true crimes into novels) updated the facts of the case. In her book, *What Really Happened*, the action in the Raydon (Bravo) household is interspersed with scenes of the trial of Eva Raydon for the murder of her husband. Birtley Raydon's childlike wife (whose extravagance in the novel is for clothes rather than drink) is running rapidly through the couple's money (mostly her own), and Birtley suggests cost-cutting exercises. Chief among these is the dismissal of Eva's friend and housekeeper, Adelaide Strain.

Like Mrs Cox before her, Mrs Strain is desperate to retain her job to support her own child. When Birtley dies, Eva is suspected because of the revival of her (platonic) relationship with Colonel Mintlaw (Dr Gully's fictional counterpart). The book ends with a verdict of not guilty, although Lowndes leaves the reader in no doubt as to the identity of the real murderer. The author went on to dramatise her novel six years later (under the same title), although it was not staged until 1936.

In the same year as Lowndes's novel, Jessie Louise Rickard's *Not Sufficient Evidence* was also published. Robert Esmond is the fictional Bravo, drawn to the beautiful widow Nydia, who relinquishes her married lover to become Mrs Esmond. Robert, however, is jealous of Nydia's female companion, and proposes to break her grip on the household. On the night he suggests that she find another job, he dies a horrible death from poison. Once more, the poisoner's identity is readily identified. As in Lowndes's work, Rickard is more concerned with character and motivation than with mystery.

It was inevitable that Joseph Shearing (the pseudonym of Margaret Long), the master of Victorian crime faction, should eventually tackle the Bravo case. In the 1947 novel, *For Her to See*, Shearing concentrates on Mrs Cox, here called Olivia Sacret. Sacret, a widow of a minister from the West Indies, is invited by her old schoolfriend, Susan Rue, to keep home for her and her new husband, Martin. Susan is unaware that Olivia is keeping incriminating letters concerning Susan's intimacy with Sir John Curle, a married physician. Matters are complicated by the arrival of Mark Bellis, a painter who has leased Olivia's house, who learns of the letters; and by the death of Sir John Curle's wife, which leaves him free to marry Susan if she can obtain a divorce. Events run their course in a similar fashion to the Bravo case, as Martin Rue's death is followed by two inquests. The novel goes beyond the inquests and the eventual death of Susan Rue, to show the scheming Mrs Sacret receiving her just desserts.

In 1972, Elizabeth Jenkins examined the Bravo case from the standpoint of a different character, in her novel *Dr. Gully*. Jenkins shows how the case and the resulting publicity affected the good doctor and his devoted family. All the characters retain their factual names, the details of the events are followed closely, and we are presented with a sympathetic portrayal of Gully and of his relationship with Florence. The novel amounts to a fictional biography of a dedicated physician destroyed by the moral code of his day.

FACTIONAL WORKS:
Marie Belloc Lowndes, *What Really Happened* (London: Hutchinson & Co., [1926]).
Mrs Victor Rickard, *Not Sufficient Evidence* (London: Constable & Co., 1926).
Marie Belloc Lowndes, *What Really Happened* (London: Ernest Benn, 1932). (**P**)
Joseph Shearing, *For Her To See* (London: Hutchinson and Co., [1947]).
Elizabeth Jenkins, *Dr. Gully* (London: Michael Joseph, 1972).

FURTHER READING:
John Williams, *Suddenly at the Priory* (London: William Heinemann, 1957).

FILM ADAPTATIONS:
So Evil My Love, d. Lewis Allen. GB: Paramount, 1948. Screenplay by Leonard Spigelgass and Ronald Miller, based on the novel, *For Her to See* by Joseph Shearing.

BRIGHTON TRUNK MURDERS GB 1933

In 1933, Brighton became the scene of two grotesque murders, which were memorable more for the identical method of disposal of the corpses than for the killings themselves. In June, a suitcase was opened in the left-luggage office of Brighton Station and found to contain the torso of a woman. The day after the body's discovery, another suitcase was discovered in King's Cross Station, London, containing a pair of woman's legs. Subsequent investigations proved that the legs belonged to the body in Brighton. All that resulted from forensic investigations was that the woman had been thirty years old, was five months pregnant and had seen a chiropodist recently. The body was never identified, and the case remains unsolved.

Further investigations in Brighton resulted in the discovery of another trunk in the house of Tony Mancini, a petty thief. Inside was the body of Violette Kaye, Mancini's mistress. In his subsequent trial, Mancini claimed that he had found Violette's body and had hidden it in the trunk because he felt his criminal record would condemn him in the eyes of the police. He was acquitted, but in 1976 he confessed to a reporter that he had murdered Kaye after a quarrel.

T. C. H. Jacobs's novel, *Broken Alibi* (1957), posits a fictional solution to the first Brighton trunk crime. Chief Detective Superintendent John Bellamy investigates a crime with all the features of the first trunk murder—female torso, legs recovered in another suitcase, second trunk found with body—in the fictional seaside resort of Lighton. Even the name of the suspect in the second crime, Arnoldi, recalls that of Tony Mancini. The intricate solution to Jacobs's first murder involves a will, an impersonation, an innocent man set up as murder suspect, and a conclusion in the South of France.

FACTIONAL WORKS:
T. C. H. Jacobs, *Broken Alibi* (London: Stanley Paul, 1957).

FURTHER READING:
Bernard Taylor and Stephen Knight, *Perfect Murder* (London: Grafton Books, 1987).

MARQUISE DE BRINVILLIERS FRANCE 1676

Marie d'Aubray, the Marquise de Brinvilliers, attained her title by marriage in 1651. She had already obtained a reputation for promiscuity, so it was no surprise that shortly after her marriage the Marquise took a lover, a young reprobate by the name of Sainte-Croix. When her parents discovered this, they had the man thrown into prison. Here, Sainte-Croix met a poisoner, Exili or Eggili, and during the six months of his imprisonment, the Marquise's lover became a willing pupil of his cell-mate.

Upon his release, Sainte-Croix returned to the Marquise and educated her in his new-found art. During the following years, mysterious deaths occurred in the Marquise's family, including that of her father and two brothers. Her sister-in-law suspected one of her brothers' servants, La Chaussée, and had him arrested. It transpired that the servant had been brought into the brother's household by the Marquise. While he was being interrogated, a warrant was made out for the arrest of Marie herself. She promptly fled to the Netherlands.

In the meantime, Sainte-Croix had died, leaving incriminating evidence against the Marquise. She was finally arrested in 1676 and stood trial. A confession discovered on her arrest made the court's decision a foregone conclusion. The Marquise was sentenced to death by torture. Her quiet and penitent acceptance of the horrors that followed shifted public opinion in her favour, and during her last days and following her execution, she was regarded by some as a saint!

John Dickson Carr gave the Brinvilliers case a supernatural treatment in his 1937 novel, *The Burning Court.* Set in twentieth-century Philadelphia, it charts a series of poisonings in the city, which seem to show the ghostly influence of the seventeenth-century French poisoner. A crime novelist pursues two theories: either the murders have been supernaturally induced or they may be the work of a descendant of the Marquise. As with most of his crime faction works, Carr uses the facts as a springboard to create a totally different crime and criminal.

A closer reconstruction of the Marquise's crimes appeared in William Fifield's 1957 bodice-ripper, *The Devil's Marchioness.* The novel takes us from Marie's meeting with Sainte-Croix and their mutually sinister attraction, through the details of their crimes, to the Marquise's ultimate execution. The story is full of vivid period detail, and is so well-researched that the reviewer for the *Times Literary Supplement* felt as though 'a veteran crime reporter were submitting a thesis for a doctorate in French history; everything known about Mme. de Brinvilliers is here set down in chronological order'.

FACTIONAL WORKS:
John Dickson Carr, *The Burning Court* (London: Hamish Hamilton, [1937]).
William Fifield, *The Devil's Marchioness* (New York: Dial Press, 1957).

FURTHER READING:
Virginia Vernon, *Enchanting Little Lady* (London: Abelard-Schuman, 1964).

WILLIAM BRODIE GB 1788

William Brodie was the classic example of a man with a double life. He came from a respectable and prosperous family, and like his carpenter father before him, was eventually elected deacon of his guild, obtaining a position on the City Council of Edinburgh. His nights, however, were spent in gambling and debauchery, and he eventually turned to burglary to supplement his dwindling fortune. Brodie probably began his criminal career in 1768, with a bank break-in. At first he worked alone, but was soon the leader of a small gang.

Brodie's position in the City gave him access to valuable information concerning the richest citizens of Edinburgh. It was not unusual for an eminent businessman known to Brodie to leave Edinburgh for a few days and return to find his premises burgled. In March 1788, the gang attempted their greatest job, the robbery of the Excise Office of Scotland. However, the plan went awry when Brodie, positioned as lookout, lost his nerve and bolted after several Office employees returned to collect some papers. The other members of his gang were lucky to escape.

A reward had been offered for information concerning one of Brodie's previous jobs. Whether influenced by his boss' craven attitude or the sum available for turning informer, one of the gang claimed the reward—without naming Brodie himself. The deacon, unaware of this, fled to London and across the Channel to Amsterdam, where he was eventually arrested. The trial of Brodie and one of his henchmen took place in Edinburgh. The jury found them guilty of burglary (a capital offence at that time) and they were both hanged.

The tale of William Brodie made a profound impression on another Scotsman, Robert Louis Stevenson. As a child, the author had a cabinet in his possession which had been built by Brodie himself. The notion of a respectable appearance concealing a criminal mind is one that recurs in Stevenson's work. Brodie has often been quoted as the prototype for the author's most extreme interpretation of this principle, *The Strange Case of Dr. Jekyll and Mr. Hyde* (1886), but the connection between the facts and this horror-fantasy is tenuous.

However, in an earlier work Stevenson recognised his debt to the true story. In his teens he had written a play about Brodie which he recited in school. He worked on several versions of the drama, finally enlisting the help of the one-legged playwright W. E. Henley (the prototype for another Stevenson villain, Long John Silver), with whom he'd become acquainted.

Privately printed in 1880, Stevenson's play was finally staged two years later in Bradford under the title *Deacon Brodie; or, The Double Life*, (it was commercially published in 1892). The play was a melodrama, originally presenting the deacon as a black-hearted villain of little subtlety, although the later revisions portrayed Brodie as wracked with guilt (more akin to the Jekyll-Hyde struggle that obviously intrigued Stevenson). He is given ample opportunity to display the righteous side of his nature in scenes with his dying father and his illegitimate children. But his thieving nature gets the better of him and he carries out the robbery of the Excise Office before the audience. The play ends with a drastic change of historical fact—the deacon is run through by a sword rather than hanged.

In 1901, Dick Donovan used the famous thief as the subject for his novel, *Deacon Brodie; or, Behind the Mask*, one of several fictional biographies of criminals by this author. In a highly sensationalised plot, Brodie is trapped into proposing marriage, a commitment he evades by having his bride-to-be kidnapped (she dies trying to escape). The nefarious exploits of his gang are more accurate, culminating in the Excise robbery and his flight from justice. Donovan concludes by adding a fictional twist, in the attempts of a quack doctor to resuscitate Brodie's body after the hanging.

This resuscitation theory once again appears in Forbes Bramble's *The Strange Case of Deacon Brodie* (1975)—the novel's title emphasising the Jekyll-Hyde connection. As with Stevenson's and Donovan's tales, names of the historical characters are retained—Brodie himself, his mistress, the members of his gang. Bramble ends his novel with a suggestion that Brodie has survived his execution. A close recounting of the crimes and a glossary of slang terms show an inclination toward authenticity lacking in the previously discussed works.

FACTIONAL WORKS:

Robert Louis Stevenson, *The Strange Case of Dr. Jekyll and Mr. Hyde* (London: Longman, Green & Co., 1886).

W. E. Henley and Robert Louis Stevenson, *Deacon Brodie; or, The Double Life* (London: David Nutt, 1892). (**P**)

Dick Donovan, *Deacon Brodie; or, Behind the Mask* (London: Chatto & Windus, 1901).

Forbes Bramble, *The Strange Case of Deacon Brodie* (London: Hamish Hamilton, 1975).

FURTHER READING:

John Sibbald Gibson, *Deacon Brodie: Father to Jekyll and Hyde* (Edinburgh: Paul Harris, 1977).

FILM ADAPTATIONS:

Doctor Jekyll and Mr. Hyde, d. Rouben Mamoulian. US: Paramount, 1932. Screenplay by Samuel Hoffenstein and Percy Heath, based on the story by Robert Louis Stevenson.*

ELIZABETH MARTHA BROWN GB 1856

Elizabeth Brown lived with her husband John, who was twenty years her junior, near Broadwindsor, Dorset. On the morning of 6th July 1856, Elizabeth rushed to the nearby cottage of John's cousin Richard Damon, claiming that she had discovered her husband at the door of their cottage, his head covered in blood. When she asked him what had happened, he had groaned 'the horse'. She claimed that he had clung to her so tightly that it wasn't until two hours later that she was able to go for help. By the time Damon reached his cousin's cottage, John Brown was dead.

The implication was that Brown's horse had kicked him in the head, but Damon's suspicion was aroused when he went to the field where the horse was kept and found the gate still shut and the halter untouched. There was no blood on the horse's hooves or on the ground in the field. Elizabeth claimed that her clothes had been soaked in blood, but no such stained clothing was found. Also an axe was missing from the cottage. The coroner was to state at Elizabeth's trial that Brown's injuries were not consistent with those caused by a horse's hooves.

On 21st July, Elizabeth Brown stood in the dock at Dorchester, charged with her husband's murder. Prosecution claimed that she was jealous of a local girl who had walked alongside Brown as he went to work the day previous to his death. After deliberating for four hours, the jury returned a guilty verdict. Prior to her execution on 9th August, Elizabeth confessed to the murder. She had quarrelled violently with her husband when he came home drunk and struck him with the axe.

Among the spectators at the execution was a young architect's apprentice, Thomas Hardy. He watched with fascination as the handsome woman walked stoically to her death. Calcraft, the hangman, neglected to tie the woman's dress to spare her modesty, and had to climb back after the hanging to do so. This gave the event a sexual frisson that deeply affected the sixteen-year-old youth. Combined with the fact that he could plainly see her features through the rain-soaked hood that covered her head, it left a strong impression that haunted Hardy throughout his life.

Was *Tess of the D'Urbervilles* (1891) an imagined biography of the woman he saw hanging in Dorchester all those years before? Hardy himself affirmed that he had that last image of Elizabeth Brown in mind when he was writing his famous novel. The sexual charge that Tess generates in the reader is just as palpable as the one that Hardy had experienced on the day of the hanging, so much so that the author was forced to bow to the strictures of Victorian morality and rewrite the novel for its initial publication. His definitive version of the work was not to appear until 1912.

Apart from the aura of sexuality, the murder of Alex D'Urberville by Tess, and her untimely end, there is little to connect the real servant-girl and the fictional country girl seduced by her cousin and rejected by her husband. It is doubtful, however, if Hardy's sympathy for the plight of nineteenth-century womanhood would have been communicated so effectively to his readers had he not seen the hanging in 1856 and felt that sympathy so powerfully himself. The novel would have been a different work entirely without Hardy's experience at Elizabeth Brown's execution.

FACTIONAL WORKS:
Thomas Hardy, *Tess of the D'Urbervilles* (London: Osgood, McIlvaine & Co., 1891).

FURTHER READING:
Patrick Wilson, *Murderess* (London: Michael Joseph, 1971).

FILM ADAPTATIONS:
Tess, d. Roman Polanski. France/GB: Renn-Burrill, 1979. Screenplay by Roman Polanski, based on the novel *Tess of the D'Urbervilles* by Thomas Hardy.*

GEORGE BROWNE GB 1573

George Sanders was a wealthy merchant tailor from London. From the testimony of George Browne at his subsequent trial, it transpires that Browne was in love with Sanders's wife Anne. Browne was encouraged by a friend, Anne Drury, who promised to arrange a marriage after Sanders was dead; Browne set about to accomplish this. He was informed by Drury that Sanders would be travelling from Woolwich to St. Mary Cray in Kent in March 1573. Browne waylaid Sanders and his servant, John Bean at Shooter's Hill and stabbed them both, leaving them for dead.

Bean managed to crawl away for help, was carried to Woolwich and died, but not before naming Browne as his master's murderer. Browne, in fear of his life, obtained money from Anne Drury and attempted to flee, but was arrested at a relative's house in Rochester. He confessed to the murders and named Drury and her servant, Roger Clement as his accomplices. He sought to divert any hint of complicity from Anne Sanders herself, but Anne Drury accused her, in correspondence, of instigating the murder and of assisting the murderer financially. All four were executed.

The killings were well-publicised, first in *A Brief Discourse* (1573) by Arthur Golding, and later in Holinshed's *Chronicles* (1577) and Stow's *Annals* (1592). The story found its way onto the Elizabethan stage via an anonymous play entitled *A Warning for Faire Women* (1599). Yet another of the many domestic tragedies attributed to Shakespeare, the plot follows the facts closely. Browne meets Anne Sanders at a feast and employs Anne Drury to work on her, poisoning her mind against her husband and predicting a remarriage after her husband's imminent death. The soon-to-be widow accepts the prediction. Browne, in the meantime, has made two attempts on the husband's life; the third attempt at Shooter's Hill succeeds. Fleeing from the scene of the crime, Browne attracts attention by the blood on his clothes. Anne Sanders, receiving her husband's bloodstained handkerchief as proof of his death, is plagued with guilt. When Browne arrives to woo her, he is

shunned and escapes to Rochester, where he is caught. The play ends with a
series of executions. Crude as the play is when compared to such established
Elizabethan drama as that of Shakespeare and Marlowe, it holds its own with
other domestic tragedies of the period, even the better-known *Arden of Faversham* (see entry on 'Alice Arden').Of particular interest are the dumb shows
between Tragedy, Lust, Murder, Mercy and others, providing a symbolic
commentary on the action, and reminding one of the close chronological ties
between Elizabethan drama and medieval morality plays.

FACTIONAL WORKS:
Anon., *A Warning for Faire Women* (London: Valentine Sims, 1599). (**P**)

FURTHER READING:
Charles Dale Cannon, ed., '*A Warning for Faire Women': a Critical Edition* (The Hague: Mouton,
1971). Contains some of the original sources.

DR. ROBERT BUCKANAN USA 1893

Buckanan studied in Edinburgh before moving to North America (English
criminologists seem to prefer the Scottish spelling of Buchanan although
Americans use the 'k'). He married at twenty-four, but after arriving in New
York, he fell under the spell of a brothel proprietor, Anna Sutherland. Sutherland had amassed a small fortune from her trade, and Buckanan divorced his
wife and married Anna in 1890. Her will was altered in his favour prior to the
wedding. The new Mrs Buckanan became her husband's receptionist, but her
flamboyant manner offended the doctor's patients. He was rising in medical
circles and Anna was becoming an embarrassment to him. In 1892, Buckanan
booked passage on a ship to Edinburgh. Four days before his departure, Anna
died, presumably from a cerebral haemorrhage. Buckanan collected his wife's
money and boarded the ship. Suspicion was aroused by his remorseless
behaviour and Anna's body was exhumed. The corpse revealed traces of
morphine poisoning. As a rule, morphine produces contraction of the pupils,
but the corpse's pupils showed no contraction. Nonetheless, Buckanan—who
had returned to New York with his first wife—was arrested.

At his trial in 1893, the prosecution showed how Buckanan might have
disguised the symptoms of morphine poisoning. They killed a cat with
morphine, and treated the eyes with belladonna—no contraction of the
pupils was visible. If that was not enough, Buckanan insisted on entering
the witness box, where he alienated the jury with his blustering evasions. He
was found guilty and executed in Sing Sing two years later.

John Dickson Carr's detective novel, *The Sleeping Sphinx* (1947), transfers the Buckanan murder to the twentieth century. Following a gruesome
party game involving the death masks of famous murderers, a young girl
dies apparently from a cerebral haemorrhage. Dr Gideon Fell, Carr's series
detective, is brought in to investigate, and uncovers a case of murder by the

identical method employed by Buckanan (and directly inspired by it). Carr uses his plot to pass on information involving other famous poisoning cases.

FACTIONAL WORKS:
John Dickson Carr, *The Sleeping Sphinx* (New York: Harper & Bros., 1947).

FURTHER READING:
Rupert Furneaux, *The Medical Murderer* (London: Elek Books, 1957).

BURKE AND HARE GB 1828

William Burke and William Hare were Irish labourers, living in a boarding-house in the West Point district of Edinburgh. On the death of the owner, Hare and his common-law wife, Maggie Laird, took over the running of the establishment. This was the time of the resurrectionists, or 'body-snatchers', who stole freshly buried bodies and sold them to medical colleges for lucrative sums. On the death of one of the boarding-house lodgers, Burke and Hare filled his coffin with tree bark, and sold his body to local anatomist and lecturer, Dr Knox. They had hit on a new vocation, with an eager employer.

Unfortunately for the working-class residents of Edinburgh, the two apprentice body-snatchers were not content to wait for their 'merchandise' to die of natural causes. When one of Hare's lodgers became ill with fever, they hastened his demise with a pillow over the face. Their *modus operandi* was to select weak men or elderly women, ply them with drink and suffocate them. They came close to discovery several times by murdering well-known low-life characters, but each time Knox turned a blind eye or deliberately deflected suspicion from them.

By now, both Hare and Burke had set up independent lodging-cum-slaughter-houses. They were finally caught when two beggars discovered the body of a recently murdered widow in Burke's establishment. Burke, Hare and their two wives were drunk when the police came to arrest them, and their conflicting alibis aroused suspicion. By the time their trial began in December 1828, Hare had turned King's evidence and Burke had signed a confession.

Only Burke and his common-law wife, Helen McDougal, were tried; McDougal won the unique Scots verdict of 'not proven', but Burke was found guilty and executed. Hare disappeared, although legend has it he was blinded after being thrown into a pit of lime when his identity was discovered.

The first factional account to cover the notorious Edinburgh body-snatchers was the rare, anonymously-authored *The Murderers of the Close* (1829). This novel's only distinction today is that its illustrations were provided by Robert Seymour, first illustrator of Charles Dickens's *The Pickwick Papers*. The author of the 1829 work made no secret of the novel's basis in fact—its sub-title was 'a tragedy based on real life'.

Of more lasting literary merit, although shorter in length, is Robert Louis Stevenson's often-anthologised story 'The Body-Snatcher', first published in the *Pall Mall Magazine* for Christmas 1884 (its first book appearance was as a separate pamphlet in New York in 1895). At first glance the tale of Stevenson's resurrectionist Gray and his hold over anatomist Wolfe Macfarlane, bears little similarity to the Burke and Hare case. There is no suggestion of the two Edinburgh body-snatchers having an influence over Knox—in fact the opposite appears to be the case—and, unlike Knox, Macfarlane murders his supplier.

But similarities abound. Like Burke and Hare, Gray and his assistant are from Ireland—Fettes, Macfarlane's assistant, hears their 'grumbling Irish voices' as they deliver one specimen. Also they supplement their supply by murder. Like David Paterson, Knox's assistant, Fettes recognises one of the corpses and suspects foul play; and like Knox, Macfarlane turns a blind eye. The story ends on a satisfying supernatural note, appropriate to a case involving the traffic of dead bodies.

In 1931, another Scottish author, James Bridie, adapted the Burke and Hare story for the stage in his play, *The Anatomist*. Unlike Stevenson's tale, Bridie's drama retains the murderous duo's names, along with that of Dr Knox, who as the title suggests is the main protagonist. Knox is shown as a dedicated physician, forced to deal with the likes of Burke and Hare, but ignoring their nefarious crimes because of his fanaticism for the progress of medical science. He is opposed by his young student, Dr Anderson, who—like the real Paterson before him—recognises the body-snatchers' latest corpse as a young girl he had met at a tavern the night before. His disclosure leads to Burke's execution and Knox's disgrace. Anderson's girlfriend, Mary Dishart, has refused to marry him because of his devotion to Knox, whom she abhors; ironically, she finds herself shielding Knox from an angry mob at the end of the play.

Inge Goodwin's novel, *Bury Me in Lead* (1952), is another close reconstruction of the case, again with a fictional young student doctor committed to Knox's cause. Here, however, the assistant manages to assuage his doubts and assist the body-snatchers. His feelings of guilt at the depths to which he must descend to forward the cause of medical science constitutes a major part of the novel's plot. The astute *Times Literary Supplement* reviewer concluded that the story 'which might easily have been a melodrama, [turned into] a realistic analysis of human behaviour'.

Welsh writer Dylan Thomas produced the most poetic adaptation of Burke and Hare's crimes in his published screenplay, *The Doctor and The Devils* (1953). Fallon and Broom are the author's fictional body-snatchers, and Dr Rock, the far-sighted, egotistical medical lecturer. Thomas's script was never filmed in his lifetime; in 1985 it was adapted for the screen by Ronald Harwood and turned into a mediocre movie.

Thomas paints a portrait of an arrogant Dr Rock, who has a number of enemies in the community. He is well aware of Fallon's and Broom's murderous activities, but regards the end as justifying the means. As he tells a fellow-doctor, 'we are anatomists, not policemen; we are scientists, not moralists'. Rock is nearly discovered when another doctor, Murray, sees his prostitute-lover's body among the recently-delivered corpses. However, Murray has enough respect for his tutor to warn him, so that he might escape the law. This Rock refuses to do, and is ultimately saved by the city's professional and social elite, who close ranks to protect one of their own members.

1974 saw the publication of Elizabeth Byrd's novel *Rest Without Peace*, which followed the facts faithfully, and concluded with Hare's blinding in the lime-pit, as per tradition. Peter Barnes's 1986 radio sketch, 'The Perfect Pair' presents Burke, Hare and Knox as a music-hall comedy trio. In song and dialogue, they discuss business and agree a verbal contract. This short play was published in his collection, *The Real Long John Silver and Other Plays*.

Inga Dunbar's *Tanner's Close* (1993) constructs a convoluted plot, centring on two girls, illegitimate daughters of William Burke (unbeknown to him) who are adopted into different families and are brought up in different social positions. Edina is taken in by Lady Alison Hamilton as her own child, while Mary Paterson, after running away from her adopted family, takes to the streets. Only two aspects of this complex novel are worthy of comment: the fact that Burke and Hare—rather than Knox—are firmly in the centre of the action; and the idea that Burke unwittingly murdered his own daughter—his last, and perhaps most famous victim, Mary.

FACTIONAL WORKS:
Anon., *The Murderers of the Close* (London: Cowie & Strange, 1829).
Robert Louis Stevenson, *The Bodysnatchers* (New York: Merriam Co., [1895]).
James Bridie, 'The Anatomist', in *The Anatomist and other Plays* (London: Constable & Co., 1931). (P)
Inge Goodwin, *Bury Me in Lead* (London: Allan Wingate, 1952).
Dylan Thomas, *The Doctor and the Devils* (London: J. M. Dent & Sons, 1953). (P)
Elizabeth Byrd, *Rest Without Peace* (London: Macmillan, 1974).
Peter Barnes, 'The Perfect Pair', in *The Real Long John Silver and Other Plays* (London: Faber & Faber, 1986). (P)
Inga Dunbar, *Tanner's Close* (London: Simon & Schuster, 1993)

FURTHER READING:
Hugh Douglas, *Burke and Hare, The True Story* (London: Robert Hale, 1973).

FILM ADAPTATIONS:
The Body Snatcher, d. Robert Wise. US: RKO, 1945. Screenplay by Philip MacDonald and Carlos Keith, based on the story by Robert Louis Stevenson.
The Doctor and the Devils, d. Freddie Francis. GB: Brooksfilms, 1985. Screenplay by Ronald Harwood, based on the screenplay by Dylan Thomas.

HARRIET BUSWELL MURDER GB 1872

The body of Harriet Buswell, alias Clara Burton, was discovered in her lodgings at 12 Great Coram Street on Christmas Day, 1872. She was lying on her bed and her throat had been cut. There were several tantalising clues at the scene of the crime: prints of a hand and thumb on Harriet's body indicated that she was forcibly held down while the murder was committed. In 1872, however, the significance of fingerprinting as a means of identifying suspects was not yet appreciated. Also in the room was a half-eaten apple. The police attempted to make a caste of the bite-marks, but it was too indistinct. The authorities were reduced to tracing witnesses who saw Harriet Buswell during her last hours. She was a prostitute (hence the alias) who frequented the West End and brought her clients back to her room. Karl Whollebe, a German surgeon's assistant working aboard a ship, the *Wangerland*, was arrested after his suspicious movements on Christmas Eve and Christmas Day were reported. He was placed in an identity parade together with his friend, Dr Gottfried Hessel, the *Wangerland's* chaplain. Two witnesses who had seen Harriet with a man on Christmas Eve identified Hessel as that person.

Hessel was detained in custody. Several more witnesses came forward to identify him as Harriet's companion on the night of her murder. Also a maid at the hotel where the two Germans were staying remembered the chaplain asking for turpentine to remove stains from his clothes; and several blood-stained handkerchieves had been sent to the hotel laundry from Hessel's room. Counter to this testimony, however, was the evidence of the hotel proprietor who had heard Hessel coughing in his room at the very time of the murder. Whollebe claimed that Hessel had been sick that evening and had remained in the hotel. The hotel proprietor's testimony helped to cast doubt on the police case when Hessel was brought to court. The chaplain was set free, and the police were lambasted by the press for what was seen as a near miscarriage of justice. Hessel was offered a public apology from Prime Minister Gladstone, and financial compensation from the British public. He left England aboard the *Wangerland*. The case remains officially unsolved.

Joseph Shearing's *Moss Rose* (1934) presents the story of Belle Adair, a chorus-girl who has a room in a seedy boarding-house next to that of Daisy Arrow, a prostitute. Daisy brings a man home on Christmas Eve, and Belle sees the man leave the house the following morning. Belle discovers Daisy's body and removes a German Bible from the room. When the police investigate, she denies any knowledge of the murder or of Daisy's visitors that night.

A suspect is found, a German ship's pastor, Maarten Morl. He is tried and acquitted—the ship's doctor and his daughter, who is Morl's fiancee, provide the pastor with an alibi. But Belle has recognised the man and blackmails him into taking her back to Germany. She is aware that the doctor and his daughter have lied on oath; back in Germany she learns the reason, and discovers the truth about Daisy's death—at her own cost. Shearing presents an intriguing portrait of a desperate, impoverished woman at the end of her tether, and the disturbed young man who fascinates her.

REFERENCE:

Joseph Shearing, *Moss Rose* (London: William Heinemann, 1934).

FURTHER READING:

H. R. F. Keating, ed., *Blood on My Mind* (London: Macmillan, 1972).

FILM ADAPTATIONS:

Moss Rose, d. Gregory Ratoff. US: TCF, 1947. Screenplay by Jules Furthman and Tom Reed, based on the novel by Joseph Shearing.

WALTER CALVERLEY GB 1605

Calverley lived in Yorkshire, near Wakefield. He came from a good family and married a lady with a sizeable dowry. At first they led a contented life and had three children together. However, Calverley's behaviour changed for the worse. He began gambling heavily and squandering his wife's dowry. He would curse his wife and children, blaming them for his reduced circumstances. His behaviour was indicative of mental illness. On 23rd April 1605, Calverley, in a rage, stabbed two of his three sons to death and wounded his wife. His third son was being tended by a nurse twelve miles away, and Calverley was apprehended en route there to complete his murderous intentions. He was brought before a magistrate but refused to plead. He did indicate, however, that his wife had implied the boys were not his. He was sentenced to be pressed to death, *la peine fort et dure* as this mode of execution was known.

The prime source of information on the murder is an anonymous pamphlet entitled *Two Unnatural Murders*, published in 1605. The case became something of an Elizabethan *cause célèbre*, and was twice dramatised. The first play, George Wilkins's *The Miseries of Enforced Marriage* (1607), was based on the unfounded rumour that Calverley had been an unwilling husband, already betrothed to another lady. Wilkins's Calverley, called Scarborrow in the play, is driven to contemplating murder by the thought of the marriage that might have been. However, he is prevented from committing the deed in the nick of time as news arrives that he has acquired an inheritance. The play ends on a note of reconciliation.

The more important play from an historical and literary point of view is the anonymous drama, *A Yorkshire Tragedy* (1608), which follows the pamphlet source letter for letter. This short work, consisting of eight scenes only, was attributed to William Shakespeare on the title-page. Some critics have suggested that the play might in fact be the original tragic ending to George Wilkins's tragi-comedy cited above, or a separate play by the same author. Although much of the dialogue and description is lifted directly from *Two Unnatural Murders*, there is a heightened moral tone in the dramatic work. Diabolic possession is suggested as a reason for Calverley's actions (Elizabethans equated mental illness with demonic control of the soul and body). Also, Calverley's lamentations in the final scene would have emphasised to the Elizabethan audience the justice of his impending fate in a much stronger manner than presented in the pamphlet.

REFERENCES:

George Wilkins, *The Miseries of Inforst Mariage* (London: Printed for G. Vincent, 1607). (**P**)

Anon., *A Yorkshire Tragedy* (London: R. B. for Thomas Panier, 1608). (**P**)

FURTHER READING:

Keith Sturgess, ed., *Three Elizabethan Domestic Tragedies* (Harmondsworth: Penguin, 1972). Includes the section of *Two Unnatural Murders* relating to the case.

JAMES CAMB GB 1948

The liner *Durban Castle* was travelling from Cape Town to England on 18th October 1947 when one of the passengers, actress Gay Gibson, was reported missing. On answering a call from Miss Gibson's cabin that morning, a watchman later claimed he had met a deck steward, James Camb, in the doorway to the cabin. According to the watchman, Camb had indicated that everything was all right, although he later denied the watchman's story. When scratches were discovered on his wrist, he put these down to heat rash. The ship docked and Camb was questioned by the police, whereupon he altered his story. He claimed that Gibson had invited him into her cabin and that, during sexual intercourse, she had had a fit and died. He had pushed the body through the porthole to avoid any implication in her death.

In 1948, Camb appeared at Winchester Assizes charged with murder. The prosecution alleged that he had forced his attentions on Gibson and had strangled her when she struggled (the scratch marks on his wrist were cited). Camb stuck to his version of the story, but the disposal of the body was cited against him and he was sentenced to death. Because the hanging clause in the Criminal Justice Bill was under debate in Parliament at the time, Camb's sentence was commuted to life imprisonment. He was released in 1959, still protesting his innocence.

Q. Patrick's short story, 'Girl Overboard', was published in 1950 in the crime fiction anthology, *Four and Twenty Bloodhounds*. Patrick's detective, Lieutenant Timothy Trant, investigates the case of a missing lady onboard ship— a case that recalls that of Camb. As in its factual basis, the plot revolves around a motive of sexual gratification. Trant, however, solves the disappearance-cum-murder with the help of a fictional clue and a broken fictional alibi.

FACTIONAL WORKS:
Q. Patrick, 'Girl Overboard', in Anthony Boucher, ed., *Four and Twenty Bloodhounds* (New York: Simon & Schuster, 1950).

FURTHER READING:
Julian Symons, *A Reasonable Doubt* (London: Cresset Press, 1960).

ELIZABETH CANNING GB 1754

On 1st January 1753, eighteen-year-old Elizabeth Canning left her aunt's house at Houndsditch to travel to the home of Edward Lynn, who had employed her as a servant. She disappeared for four weeks. On 29th January, she stumbled into her mother's house in a dishevelled state, covered in bruises and wearing only her shift. She claimed that she had been accosted by two men who knocked her unconscious and took her to a house on the Hertford Road. Here she was kept prisoner by two old women whom she identified as Susannah Wells and Mary Squires.

The two were arrested and held in custody, while Elizabeth related her story to the magistrate, the novelist Henry Fielding. Squires and Wells were charged with abduction. At their subsequent trial, they were both found guilty and sentenced to death. However, Mary Squires's claim that she had been out of London the day in question was investigated by certain doubting officials, and sufficient evidence was obtained on her behalf to suggest that Canning had lied. The two women were pardoned; Canning herself was arrested for perjury.

By this time, with blanket coverage of the case in the newsheets and pamphlets of the day, most of London was divided between Canningites, who believed the servant-girl's tale, and those who considered her a vicious liar. In this atmosphere, Canning was brought to trial in April 1754. After a obscure first verdict ('guilty of perjury, but not wilful and corrupt'), the jury returned a second verdict of guilty, but with a recommendation to mercy. She was sentenced to seven years' transportation to America, where she married and settled in Connecticut, and died in 1773.

In 1947, Lillian de la Torre—who had produced a factual study of the case two years before (*Elizabeth is Missing*)—published her short story, 'The Disappearing Servant Wench', in her collection of short pieces, *Villainy Detected*. The tale has none other than Dr Samuel Johnson investigating the mystery. Johnson was to appear over the years in a host of de la Torre's pastiche detective short stories, all narrated by his biographer, James Boswell. In 'The Disappearing Servant Wench' the good doctor promotes a medical solution to the case, after unintentionally hypnotising the girl. De la Torre provides her own claimant for the villain, along similar lines to her factual solution of the mystery.

Josephine Tey's novel, *The Franchise Affair* (1948), provides a twist to the Canning story by bringing it into the twentieth century. Betty Kane, a young schoolgirl, accuses the eccentric Sharpe family of abducting her to their country house, The Franchise. Country solicitor Robert Blair takes up the case, and in the process, falls in love with the daughter, Marion Sharpe. His investigations provide a simple possible solution to the Canning case, although certain features of the plot are uniquely anachronistic to the true case. The novel gives an engrossing view of ordinary post-war village life and of the petty jealousies that the case arouses in such an environment.

FACTIONAL WORKS:
Lillian de la Torre, 'The Disappearing Servant Wench', in *Villainy Detected* (New York: Appleton, 1947).
Josephine Tey, *The Franchise Affair* (London: Peter Davies, 1948).

FURTHER READING:
John Traherne, *The Canning Enigma* (London: Jonathan Cape, 1989).

FILM ADAPTATIONS:
The Franchise Affair, d. Lawrence Huntington. GB: ABP, 1950. Screenplay by Robert Hall and Lawrence Huntington, based on the novel by Josephine Tey.

CARAVAGGIO ITALY 1606

Michelangelo Merisi was born in the town of Caravaggio in 1573, and took the name of his birthplace as his own. At the age of eleven, he went to Milan to study art, and later moved to Rome. From the beginning of the seventeenth century, he began to execute the religious paintings that were to establish his reputation—*The Crucifixion of St. Peter, The Conversion of St. Paul,* and *The Burial of Christ* among them. He had a violent temper, and his name appeared in many court records for various misdemeanours ranging from slander to malicious wounding.

In May 1606, Caravaggio and a young man from Terni, Rannuncio Tommasoni, got into a brawl over a ball game, and Tommasoni was killed. Although Caravaggio himself was seriously wounded, he fled from Rome to escape arrest. He turned up in Naples, and became something of a celebrity for his painting of the *Death of the Virgin Mary*, when word spread that he had used the corpse of a notorious prostitute as the model for the Madonna. In 1607, negotiations began to obtain him a pardon; despite this, he travelled to Malta, where he was knighted. He moved to Syracuse and Palermo before returning to Naples in 1609.

In that year, he was set upon by a gang of hired assassins, who evidently left him badly disfigured and gravely wounded. But this was not the end of Caravaggio's short, eventful life. He left Naples in 1610, and got as far as Porto Ecole, near Grosseto, presumably on his way back to Rome. Here, he was arrested in error, and thrown into prison. He was released a few days later, but died of malaria on the beach at Porto Ecole.

Frank McGuinness's 1987 play, *Innocence*, takes as its subject the day in May 1606 when Caravaggio committed murder. In Rome, Caravaggio lives with a prostitute, while painting, pimping for a cardinal, wrestling with his deep sense of sin and his fear of death, his disgust at both his homosexuality and his violent temper. He is visited by his brother, who tries to persuade him to return home and marry so that he may father a child who will inherit the family estates.

They quarrel and part, and Caravaggio, needing an outlet for his murderous passions, kills a man in a brawl. In hiding from the authorities, he dreams of his sister, who died in childbirth, and also of the whores and male prostitutes, whom he has used for his models and who accuse him of neglecting them and driving them to their deaths. He claims that he has immortalised them in his paintings; unfortunately, by doing so, he has also cruelly reminded himself of his own mortality.

FACTIONAL WORKS:
Frank McGuinness, *Innocence* (London: Faber & Faber, 1987). (**P**)

FURTHER READING:
Roger **P**. Hinks, *Michelangelo Merisi da Caravaggio* (London: Faber & Faber, 1955).

EDITH CAREW JAPAN 1897

Edith Porch, daughter of a mayor of Glastonbury, met Walter Carew in 1869 and married him shortly after. Walter secured a job in Singapore and moved there with his new wife, where they had two children. When a post in Yokahama came up, the family transferred to Japan. Here, Edith fell in love with a bank clerk, Henry Dickerson, and an affair developed. Walter seemed unconcerned about the relationship. He had already confessed to his wife of an earlier affair with a girl called Annie Luke.

In the autumn of 1896, Walter Carew fell ill from what was diagnosed as a stomach inflammation. He seemed to be recovering after treatment, when a relapse occurred. He died in hospital. His doctor became suspicious after he received a letter stating that Edith Carew had bought three bottles of arsenic from a local chemist. He ordered a post-mortem and arsenic was indeed found in Walter Carew's system, whereupon Edith was arrested for murder. Letters were produced addressed to Walter supposedly from Annie Luke, who had arrived in Japan and wished to arrange a meeting. Other letters addressed to the coroner and Edith's counsel and signed 'A.L.' seemed to suggest that the writer had poisoned Walter and was contemplating suicide.

At Edith's trial, the prosecution produced their own set of letters, written by Dickerson to Edith concerning their passionate affair. The implication was that Edith had poisoned her husband so that she could go to Dickerson, and had written the Annie Luke letters to draw suspicion away from herself. Edith's counsel responded by taking out a private prosecution against Mary Jacob, the Carews's governess, claiming that *she* had written the letters and was responsible for Walter's death. It was also suggested that Walter had taken the arsenic himself as a cure for an unspecified disease. But to no avail. The jury took half an hour to find Edith guilty of her husband's murder, which immediately resulted in the collapse of the case against Mary Jacob. Edith was sentenced to death, but the British Minister in Japan commuted the sentence to life imprisonment, to be served in Britain. She was released in 1910, and died in Wales in 1958.

Meira Chand, who has lived in Japan and written several novels set in the Far East, published *The Painted Cage* in 1986. The author admits that the plot was based on the Carew case, but states that the novel 'makes no claims to solving the enduring controversy about the verdict of the trial', and that the facts were 'no more than a springboard for the leap into fiction'. Chand's Edith is Amy Redmore, married to Reggie and accused of his murder. The story is told in flashbacks during the trail itself. Chand sees Amy as a passionate woman, whose strong sexuality repels her physically frail husband. When the relationship becomes irreconcilable, Amy takes several lovers—a fact that will weigh heavily against her at her trial. As with several other novels about the British in the Far East, the local exotic atmosphere is seen as having a liberating—and tragic—effect on the ex-patriates.

FACTIONAL WORKS:
Meira Chand, *The Painted Cage* (London: Century Hutchinson, 1986).

FURTHER READING:
Molly Whittington-Egan, *Murder on the Bluff: the Carew Poisoning Case* (Glasgow: Neil Wilson Publishing, Ltd., 1996).

MARGARET CATCHPOLE GB 1797

Margaret Catchpole was the daughter of a Suffolk labourer. She worked as a servant in Ipswich at the house of a Mr Cobbold. In the course of her career there, she saved one of the Cobbold children from drowning. She fell in love with William Laud, the son of a local boatman—and a smuggler. When Laud found himself in some difficulties in London, he contacted Margaret, who stole her employer's horse and rode to London disguised as a sailor. She was arrested and tried for theft in 1797. She was sentenced to death, but her employer managed to have the sentence commuted to seven years' transportation.

Before the sentence could be carried out, Margaret escaped from Ipswich gaol. Recaptured and once more sentenced to death by the same judge, her sentence was again commuted to transportation—this time for life. In 1801 she left England for Australia, where she apparently obtained her freedom after several years, and married happily. She died in New South Wales in 1841.

Evidently she wrote to the Reverend Richard Cobbold, the son of her former employer, giving him permission to recount her life story, on condition that he 'let my husband's name be concealed for mine and my children's sake'. This Cobbold did in his 1845 novel, *The History of Margaret Catchpole*. He gives Laud a rival for Margaret's love in the character of an honest local man, John Barry. After fighting with the smuggler for Margaret's hand and realising that her affection lies with Laud, Barry leaves England to make his fortune. Laud helps Margaret escape from Ipswich gaol, but is mortally wounded in the process.

When Margaret is finally released from prison in Australia, she is reunited with Barry, who has reached a prominent position in the new colony. They renew their acquaintance and are finally married. According to Cobbold, the correspondence quoted in the novel is Margaret Catchpole's own, and the letters certainly give the novel authenticity. Whatever else of Cobbold's narrative is based on truth, his novel formed the basis for all future factional treatments of the case.

Edward Stirling dramatised Cobbold's work under the same title in 1845. The play, which was staged at the Surrey Theatre in London that year, follows the important events of Cobbold's narrative—the courting of Margaret by Laud and Barry, their fight, Margaret's theft of the horse and ride to London, her arrest and escape, her transportation, her eventual marriage to Barry. One addition to the drama is the inclusion of comic scenes involving a trio of country bumpkins: Muffin Pegs, Gooseberry Pip and Sally.

In G. G. Carter's novel of 1949, *Margaret Catchpole*, the author tries to invest the story with gritty realism, concentrating on the smuggling sub-plot of the original. In an early scene, William Laud and his psychopathic smuggler companion, John Luff (who appears as a minor character in Cobbold's original) are nearly trapped by excise-men. One of them is Lieutenant Edward Barry, John's brother. Laud loses his eye in the ambush, Barry is wounded and Luff graphically mutilates another adversary.

Two of Margaret's brothers join Laud in his smuggling activities—one is killed by hounds while poaching, the other becomes an alcoholic and is murdered by Luff. Laud's (and Barry's) scenes with Margaret are more romantically portrayed than in Cobbold's love story. The novel is well-researched, with good nautical and geographical detail. It has two faults: the excruciating pseudo-eighteenth-century language ('There'll be rum goings-on at Cliff House afore long, mark my words!'), an error common to many historical novels of the period; and the overemphasis on the character of Luff who is more charismatic than the other three leads.

Monica Mugan's 1972 novel, *Smuggler's Wench*, shows some novelty in its title but little elsewhere. Most of the action follows Cobbold's narrative religiously. One new character is introduced—young Tom, who is onboard the transport ship with Margaret and helps her discover a mutiny. He stays with her in Australia and is eventually adopted by her and Barry.

FACTIONAL WORKS:
[Richard Cobbold], *The History of Margaret Catchpole* (London: Henry Colburn, 1845).
Edward Stirling, *Margaret Catchpole* (London: J. Duncombe, [1845]). (**P**)
G. G. Carter, *Margaret Catchpole* (London: Constable & Co., 1949).
Monica Mugan, *Smuggler's Wench* (London: Robert Hale, 1972).

FURTHER READING:
Leslie Stephen , ed., *Dictionary of National Biography*, vol. 9 (London: Smith, Elder & Co., 1887).

BEATRICE CENCI ITALY 1599

Francesco Cenci was a wealthy despot and the son of the pope's treasurer who used his wealth to buy his way out of trouble. He ruled his family with a rod of iron, and paid particular attention to his daughter, Beatrice. He was later accused of having raped her, and when a nobleman asked for her hand, Francesco told him that Beatrice was his mistress.

Eventually, Cenci's family decided to rid themselves of their persecutor. Beatrice, along with her two brothers, her stepmother and two accomplices, drugged her father by putting opium in his wine, drove nails though his brain and throat, and finally tossed him from an upstairs window. When his body was discovered the next day, the authorities decided he had fallen from a window in a drunken state! However, doubts remained, and a month later an investigator was told by a servant of a bloodstained sheet she had been ordered to wash. The family, aware that their secret might come out, tried to silence the two accomplices. One of them was murdered, but the other was taken into custody before they could reach him, and he confessed to the conspiracy against Francesco Cenci.

The Cencis were arrested and tortured. Beatrice, despite suffering horrific pain, denied the murder. However, her two brothers confessed. The four members of the family were condemned to death, and appealed to the Pope. He might have granted a reprieve, but another case of parricide was being investigated at the time and he felt an example was needed. Beatrice, her stepmother and brother Giacomo were executed; her brother Bernardo was sentenced to life after a last-minute pardon.

The factional accounts of the family began in 1819 with the publication of Percy Bysshe Shelley's only dramatic work, *The Cenci*. Shelley accepts Francesco as a despotic, sadistic brute who deserves his fate, but in his version, Beatrice petitions the Pope for protection against her father's cruelty. When her father holds a banquet to mark the death of two of his sons, she appeals to the guests to help her family escape his clutches. But Francesco convinces them that she is mad and threatens to rape her when they have left.

In this situation, the family are forced to take the law into their own hands, and Beatrice grudgingly accedes to the murderous plans of her step-mother and brothers. A first attempt ends in failure, but the second succeeds and the plot follows historical fact to conclude with a sentence of death on the four murderers. Shelley avoids the charge of incest against Francesco; although guilty of many crimes, the father in his version only threatens his daughter with rape.

In 1935, Antonin Artaud, French dramatic theorist and founder of the Theatre of Cruelty, chose the appropriately barbaric plot of the Cenci murder for his play, *Les Cenci*, which he saw as a prefiguration of his movement. He took as his sources both Shelley and Stendhal (who had written a factual account of the case), and retained Shelley's fictional Cardinal Camillo, who investigates the murder. As with Shelley's drama, Artaud's Francesco is again the villain of the piece. After murdering his sons and sexually abusing his daughter, he is ripe for the vengeance that is brought upon him. Artaud used all the tricks of stagecraft to achieve his effect: ritualistic chant, integrated lighting effects, symbolic set design, theatre-in-the-round. He himself played Francesco Cenci in the original production, but the novelty of his approach alienated the audiences, and the play was an initial failure. It was published in the author's *Oeuvres Complètes* in 1964 and translated in 1969.

In 1955, Frederic Prokosch's masterly novel, *A Tale For Midnight*, revisited the Cenci tragedy. Against an authentically-historical background of flood and plague in sixteenth-century Rome, the evil actions of the Cenci family are played out, mirroring the natural pestilence around them. Beatrice is seen as the prime mover in the murder, seducing one of the accomplices, Olimpio to achieve her goal. It is she who ropes her stepmother and brothers into the plot. After one failed attempt, the murder is committed (by Olimpio and another, Marzio—no other member of the family takes part). The Royal commissioner, Carlo Tirone, investigates and discovers the murder weapons.

Beatrice is blackmailed by a wood-carver, Claudio Crespi, who has seen the disposal of the body, and she buys him off. Before her trial, she gives birth to Olimpio's child. Meanwhile, her brother Giacomo tries unsuccessfully to poison Olimpio, who is finally seen off by a friend of the Cenci family, Monsignor Guerra, a late character in the plot. Beatrice's lawyer dreams up the incest charge as mitigation—but to no avail. Beatrice, her stepmother and brothers go to their deaths.

Three years after Prokosch's work appeared, Italian novelist Alberto Moravia published his drama, *Beatrice Cenci* (translated in 1965). Using one location (the castle of La Patrella where the murder took place) and six characters (Cenci, his wife and daughter, the two murderers and Carlo Tirone, the investigator), Moravia presents the tale in a contemporary manner, echoing a view of the futility of life and the randomness of catastrophe more akin to the current existentialist theories than to the Romantic presentation of Shelley. At the beginning of the play, the wilful and determined Beatrice is awaiting a reply to a letter she has written to her brothers, begging them to rescue her from her life of misery. Olimpio, who lusts after Beatrice, ensures that the letter will fall into her father's hands, in the hope that she will submit to him to obtain his assistance. She does, but deceives him afterwards that her father has discovered their love-making and intends to kill them both. Olimpio thus consents to the murder plan partly to save his own life. Following the murder, however, Beatrice readily confesses to the crime rather than spend her life with Olimpio—feeling that she has replaced one prison for another.

FACTIONAL WORKS:

Percy Bysshe Shelley, *The Cenci* (London: Printed for C. & J. Ollier, 1819). (**P**)

Frederic Prokosch, *A Tale for Midnight* (Boston: Little Brown, [1955]).

Alberto Moravia, *Beatrice Cenci* (London: Secker & Warburg, 1965). First published in Italian in Teatro, 1958. (**P**)

Antonin Artaud, *The Cenci* (London: Calder & Boyars, 1969). First published in French as *Les Cenci* in *Ouevres Completes*, IV, 1964). (**P**)

FURTHER READING:

Corrado Ricci, *Beatrice Cenci* (London: William Heinemann, 1926).

JOHN REGINALD HALIDAY CHRISTIE GB 1953

Probably the most notorious British mass-murderer of his day, Christie had a prison record for minor offences before he began his murder spree. This did not prevent him from getting a job as constable in the War Reserve

Police during the Second World War. He probably committed his first murder as early as 1939. His general *modus operandi* was to persuade his women victims that he had a medical background and could cure some ailment such as migraine or catarrh—or could provide an abortion. He would invite a woman back to his house at 10 Rillington Place in London, then gas her, sexually assault her while she was unconscious (or while strangling her), and finally kill her and dispose of the body under the floorboards or in the grounds of his house.

Christie probably would have made headline news even without the arrival of Timothy Evans and his wife as lodgers. It now appears that Mrs Evans and her child were murdered by Christie; but it was Evans himself who was arrested, tried and executed for the murders. In 1953 Christie left Rillington Place. The new occupier discovered bodies in a papered-over cupboard. Police found more corpses in the garden. After a nationwide search, Christie was arrested. His defence at his trial was one of insanity, but he was found guilty of first-degree murder and hanged in 1953.

The murderer of 10 Rillington Place appeared on the stage in an early play by Howard Brenton entitled *Christie in Love*. It was first performed in 1969 and published the following year. This one-act drama begins with the discovery of the bodies at Christie's home. Christie is interrogated by a police inspector and constable and re-enacts the murders for them, displaying his hatred of women. The two policemen, although horrorified at the crimes, appear equally misogynistic in their attitudes and speech. They end by stringing Christie up. The main theme of Brenton's play seems to focus on society's unwillingness to deal dispassionately with what it cannot comprehend.

FACTIONAL WORKS:
Howard Brenton, 'Christie in Love', in *Christie in Love, Heads [and] The Education of Skinny Spew* (London: Methuen, 1970). (**P**)

FURTHER READING:
Ludovic Kennedy, *Ten Rillington Place* (London: Victor Gollancz, 1961).

THE CLEVELAND TORSO CASE USA 1934

In September 1934, a mutilated female corpse was found on Euclid Beach in Cleveland, Ohio. The head of the corpse was missing and was never recovered; the body remained unidentified. In September 1935, two headless male bodies were also discovered in Cleveland. The genitals had also been removed from the bodies. One of the corpses was identified as that of twenty-eight-year-old Edward Andrassy, who had a police record for carrying a concealed weapon. It was speculated that Andrassy and the second man had been victims of a gangland killing, possibly with Mafia connections. Another suggestion was that the two were murdered by a jealous homosexual.

In January 1936, a fourth headless torso of forty-one-year-old prostitute, Florence Polillo was found. This reminded police investigating the 1935 murders of the unidentified female corpse of 1934. The jealous homosexual theory was thrown out—now they were looking for a psychopath. The murders continued until May 1938, by which time the number of torsos had reached thirteen. In July 1939, a bricklayer named Frank Dolezal was arrested for the murder of Florence Polillo. He confessed and was sentenced to manslaughter, despite retracting his confession. He was found hanging in his cell soon after.

At the time of the murders, Elliott Ness—of *The Untouchables* fame—was Safety Director of Cleveland, and had some input into the investigations, although most of the footwork was done by Sergeant James Hogan, Cleveland's Head of Homicide. Ness believed that the murderer was a powerfully-built Cleveland socialite with a history of mental illness and a knowledge of medicine. Ness had confronted the man with his suspicions, but after the suspect had been committed to a psychiatric hospital, he realised that he would never be able to bring his suspect to justice.

John Peyton Cooke's *Torso* (1993) places the murderer and victims squarely in the gay underworld of 1930s Cleveland. Chronicling the case from the murder of Eddy Andrassy (shown in all its bloody details), Cooke's harrowing novel of psychopathic perversity takes us through the subsequent murders and investigations to the final unmasking (and suicide) of the murderer. The investigation is conducted by Hank 'Lucky' Lambert, although Ness is on hand to make significant contributions. As he pursues his inquiries through the gay sub-culture of pre-war America, Hogan comes to terms with his own sexuality. Although the murderer is fictional, Cooke states in an afterword that he was based on Ness's suspect.

FACTIONAL WORKS:
John Peyton Cooke, *Torso* (London: Headline, 1993).

FURTHER READING:
Colin Wilson , ed., *Murder in the 1930s* (London: Robinson, 1992).

CHRISTINA COLLINS MURDER GB 1839

In June 1839, Christina Collins, a Liverpool dressmaker, took a barge on the Trent and Mersey Canal to Preston Brook, where she caught a Pickford boat to London. She was on her way to join her husband, Robert Collins, who had recently secured a job in the capital. The crew of the Pickford boat were James Owen, the captain, George Thomas, William Ellis and young William Musson. Two days after the boat left Preston Brook, Christina's body was found in the canal near Rugeley.

The crew were tried in July of that year, accused on four indictments— murder, rape, common assault and theft. For legal reasons, the trial was postponed; by the second trial, only the charge of murder was pursued, and Musson was set free. Witnesses were presented who testified to the crew's drunken state, and Christina's attempt to change boats along the route, after complaining that the men were harassing her. Others testified that the men had threatened and cursed her. Screams had been heard near the place where Christina's body was found. She was believed to have been suffocated and drowned.

The boatmen pleaded not guilty, suggesting that the girl had committed suicide. The jury, however, decided otherwise, and they were condemned to death. Ellis was reprieved at the last minute and transported for life; Owen and Thomas were hanged.

Colin Dexter used the details of the case for his Chief Inspector Morse novel, *The Wench is Dead* (1989). Morse, recovering from an operation on a perforated ulcer, is given a pamphlet concerning the murder of Joanna Franks, seemingly murdered on the Oxford Canal in 1859 (the pamphlet, in fact, is a clever pastiche of John Godwin's work cited below). Certain facts in the case lead Morse to believe the executed men to be innocent, and with the help of his assistant, Detective Sergeant Lewis and a young woman librarian at the Bodleian, the Chief Inspector investigates the century-old case. The structure of the plot suggests Josephine Tey's classic historical detective novel, *The Daughter of Time* (1951), which features a hospitalised policeman whiling away the hours re-interpreting an old crime (in Tey's book, the crime was the supposed murder of the Princes in the Tower by Richard III).

FACTIONAL WORKS:
Colin Dexter, *The Wench is Dead* (London: Macmillan, 1989).

FURTHER READING:
John Godwin, *The Murder of Christina Collins* (StaVordshire: StaVordshire County Library, 1981).

WILLIAM CORDER GB 1828

Undoubtedly the most famous 'literary' crime in England was the Red Barn murder of 1827, which inspired a popular melodrama and many fictional versions of the story. The crime was committed by William Corder, son of a wealthy farmer at Polstead, Suffolk. His victim was Maria Marten, daughter of the local mole-catcher. Corder and Maria had become lovers in 1826. When Maria became pregnant, William promised to marry her. The child died, and the prospective husband backed down. Maria's parents, however, were insistent that the marriage should go ahead.

On 18th May 1827, Corder apparently told Maria that they were to be married in secret later that day and persuaded her to meet him at the Red Barn on the Corder estate. She was to come disguised, and they would drive to Ipswich, where the marriage would take place. Maria kept her appointment and was never seen alive again. Corder told the girl's gullible parents that she was on holiday in the Isle of Wight. He then borrowed money from his mother and set off for London, where he promptly advertised for a wife, married one of the applicants and settled down as a teacher.

Back in Polstead, Mrs Marten was plagued by dreams that her daughter had been murdered at the Red Barn. She persuaded her husband to search the barn—as she feared, Maria's body was discovered in the very spot she had pictured in her dreams. Corder was arrested and returned to Bury St. Edmonds for his trial. His defence was that Maria had shot herself and that he had merely concealed the body. He was found guilty and sentenced to death. Before his execution on 11th August 1828, he made a full confession.

It is generally accepted that the Red Barn case owes its factual (and factional) longevity in the field of criminology to the dramatisation of the events early in the nineteenth century. What is less well known is that the play itself—and the whole myth of Maria Marten—owes its existence primarily to a novel published in the very year of the trial. Most of the focal points of the subsequent legend—the virtuous and noble Maria, the despicable, evil Corder, a fortune-teller's prediction of romance for the girl, Corder's poisoning of the child—were presented here for the first time.

The novel was called *The Red Barn*, and the author was William Maginn, an impoverished hack specialising in potboilers such as this work. Maginn makes no secret of the novel's basis in truth (the sub-title is 'a tale founded in fact'). Although Corder's name is changed to Barnard, Maria retains her rightful surname. The plot begins with Maria being informed by a gypsy fortune-teller, Hannah Woods, that she will find romance with a young man on horseback at Polstead Fair. She already has a secret admirer—shy Harry Everton—who is favoured by her parents.

At the fair, Maria is approached by two young men on horseback. One is Stafford Jackson, a smuggler and member of the 'fancy' (and based on a character called Peter Mathews who featured in the original case). The other is William Barnard (alias Corder), whom Jackson eventually introduces to the vices of London. Maginn's theory is that Corder was corrupted by London life which made him dissatisfied with his mundane existence in Polstead. At a subsequent dance in Polstead, Maria convinces herself that Barnard is the man in Hannah Wood's prediction, but Barnard seduces the fortune-teller instead. Jackson, who is really interested in Maria himself, has in fact persuaded Hannah to lure Barnard away from Maria. When Maria rebuffs Jackson's advances, he attempts to kidnap her. She is saved by the ever-constant Harry Everton.

Jackson continues to prey on Barnard. When Barnard's father eventually cuts him off from his inheritance, Jackson persuades him to join his criminal activities. When Barnard finally realises that he is being conned by Jackson, he returns to Polstead and Maria. His father dies and he inherits the estate. He begins to court Maria in the Red Barn, which serves as their constant trysting-place. However, when Maria becomes pregnant and gives birth, Barnard callously poisons the child.

Meanwhile, Hannah Woods, in an effort to free Jackson from jail, returns to Polstead to blackmail Barnard. She threatens to tell the authorities of his criminal affairs in London. With Maria pressing him into marriage and Hannah bribing him for money, Barnard decides to cut his losses. He lures Maria to the Red Barn, where he murders her. The story follows its source to the ultimate conclusion, with Barnard moving to London to marry a wealthy bride, Maria's mother dreaming of her murder and Barnard being arrested and hanged after the discovery of Maria's corpse. The fictional side of the plot is concluded when Jackson is killed while robbing a coach, by none other than Harry Everton.

Many stage versions of the Corder case appeared in the years following the trial. The story seemed to strike a chord in pre-Victorian society. Most of these dramas took features from Maginn's novel, features that added to the myth of Maria Marten and the Red Barn. The standard dramatisation was not published until the end of the century—and appropriately enough, it was the showpiece of play publishers Samuel French Ltd., who produced it. *Maria Martin; or, The Murder in the Red Barn* (the misspelt surname was a feature of many newspaper reports of the case) follows Maginn's portrayal of the two principal characters—Corder as a dyed-in-the-wool villain, Maria as a steadfast if not entirely virtuous heroine. The action, in two short acts, takes the plot from the lovers' decision to leave the village, through the murder itself, to Corder's last night in the condemned cell.

Three features of the play show a marked difference from both Maginn's fiction and the case's facts. The comical love-making of Maria's sister, Anne with local yokel Timothy Bobbin acts as a contrast to Corder's cynical relationship with Maria. The reason that Corder gives for Maria's murder is that he believes the child is not his. Finally, Corder is visited in the condemned cell by Maria's ghost, and breaks down in remorse and terror.

A minor fictional version of the case appeared in 1831, with Robert Huish's novel, *The Red Barn*. Again, the source was emphasised, with the inclusion at the end of the book of documents relating to the genuine crime. The book's only novelty is a sub-plot involving a gang of child pickpockets, nine years before the appearance of Charles Dickens's *Oliver Twist*.

In the third decade of the twentieth century, Montagu Slater prepared a 'traditional acting version' of the evergreen true-crime melodrama. His 1928 play, *Maria Marten*, includes an introduction which places the Corder plays within the context of nineteenth-century melodrama as a whole, and investigates the importance of seduction as a plot-device in such works. Slater's own play is based upon a hand-written copy composed by John Latimer of the Queen's Theatre, Battersea.

Once again the comic wooing of Anne Martin by Tom Bobbin is featured, but here it dominates and disrupts the dramatic plot. The gypsy fortune-teller is a man, Ishmael, out to avenge the seduction and death of his daughter by Corder. Corder, unaware of Ishmael's identity, asks him to win Maria to his favour, but Ishmael warns Maria of her eventual fate in the Red Barn. The gypsy also supplies Corder with the poison to kill Maria's child, in the hope of incriminating him further. Corder learns of Ishmael's intentions and kills him. The final ironic, if far-fetched, touch is that the Bow Street officer who arrests Corder is none other than Ishmael's son!

Novels based on the crime continued to appear in the twentieth century. Almey St. John Adcock's 1948 book, *The Warped Mirror*, is a minor affair. The only interesting change from the previous melodramas is the sympathetic portrayal of Corder and the more realistic portrayal of Maria. It was left to Philip Lindsay to present a well-researched and enjoyable novelisation of the crime in his *Shadow of the Red Barn*. Lindsay admits to returning to the earliest factual book on the case for his details—J. Curtis's *An Authentic and Faithful History of the Mysterious Murder of Maria Marten* (1828).

The principal character in Lindsay's book is Tom Barsett, known as 'The Corinthean', a London swell with a grudge against Corder. Barsett tackles Maria's mother over her complicity in her daughter's affair with Corder, learns of her fear for her daughter's fate after her disappearance, and—in a novel twist—puts the idea in her head of incriminating Corder, thus leading to her story of the dream. The Corinthean has designs on Corder's London wife, who rejects him after her husband's execution, telling her troublesome admirer that she is carrying Corder's child.

Brian J. Burton, an authority on Victorian melodrama, turned his attention to the story in 1963, when his version of the old play, called *The Murder of Maria Marten; or, The Red Barn*, opened at the Opera House in Harrogate. It was published the following year in Birmingham. Burton collated several of the earliest texts, mixing details from their plots with those from one of the nineteenth-century novels. All the standard trimmings are there—the gypsy fortune-teller, the poisoned child, the appearance of Maria's ghost in the condemned cell. In Burton's version, Nell Hatfield, the gypsy, attempts to cause Corder's downfall to avenge her sister, who had been killed by him. She is in turn avenged by her brother, the Bow Street Runner who arrests Corder.

In 1979, Burton returned to Corder in his one-act melodrama, *The Gypsy Curse*, an attempt to reproduce the style and atmosphere of its predecessors of the last century. In effect, the play is a 'prequel' to *Maria Martin*. Corder is seen seducing and abandoning a gypsy girl (presumably Nell Hatfield's sister). When she dies, the gypsies place a curse on him—a curse that those familiar with the story know will take its course.

FACTIONAL WORKS:
[William Maginn], *The Red Barn* (London: for Knight & Lacey, 1828).
[Robert Huish], *The Red Barn* (London: for J. Bennett, 1831).
Anon., *Maria Martin; or, The Murder in the Red Barn* (London: Samuel French Ltd., [1877]). (P)
Montagu Slater, *Maria Marten, or, The Murder in the Red Barn* (London: Gerald Howe, 1928). (P)
Almey St. John Adcock, *The Warped Mirror* (London: Jarrolds, [1948]).
Philip Lindsay, *Shadow of the Red Barn* (London: Hutchinson and Co., 1952).

Brian J. Burton, *The Murder of Maria Marten, or, The Red Barn* (Birmingham: C. Combridge, 1964). (**P**)

Brian J. Burton, 'The Gypsy Curse', in *Three Hisses For Villainy* (Birmingham: Combridge Jackson, 1979). (**P**)

FURTHER READING:
Peter Haining, *Buried Passions* (1980: Sudbury, Spearman).

FILM ADAPTATIONS:
Maria Marten, or The Murder in the Red Barn, d. George King. GB: George King, 1935. Screenplay by Randall Faye, based on the anonymous play of 1877.*

CRAIG AND BENTLEY GB 1952

On 2nd November 1952, two youths were cornered on the rooftop of a Croydon warehouse by police. One, Derek Bentley, was taken into custody; the other, Christopher Craig, held police at bay with a gun. According to later police evidence, Bentley shouted, 'Let him have it, Chris' to his friend. Craig fired several times, wounding Detective-Constable Frederick Fairfax, and killing PC Sydney Miles outright. When he ran out of bullets, Craig jumped from the roof, fracturing his spine. He too was taken into custody, and the two were charged with the murder of PC Miles.

At their trial in December, further facts were elicited about the two. Bentley, nineteen years old, was educationally sub-normal and suffered from periodic epileptic fits. Craig, sixteen, had a grudge against the police; his brother, Niven, had been sentenced to twelve years imprisonment for armed robbery just three days before the killing. Bentley's defence lawyers made much of the interpretation of his words to Craig. They suggested that he was telling his friend to hand the gun over; the prosecution obviously interpreted the words as an incitement to shoot.

The jury took less than two hours to find both of them guilty. Craig, too young to hang, was sentenced to be detained. Bentley received the death sentence. His subsequent appeal was rejected—as were the petitions and appeals for clemency from other quarters—and he was hanged on 28th January 1953. His father, and subsequently his sister Iris, continued to campaign for a posthumous pardon, without success.

Ludovic Kennedy, a tireless campaigner against capital punishment (see the sources quoted under 'Christie' and 'Hauptmann'), produced a play based on the Craig and Bentley case, *Murder Story* (1956). The action opens in the living room of the Tanner's house, after Jim Tanner, a backward youth, has gone out with a friend of whom his parents disapprove; the first act ends with the Tanners learning that Jim has been arrested for the murder of a policeman.

Act two moves to the condemned cell, where Tanner's simplicity wins the sympathy of the warders—one of whom (Graves), acting as Kennedy's mouthpiece, condemns the unfairness of Tanner's fate, while the real murderer is imprisoned for life. Act three begins with the murdered police-man's wife signing a petition for clemency, before the action returns to the condemned cell, where a padre gives a graphic account of the procedure for execution. The play ends with the padre visiting the Tanner family at the hour of Jim's execution to comfort them; even he is convinced that the hanging is unjust. Kennedy finishes the published version of his play with a defence of his anti-capital punishment stance.

FACTIONAL WORKS:
Ludovic Kennedy, *Murder Story* (London: Victor Gollancz, 1958). (P)

FURTHER READING:
M. J. Trow, *Let Him Have It, Chris* (London: Constable & Co., 1990).

THOMAS NEILL CREAM GB 1892

Born in Glasgow and raised in Canada, Cream had his first serious encounter with the law in Chicago in 1881, where he was accused of poison-ing his mistress's husband. He had drawn attention to himself by letters written to the coroner, a form of self-advertisement that was to mark the rest of his murderous career. Although he was given a life sentence, he was released from prison after ten years. Cream emigrated to England in 1891, settling in London.

Here he pursued his poisonous pastime, handing out capsules of strych-nine to unsuspecting prostitutes. His first victim was Ellen Dunworth, who was discovered writhing in agony in Waterloo Road on October 1st 1891. Shortly afterwards, the police received a letter from an 'A. O'Brian, detective', offering to name the murderer for a sizeable fee. Three more prostitutes were to die in a similar manner before Cream was arrested, mainly through his own actions—his letters to the police and other individuals were bound to draw suspicion upon him eventually. Cream was tried in October 1892, a year after his first London murder. A prostitute who had accepted his pill but hadn't swallowed it was the star witness for the prosecution.

Found guilty of murder, Cream was hanged in November 1892. Legend has it that on the scaffold, Cream shouted, 'I am Jack the. . .' before the trap-door and noose cut his words short. This has lead various criminologists to suggest that Cream was Jack the Ripper, forced to change his *modus operandi* for fear of early detection.

John Cashman's 1973 novel, *The Gentleman from Chicago*, presents the 'autobiography' of Thomas Neill Cream. The poisoner narrates his life story from his childhood in Canada, through his murderous career either side of the Atlantic, to his last days in the condemned cell. Cashman, a barrister, specialised in fictional biographies of Victorian murderers (see entries on 'Charles Peace' and 'Kate Webster'), strongly rooted in fact but with much fictional embroidering. Cream's autobiography is presented 'with hilarious sanctimoniousness' (to quote one review of the novel). By employing the framing device of a doctor's report on the veracity of the book, Cashman provides much useful information concerning aspects of the Cream case.

In Donald Thomas's *The Ripper's Apprentice* (1986), Cream is pitted against the author's series detectives, Inspector Swain of Scotland Yard and his assistant, Sergeant Lumley. Lumley is on hand when Ellen Dunworth dies, and Swain goes undercover to unmask the murderer among three suspected doctors. The period detail is strong, and Thomas is particularly good at portraying the sexual and religious tensions existing underneath the veneer of polite Victorian society.

FACTIONAL WORKS:
John Cashman, *The Gentleman From Chicago* (New York: Harper and Row, [1973]).
Donald Thomas, *The Ripper's Apprentice* (London: Macmillan, 1986).

FURTHER READING:
Richard D. Altick, *Victorian Studies in Scarlet* ((New York: W. W. Norton & Co., 1970).

ALICE CRIMMINS USA 1968

On 14th July 1965, Alice and Edmund Crimmins, the four-and five-year-old children of divorcee Alice Crimmins, were reported missing from their home in New York. Young Alice's body was found later that day—she had been strangled. Eddie's body was discovered later. At first, the police suspected abduction, but later formed the theory that Alice Crimmins had killed her daughter in a rage, and then had arranged for her son to be murdered because he had witnessed his sister's death.

In her trial in 1968, which dwelt on the details of her active sex life, Alice was found guilty of the manslaughter of her daughter and was sentenced to twenty years' imprisonment. An appeal was upheld on the basis that several members of the jury had visited the scene of the crime before the trial.

In her 1971 retrial, Alice was accused of her daughter's manslaughter and her son's murder. The police case in the retrial was that she had killed her children to prevent her husband from receiving custody. She was once more found guilty of manslaughter (again, a twenty year sentence) and of murder (life imprisonment). The life sentence was lifted on appeal, and Alice Crimmins served four years in prison before being transferred to a work-release programme. Shortly after, she was paroled.

In Mary Higgins Clark's novel, *Where Are The Children?* (1975), Alice Crimmins becomes Nancy Harmon, acquitted of the murder of her two young children in California. Seven years later, she is married to Ray Eldridge and living with their two children in Cape Cod. When the Eldridge children disappear, Nancy is suspected by the police. Is Nancy guilty of the first murders? And will her second family be found alive? The first question is answered early in the novel; the suspense of the plot lies in the unravelling of the second.

In her 1977 novel, *The Investigation*, ex-policewoman Dorothy Uhnak returns the story to its New York setting. Joe Peters of the District Attorney's Investigation Squad is called in on the case of Kitty and George Keeler, whose two children have been found brutally murdered close to their home. Kitty is the prime suspect, but the investigation becomes increasingly difficult for Joe as he finds himself falling in love with her. The eventual solution involves political corruption and organised crime.

FACTIONAL WORKS:
Mary Higgins Clark, *Where Are the Children?* (New York: Simon & Schuster, 1975).
Dorothy Uhnak, *The Investigation* (New York: Simon & Schuster, 1977).

FURTHER READING:
Kenneth Gross, *The Alice Crimmins Case* (New York: A. A. Knopf, 1975).

HAWLEY HARVEY CRIPPEN GB 1910

The Crippen case seems to have acquired a fame (or notoriety) out of all proportion to the murder that he committed. This probably has much to do with the fact that the American-born doctor, like the solicitor Armstrong after him, is a classic example of the 'worm that turned'—the harassed, dominated husband who resorted to the ultimate crime to ease his existence. Crippen, born in Michigan, married a stage actress, Belle Elmore, and moved to London in 1900. His wife made the doctor's life a misery, scolding him in front of friends and leaving him to do the housework. Crippen, in the meantime, had fallen in love with a secretary, Ethel Le Neve.

In 1910, Belle disappeared—the doctor told her friends that she had returned to the States and had died there. In the meantime, Ethel moved into the Crippen house and took to wearing Belle's jewellery. The police were informed, but a search of the house revealed nothing. But Crippen was apprehensive. He had poisoned Belle with hyoscine and buried her body in the cellar. He booked passage on a liner to Canada, taking his young mistress with him disguised as a boy. On learning of his flight, police searched his house again, and discovered the corpse in the cellar. A warrant for his arrest was issued. The captain of the fugitives' liner was suspicious of these two unusual passengers and sent a message by wireless to Scotland Yard—the first time the invention had been used in a murder hunt. Inspector Dew was dispatched by a faster ship and apprehended the doctor and his 'son' before they could set foot in Canada. Ethel was acquitted as an accessory, but Crippen was tried at the Old Bailey, found guilty and hanged in Novemer 1910.

Crippen has led a varied life in fiction and drama. Catherine Meadows's novel, *Henbane* (1934), features the shy American Dr Moon, married to the extravagant Flora, but in love with his typist, Maria. Meadows gives a sympathetic portrayal of the downtrodden medic, and her plot follows the original case with reasonable accuracy.

Less faithful to the facts was Ernest Raymond's masterly novel of 1934, *We, The Accused*. Here the doctor is transformed into a teacher, Paul Presset, who desires fellow-teacher Myra Bourne. Like Crippen and Le Neve, Presset and Myra flee from the police after the murder of his wife; but in Raymond's novel, their flight takes them around England rather than abroad. The author's success is in the minutiae of the legal web that is spun around the couple. The police manhunt, Presset's trial, his time in jail, the preparation for his execution, and the final scene in the execution shed all hold the reader's attention with their meticulous detail. Once more, the Crippen character is seen as a pathetic victim of circumstance.

In Edward Hale Bierstadt's 1935 novel, *Satan was a Man*, the protagonist, Carroll Lindsay, recreates the murders committed by Jack the Ripper, Lizzie Borden and Crippen after dreaming of the real-life killers themselves (see the entry on Jack the Ripper for details of the novel's convoluted plot).

Paul Dornhorst's play, *They Fly by Twilight*, was produced on the London stage in 1937 and published in 1939. Grocer George Martin finds his marriage to ex-music hall singer Flo is a nightmare. Flo is extrovert, George is bookish and reserved. When he falls for Mary Williams, the niece of one of Flo's theatrical friends, it seems George's life may change for the better. But Flo discovers the relationship and threatens to ruin Mary's reputation. In desperation, George strangles her. When Mary discovers that Flo is dead and buried beneath the scullery floor, she agrees to run off with George. At the last moment, however, they realise that their life together will be one of duplicity and fear, and they decide to spend one last night together before George turns himself over to the police.

Hilda Lewis's 1940 novel, *Said Doctor Spendlove*, presents a close adaptation of the case. Dr Charles Spendlove overdoses his nymphomaniac wife Dixie with hyocine after they argue over his mistress, Elsie Palmer, who is pregnant with his child. After Spendlove disposes of Dixie's body, he invites Elsie to move in, telling her that his wife has left him. But when Inspector Rose calls to question the doctor, he and his mistress flee disguised as father and son. The body is discovered, the escapees arrested on board ship and returned to stand trial—just as in the original.

The protagonist of Sydney Horler's novel, *The Man Who Did Not Hang* (1948), is Horace Harvey Pring, whose name echoes Crippen's. A patent medicine salesman like the real doctor, Pring is burdened with an unfeeling wife who has theatrical pretensions. The plot centres heavily on Esther Pring's character—her pursuit of a stage career (as Mai Hawthorne, a name she insists upon at home), her unscrupulous dealings in her efforts to achieve this goal, and her active love-life away from her husband. After Horace takes his secretary, Elsie Dean, as mistress, tragedy ensues. An observant policeman notes the similarity to the Crippen case, with the essential difference revealed in the title.

Ursula Bloom's *The Girl Who Loved Crippen* (1955) tells the story from the viewpoint of Ethel Le Neve. As is Bloom's trademark, the novel is heavily romanticised. Michael Hooker's novel, *Dr. Crippen* (1962), is based on Leigh Vance's script for the film of the same name. Once again, a sympathetic portrait of the doctor is provided and Le Neve is seen as an innocent party. The novel (and Vallance's script) suggests that the murder was an accident, the doctor inadvertently overdosing his wife while trying to deaden her passion with hyoscine.

Richard Gordon, in *The Private Life of Dr. Crippen* (1981), views the case as it touches the life of Eliot Beckett. Beckett is a dedicated doctor, first seen working at a Swiss clinic, where he meets American heiress Nancy Granger and her sister, Jane. Jane is suffering from pthisis, and Nancy has heard of a patent medicinal cure offered by a Dr Crippen in London. Eliot is sceptical, but offers to look Crippen up when he returns to London, where he is to set up a surgery for the poor. Nancy, intrigued by the taciturn doctor, travels to London with him. Here they make the acquaintance of Crippen and his circle: his wife Belle, his secretary Ethel Le Neve and Belle's friends, the Martinellis.

Eliot is party to the many developments in the case—he knows of Crippen's relationship with Ethel, he learns that Crippen doses Belle with hyoscine to subdue her sexual appetite, he hears from his medical friend, Bernard Spilsbury (the forensic scientist who gave evidence at Crippen's trial), the results of the post-mortem on Belle's body. Eliot believes Crippen to be guilty of nothing more than manslaughter, accidentally overdosing his wife. Gordon also suggests another possible solution to the case when he points out that henbane, the source of hyoscine, can be mistaken for parsnips; thus Belle might have poisoned herself inadvertently.

As expected from the author of the famous Doctor series of novels, the medical background in this novel is riveting, but his plot suffers from an excess of detail. The author does, however, provide an amusingly ironic coda to his story, with Eliot providing Crippen a sedative for his last hours—hyoscine.

Detective novelist Peter Lovesey gives a new twist to the Crippen story in *The False Inspector Dew* (1982). The date is 1921, and dentist Walter Baranov, who is married to a dominant ex-actress, falls in love with Alma Webster, a florist. When his wife decides to return to America, Walter plans to murder her with Alma's help. But, with the Crippen murder in mind, they agree to add a few touches to the previous method to ensure that theirs is a perfect murder. The first half of the novel traces the parallels between their affair and that of Crippen and Le Neve. Once aboard the S.S. Mauretania, the tone becomes farcical, with Walter forced into a charade that he eventually comes to enjoy, and with author Lovesey keeping the last of many delicious plot twists well concealed.

In his 1988 novel, *Dr. Crippen's Diary*, Emlyn Williams provides the reader with the 'newly-discovered' document, which chronicles the life of the medic from his twenty-first birthday to his arrest on board ship in 1910. His disillusionment with his brash wife follows quickly after the marriage, and he is soon using hyoscine to placate his wife's strong sex-drive. The murder itself is seen as an accident involving mistaken bottles of medicine, and Ethel Le Neve is innocent of any knowledge of the crime (Crippen persuades her that Belle is still alive, and that she will have him arrested if they do not flee together). Williams's adopts a light tone and his attempts at Crippen's Americanisms are on the whole successful.

FACTIONAL WORKS:
Catherine Meadows, *Henbane* (London: Victor Gollancz, 1934). US title: *Dr. Moon*.
Ernest Raymond, *We the Accused* (London: Cassell & Co., 1935).
Edward Hale Bierstadt, *Satan Was a Man* (New York: Doubleday, 1935).
Paul Dornhorst, 'They Fly by Twilight', in Sydney Box, ed., *Five Plays of Our Time* (London: Thomas Nelson, 1939). (**P**)
Hilda Lewis, *Said Dr. Spendlove* (London: Jarrolds, 1940). US title: *The Case of the Little Doctor*.
Sydney Horler, *The Man Who Did Not Hang* (London: Quality Press, 1948).
Ursula Bloom, *The Girl Who Loved Crippen* (London: Hutchinson and Co., [1955]).
Michael Hooker, *Dr. Crippen* (London: Brown, Watson Ltd., [1962]).
Richard Gordon, *The Private Life of Dr. Crippen* (London: William Heinemann, 1981).
Peter Lovesey, *The False Inspector Dew* (London: Macmillan, 1982).
Emlyn Williams, *Dr. Crippen's Diary* (London: Robson, 1988).

FURTHER READING:
Tom Cullen, *Crippen: The Mild Murderer* (London: Bodley Head, 1977).

FILM ADAPTATIONS:
Dr. Crippen, d. Robert Lynn. GB: ABP, 1962. Screenplay by Leigh Vance, novelised by Michael Hooker.

THE CROYDON POISONINGS GB 1928–29

The Sydney family of Croydon seemed a close-knit, happy family to most of their neighbours. Mrs Violet Sydney and her daughter Vera lived at 29 Birdhurst Rise. Her daughter, Grace Duff lived in the same road with her husband, Edmund and their three children. And in nearby South Hill Park Road, Violet's son, Thomas lived with his wife and children. The families would frequently gather at 29 Birdhurst Rise on Sundays for dinner.

On 27th April 1928, Edmund Duff died after a brief, unexpected illness; a poorly-executed post mortem resulted in a verdict of death by natural causes. Grace, a penniless widow, was reduced to living off a family handout of £400 per year. On 15th February 1929, Vera Sydney died after a few days' illness. Despite the fact that she and her aunt, Mrs Greenwell, had both been ill after the same lunch on 13th February, her death was attributed to gastric influenza.

On 5th March, Violet Sydney died after taking some medicine. She had complained about the taste and told her doctor that she had been poisoned. At first, the death was again attributed to natural causes, but a subsequent post-mortem on mother and daughter revealed a strong presence of arsenic in both bodies. Arsenic was also found after a further post-mortem on

Edmund's corpse. An inquest was held into the three deaths, at which Grace Duff and Thomas Sydney were the principal witnesses. The jury returned a verdict of murder by person or persons unknown. The police dropped their investigations in September 1929, and the case remains officially unsolved.

Julian Symons, who had investigated the case in one of a collection of non-fiction essays (see source quoted below), set his 1978 detective novel, *The Blackheath Poisonings*, in Victorian times. Harriet Collard is the fictional Violet Sydney, widowed daughter of a deceased toy manufacturer, Charles Mortimer, who had built their home, Albert House, in the style of an East Anglian church. Here, Harriet lives with her unmarried daughter, Charlotte, and her nephew, Bertie. In nearby Victoria Villas, another house built by Mortimer (this time in the Italian Palladian style), lives Harriet's daughter, Beatrice Vanderbilt, her husband, Roger, and her young stepson, Paul. Also living at Victoria Villas is Harriet's son, George, and his young wife, Isabel.

They often gather together at Harriet's house for Sunday dinner, and following one such meal, Roger Vanderbilt is taken ill and soon dies. Although the doctor certifies death by natural causes, Roger's son Paul suspects foul play. When a second death results, the young detective feels obliged to dig deep into his family's relationships and secrets. A trial results, at which Isobel Collard (secretly loved by Paul) is found guilty of murder. A third murder occurs before Paul can bring the mystery to a satisfactory conclusion and free Isabel. Symons obviously used the Croydon poisoning case as the springboard from which to launch his more intricate and atmospheric thriller. The solution itself is at odds with the original facts, the murderer being one of the additional relatives invented by the author.

FACTIONAL WORKS:
Julian Symons, *The Blackheath Poisonings* (London: Collins, 1978).

FURTHER READING:
Julian Symons, *A Reasonable Doubt* (London: Cresset Press, 1960).

EMMA CUNNINGHAM CASE USA 1857

Dr Harvey Burdell was a dentist who lived in a large house in Bond Street, New York, which he sublet as a boarding establishment to a widow, Mrs Emma Cunningham. On 31st January 1857, Burdell was attacked in his bedroom. Despite the fact that he was stabbed twelve times and had fought for his life before finally being strangled, no one in the house heard a thing, or so they were later to testify. Apart from the dentist and the widow, there were Mrs Cunningham's two daughters and two sons, three boarders—George Snodgrass, John J. Eckel and the Hon. Daniel Ullmann—and two maids.

There were plenty of suspects for the police to choose from; no one seemed to have a kind word to say about the deceased man. On hearing of Burdell's death, Eckel had supposedly danced a jig, and Snodgrass went out and got drunk to celebrate. Despite the fact that Burdell and Mrs Cunningham were forever fighting, she claimed that she had gone through a secret marriage ceremony with him and was therefore the owner of his estate. The authorities finally fastened on the trio of Cunningham, Eckel and Snodgrass as suspected murderers. They were duly arrested, although Snodgrass was later discharged.

Emma Cunningham was the first to stand trial. Unfortunately for her, she was left-handed, and Burdell had been stabbed by a left-handed person. However, she was defended by Henry L. Clinton, who tore apart the prosecution's circumstantial evidence. He insisted that the dentist and widow were indeed man and wife, calling her 'Mrs Burdell' throughout the trial—despite the fact that the clergyman who had married them couldn't identify Burdell as the groom (the State's theory was that Eckel had impersonated Burdell). He also claimed that 'Mrs Burdell' was expecting a child. The jury took half an hour to decide on the widow's innocence. The case against Eckel thus crumbled and he too was set free.

However, the story didn't end there. Cunningham's 'pregnancy' turned out to be a fraud. She had bribed a doctor to produce a new-born baby for her, but the authorities were onto the caper. The baby was identified before it was passed to Mrs Cunningham, and police broke in as she was cradling the child after its 'delivery'. She was once more arrested, this time for attempted fraud. The case, however, was dropped and the widow vanished into obscurity. Burdell's murderer was never caught. The 'bogus baby', however, became a celebrity, making regular appearances at P. T. Barnum's Museum!

Raymond Paul, in his novel *Murder by Gaslight* (1987), put his barrister-detective Lon Quincannon on the Burdell case. The story begins with Burdell's death at the hands of an unknown assailant. The action then returns to 1856 as the narrator, Toby Brendon, a new arrival in New York, makes the acquaintance of the flamboyant Quincannon, who saves him from a trumped-up murder charge. Brendon, appointed to a solicitor's firm, is involved in a divorce case concerning the beautiful Demis Hubbard, who is staying with her cousin, Harvey Burdell.

He is asked by Mrs Cunningham to help her in a breach-of-promise case against the dentist, and is called in by Quincannon when Burdell is found murdered. The fictional Brendon and Quincannon take the place of the factual Henry Clinton in defending the widow at her murder trial. Having obtained Mrs Cunningham's freedom, the two solve the murder in a turn of events which are at odds with the facts of the real case.

As with Paul's other detective novels (see the entry for the 'Richard P. Robinson Case'), the tale is full of strong period flavour and engaging characters, both fictional and factual. The New York Police Riots of 1857 and the closing of the notorious Shepherd's Fold orphanage run by the brutal Reverend Edward Cowley are intermingled with the progress of the Cunningham trial. So too is Brendon's search for the secret of his parentage.

The whole is an engaging thriller and a vivid, lively representation of New York life in the mid-nineteenth century.

FACTIONAL WORKS:
Raymond Paul, *Murder by Gaslight* (New York: W. W. Norton, 1987).

FURTHER READING:
Joan Kahn, ed., *Some Things Dark and Dangerous* (New York: Harper and Row, 1970). Includes Edmund Pearson's essay, 'The Murder of Dr. Burdell'.

JOHN CURRIE GB 1914

Currie was born in Staffordshire of Irish Catholic parents. He worked in the Minton pottery firm as a ceramic decorator, before going to Hanley School of Art and finally winning a place at the Royal College of Art. He married in 1907 while living in Bristol, where he was working as an art master. He moved to Dublin as an art inspector, a position he held for two years before returning to England and enrolling at the Slade School of Fine Art in London. All this time he had been building a reputation as an artist of merit.

At the Slade he met, among others, Paul Nash, Stanley Spencer, Gaudier-Brzeska and the East London-born Jewish artist, Mark Gertler. He found a patron in Edward Marsh, to whom he would introduce his fellow-artists such as Gertler. From the enthusiasm for modern art that he gained with Currie and Gertler, Marsh built up a formidable collection of modern British painting. The two artists founded their own school, calling themselves the 'Later Primitives'.

In 1911, Currie separated from his wife and moved in with a model, Dolly Henry. Although a warm and attractive personality, Dolly was also possessive and jealous of Currie's attention to his art. Gertler for one was disturbed by their violent arguments, which often came to blows. Currie broke from Dolly several times, but they would always eventually reconcile. Her relationships with other men preyed on his mind and made him sometimes suicidal.

On 8th October 1914, Currie went to Dolly's house in Chelsea and shot her, then turned the gun on himself. Dolly died instantly but Currie was taken to an infirmary, where he died the following day. An inquest found him guilty of Dolly's murder and his own suicide, on the grounds of temporary insanity.

Gertler later made the acquaintance of Gilbert Cannan, a dramatist and novelist. The appearance in 1916 of Cannan's novel, *Mendel*, caused a minor scandal within Gertler's circle. The story of Mendel Kuhler, son of a Polish Jew, who is born into the East End slums but finds fame as an artist, was a thinly-disguised biography of Gertler himself. Gertler's affair with fellow Slade School student, Dora Carrington, was echoed in Kuhler's passion for Greta Morrison. There were fictional sketches of other members of the contemporary art scene—C. B. W. Nevinson, Sir William Rothenstein,

Edward Marsh. And chief among the factional creations was the flamboyant, erratic and volatile James Logan.

Logan, an artist from the North, admires the younger Kuhler's work. Like Kuhler, he derides the English middle classes for their lack of passion. As a child he suffered from rickets, which has left him with a visible lump on his head. Because he is 'lop-sided' he tells Kuhler, 'I need you to balance me'. Together, the two artists decide to exhibit their new ground-breaking art. Logan meets Nellie Oliver, a Lancashire girl who becomes his mistress. Like her real-life prototype, Nellie is envious of her lover's passion for his art—'a woman is more important than the biggest picture ever painted'.

The three travel to Paris, partly for inspiration and partly in the hope of resolving the power struggle between Logan and Nellie. Logan wants Kuhler there for moral support: 'without you, Oliver would gobble me up'. The trip is a disaster—Oliver sleeps with another artist, and Kuhler has to hide the fact from Logan. Back in England, the relationship has turned to one of continuous physical and mental abuse. But Logan cannot make a break from her: 'She's all the religion I've got', he tells Kuhler, 'It is extraordinary how near love is to hate, and how rotten love becomes when hate is suppressed—stale and tasteless and vapid'.

Disgusted by his friend's turmoil and the effect it has on his art, Kuhler tells Logan that he must break with either him or Oliver. He later hears that Logan has separated from her, but is acting in a peculiar manner. When he and Greta Morrison see Logan at a restaurant, he is a shadow of his former self. He ignores them; Oliver then appears and Logan leaves with her. The following day, Kuhler learns that Logan has killed Oliver and attempted suicide. He visits Logan's death-bed, a visit that helps him come to terms with the faults in his own life and art.

The novel was lambasted by Gertler and his circle. Carrington, to whom it was dedicated, called it 'ugly, and so damned vulgar' and Gertler himself referred to it as 'a piece of cheap trash' (probably because many of his views of his fellow-artists were so accurately captured in the book). Logan's passionate and viscerous language persuaded Freda Lawrence that her husband, D. H. Lawrence must have been the model for the artist. But contemporary views of Currie suggest that Cannan captured his temperament perfectly in his explosive portrait of an artist in torment. James Logan is definitely the most vibrant character in this fascinating novel of turn-of-the-century bohemian London.

FACTIONAL WORKS:
Gilbert Cannan, *Mendel* (London: Fisher Unwin, 1916).

FURTHER READING:
John Currie, *Paintings and Drawings 1905–14* [exhibition catalogue] (Stoke-on-Trent, City Museum and Art Gallery, 1980).

RICHARD DADD GB 1844

Richard Dadd was born in 1817, the son of Robert Dadd, who worked as a chemist. Richard entered the Royal Academy schools in 1837, where he won three silver medals and established himself as a painter of some note. In 1842, he joined Sir Thomas Phillips on a journey to Egypt, but suffered an attack of sunstroke and was sent back to England. By the time he had reached home shores, he was suffering from paranoid schizophrenia. He returned to his studios, painting in a frenzy, although most of his head-and-shoulder portraits displayed a red slash across the throat—an uncanny indication of what was to come.

Dr Alexander Sutherland of St. Luke's Hospital was consulted. He suggested to Robert that Richard be kept under close and constant supervision. The older Dadd began planning a trip to Gravesend; but Richard proposed an alternative, Cobham Park in Kent, where he had sketched as a schoolboy. Dadd father and son put up at the village of Cobham, where Richard pestered his father to take a late night stroll. The following morning, two villagers discovered the body of Robert Dadd in Cobham Park; he had been stabbed and his throat had been cut.

Richard Dadd escaped to the continent. He was arrested near Montereau, having attempted to cut the throat of a fellow-passenger in a stagecoach. Escorted back to England, he stood trial at Rochester on 29th July 1844. He was committed to the State Criminal Lunatic Asylum at Bethlem Hospital, London. Here he continued his painting, specialising in fantastic illustrations of fairies and goblins; one of his most famous works was *The Fairy Feller's Master Stroke*. In 1864, the State Criminal Lunatic Asylum was transferred to Broadmoor, where Richard Dadd died in 1886, aged seventy.

French author Isaure de Saint Pierre published her novel, *L'Oeil D'Osiris* in 1980; it was translated as *Richard Dadd—His Journals* in 1984. As the English title suggests, the novel is—like Guy de Maupassant's famous short story—'The Diary of a Madman'. Dadd, incarcerated in Broadmoor, looks back over the events that placed him there. He returns constantly to the stagecoach where he attempted his second murder. Both murderous attacks were triggered by his belief that the victims were possessed by demons. He recalls his childhood, his meeting with Sir Thomas Phillips, who seduced him before their trip to Egypt and their continuing affair after they arrived in Africa. He remembers again the gradual onset of his insanity, as he becomes convinced that he is the servant of the Egyptian god, Osiris. He relives the violent murder of his father and his escape and capture on the continent.

As befits the memoirs of a madman, the narration is fragmented and frenetic, which makes the story difficult to follow, especially for one unfamiliar with Dadd's life. The work is well-researched—the author visited many of the places associated with Dadd, both in England and abroad, and had access to much archival material, correspondence and memorabilia. Dadd comes across as a pathetic and sympathetic character, lost in the depths of his malady, and, to some extent, taking solace in his mad and fantastic beliefs to distance himself from the monotony of his imprisonment.

REFERENCE:
Isaure de Saint-Pierre, *Richard Dadd: His Journals* (Henley-on-Thames: Ellis, [1984]). First published in French as *L'Oeil d'Osiris*, 1980.

FURTHER READING:
Jonathan Goodman , ed., *The Art of Murder* (London: Piatkus, 1990).

MICHAEL DAVIES GB 1953

While passing the bandstand on Clapham Common in London on 2nd July 1953, John Beckley and Matthew Chandler made a sarcastic comment about a group of teddy boys nearby. The gang, known as the 'Plough Boys', chased after the two youths, punching and kicking them as they went. Beckley and Chandler tried to climb onto a bus at a request stop but were dragged off. Chandler managed to climb back on, bleeding from stab wounds; Beckley fell to the ground. His body was later discovered by the bus stop.

After they were questioned by police, six youths were charged with the murder of John Beckley. Four were acquitted but found guilty of common assault. Two stood trial for murder, but when the jury failed to reach a verdict, only one was sent for retrial. He was Michael Davies, a twenty-year-old labourer. A witness on the bus had identified him as the ring-leader in the attack and blood had been found on his inside breast pocket.

Davies proclaimed his innocence, although he admitted to the charge of assault. Nonetheless, he was found guilty and sentenced to death. Appeals were rejected, but ten days before the date of his execution, Davies's sentence was commuted to life imprisonment. Seven years later he walked free, still proclaiming his innocence. The doubts raised during his trial led to a change in the law stating that evidence given by accomplices had to be corroborated.

Seven years after the events, Julian Symons tackled the Clapham Common murder in his novel, *Progress of a Crime*. On Bonfire Night, a man is stabbed to death on a village green by a gang of teddy boys. Young reporter Hugh Bennett sees the murder, but begins to question his view of events as the trial against the youths progresses. Symons's interest in the story focuses on the role played by the media in murder trials, and the value or lack therof in eyewitness testimony—both issues investigated through the sympathetic eyes of Bennett. Apart from his examination of reports of the Davies case, the author researched his novel by working briefly as a newspaper reporter.

FACTIONAL WORKS:
Julian Symons, *Progress of a Crime* (London: Collins, 1960).

FURTHER READING:
Tony Parker, *The Plough Boy* (London: Hutchinson and Co., 1965).

DAISY DE MELKER SOUTH AFRICA 1932

In 1932 a teenage boy named Rhodes de Melker died, presumably after contracting malaria. His father, William Cowle had died in 1923, apparently of a cerebral haemorrhage. Rumors began to spread regarding the boy's mother, Daisy de Melker, and the short life-spans of the men in her family. After William Cowle died, she had married Robert Sproat, who died four years later. Again the cause of death was given as cerebral haemorrhage. In each instance, Daisy had collected a sizeable insurance cheque.

Police became suspicious when they discovered that prior to Rhodes's death, arsenic had been bought by a 'Mrs Sproat'. The son's body was exhumed and found to contain arsenic; when exhumations were carried out on Mrs de Melker's two deceased husbands, strychnine was discovered. Daisy de Melker was arrested and charged with the three murders. As she was a trained nurse by profession, she would have had a working knowledge of poisons. She maintained her innocence throughout her trial, but the weight of evidence was against her. She was found guilty and executed in Johannesburg.

The fictionalised Daisy appeared two years after her hanging as Julia Taplin, a greedy, ambitious woman who uses her sexual attraction and her wiles to get her own way. In the course of Sarah Gertrude Mullins's novel, *Three Men Die*, she marries then murders first the weak Alexander Bishop and then the greedy Henry Biddington. However, after falling for Paul Foster, she finds not only her third husband barring her way to avaricious success, but also her son, Johnnie, who has been her sole comfort through her previous 'losses'. Millin provides an intriguing portrait of a *femme fatale* with one solution in her quest for sexual and monetary fulfilment. The setting, like that of the factual case, is South Africa.

FACTIONAL WORKS:
Sarah Gertrude Millin, *Three Men Die* (New York: Harper & Sons, 1934).

FURTHER READING:
Benjamin Bennett, *Up for Murder* (London: Hutchinson & Co., 1974).

HANNAH DOBBS CASE GB 1879

In May 1879, the badly decomposed body of an old woman was found in the cellar of a lodging house in Euston Square, London. Although a rope was tied around her throat, the injuries were not consistent with suicide by hanging or with strangulation. A blood stain found in a room above implied that the woman had been murdered upstairs and the body hidden in the cellar. It was estimated that the body had lain in the cellar for two years.

Eventually the body was identified as that of Matilda Hacker, aged about sixty-six at the time of her death. Hacker was an eccentric lady who had a habit of moving frequently under a variety of aliases. She had moved into the house in Euston Square as a lodger in September 1877, but had remained a recluse, seldom seen by the other lodgers. The only person who could recall her in any detail was Hannah Dobbs, a servant who collected the rents. It was known that Dobbs had pawned a watch in 1877, shortly after Matilda Hacker disappeared, and she was the only person in the house with any reason to visit the cellar regularly.

Dobbs was arrested for the murder. At her trial, the defence tried to cast doubt on the evidence, suggesting that proof of murder had not been irrefutably established. They also attempted to implicate the landlady and her husband, Mrs and Mr Bastendorff, in Matilda Hacker's death. Hannah herself cast suspicion on another lodger called Finley who had owned a revolver. She needn't have worried; the jury was unimpressed by the prosecution case and found Hannah not guilty.

Ronald Pearsall's 1989 novel, *Sherlock Holmes Investigates the Murder in Euston Square*, sees the great detective sleuthing from his armchair in an attempt to solve the Hacker murder. After the detective has read the newspaper reports of the trial, Watson presents Holmes with a document in his rooms at 221b Baker Street. The document contains statements made by twelve characters, some true, some fictional, all involved with the case. The statements themselves are related, with Holmes's and Watsons's comments on each one. After Holmes visits a thirteenth (fictional) person, he presents his solution. Pearsall's answer to the mystery is far-fetched to say the least, but immensely enjoyable, and in the spirit of Conan Doyle's own canon of often fantastic stories.

FACTIONAL WORKS AND FURTHER READING:
Ronald Pearsall, *Sherlock Holmes Investigates the Murder in Euston Square* (London: David & Charles, 1989). The preface reconstructs the facts from contemporary newspaper reports.

CAPTAIN JOHN DONELLAN GB 1781

Donellan lived at Lawton Hall near Warwick with his wife, his mother-in-law, and his wife's brother Sir Theodosius Boughton who was a sickly young man of twenty. In February 1781, shortly after taking a course of medicine, Sir Theodosius fell ill, and after several hours of agony, died. Captain Donellan was later seen washing out the medicine bottle. The local doctor performed an autopsy and concluded that Sir Theodosius had been poisoned by a distillation of laurel leaves.

Suspicion fell on the captain, who was arrested and tried for murder. It transpired that Donellan's brother-in-law was to come into an annuity of two thousand pounds a year upon his twenty-first birthday; if he died prior to that day, most of the money would pass to his sister. The captain maintained his innocence throughout the trial, suggesting that his covetous mother-in-law had murdered her own son. Found guilty, he was hanged in April 1781.

The Donellan case supplied the inspiration for Joseph Shearing's novel, *Laura Sarelle* (1940). The title character, a headstrong and neurotic girl, lives with her brother, Sir Theodosius at Leppard Hall in the 1840s. She is fascinated by a portrait of her namesake who, according to legend, poisoned her cousin with a sleeping draught and herself died of consumption. Laura learns that her eighteenth-century ancestor had in truth married an adventurer, Captain Avershaw, who had murdered her brother with laurel water.

Laura's relationship with her own brother is one of mutual hatred. Forced into a loveless marriage with a Jamaican planter, Harry Mostyn, Laura decides that history must be repeated so she can rid herself of both her detested brother and unwanted husband. An intriguing plot; but Shearing's novel is full of purple prose and little feel for period detail.

Donellan also makes a token appearance in Lillian de la Torre's short story 'The Stroke of Thirteen', from the collection *The Detections of Dr. Sam: Johnson* (1960). Although reference is made to the captain's trial in 1781, the plot concerns an earlier misdemeanour by the vicious Donellan. Unlike so many of de la Torre's short detective pastiches featuring the ubiquitous doctor and his biographer, James Boswell, the story is totally fictional.

FACTIONAL WORKS:

Joseph Shearing, *Laura Sarelle* (London: Hutchinson & Co., 1940). US title: *The Crime of Laura Sarelle.*

Lillian de la Torre, 'The Stroke of Thirteen' in *The Detections of Sam. Johnson* (New York: Doubleday, 1960).

FURTHER READING:

Brian Lane, ed., *The Murder Club Guide to the Midlands* (London: Harrap, 1988).

SAMUEL DOUGAL GB 1903

Dougal was born in 1846. He joined the army at the age of twenty, and left it ignominiously in 1896, after serving a twelve-month sentence for forgery. Within the next three years, he had met a wealthy spinster, Camille Holland, married her and moved with her to Moat Farm House. However, it transpires that Dougal had already been married twice during his army days; his wives had both died under suspicious circumstances. Also, unbeknown to Camille, he was already married and his current wife was still alive.

Even when established at Moat Farm House with his new spouse, Dougal could not subdue his passion for other women. He attempted to seduce Camille's maid, who reported the incident to her mistress. A few days later, Dougal and Camille went 'into town to do a little shopping'. That evening, Dougal returned alone, saying that his wife had gone to London on a short trip. When she failed to return, the maid left for her mother's house. Dougal's other wife appeared, and stayed at the House with her husband until 1902. Maids and servant-girls came and went, often providing Dougal with his sexual pleasures; he was responsible for fathering several children among the local female population.

His lascivious behaviour, together with Camille's disappearance, fuelled many rumours and when Dougal forged a cheque to obtain some of Camille's savings, the police moved in. On 27th April 1903, a search of the House and its grounds revealed the decomposed remains of Camille's body in a drainage ditch. A bullet was found inside the skull. Dougal was charged with murder, tried and found guilty. Shortly before his execution on 8th July, he confessed to the killing.

Douglas G. Browne, who would later write on the Wallace Case, turned to the Dougal murder in 1948 for his novel, *Rustling End*. As in most of Browne's novels, the detective is Harvey Tuke of the Department of Public Prosecutions. Browne takes as the basis of his plot a suggestion made by F. Tennyson Jesse that Dougal may have met fellow-murderer George Chapman (hanged for the murder of his barmaid Maud Marsh in 1903, and responsible for the deaths of two other women) when Chapman was running a public house in the locality of the Moat Farm in 1899. Although Browne's Chapman, Herbert Detmold, is a minor character in the plot, Tuke concentrates his attention on James Hipwell Prowse, a close facsimile of Dougal. The case is given a contemporary setting. One chilling scene, in which Prowse and Detmold meet, has the men sensing their murderous affinity and shying away from each other without knowing the reason.

R. J. White, who also tackled another true crime case in fiction (see the entry on the 'Gardiner Case'), novelised the tale of Samuel Dougal in 1961. *The Smartest Grave* is a closer reconstruction of Dougal's misdeeds, with Captain Dugdale marrying the wealthy Cecile Germaine and taking her to Moat House, where she is murdered. Inspector Brock is the policeman placed in charge of the case of Cecile's disappearance, and his mental tug-of-war with Dugdale gives the final chapters of the book plenty of suspense. In the concluding scene when Brock visits Dugdale in the condemned cell, White takes the opportunity to present his interpretation of Dougal's psychological make-up and answer some of the mysteries surrounding Dougal's actions at Moat Farm House. White's novel won a Crime Club competition for the best crime novel of that year written by a University don.

FACTIONAL WORKS:
Douglas G. Browne, *Rustling End* (London: Macdonald, 1948).
R. J. White, *The Smartest Grave* (London: Collins/Crime Club, 1961).

FURTHER READING:
Richard T. Altick, *Victorian Studies in Scarlet* (London: J. M. Dent and Co., 1972).

MARQUISE DE DOUHAULT FRANCE 1789-1817

In 1764 at the age of 23, Adélaide-Marie-Rogres Lusignan de Champignelles married the Marquis de Douhault. After twenty years of marriage, her father died. Her scheming brother managed to obtain large portions of the estate which were rightfully due to the Marquise and her mother. In 1787, following her husband's death, the Marquise was persuaded by her sister to attempt to reclaim the inheritance, for the benefit of their destitute mother.

She set off for Paris at the end of that year, stopping at the house of a relative at Orléans at the beginning of 1788. It appears she was drugged there with a pinch of snuff. When she recovered her senses, she found herself in the Salpêtrière, an asylum in Paris, under a different name. Here she was detained for over a year, while her brother claimed part of her estate by marriage, her death having been assumed by this time.

The Marquise managed to obtain her release in 1789, and was recognised by her friends and former servants. Her brother, however, refused to acknowledge her and used his new-found wealth to prevent her from establishing her identity in law. After twenty-eight years of fruitless efforts to regain her position and rightful inheritance, the Marquise died in 1817.

Wilkie Collins read the Marquise's sad tale in 1856 in Maurice Mejan's *Recueil des Causes Célèbres*, a book he picked up in Paris. It struck a chord in the writer's own life: once while he was walking with his brother Charles and the artist John Everett Millais, he was approached by a woman dressed in long white robes who suddenly ran off. Collins pursued her and later told Millais that the young lady 'of good birth and position' was being kept prisoner by a man in a villa in Regent's Park. The lady, Caroline Graves subsequently became the author's mistress.

Collins amalgamated elements of the Douhault case and his own meeting with Caroline Graves—forced imprisonment, a fraudulent claim after a supposed death, denial of identity, the mysterious appearance of a woman in distress—to form the basis of his 1860 novel, *The Woman in White*. The novel's chief narrator, Walter Hartright, crosses the path of a curious woman 'dressed from head to foot in white garments', who walks with the young man to London. Later, when Walter takes up the post of drawing-master to Laura Fairlie, he notices a strong resemblance between Laura and the mysterious woman.

It transpires later that the woman in white is Anne Catherick, who holds a secret relating to Laura's future husband, Sir Percival Glyde. Anne is being held in an asylum by Sir Percival and his mentor, Count Fosco. The two villains are intent on robbing Laura of her wealth. After the marriage of Laura and Sir Percival, Anne Catherick dies and is buried as Laura, who is now herself interred in the asylum.

Walter, who has fallen in love with Laura, rescues her and they are married. With the help of Laura's half-sister, the strong-willed and resourceful Marion Halcombe, she is restored to her rightful property. Sir Percival is killed attempting to burn documents which would prove Laura's case. Fosco, a member of an Italian secret society, is assassinated by his colleagues for betrayal. Thus the novel has a more satisfying conclusion than the Douhault case itself.

Collins was persuaded to dramatise the novel for copyright reasons, and this stage version was self-published in 1871. It had been 'tried out' in Leicester in 1870 before opening at the Olympic Theatre in London. It made its American debut in 1873. Few copies of the original edition have survived, but, to all intents and purposes, the play closely followed the novel.

FACTIONAL WORKS:
Wilkie Collins, *The Woman in White* (London: Sampson, Low, Son & Co., 1860).
Wilkie Collins, *The Woman in White* (London: published by the author, 1871). (**P**)

FURTHER READING:
Clyde K. Hyder, 'Wilkie Collins and The Woman in White', in *PMLA*, vol. 54 (1939).

FILM ADAPTATIONS:
The Woman in White, d. Peter Godfrey. US: Warner, 1948. Screenplay by Stephen Morehouse Avery, based on the novel by Wilkie Collins.*

DRUCE-PORTLAND CASE GB 1907

Though not as celebrated as the Tichbourne Claimant case, which it strongly resembles, the Druce-Portland affair has many interesting features of its own. For nine years the claim of George Hollamby Druce that he was the heir of the Duke of Portland was the subject of the day. The case arose from an allegation made in 1898 by the daughter-in-law of Thomas Charles Druce, that her father-in-law had in fact been John Bentinck, the fifth Duke of Portland.

She claimed that the eccentric duke had led a double life as both Portland and Druce, until he had tired of the charade and staged Druce's death in 1864 (the Duke himself died fifteen years later). She alleged that Druce's coffin, buried in Highgate Cemetery, contained nothing but lead. She attempted to have the coffin opened, but Druce's son Herbert refused an exhumation, a decision that was upheld in court.

In 1907, George Hollamby Druce forced Herbert's hand by charging him with perjury, as Herbert had stated he had seen his father's body in the coffin. Witnesses were called to support the theory of Druce's double life. One such witness—an American named Robert Caldwell—claimed to have aided in the burial deception by supplying the lead. He was subjected to a blistering cross-examination by Herbert Druce's lawyer, Horace Avory, and subsequently fled to America to escape a warrant for his arrest on a charge of perjury. Two more witnesses for the prosecution were similarly charged before the trial was eventually concluded by the opening of Thomas Druce's coffin. The corpse inside was positively identified as that of Druce. The affair fizzled out on an anti-climactic note.

In 1933, R. Austin Freeman utilised the facts of the case for his detective novel, *Dr. Thorndyke Intervenes*. Christopher Pippet, an American, arrives in England to discover whether he is the descendant of the Earl of Winsborough and rightful heir to his estate. Like its factual counterpart, the Pippet-Winsborough case stems from the possibility of the earl leading a dual existence (as earl and publican). and that a death had been faked. The discovery of a decapitated head in a railway cloakroom, and the theft of a shipment of platinum adds to the suspense. Freeman's forensic detective, Dr John Thorndyke, solves all three mysteries.

FACTIONAL WORKS:
R. Austin Freeman, *Dr. Thorndyke Intervenes* (London: Hodder & Stoughton, 1933).

FURTHER READING:
Theodore Besterman, *The Druce-Portland Case* (London: Duckworth, 1935).

DRUMSHEUGH CASE GB 1810

Twenty-eight-year old Marianne Woods and her friend Jane Pirie, a year younger, were mistresses of a small girls' school near Drumsheugh Gardens in Edinburgh at the beginning of the nineteenth century. Apart from Woods and Pirie, the school was co-managed by Miss Woods's aunt Ann, an ex-actress. Among the girl-boarders at the time of the scandal was Jane Cumming, the sixteen-year-old illegitimate, half-caste granddaughter of Lady Helen Cumming Gordon. Cumming, who had had a lenient upbringing, was frequently in trouble at school.

On 14th November 1810, Jane visited her grandmother. The story she related at this time caused Lady Gordon Cumming to contact the other parents and guardians and persuade them to withdraw their children from the school. Her influence was such that within two days, all the pupils were removed. Miss Woods's request for a reason was met with stony silence. Eventually the truth emerged. Jane Cumming had told her grandmother that Marianne Woods and Jane Pirie were involved in a lesbian relationship, and that one of the maids had seen them in a compromising position through a keyhole of the drawing-room door at the school.

As soon as they were aware of the allegations, Woods and Pirie brought an action of defamation of character against Lady Cumming Gordon, claiming £10,000 for loss of income and the ruin of their establishment. The trial began on 8th December. In the course of a long series of hearings, it transpired that the drawing-room door had no keyhole and that the sofa on which Woods and Pirie were spotted was not even visible from the opened door. The maid denied Jane Cumming's statement. A second girl, Janet Munro, confirmed Cumming's accusation but seemed to have been influenced by her friend.

In June 1811, the trial reached its conclusion, with the judges split four to three in favour of the defendent, Lady Cumming Gordon. In October, the 'pursuers', Woods and Pirie, petitioned for a review of the case on the grounds of the close decision. Their petition was granted, and a second trial resulted in a four-three split between the judges in their favour. Lady Cumming Gordon appealed to the House of Lords; seven years later, the appeal was dismissed.

In December 1819, the pursuers placed their claim for damages, which were estimated at just under £9,500. Even then Lady Gordon Cumming fought the payment for over a year, before offering £3,500. The final result was never recorded in the newspapers, which had by this time lost interest.

120 years later on the other side of the Atlantic, Dashiell Hammett suggested to his partner, Lillian Hellman, that the story of Pirie and Woods would make a good subject for drama. He had recently read William Roughead's account of the case, 'Closed Doors'. Hellman's subsequent play, *The Children's Hour*, was staged in New York in 1934 and published the same year. It made her reputation as a leading American dramatist.

The story is transferred to contemporary America. In a girl's boarding school in Massachusetts, young Mary Tilford, a liar and thief, is constantly in trouble with Karen Wright and Martha Dobie, the schoolmistresses. She informs her aunt, the wealthy benefactor of the school, that Martha is jealous of Karen's forthcoming marriage to local doctor, Joseph Cardin, and that the women have had a lesbian relationship.

The facts of the slander and the resulting suit are heavily based on the Drumsheugh incident, right down to the non-existent keyhole. In Hellman's version, however, the two ladies lose their slander suit, mainly because Martha's aunt, an ex-actress named Lily Mortar, who has helped with the running of the school, refuses to testify for them in court. Also, Mary Tilford blackmails a friend of hers into backing up her lies. Reduced to bankruptcy, Karen and Martha are left in the deserted school. Martha confesses her unrequited love for Karen and commits suicide in her room. Mrs Tilford, finally convinced of her niece's falsehood, arrives—too late—to apologise for her actions.

Hellman's play was controversial when it first opened, but proved to be a box-office success. When it was filmed in 1936, the stricter Hollywood morality code ensured that Hellman's script was devoid of all traces of the lesbian relationship—the slander was based on Martha's supposed affair with Karen's fiance. In 1961, the play was filmed again by a more liberal Hollywood, with the lesbian overtones restored.

FACTIONAL WORKS:
Lillian Hellman, *The Children's Hour* (New York: A. A. Knopf, 1934). (**P**)

FURTHER READING:
Lillian Faderman, *Scotch Verdict* (New York: Morrow, 1983).

FILM ADAPTATIONS:
The Children's Hour, d. William Wyler. US: UA/Mirisch, 1961. Screenplay by Lillian Hellman, based on her play.*

ARNAUD DU TILH ('MARTIN GUERRE') FRANCE 1560

In 1548, Martin Guerre, a twenty-four-year-old peasant farmer, departed from his village of Artigat in the Languedoc region of France, leaving behind his wife, Bertrande, and a young son. For eight years, nothing was heard of him. Then in 1556, a man turned up in the village claiming to be Martin. He was much changed—for one, he was bearded—but his sisters accepted him as their brother, as very soon did the rest of Artigat. Even his wife appeared to recognise him. The newly-returned prodigal settled down to his farm and his impending inheritance (the Guerres had other land in Hendaye on the Spanish border).

In 1558, a quarrel erupted between Martin and his Uncle Pierre over his inheritance and the money still owed him from the time of his travels. Pierre spread rumours that the man was an impostor. The village soon split between those who now believed Pierre and those who sided with Martin. Illegally using Bertrande's name, Pierre had his nephew arrested, claiming that the impostor was Arnaud du Tilh from the nearby village of Sajas.

At his trial in Rieux, Guerre/du Tilh was found guilty of imposture and sentenced to death. He appealed to the Parlement of Toulouse, and his appeal was heard in April 1560. Bertrande alleged that she had been forced to bring an accusation against her husband and Martin's sisters still asserted that the accused was their brother. As the judges were about to make their final decision, a man with a wooden leg hobbled into the court and claimed that *he* was Martin Guerre.

The judges ordered that the two Martins be placed side by side. The sisters eventually identified the newcomer as their brother. Finally, Bertrande stood before the one-legged man and asked for his pardon, admitting that he was her husband. Du Tilh, who confessed before his execution and returned to his genuine name, was once more sentenced to death. He was executed in front of Martin Guerre's house.

Any investigation of the case must hinge on Bertrande's role in the affair. Was she taken in by the false 'Martin'? Did she go along with the impersonation for her own ends? Or was a wife's role in medieval France so subservient that she dared not act on her own? Janet Lewis's novel, *The Wife of Martin Guerre* (1941) relates the story solely from Bertrande's point of view. Lewis sees her as a dupe of du Tilh, initially accepting him unreservedly as her returned husband. However, when she begins to suspect he is an impostor, she is tortured by religious guilt for her unwitting adultery—a guilt that finally destroys a relationship she is far from loath to accept.

Lewis based her novel on a factual version of the story written by Alexandre Dumas *père* which places Bertrande as the sole instigator of both her own and du Tilh's downfall. Since then, after reading what is accepted as the most authentic record of the case—that of Jean de Coras, the recorder at the Toulouse trial—she realised Pierre's role in instigating the trial. She accepted afterwards that 'if I were to write the story of Bertrande today it would have to be a different story'. Nevertheless, her novel is still a gripping tale of confusion, deception, guilt and redemption, with an authentic background and a touching finale. Her Bertrande is a spirited and sympathetic character. The story was successful enough to be adapted into an opera in 1958 with music by William Bergsma and a libretto by Lewis. This success has recently been echoed in the popularity of the West End musical, *Martin Guerre*, written by Bloublil and Schonberg.

FACTIONAL WORKS:
Janet Lewis, *The Wife of Martin Guerre* (San Francisco: Colt Press, 1941).

FURTHER READING:
Natalie Zamon Davis, *The Return of Martin Guerre* (Cambridge, Mass.: Harvard University Press, 1983).

PAULINE DUBOISSON FRANCE 1953

It is surprising that Pauline Duboisson did not receive the death penalty at her trial in 1953—the details of her previous sexual adventures did much to alienate the French public. At the age of sixteen, during the German occupation, she had taken a German officer as her lover. Listed as a collaborator by the French Resistance, she was treated accordingly at the end of the war; her head was shaved in public. She kept a diary of her subsequent lovers, among whom was listed Felix Bailly, a fellow student at Lille University. For two years they had a passionate, stormy relationship, before Bailly left her in 1949.

Eighteen months and many diary entries later, Pauline and Felix met again. According to her the relationship was resumed; Felix's friends, on the other hand, suggested that he was afraid of her advances and asked them to protect him. On 17th March 1951, Pauline gained entrance to Felix's flat and shot him three times. She then tried to gas herself. During the months before her trial, she attempted suicide again. In 1953 she stood in the dock charged with assassination (premeditated murder, for which the penalty was death). The jury, however, found her guilty of manslaughter and she was sentenced to life imprisonment.

French playwright Michel Vinaver followed the trial closely in the pages of the national newspaper *Le Monde*. Over thirty years later he employed these clippings for his play, *Portrait d'une Femme* (published in England in 1989 as *Portait of a Woman*). Scenes of the trial of Sophie Auzzaneau (Vinaver's Pauline) are intertwined with images from her life and her affairs. Vinaver was fascinated by Duboisson's failure to connect emotionally with the court proceedings. Consequently, he juxtaposes accurate representations of Pauline/Sophie's bland responses to questioning at her trial with scenes from her full-blooded, passionate life—presenting us with a portrait of a woman unable to discuss or dissect passion, but more than able to experience and react to it.

FACTIONAL WORKS:
MichelVinaver, 'Portrait of aWoman', in David Bradby and Claude Schumacher, eds. *New French Plays* (London: Methuen, 1989). First published in French as 'Portrait d'une Femme', 1989.

FURTHER READING:
Derick Goodman, *Crime of Passion* (London: Elek, 1958).

CLAUDE DUVAL GB 1670

Claude Duval was born in Normandy and moved to Paris in his early teens. There he fell in with the large colony of English exiles from the Civil Wars, and when Charles II claimed the English crown, Duval went to England as a pageboy. Restoration England was a period of turmoil for cavalier soldiers, their services no longer required. Many turned to robbery to supplement their income—Duval followed this path with much success.

Contemporary tales of his exploits invariably expound upon his gallantry and manners and his prowess with women. There is a famous encounter on Hounslow Heath, where he is reputed to have danced with a young lady whose coach he was in the process of robbing. Inevitably, Duval was caught, supposedly while in a drunken stupor, tried and sentenced to death. His gallantry was so renowned that there was talk of a pardon from the King. But in 1670 at the age of twenty-seven, Duval was hanged at Tyburn.

Not surprisingly, Duval became a popular figure during the early nineteenth century in the heyday of Newgate fiction. Despite that, only two works appear to have survived in print. Thomas P. Taylor's play, *Claude Duval, The Ladies' Highwayman*, was staged in 1842, but was not published until around 1885. The one-act farce features a fictional incident in the highwayman's career, encapsulating his attraction to women and his chivalry to those he robbed. The tone is set by the name of one character, the Marquis of Honeybum.

More substantial, but no greater from a literary standpoint, is Emma Robinson's historical soufflé, *Whitefriars* (1844), in which Duval threads his way through the complex narrative, helping the novel's hero—Reginald, Lord Mervyn—at every turn. Robinson's narrative begins as Duval takes Mervyn, the bastard infant of the Earl Aumerle, to the Tower of London, where the Earl is held on a charge of treason. Throughout the book, Lady Aumerle and her lover Colonel Blood conspire against Mervyn, but Duval always appears in time to assist the hero. Together, they traverse the Great Fire of London, the Popish Plot (see 'Sir Edmund Godfrey Murder') and The Rye Plot before Duval finds himself on his way to the gallows and Mervyn comes into his inheritance.

The novel is a half-baked mixture of crowded incident, hilarious hairbreadth escapes and sloppy character development, indicative of the many talentless writers who tried to follow in the footsteps of Sir Walter Scott.

FACTIONAL WORKS:
[Emma Robinson], *Whitefriars; or, the Days of King Charles* (London: Henry Colburn, 1844).
Thomas P. Taylor, *Claude Duval, the Ladies' Man* (London: T. C. Dick, [1885]). (**P**)

FURTHER READING:
Patrick Pringle, *Stand and Deliver: the Story of the Highwaymen* (London: Museum Press, 1951).

CHRISTIANNA EDMUNDS GB 1872

Christianna Edmunds, forty-two years old, lived with her mother in Brighton. She developed a consuming passion for her physician, Dr Beard, who treated her for nervous headaches. Although he was married, she bombarded the doctor with letters confessing her desire for him. When these failed to elicit a response, Edmunds decided to poison Mrs Beard. She brought strychnine from a chemist and sent a box of treated cakes to the doctor's wife. Servants who ate them complained of a bitter taste. The doctor saw through her plan and broke with her.

To vindicate her name with Dr Beard, Edmunds tried to divert suspicion onto a local shopkeeper. She persuaded a young boy to order sweets from the shop for her, dosed them with strychnine and returned them to the shop, again using the boy as go-between. When the sweets were re-sold, young Sydney Barker died a horrible death from the poison. At the inquest, Edmunds attracted attention by saying she had almost been poisoned herself. Not content with this, she sent anonymous letters to the boy's father, insisting that he prosecute the shopkeeper.

Police checks on the sale of strychnine led them to Christianna Edmunds. The boy who had acted as go-between identified her; handwriting experts matched her writing with that in the anonymous letters. At her trial in 1871, Edmunds pleaded insanity, a plea that was rejected by the jury. Sentenced to death, she was sent instead to Broadmoor for life by order of the Home Secretary.

John Dickson Carr transferred the details of the Edmunds murder to a modern setting in his 1939 detective novel, *The Black Spectacles*. The deaths of a number of children via poisoned sweets from a village shop owes much, as the police hero rightly surmises, to the Edmunds case of 1872. Carr's private detective, Dr Gideon Fell, who assists the police in their investigation of these and a subsequent (and more intricate) murder, provides an interesting thesis on the psychology of poisoners, citing several genuine cases.

FACTIONAL WORKS:
John Dickson Carr, *The Black Spectacles* (London: Hamish Hamilton, 1939). US title: *The Problem of the Green Capsule*.

FURTHER READING:
Richard and Molly Whittington-Egan, *The Bedside Book of Murder* (Newton Abbot: David & Charles, 1988).

RUTH ELLIS GB 1955

Ellis was the manager of the Little Club in London. There she met a young aspiring racing driver, David Blakely. They became lovers, but the relationship was stormy, with scenes, jealousies and drunken binges. At first, Blakely was emotionally dependent on Ruth, but in the latter stages of their brief affair, Ruth became subservient to his whims.

In 1955, after they had again quarrelled and parted, Ruth suffered a miscarriage. She went to the house of mutual friends where she knew Blakely was staying and created a disturbance. When Blakely went to a local pub, she followed him and shot him as he left. She readily confessed to the murder and was found guilty. Despite a strong campaign for a reprieve, she was hanged on 21st July 1955—the last woman in Britain to die under the death penalty.

Mike Newell's film *Dance With a Stranger* was released in 1985. Dramatist Shelagh Delaney's script was reworked as a novel by Kenneth Harper. The story presents Blakely and Ellis as two innocents trapped in a mutually-destructive relationship that neither can control. Alternatively passionate in their love and hatred of each other, they find themselves at a point of no return. As well as providing a sympathetic portrait of Ruth, the treatment also investigates the plight of Ruth's long-time companion, Desmond Cusson, who occasionally provides her with a secure home and a settled family life, but who receives little affection for his pains.

FACTIONAL WORKS:
Kenneth Harper, *Dance with a Stranger* (London: Panther, 1985).

FURTHER READING:
Laurence Marks and Tony Van Den Bergh, *Ruth Ellis: A Case of Diminished Responsibility?* (London: Macdonald & James, 1977).

FILM ADAPTATIONS:
Dance with a Stranger, d. Mike Newell. GB: Goldcrest, 1985. Screenplay by Shelagh Delaney, novelised by Kenneth Harper.

JOSEPH BROWNE ELWELL MURDER USA 1920

Joseph Elwell was the American bridge expert *par excellence* at the beginning of the century. Author of several books on the game (although later it was discovered they were in fact written by his wife), Elwell was a vain man who married into wealth and used his bridge expertise to fleece his rich acquaintances. Despite his baldness, which he concealed with a wig, and his false teeth, he was a notorious philanderer who kept an index of his conquests (disguised as a list of chosen bridge partners). A man such as Elwell was bound to make enemies.

On 11th June 1920, his housekeeper found him sitting in his bedroom, dying from a bullet lodged in his forehead. There was no evidence of theft—large amounts of money and valuables were discovered untouched. Police investigated his 'love index' for possible suspects, but most of the listed women had alibis, and it was unlikely that the pretentious Elwell would have been seen by a woman-friend without his false teeth and wig, as the housekeeper discovered him. Many theories were proposed—jealous husbands or lovers, equally jealous bridge-players, indebted gambling cronies—but the murder still remains officially unsolved.

Two years later Hannah Gartland's novel, *The House of Cards*, appeared. Gartland's fictional Elwell is Gregory Barwood, the keeper of a fashionable gambling den who is involved in the illegal traffic of liquour. When Barwood is discovered shot in his house one morning, the news causes consternation in society circles, especially among his women acquaintances, who are anxious to have their names kept out of the press. Stephen Wallace, the district attorney and James Macoy, a young reporter join forces to discover the murderer.

The investigation is complicated by the fact that most of Wallace's acquaintances are ex-pupils of Barwood's. Furthermore, he discovers that his wife visited Barwood the night before the murder. Following a trail of blackmail, organised crime and adultery, Wallace and Macoy unmask the murderer—but their findings cannot be broadcast to the world at large. So the Barwood case, like that of Joseph Elwell, has to remain officially unsolved.

In 1926, S. S. Van Dine introduced readers to his detective, Philo Vance, in *The Benson Murder Case*. Vance, an American equivalent of Dorothy Sayers's Lord Peter Wimsey, is a socialite, a lover of the fine things in life and an amateur sleuth. His friend, the district attorney of New York County, allows him to watch the police in action on a murder case. Alvin Benson, a wealthy New York sportsman, has been shot through the forehead in circumstances duplicating the Elwell case. Vance immediately finds a clue that will identify the murderer, but conceals it while the police pursue fruitless lines of enquiry. Finally, he puts the despairing district attorney out of his misery and solves the case. In one of the footnotes that Van Dine employs to give his novel a sense of authenticity, the author identifies the similarity between the fictional case and its factual basis.

FACTIONAL WORKS:
Hannah Gartland, *The House of Cards* (New York: Dodd Mead & Co., 1922).
S. S. Van Dine, *The Benson Murder Case* (New York: C. Scribner's Sons, 1926).

FURTHER READING:
Jonathan Goodman, *The Slaying of Joseph Browne Elwell* (London: Harrap, 1987).

FILM ADAPTATIONS:
The Benson Murder Case, d. Frank Tuttle. US: Paramount, 1930. Screenplay by Barlett Cormock, based on the novel by S. S. Van Dine.

EYRAUD AND BOMPARD FRANCE 1890

In 1889, the decomposed body of solicitor Toussaint-Augssent Gouffé was discovered near a river in Lyon; he had been strangled. The remains of a trunk nearby led the police to determine that Gouffé had been murdered in Paris and his body taken by train in the trunk to Lyon, where it was dumped. The authorities widened their search to find Gouffé's last known companions in Paris, an army deserter by the name of Michel Eyraud and his prostitute mistress, Gabrielle Bompard. In 1890, Bompard was arrested in Paris.

She claimed that Eyraud had forced her to assist him in the murder of the solicitor, who was investigating a bankruptcy charge against him. Gouffé was lured to Bompard's room where he was killed and thrown into the trunk. The pair robbed his apartment and escaped to America after disposing of the body in Lyon. There they split up, and Bompard returned to France. Eyraud was arrested in Cuba and extradited to France. At the subsequent trial, he was sentenced to death and Bompard to twenty year's imprisonment.

The German author Joachim Maass saw Gabrielle Bompard as the driving force behind the murder—the quintessential *femme fatale*. To this end, when he wrote his novel *Der Fall Gouffé* (1958—translated two years later as *The Gouffé Case*), he took liberties with the facts to develop and dissect Bompard's character. The first half of Maass's novel follows the details of the case faithfully until the trial, when Bompard is acquitted. She returns to America, pursued by Gouffé's nephew Jaquemar, who intends to lay a trap for her. However, like his uncle before him, he falls for her and is himself caught and destroyed in a plot of his intended victim's devising. The novel is an intriguing portrait of a calculating, egocentric woman, intent on satisfying her own desires.

FACTIONAL WORKS:
Joachim Maass, *The Gouffe Case* (London: Barrie & Rockliff, [1960]). First published in German as *Der Fall Gouffe*, 1952.

FURTHER READING:
Leonard Gribble, *Strange Crimes of Passion* (London: Long, 1970).

LAURA FAIR CASE USA 1871

In 1863, Laura Fair, a boarding-house proprietor in Virginia City, made the acquaintance of Alexander P. Crittenden, a rising lawyer. After her second husband's suicide, Laura had tried a career on the stage, but moved to Virginia at the beginning of the gold rush to establish the Tahoe House for boarders. Crittenden came from a Southern family of distinction and was visiting Virginia on business when he first met Laura. From the beginning, he led her to believe that he was a widower. When Laura eventually learned that Mrs Crittenden was very much alive, the lawyer hastily told her that they were separated. Laura's mother was shocked by the adulterous affair and ordered Crittenden out of the house.

He took Laura with him. He even persuaded his mistress and his wife to share the same house for a time! Laura left Crittenden in 1867, threatening to go to Havana, but he persuaded her to return to him until his separation was finally made legal. Three years later, she was still waiting. When she showed interest in a boarder at Tahoe House, Crittenden reacted jealously. Laura married the man anyway; the marriage lasted four months, and she divorced her husband on grounds of adultery. She assumed that Crittenden would now leave his wife for her, but she learned that the couple were reunited.

On 3rd November 1870, Crittenden met his wife aboard a San Francisco ferry, the *El Capitan*. Unknown to him, Laura had followed. Dressed in black with a veil over her face, she approached the couple as they sat on the upper deck, drew a pistol from her cloak and shot Crittenden through the chest. He died two days later. Laura was taken to a San Francisco jail, where she raved for hours before being sedated.

At her trial in 1871, Laura put forward a plea of 'emotional insanity', claiming that she had blacked out before shooting her lover. She was found guilty of first-degree murder and sentenced to death. Her lawyers appealed, and she was granted a retrial on a legal technicality. By then public opinion was in Laura's favour, and at her second trial in September 1872 she was acquitted. She continued to court publicity, pursuing expensive law suits and lecturing on her trials. She died in San Francisco in 1919, at the age of eighty-two.

In Mark Twain's first novel, *The Gilded Age* (1873), which was co-written with Charles Dudley Warner, Laura Fair is reflected in the character of Laura Van Brunt. Laura is orphaned when her parents are killed in a steamboat explosion (Twain's own brother had died in 1858 in a similar accident), and the five-year-old girl is adopted by the Missouri-bound Hawkins family. During the Civil War, she is seduced by Colonel George Selby, who goes through a mock marriage ceremony and later abandons her. Laura moves to Washington, where her beauty attracts many admirers. However, her experiences with Selby have soured her, and she turns down their advances. When she meets Selby again at a party, she intends to berate him, but he charms her once more and they renew their relationship. Their affair scandalises the capital.

Laura learns that Selby intends to leave for England with his wife and family. She catches up with them in New York and shoots him in a hotel parlour. Found not guilty at her subsequent trial, she is persuaded, like her genuine counterpart, to travel the lecture circuit with the story of her tragic life. Unlike her counterpart, however, her debut is a disaster. She is laughed off stage, and dies the following morning from heart disease. Twain and Warner use Laura's tale as one anecdote in a lengthy, incident-filled novel. The book gives a panoramic view of American life in all its aspects during the nineteenth century, casting a particularly jaundiced eye on the greed and financial chicanery of post-Civil War America.

FACTIONAL WORKS:

Mark Twain and Charles Dudley Warner, *The Gilded Age* (Chicago: F. G. Gilman & Co., 1873).

FURTHER READING:

Joseph Henry Jackson, ed., *San Francisco Murders* (New York: Duell, Sloan & Pearce, 1947).

STARR FAITHFULL DEATH USA 1931

The body of Starr Faithfull, a young New York socialite, was found washed ashore on Long Beach on 8th June 1931. Starr had been a familiar face at the parties and speakeasies that were a feature of the Prohibition period. During the inquest and subsequent investigations, it emerged she had been a nymphomaniac. She kept a diary outlining her amorous conquests and she was once found beaten and naked in a hotel room. She took drugs and drink in equal measure and had received psychiatric treatment. There were rumours that her uncle, Andrew J. Peters, had abused her as a child.

Evidence of recent sexual intercourse and bruising on the upper part of her body led some reporters to assume that she had been thrown from one of the many pleasure steamers that passed Long Beach (she had attended a party on board one such steamer shortly before her death). Others favoured a verdict of suicide. Starr Faithfull's true fate still remains a mystery.

Four years after her death, novelist John O'Hara used the facts of the mystery for his work, *Butterfield 8*. The character of Gloria Wandrous, the alcoholic nymphomaniac living on Park Avenue is a fictional portrait of Starr Faithfull. Gloria has been sexually abused as a young girl, and now shows a tendency towards slow self-destruction through drink and casual relationships. The sole redeeming feature in her life is her platonic love for a penniless artist, Eddie Brunner. O'Hara knew his subject; he was familiar with New York night-life and had met Starr Faithfull cruising speakeasies. After her death he was allowed to read her diaries, which helped to develop his pathetic Gloria. Despite the possibility of murder in the true story, Gloria commits suicide, throwing herself under the wheels of a paddle steamer.

Sandra Scoppetone's 1977 novel, *Some Unknown Person*, provides an imaginative fictional solution to the death of Starr Faithfull, juxtaposing scenes of her life with those of the fictional character, Orlando Antolini. The book follows Faithfull and Antolini from youth, to Starr's death, and finally Antolini's hospitalisation after a stroke in 1977, when he reminisces from his hospital bed. Scoppetone's solution involves an accidental homicide and a (fictional) murderer who receives ironic justice in the final chapter. Although Starr's demise is the author's invention, the facts of her life are followed accurately.

William Palmer's 1995 novel, *The Contract*, is a closer recreation of Starr Faithfull's life, narrated by Starr and her mother. Palmer provides her life story, concentrating specifically on her early teens, when her uncle, Andrew

Peters first noticed her. Her drug addiction is seen as a direct result of his brutal attention. When Starr finally confesses the relationship to her mother, her stepfather, Stanley takes advantage of the situation by blackmailing Peters. But rumours lead Peters to withdraw his support; and when Starr suspects that her younger sister, Tucker has been sent to Uncle Andrew to make amends, she cannot stand any more. Palmer makes no direct conclusion regarding Starr's death, although he speculates on a few theories. The novel is a convincing portrait of a dysfunctional family and of a young life wasted, if not maliciously destroyed.

FACTIONAL WORKS:
John O'Hara, *Butterfield 8* (New York: Harcourt, Brace & Co., 1935).
Sandra Scoppetone, *Some Unknown Person* (New York: Putnam, 1977).
William Palmer, *The Contract* (London: Jonathan Cape, 1995).

FURTHER READING:
Charles Franklin, *Woman in the Case* (London: Robert Hale, 1967).

FILM ADAPTATIONS:
Butterfield 8, d. Daniel Mann. US: MGM, 1960. Screenplay by Charles Schnee, based on the novel by John O'Hara.

HENRY FAUNTLEROY GB 1824

Fauntleroy was the son of one of the founders of the March, Sibbald and Co. Bank in London. On his father's death in 1807, Henry was taken into partnership. In 1815, he began his criminal career by forging a power of attorney over control of stock entrusted to the bank, and promptly sold it. After nine years of such fraudulent activity, he was finally arrested. At his trial in October of 1824, Fauntleroy claimed that his frauds had been perpetrated because of the bank's instability, and that he had used the money to pay off demands on the bank. However, rumours circulated concerning his extravagant life-style which severely prejudiced his case. He was found guilty of forgery, a capital offence at that time, and was hanged in November.

Four years after his death, Fauntleroy appeared in fictional form as Richard Crauford in Edward Bulwer Lytton's novel, *The Disowned*. The Byronic hero, Angerson Mordaunt, has lost his property and is posing as a poor writer named Glendower. He meets his old friend Crauford, who sees Mordaunt as the perfect accomplice for one of his sizeable fraud schemes. To persuade Mordaunt to help him, he reduces him to further poverty by antagonising any prospective publishers. However, when he proposes his scheme, Mordaunt refuses to participate. He eventually regains his wealth, but is accidentally killed, while Crauford is arrested and hanged for fraud.

Bulwer Lytton uses the two characters to compare and contrast the good and evil faces of Victorian life and capitalism. The novel includes many of the features of Fauntleroy's trial and execution.

When Theodore Hook came to write his novel *Maxwell* in 1830, he employed not the facts but the fables concerning the Fauntleroy case—in particular the fraudster's execution. Because Fauntleroy's relatives had sealed his coffin immediately after his death, a rumour circulated that he had escaped the gallows. One particular legend claimed that Fauntleroy had cheated death by swallowing a silver tube that allowed him to breathe when the noose tightened around his throat. Hook used this story as part of a broader aspect in his novel. The merchant, Hanningham, convicted of murder and fraud, manages to turn up in the Azores after his funeral. Hook's solution follows the legend of Fauntleroy's silver tube. In Hanningham's case, moreover, the device prevents a miscarriage of justice, since Hanningham is eventually cleared of the charges against him.

FACTIONAL WORKS:
Edward Bulwer Lytton, *The Disowned* (London: Henry Colburn, 1829).
Theodore Hook, *Maxwell* (London: Henry Colborn & Richard Bentley, 1830).

FURTHER READING:
Horace Bleackley, ed., *The Trial of Henry Fauntleroy* (Edinburgh & London: W. Hodge & Co., 1924).

FIELD AND GRAY GB 1920

The body of a typist named Irene Munro was discovered on 20th August 1920 on a stretch of shingle beach known as the Crumbles near Eastbourne. She had been beaten about the head; a large bloodstained stone lay nearby. Investigations uncovered the fact that two men had been seen accompanying Irene to the beach on the previous day. From descriptions given by witnesses, police brought in two local men for questioning, unemployed labourers Jack Field and Thomas Gray.

They were released on insufficient evidence, but subsequent enquiries uncovered new facts. Although they had no money, on the day in question they could afford drinks in a local pub. Also, shortly after the murder, both men had tried to enlist. At their trial, defence lawyer Edward Marshall Hall tried to prove that Irene Munro was too refined to associate with them; but it transpired that the seventeen-year-old had had casual relationships with older men. Although each ultimately accused the other of the murder, they were both found guilty and hanged in February 1921.

Winifred Duke's novel, *Room For a Ghost* (1937) takes the facts of the Crumbles murder, as it became known, and adds a few twists to present an inverted detective story. The murderer is seen committing the crime early in the book, and interest is maintained by following the sparse clues which eventually lead police to their suspect. Duke blends the factual murder duo into one fictional character, Jack Wood. Most aspects of the case are followed rigorously, however, with the victim—Irene, a typist—vacationing in the fictional South coast of Westbourne in August.

FACTIONAL WORKS:
Winifred Duke, *Room for a Ghost* (London: Jarrolds, [1937]).

FURTHER READING:
Douglas G. Browne and Alan A. Brock, *Sir Bernard Spilsbury: His Life and Cases* (London: George Harrap & Co., 1951).

ISIDOR FINK MURDER USA 1929

A 'locked room mystery' that could be straight out of a John Dickson Carr novel, the Fink case still remains officially unsolved. The victim was a thirty-year-old Polish refugee who had arrived in America eleven years earlier. Fink ran his laundry from one room at 4 East 132nd Street in New York. For fear of burglary, the doors of the room were locked at all times and the windows were fitted with iron bars.

On 9th March 1929, Fink's neighbour was disturbed by the sound of three shots. A policeman called to the scene found the front door locked. When the room was broken into, the body of Isidor Fink was discovered on the floor—he had two bullets in his chest and a third in his left wrist. His money was undisturbed, and as usual, all the windows and doors had been securely locked from the inside.

At first the theory was suicide, but no gun could be found in the room. No hidden compartments, secret passageways or trap-doors were discovered; the room was seemingly impregnable. Several wild theories were proposed by the press, but although the police by then suspected murder, they could come to no firm conclusions and the case was left unsolved.

Surprisingly, the mystery failed to inspire the well-known crime fiction writers of the period. Not even John Dickson Carr thought it worthy of consideration. It was left to crime reporter, playwright and fiction writer Ben Hecht to adapt the Fink case. The story was told from the standpoint of a newspaper reporter like himself in his short story, 'The Fabulous Laundry-man', published in the 1936 collection, *Actor's Blood.*

Crime reporter Dick McCarey is drowning his sorrows in a Harlem speakeasy when a fellow newsman finds him. McCarey tells of the case he has just covered. A laundryman, Meyer, has been found dead in his locked apartment, two bullet wounds in his head and—Hecht's macabre fictional touch—his right hand chopped off and missing. McCarey sees a clue in Meyer's lifestyle, locked away and friendless in a run-down hovel. He is convinced that the police know who murdered Meyer, but are covering up—and his editor has removed him from the story. The reason lies in the fantastic truth of the laundryman's identity. More plausible is Hecht's solution to the locked-room aspect of the mystery.

FACTIONAL WORKS:
Ben Hecht, 'The Fabulous Laundryman', in *Actor's Blood* (New York: Covici Friede, 1936).

FURTHER READING:
Richard and Molly Whittington-Egan, *The Bedside Book of Murder* (Newton Abbot: David & Charles, 1988).

GUIDO FRANCESSCHINI ITALY 1698

Francesschini came from a noble but impoverished Arezzo family. Out of financial desperation, he married twelve-year-old Francesca Pompilia Comparini of Rome in 1693. Her family were not wealthy, but what property they had would pass to Francesca Pompilia on her father's death. In the meantime, Guido's wife brought with her a reasonable dowry. The couple moved to Arezzo along with Francesca's parents (part of the marriage settlement was an agreement that Guido would provide for his in-laws). However the two families found it hard to live together in harmony and quarrels ensued.

Matters came to a head when Francesca's mother, Violante, confessed that her daughter had been adopted at birth and that she had fooled her husband, Pietro, into believing the child was his. As a result, Pietro refused to pay the rest of his 'daughter's' dowry. Guido began to mistreat his wife, who turned to a young priest, Guiseppe Caponsacchi, for affection. In April 1697, Caponsacchi helped Francesca to escape, while her husband and brother-in-law lay in a drugged sleep. The couple were overtaken at Castelnuovo on their way to Rome and arrested.

They were led to Rome where the young priest was tried for abduction and theft. He was banished to Civita Vecchia and Francesca was sent to a nunnery to await trial. The Francesschini family were unhappy with the trial's result; there was still no decision on the dowry, and the recent court cases were eating into their meagre funds. Francesca was released from the convent and gave birth to a boy, but the identity of the father was uncertain. Guido could contain himself no longer. He hired a group of assassins and attacked the Comparini house, killing Violante and Pietro and mortally wounding Francesca. She lived long enough to name Guido as her murderer. He was arrested, tried and sentenced to death. He appealed to Pope Innocent XII, on the novel grounds that as he had avenged himself on an adulterous wife, he should not have been tried for murder. But the Pope refused his appeal, and he was executed along with his accomplices in February 1698.

The poet Robert Browning discovered the facts of the case in a publication known as *The Old Yellow Book*, which contained pamphlets relating to the trials. Browning was so fascinated by the story that he researched it further, and made it the basis for his epic poem, *The Ring and the Book* (1868–9). Although Browning's work falls outside the scope of this study, it did inspire two factional studies. In 1927 Arthur Goodrich and Rose A. Palmer opened a stage version in New York entitled *Caponsacchi*. The story of Caponsacchi and Francesca Pompilia is bracketed between scenes of Caponsacchi's trial; in this adaptation, Guido manages to cast suspicion for the murders on the priest. Caponsacchi is seen as an honourable, saintly man who helps Francesca for altruistic reasons. When Guido captures his wife and the priest after their escape, Caponsacchi moves the crowd to prevent Guido from killing them on the spot. Guido is persuaded to take his case to the Pope. On reaching Rome, he sets his hired assassins on Francesca Pompilia and her parents. Caponsacchi is left to prove his innocence and Guido's guilt.

A more enterprising adaptation is Naomi Royde-Smith's novel, *For Us in the Dark* (1937), which transports the seventeenth-century Italian murder story to twentieth-century England. It is 1917, and Violet Comper's husband has left for war service in Egypt. Violet's grandfather has left a fortune in his will, the interest on which will pass to her, on the condition that she has a child. Thus, Violet persuades a pregnant woman to part with her newborn daughter. They name her Francie and raise her as Major Comper's own child. She will inherit his estate at the age of twenty-one or upon marriage; in the meantime, her father and mother are well provided for.

With Violet's assistance, the vicious and impoverished Lord Trehick marries Francie and whisks her and her parents off to his crumbling estates in Cornwall. However, once he learns that Francie's father has illegally spent much of the inheritance, he forces Mr and Mrs Comper to leave. Francie is befriended by a neighbour, Jan Torrington, who helps her escape from the clutches of her callous husband. A murder follows.

FACTIONAL WORKS:
Arthur Goodrich and Rose A. Palmer, *Caponsacchi* (New York: Appleton & Co., 1927). (P)
Naomi Royde-Smith, *For Us in the Dark* (London: Macmillan, 1937).

FURTHER READING:
Beatrice Corrigan, *Curious Annals. New Documents Relating to Browning's Roman Murder Story* (Toronto: University of Toronto Press, 1956).

LEO FRANK USA 1913

In 1913, Frank was superintendent of the National Pencil Company in Atlanta, Georgia. In April of that year, the body of a fourteen-year-old employee, Mary Phagan, was discovered in the basement of the company's premises. She had been beaten about the head. Notes supposedly written by the girl were found nearby, accusing a black hired hand of the beating. When Newt Lee, a black nightwatchman was arrested, another black employee, James Conley, came forward to confess that he had written the letters, but had been force to do so by Leo Frank. Frank was arrested and charged with the murder.

At his trial, Frank made a statement (by Georgia law he could not testify) refuting Conley's accusations. It was strongly believed that because he was white and his accuser was black, he would go free. But the jury found Frank, a Jew, guilty. However, the Governor of Georgia was concerned about certain inconsistencies in Conley's testimony, and commuted the death sentence to one of life imprisonment.

Almost two years after the trial, a lynch mob kidnapped the Jewish superintendent from prison and hanged him. It was not until 1982 that a former employee at the factory told a reporter that he had seen Conley with Mary Phagan's body, but had been afraid to go to the police. Subsequently, Frank was given a posthumous pardon by the state of Georgia.

Ward Greene's 1936 novel, *Death in the Deep South*, gives a close rendering of the Frank case, but with significant changes. Mary Clay, the fictionalised Mary Phagan, attends business college where her teacher is a Northerner named Robert Hale. When her strangled body is discovered in the college, the black janitor is at first suspected. However, the police and politicians are more than willing to drop the charges when they realise they could implicate the Northerner instead. Rather than anti-Semitism, it is the North-South divide in America that effectively brings about Hale's death. Northern editors place Southern prejudice in the dock; Southerners see the press coverage as a slur on their mode of justice.

Hale's guilt or innocence is never indicated by Greene. Although the novel strongly portrays the racism of both South and North, with the characterisation of the black janitor, the author himself is guilty of creating a racial stereotype worthy of any Hollywood film of that period.

FACTIONAL WORKS:
Ward Greene, *Death in the Deep South* (New York: Stackpole Sons, [1936]).

FURTHER READING:
Leonard Dinnerstein, *The Leo Frank Case* (New York: Columbia University Press, 1968).

FILM ADAPTATIONS:
They Won't Forget, d. Mervyn Le Roy. US: Warner, 1937. Screenplay by Robert Rossen and Abel Kandel, based on the novel *Death in the Deep South* by Ward Greene.

MARY FRITH GB C.1585–1659

Mary was the daughter of a London cobbler. She delighted in smoking a pipe and wearing men's clothes, although it was illegal for a woman to do so then. She earned a reputation as a forger, deceiver, trickster and prostitute (the last of which she strenuously denied). She landed in court a few times for minor offences like drinking, wearing male attire and even for appearing in a play! During the Civil War, she was employed as a spy by the Royalists. She was also a highwayman who made a career of robbing Parliamentarians, including General Fairfax. For this she was committed to Newgate, but was released on payment of £2,000. She died in her seventies at her home in Fleet Street.

Thomas Dekker and Thomas Middleton used the flamboyant Mary as the prototype for the title character of their play, *The Roaring Girle* (1611). Moll Cutpurse (as the Frith character was known, leaving no doubt as to her livelihood) is the heroine of the play, helping two lovers in distress, saving a debtor from the clutches of the Counter prison and participating in the joviality at the Three Pigeons Inn at Brentford (a genuine public house of the period). She retains the masculine traits of her original, wearing men's clothes and winning a duel against a prospective suitor. Mary herself is reputed to have played Moll several times on stage.

The character and her prototype were still sufficiently well-known seven years later for Moll Cutpurse to make a fleeting appearance in Nathaniel Field's *Amends For Ladies*. In Act Two of Field's play, Moll is seen delivering a letter from Lord Love-all to Grace, a shop-keeper's wife. Grace is obviously baffled by Moll's attire—'I know not what to term thee, man or woman'—and there is more comical by-play concerning Moll's bisexual appearance ('sword and target', 'rogue and a whore', 'y'are a good wit and can conceive') before Moll takes her abrupt departure.

Three centuries later, Ellen Galford gives Moll's story a feminist slant in her novel, *Moll Cutpurse, Her True History* (1993). The tale is told by Bridget, an apothecary's daughter, who meets Moll in her father's shop in search of a potion that will turn her into a man. Bridget dissuades her and becomes her lover, sharing in Moll's adventures. Whenever they are apart, Bridget hears of Moll's deeds from other characters. The two make the acquaintance of Middleton and Dekker and see their play in performance. Galford makes no apology for Moll's criminal activities, rather they are justified as her attempt to make her way independently in a world dominated by men, where her only option is to steal rather than sell herself. The period detail is well-observed and the novel reads like a serial, with Moll moving from one adventure to another before settling for relative peace and quiet with Bridget.

FACTIONAL WORKS:
Thomas Middleton and Thomas Dekker, *The Roaring Girle* (London: for Thomas Archer, 1611). (P)
Nathaniel Field, *Amends for Ladies* (London: G. Eld, 1618). (P)
Ellen Galford, *Moll Cutpurse, Her True History* (London: Virago, 1993).

FURTHER READING:
Judith Cook, *At The Sign of the Swan* (London: Harrap, 1986).

WILLIAM GARDINER CASE GB 1902

The murder of Rose Harsent in the Suffolk village of Peasenhall resulted in two trials for William Gardiner. There were rumours that the carpenter and the maid who sang together in the church choir were lovers. Gardiner was hauled before his Methodist church elders on the basis of these tales, but was acquitted of any immoral practice. Then on 1st June 1902, the pregnant body of Rose Harsent was found in the kitchen of her home. It was partially burnt and the throat was cut. Letters from Gardiner were also discovered in the Harsent house. The carpenter was tried in November for Rose's murder. His wife testified on his behalf and the jury could not reach a verdict. A second trial was held in January of the following year, but again the jury failed to agree. The authorities refused to proceed with a third trial, and Gardiner was set free. The case remains unsolved.

The Harsent murder case made its first factional appearance in a 1940 short story by John Dickson Carr. 'Blind Man's Hood' was published in the collection *The Department of Queer Complaints*, under Carr's pseudonym Carter Dickson. The story is one of Carr's locked-room mysteries, where the whodunit element is on a par with the question of how a seemingly impossible murder is achieved. Invited to a Christmas party at a remote house in Kent, Rodney and Muriel Hunter find the place deserted, apart from a mysterious woman, who proceeds to tell them of a murder committed in the house years before.

The details of the murder replicate that of Rose Harsent. A half-burnt corpse is discovered with its throat cut, lamp and candle nearby, broken medicine bottle on the floor. Dickson presents an intriguing, if far-fetched, solution to the crime. What starts as a straightforward detective story ends on a supernatural note that does not, however, affect the feasibility of the solution.

In 1954 Jean Potts used the minimum of details from the case for her detective novel, *Go, Lovely Rose*. The character of Mr Henshaw owes something to that of 'Holy Willie' Gardiner. Henshaw is suspected of the murder of his estranged wife Rose, whose body is discovered at the foot of her cellar steps. However, any other links between the Peasenhall case and this contemporary American detective story are extremely tenuous.

A closer examination of the facts is contained in Brian Cooper's novel, *Genesis 38* (1965). Names of the principal characters are changed, but the events of the murder of Rose Harsent and the trials of Gardiner are followed with reasonable accuracy, and Cooper presents his own solution to the case. He acknowledges his source in an introductory note to the book.

The definitive Gardiner treatment came in 1969 with the publication of R. J. White's *The Women of Peasenhall*. White's novel features his fictional detective, Inspector David Brock, who had already tackled the Moat Farm murder in a previous book (see entry on 'Samuel Dougal'). Brock is sent to Peasenhall to investigate the nature of Gardiner's relationship with Harsent and is present in the village when Rose is brutally murdered. With the help of a free-spirited Victorian lady of the village, he comes up with an unusual but satisfying solution to the mystery. As the title suggests, the answer to the case lies within the close-knit female community of the village.

FACTIONAL WORKS:

Carter Dickson, 'Blind Man's Hood', in *The Department of Queer Complaints* (London: William Heinemann, 1940).

Jean Potts, *Go, Lovely Rose* (New York: C. Scribner's Sons, 1954).

Brian Cooper, *Genesis 38* (London: William Heinemann, 1965). US title: *The Murder of Mary Stears*.

R. J. White, *The Women of Peasanhall* (London: Macmillan, 1969).

FURTHER READING:
Martin Fido and Keith Skinner, *The Peasenhall Murder* (Stroud: Alan Sutton, 1990).

THE GATTON CASE AUSTRALIA 1898

Gatton, a small town west of Brisbane, was the scene of one of Australia's most baffling and brutal murders. On Boxing Night 1898, a dance in the town had been cancelled due to poor attendance, and the few guests were making their way home. Among them were three young members of the Murphy family, a close-knit clan consisting of father and mother, six boys and four girls. Before they rode out of town towards their farm, Michael Murphy and his two sisters, Nora and Ellen, met their brother Patrick, who lived in Gatton. They were never to be seen alive again.

When they failed to return home, their brother-in-law, William McNeil, set out to find them. On the path between the town and the family homestead, he saw wheel-marks running off the track into the bush. He came across the Murphy carriage surrounded by the bodies of the three youngsters. They had been shot and bludgeoned to death, and the two girls had been raped. The police suspected that the three had been ambushed. The puzzling aspect of the case was its extreme violence, as if there might have been a motive of hatred or revenge. Also, the police were amazed by the lack of assistance given by the local community, despite the fact that the family were seemingly respected locally.

A recently released convict named Richard Burgess was questioned—he had a history of violence and sexual assault, and may have been in the vicinity—but police lacked the evidence to prosecute him. The local butcher's assistant, Thomas Day, was also suspected after blood-stained clothing was discovered in his rooms—but again nothing came of it. The Gatton mystery remained unresolved.

Rodney Hall's novel, *Captivity Captive* (1988), presents the Murphy family as a claustrophobic clan carrying the seeds of its own destruction. Ruled by a tyrannical father and a sullen, religious mother, the pressures and conflicts on the children lead to an inevitable explosion. But despite the tragic consequences, the family's strong tribal ties instinctively result in a closing of ranks against the outside world. In this masterly work, Hall provides an intriguing and believable solution to the ninety-year-old mystery.

FACTIONAL WORKS:
Rodney Hall, *Captivity Captive* (New York: Farrar, Straus and Giroux Inc., 1988).

FURTHER READING:
James and Desmond Gibney, *The Gatton Mystery* (London: Angus & Robertson, 1977).

KITTY GENOVESE MURDER USA 1964

Twenty-eight-year-old Catherine (Kitty) Genovese was returning to her apartment in Queens, New York, at three o'clock one morning in 1964 when a stranger approached her, pulled out a knife and stabbed her. Her screams woke neighbours in nearby flats and the stranger moved off, but no one came to her assistance. The stranger returned as Kitty was dragging herself along the street. Once more she was stabbed, once more she screamed, and once more her screams were ignored. Only after the murderer returned a third time did someone call the police.

From the first attack until her eventual death, Kitty had suffered for thirty-five minutes; after the phone call, the police arrived within two minutes. Eventually, Winston Moseley was arrested for Kitty's murder and charged with the murders of two other women. What fascinated the media, however, was the callous indifference of Kitty's neighbours. Thirty-eight people had witnessed the attacks from their windows, but no one had gone to Kitty's aid and only one had phoned the police. The universal plea from the witnesses was 'I didn't want to get involved'.

Science fiction and fantasy author, Harlan Ellison was fascinated by the case, and the actions of the witnesses, who 'could have saved her'. He could find no reason for their actions in real terms and decided the incident 'could only be explained in terms of magic realism, fantasy'. In Ellison's short story, 'The Whimper of Whipped Dogs' (published in book form in 1973), Beth witnesses the murder of a woman in the street below her New York flat. She is horrified to see her neighbours watching the incident with no expression of disgust or pity in their faces. Shortly after, she drifts into a short relationship with Ray, whose violent sexual appetite and crude banter repel her. She finds her own behaviour being moulded by the pressures of city life, until one night when she is attacked by an intruder and learns the truth behind her neighbours' stony expressions, Ray's behaviour, the brutality of modern urban life. Ellison's supposition is that violent deaths in the city are a cathartic sacrifice required of city dwellers to help them survive in such hellish conditions.

A more realistic view of the Genovese case is given in Dorothy Uhnak's novel, *Victims* (1986). Uhnak, a former New York police officer turned novelist, uses the Genovese story as the basis for a police procedural novel concerned with the troubled relationship between the press and the forces of law and order. A young nurse, Anna Grace, is murdered outside her apartment block in Queens. The occupants look on but do not respond.

A young Hispanic policewoman, Miranda Torres, is put on the case. Her problems stem from her role as 'liaison officer' working with Mark Stein, a Pulitzer prize-winning reporter who is fascinated by the murder witnesses' reactions. When Stein lets his desire for a good scoop interfere with Miranda's tracking of the killer, they clash. Stein's actions place both Miranda's career and her life in jeopardy.

REFERENCES
Harlan Ellison, 'The Whimper of Dead Dogs', in Thomas M. Disch, ed., *Bad Moon Rising* (New York: Harper & Row, 1973).
Dorothy Uhnak, *Victims* (New York: Simon & Schuster, 1986).

FURTHER READING:
A. M. Rosenthal, *Thirty-Eight Witnesses* (New York: McGraw-Hill, 1964).

CHESTER GILLETTE USA 1906

In 1906, Chester Gillette was working as a supervisor in his uncle's clothing factory in New York. Gillette fancied himself as a social climber, visiting the local society resorts such as Lake Skaneateles. However, his social aspirations were thwarted when Billie Brown, a factory girl with whom he'd been having an affair, announced she was pregnant. Gillette offered to marry Billie and took her on a holiday to Big Moose Lake. While there the couple went boating. Gillette hit Billie over the head with a tennis racket and threw her in the lake. He overturned the boat, left a straw hat as evidence that a second person had also drowned, and swam ashore.

When Billie's body was discovered, Gillette was arrested and questioned. His contradictory statements, together with the evidence of witnesses who had seen him drying his clothes by the lake and asking about the drowning at a nearby hotel, led to his subsequent trial and conviction for Brown's murder. After a fifteen-month appeal, he went to the electric chair in March 1908.

Eleven years later, Theodore Dreiser began work on a novel concerning a man who murders his girlfriend to leave himself free to marry another girl. He had researched many recent murder trials with similar circumstances, and was six chapters into the novel before he decided that the Gillette case was to form the basis of his plot. The book, *An American Tragedy*, was published in 1925. The tragedy, in Dreiser's opinion, was the pressure on modern Americans to attain social standing and success at the expense of personal attachments and emotions.

Clyde Griffiths, the son of a lay preacher, is brought up with his two sisters and brother as accessories to his father's calling, expected to preach on the streets with him. From an early age, Clyde is influenced by his parents' search for respectability. When his older sister becomes pregnant and is abandoned by her lover, Clyde's reaction is one of concern for the family's good name rather than for his sister's plight.

After he is involved in a car crash in which a girl is killed, Clyde flees his home town of Kansas City for New York. Here he falls in by accident with his wealthy uncle who offers him a job in his clothing factory. At his uncle's home, he meets Sondra Finchley, but makes little impression on her. Instead, he starts an affair with Roberta Alden, whom he supervises at the factory. However, Sondra soon begins to notice Clyde and he is accepted into her circle of socialite friends. In the meantime, Roberta discovers she is pregnant and insists on marriage. Clyde takes her to a doctor for an abortion, but is refused. After reading of a boating accident, he decides to do away with Roberta.

He invites her to Big Bittern Lake and takes her rowing. Once on the lake, he finds he cannot bear to go through with his plan. However, Clyde strikes her accidentally and she falls overboard. He swims to the shore, changes his clothes and goes to meet Sondra. When Roberta's body is eventually found, however, Clyde is arrested. The signs on the body point to premeditated murder, especially when Roberta's despairing letters to Clyde are found. Sondra is removed from any trace of scandal by her parents, while Clyde's uncle grudgingly puts up the money for his defence, although he believes his nephew is guilty. He is sentenced to death for first degree murder. His mother attempts to obtain a reprieve for him, but all efforts fail. Clyde is taken to his execution, still unsure in his own mind whether Roberta's death was accidental or deliberate and cold-blooded murder.

FACTIONAL WORKS:
Theodore Dreiser, *An American Tragedy* (New York: Albert & Charles Boni, Inc., 1925).

FURTHER READING:
Charles Samuels, *Death Was The Bridegroom* (New York: Fawcett, 1955).

FILM ADAPTATIONS:
A Place in the Sun, d. George Stevens. US: Paramount, 1951. Screenplay by Michael Wilson and Harry Brown, based on the novel *An American Tragedy* by Theodore Dreiser.*

SIR EDMUND BERRY GODFREY MURDER GB 1678

Sir Edmund Berry Godfrey, Justice of the Peace for Westminster, was knighted in 1666 for service during the Great Plague of the previous year. In September of 1678, Titus Oates, a disgraced cleric who had inveigled his way into the Jesuit fraternity, swore a deposition in front of Godfrey. Oates claimed that the Jesuits were behind a plot to overthrow the king, Charles II, and return the country to Catholicism. On 12th October, Godfrey disappeared. His body was discovered five days later in a ditch on Primrose Hill in North London.

His chest, torso and neck were badly bruised. His own sword had been thrust through his body, although there was no bloodstains in the vicinity. His valuables were still on the body. At first it was thought that the melancholy magistrate had committed suicide, but coming so soon after Oates's deposition, a rumour began to spread that Godfrey was the first victim of the 'Popish plot' that had been uncovered by Oates. The fervour that gripped the country was played upon by staunch Protestants like the Earl of Shaftesbury and the Duke of Monmouth for their own political gain. It took several years and many executions before the fear subsided and the Popish Plot was forgotten.

However, two questions remain: why and where was Godfrey killed? The theory still holds that the death may have been suicide by hanging, and when the body was discovered it was dumped on Primrose Hill with a sword through it. This suggestion of murder would have been devised to cause commotion or to avoid the embarrassment of a suicide. Some theorists follow the opinion which was popular at the time—that Godfrey *was* murdered by Jesuits, although Oates's deposition and subsequent statements were an exaggeration of the plot's extent.

One prime candidate for the murder is the Earl of Pembroke, a psychopathic character who had earlier that year been found guilty of manslaughter but had pleaded benefit of clergy and escaped a death sentence. Godfrey had been the foreman of the Grand Jury who had originally indicted him. Whatever the theory (all expounded in John Kenyon's 1972 book, *The Popish Plot*), the murder continues to fascinate writers after three centuries.

The first noticeable coverage of the Godfrey murder in fiction was in Emma Robinson's 1844 historical blockbuster, *Whitefriars*. An attempt to emulate Scott's fiction, Robinson's work is a poor copy of the master's style. Her hero Reginald, Lord Mervyn, happens to be present at the Great Fire of London, in the Tower during Colonel Blood's theft of the Crown Jewels, at the Rye House plot, and at the execution of his friend the highwayman Claude Duval. Significantly, he is also in France when Titus Oates leaves the Jesuit order that he has infiltrated and in his presence when he gives his deposition to Godfrey (and Colonel Blood!). Robinson sees Oates as a fanatic who believes his fable of a country-wide plot, while the likes of Monmouth and Shaftesbury use his fanaticism to their own political ends.

Mervyn agrees to take a letter from Blood warning Godfrey of an attempt on his life, but he suspects Blood's intentions and tries to hide Godfrey when Oates and Blood break in. They are taken to Somerset House, where Godfrey is killed trying to escape. The Plot continues apace, only one incident in an abysmal mélange of historical facts and figures.

John Dickson Carr's semi-fictional investigation of the case, *The Murder of Sir Edmund Godfrey*, appeared in 1936. As Carr states 'the intent is only to amuse with a detective story built on facts'. His case is closely argued, however, and well constructed. All of the major historical characters are present and a variety of suspects also make their appearance. After reviewing many scenarios, Carr develops two possible solutions to the murder. Not content with this, however, the author steps out of his fiction at the end to demolish his own suggestions .

The most recent Godfrey treatment is Jeremy Potter's 1992 thriller, *The Primrose Hill Murder*. Sam Atkins, a fictional clerk in the Navy Office under Samuel Pepys, is fascinated by the death of Godfrey. Pepys is suspected of Catholic sympathies and is a mortal enemy of the Earl of Shaftesbury, who is riding high on the wave of anti-Catholic fervour stirred up by Oates. Sam is accused of complicity in the murder and finds himself on trial. He is able to provide an alibi and is released, but when the Earl of Shaftesbury takes control of Parliament, Pepys is disgraced and thrown into the Tower. Now Sam must pursue his investigations into the case to prove his master's innocence. In the penultimate chapter, he finds himself face to face with the murderer in a showdown that almost costs him his life.

All the historical characters, from Charles II to Pembroke and Pepys to Shaftesbury, make their appearance in Potter's detailed novel. But just as important are the minor characters who are, for the most part, fictional—Sam himself, Godfrey's clerk Henry Moor, and Elizabeth the magistrate's servant with whom Sam falls in love. Potter's solution adheres to the one put forward by Stephen Knight (see source quoted below) and is in keeping with the period atmosphere that the author evokes.

FACTIONAL WORKS:

[Emma Robinson], *Whitefriars; or, the Days of King Charles* (London: Henry Colburn, 1844).
John Dickson Carr, *The Murder of Sir Edmund Godfrey* (London: Hamish Hamilton, [1936]).
Jeremy Potter, *The Primrose Hill Murder* (London: Constable & Co., 1992).

FURTHER READING:

Stephen Knight, *The Killing of Justice Godfrey* (London: Granada, 1984).

JIMMY GOVERNOR AUSTRALIA 1900

Jimmy Governor was born in 1875. Partly of aboriginal ancestry, Jimmy suffered the mental torment of never being fully accepted by any race. By the age of twenty-one, he was a tracker for the New South Wales Mounted Police. Two years later, when he married a white girl, Ethel Page, his position became unbearable. Ethel also found herself rejected by her own community.

In 1900 the Governors were living on John Mawbey's farm at Breelong, New South Wales, where Jimmy worked on the fences. The Mawbey family consisted of John and his wife Sarah, their nine children, a nephew of John's, two of Sarah's relatives and a schoolteacher named Helen Kerz. The Governor household included Jimmy, Ethel and their baby son, as well as Jimmy's brother Joe, his uncle and nephew and an aboriginal friend named Jacky Underwood. Understandably, relations between the two families were strained.

The real trouble began when John Mawbey refused to pay more than half-price for some of the fences Jimmy had erected and held back payment until the job was completed. Jimmy's uncle and Jacky Underwood, as full-blooded aborigines, were entitled to rations from the farm store (compensation would then be paid by the local authorities), but this too was refused. When Ethel went to the homestead to plead their cause, Mrs Mawbey and Helen Kerz were abusive to her.

She ran home to tell her husband. Jimmy, accompanied by Jacky Underwood, returned to the farm to ask for an apology. He carried an unloaded rifle and a club; Jackie had a tomahawk. John Mawbey and the eldest male members of the family were away for the night. When Mrs Mawbey started to insult Jimmy, he snapped. Within a few minutes, five of the Mawbey family were dead and one badly wounded. Jimmy, Joe and Jacky fled the homestead. Ethel, abandoned by her husband, was arrested but was later freed.

The three outlaws began a spree of murder, rape and destruction that terrorised New South Wales for ninety-nine days. At one time, up to two thousand men were involved in the manhunt for them. Soon Jacky, who was lame and blind in one eye, was left behind and was subsequently arrested and executed. A reward of £1,000 was offered for either brother, dead or alive. After the brothers split up, Joe was ambushed and shot to death. Jimmy was caught and tried. The jury took ten minutes to pronounce him guilty. He was hanged on 18th January 1901, seventeen days after the Commonwealth of Australia was formed.

In his novel, *The Chant of Jimmie Blacksmith* (1972), Thomas Keneally presents a sympathetic portrait of his fictional Jimmy Governor, without shirking from the violence of his retribution. Blacksmith turns his back on his aboriginal upbringing, hoping to find a place in white Australian society. Rejected and despised by his white employees for his aspirations, an outcast from black society because of his marriage to a white woman, Blacksmith is driven to exact a bloody revenge on the dominant and more oppressive group. Keneally provides a graphic description of Jimmie's revenge and the political manoeuvring that surrounds Jimmie's trial and execution.

FACTIONAL WORKS:
Thomas Keneally, *The Chant of Jimmie Blacksmith* (London: Angus & Robertson, 1972).

FURTHER READING:
Frank Clune, *Jimmy Governor* (London: Horowitz, 1959).

FILM ADAPTATIONS:
The Chant of Jimmie Blacksmith, d. Fred Schepisi. Australia: Film House, 1978. Screenplay by Fred Schepisi, based on the novel by Thomas Keneally.

HAROLD GREENWOOD CASE GB 1920

Harold Greenwood, a lawyer by profession, lived with his wife Mabel and their four children in Llanelly, Wales. Harold was not very popular in the local community, unlike his wife, who was a strongly religious woman. Following a series of illnesses, Mabel died on 16th June 1919. The doctor certified that her death was due to heart disease. Only four months later, Greenwood remarried. Vicious local gossip resulted in an exhumation of Mabel's body and arsenic was discovered. An inquest brought in a verdict of death by poisoning, and Greenwood was suspected.

At his subsequent trial, Harold was fortunate enough to have Sir Edward Marshall Hall as his defence lawyer. When the prosecution accused Greenwood of putting arsenic in the burgundy served at dinner the day before his wife's death, Marshall Hall demonstrated that Greenwood's daughter had drunk the same burgundy with no ill effects. When questioning the doctor who provided the death certificate, he suggested that Mabel could have been poisoned accidentally by her own physician. The jury acquitted Greenwood. He died nine years later, his health destroyed by the ordeal and the continuous rumours.

In 1922, Aldous Huxley's short story, 'The Gioconda Smile', was published in his collection, *Mortal Coils*. Huxley later admitted that he was inspired by a recent case in which 'the ailing wife of a Welsh solicitor was carried off, very suddenly, after eating stewed prunes and drinking a glass of wine'. As Huxley pointed out, the question of who had killed her remained. 'Because nobody was in a position to answer the question, I was forced to invent an entirely new set of circumstances in which the solution to the mystery became possible'.

The 'Gioconda smile' belongs to Janet Spence, who nurses a secret passion for Henry Hutton. Despite his innocent flirtations with Spence, Hutton is having an affair with a young girl called Doris. Meanwhile, his sick wife lingers at home. When Mrs Hutton eventually dies, Henry secretly marries Doris. Janet, proclaiming her love for him, is rejected. Rumours spread regarding Mrs Hutton's untimely death. Her body is exhumed, arsenic is discovered and Hutton is tried and found guilty. After his execution, the real murderer confesses to the shrewd local doctor, who has suspected Hutton's innocence all along.

Huxley adapted his short story for the cinema in 1947 and for the stage the following year. In both adaptations, Huxley added the character of Mrs Hutton's nurse, who is instrumental in spreading the rumours of her murder. Also, the murderer makes a confession to the doctor believing that Hutton's execution has already taken place. However, the doctor has altered the clock in the room, and thus is able to save the innocent husband.

Winifred Duke's novel, *Bastard Verdict* (1931), approaches the story after Greenwood's acquittal. Duke is interested in the effects of suspicion and rumour on her character, Harold Fieldend, the constant changes of address, the ostracism from local society. Duke never states Fieldend's guilt or innocence in the crime.

FACTIONAL WORKS:
Aldous Huxley, 'The Gioconda Smile', in *Mortal Coils* (London: Chatto & Windus, 1922).
Winifred Duke, *Bastard Verdict* (London: Jarrolds, 1931).
Aldous Huxley, *The Gioconda Smile* (London: Chatto & Windus, 1948). (P)

FURTHER READING:
Jonathan Goodman, *The Country House Murders* (London: Allison & Busby, 1987).

FILM ADAPTATIONS:
A Woman's Vengeance, d. Zoltan Korda. US: Universal-International, 1947. Screenplay by Aldous Huxley, based on his story 'The Gioconda Smile'.

CLAUDE GUEUX FRANCE 1832

Claude Gueux was born in 1804. From an early age, he had several brushes with the law. These led to a six-year sentence in Clairvaux prison—extended by six months when he assaulted a guard. Released in 1829, he was back inside Clairvaux the following year for theft. His father followed him into prison, and Gueux's violent temperament improved temporarily while he looked after the old man, who died while still in prison in 1831. According to Gueux's own testimony at his subsequent trial, he was the victim of sustained bullying by the head warder, Delacelle. He once made a grab for the warder's sword, but was disarmed.

Gueux shared a cell with another prisoner, Albin Legrand. They were suspected of having a homosexual liaison; in fact Legrand was later sentenced to hard labour for killing a prisoner during a homosexual quarrel. Legrand shared his food with Gueux, and whether because of this or because of their suspected relationship, Delacelle had Legrand removed from Gueux's cell. One day, Gueux managed to obtain an axe, and when Delacelle came on his rounds, he hit the warder several times with the instrument, then tried to kill himself with a pair of scissors.

Delacelle never regained consciousness and died the next day. Gueux, however, was revived and charged with the warder's murder. He was tried in March 1832, and proved an able jurist, confounding prosecution witnesses and making an eloquent speech in his own defence. Nonetheless, he was found guilty and executed in Troyes market-place the same month.

Victor Hugo read the facts of the case in the *Gazette des Tribunaux* (the same magazine that Stendhal had used as a source for his novel based on the Antoine Berthet case). He decided that Gueux's story might, with a little adaptation, serve as an argument against capital punishment, a personal *bête noire*. His short story, 'Claude Gueux', was published in July 1834. It was translated into English in 1865 under the title, 'Capital Punishment: Claude Gueux'. The translator was under the impression that the tale was 'a true narrative, every incident in which occurred exactly as the author tells it'. Comparison of the tale with the facts reveals this to be far from the truth.

Hugo's Claude is not a habitual criminal. His sole term of imprisonment is a result of stealing for his starving family, for which he is sentenced to five years in jail. The warder is seen as a brutal, malicious man, who informs Claude that his wife has turned prostitute. He detests Claude's benevolence towards the other prisoners and their respect for him, moving Albin from Claude's cell because he knows that Albin shares his food with his cell-mate. The relationship between Claude and Albin is portrayed as that of father and son, although in fact, Gueux was only two years older than Legrand. Because Claude relies on Albin for extra food, he is convinced that the warder is trying to starve him. Thus, the murder can be viewed as self-defence.

Claude informs the other prisoners of his murderous intentions, giving his reasons and asking for any objections. He agrees to one prisoner's suggestion that he give the warder a last chance to return Albin to his cell. Claude's legal know-how gives the proposed murder the air of a justified execution. Capital punishment is no more than murder, Hugo is saying. Claude pleads piteously with the warder for Albin's return, but to no avail. The murder is committed, and Hugo depicts it in all its brutality, as well as the subsequent suicide attempt. Claude's eloquence at his trial is accurately portrayed, as is his resolute bearing at his execution. Hugo concludes his tale with a plea for compassion and education to prevent the need for such crimes and such punishments.

FACTIONAL WORKS AND FURTHER READING:
Victor Hugo, 'Claude Gueux', in *The Last Day of a Condemned Man and Other Prison Writings* (Oxford: Oxford University Press, 1992). First published in French as 'Claude Gueux', 1834. The introduction, by translator Geoff Woollen, gives the facts of the genuine case.

JAMES HACKMAN GB 1779

Martha Reay had been apprenticed to a mantua-maker when she attracted the attention of the Earl of Sandwich. He furnished her with an education, she became his mistress and they lived together for nineteen years. During this period, James Hackman, an ensign in the 68th Regiment of Foot and a regular guest of the Earl, developed an overwhelming infatuation for Reay. Hackman left the army and became a clergyman, subsequently accepting the post of rector of Wiverton in Norfolk. However, he still harboured feelings for Reay.

The Earl and his mistress were frequent visitors to the theatre. On 7th April 1779, they attended a performance of the play *Love in a Village* at Covent Garden Theatre. Hackman, who was lodging in London at the time, followed them there. During the performance, he ran home to collect his pistols, and waited for the play to finish. As Reay was being escorted to her coach, Hackman stepped out of the crowd and shot her, turning the second pistol on himself. Reay was killed outright, but the second pistol misfired. Hackman proceeded to beat himself about the head with the butt of his weapon until he was overpowered.

He was taken before Sir John Fielding, the blind magistrate (and the brother of novelist Henry Fielding), and was committed to Newgate. James Boswell attended his trial, and had a lively discussion with Dr Johnson about the murder three days before Hackman's execution.

Constance Wright's novel, *The Chaste Mistress* (1930), provides much fictional background to the Earl of Sandwich's courtship and subsequent life with Martha. He spies her in a haberdasher's shop, and attracted by her melodious voice, proceeds to make her his mistress. In Wright's version. Hackman's love for Martha is reciprocated. However, when she appeals to the Earl to free her so she can marry the young captain, Sandwich threatens to remove her children if she does so. The author introduces Martha's companion, Mme. Galli, and Omai, the Earl's South Sea island retainer, who both act as catalysts for the tragedy by poisoning Hackman's mind.

FACTIONAL WORKS:
Constance Wright, *The Chaste Mistress* (London: John Lane, 1930).

FURTHER READING:
G. T. Crook, ed., *The Complete Newgate Calendar* (London: Navarre Society, 1926).

HALL-MILLS CASE USA 1926

In September 1922, the bodies of Reverend Edward Wheeler Hall and his mistress, choir member Eleanor Mills, were discovered by a crab-apple tree in New Brunswick, New Jersey. The Reverend had been shot through the head and Mrs Mills had been shot and her throat had been cut. Scattered around the corpses were fragments of love letters written by Mrs Mills to the Reverend. A grand jury was convened but no arrests were made. Four years later, after an intensive press campaign to re-open the case, Mrs Frances Hall and her two brothers William and Henry Stevens were charged with the double murder.

A former maid of the Halls said that the murdered couple had intended to elope together. Also, a local pig-farmer, Jane Gibson (referred to as the 'Pig Woman' by the press), gave evidence that she had seen Mrs Hall and her brother Henry with a group of people around the tree, and had subsequently heard shots. The three defendants denied the charges, even eccentric Willie Stevens made a presentable appearance in the witness box, and the jury returned a verdict of not guilty after five hours. The case remains unsolved.

Three novelists put the Hall-Mills murders to good use in very different works of fiction. Anthony Abbott put his series detective, Commissioner Thatcher Colt, on the case in the 1931 thriller, *About the Murder of the Clergyman's Mistress* (called *The Crime of the Century* in the UK). The facts were brought a decade forward, the location changed to New York, and the corpses of the minister and choir singer are discovered in a rowing boat on the East River. The narrator admits a similarity to the Hall-Mills case, and another factual murder of 1912, in which a Cape Cod minister named Clarence Richeson poisoned his pregnant lover. Unlike the real case, Abbott gives his version a satisfying conclusion.

J. J. Connington's *The Twenty-One Clues* (1941) also places the case within the framework of a detective story. In this version, the story is transferred to England, where the bodies of Rev. John Barratt and his mistress Esther Callis are discovered by a railway embankment, surrounded by love letters. The deaths have all the hallmarks of a suicide pact, as they have both been shot by a gun in the reverend's hand. The local chief constable, Sir Clinton Driffield, is called in to investigate. After another mysterious death in Barratt's congregation, ballistic clues lead to the case's solution.

Stephen Longstreet also presents a satisfactory conclusion to the tale in his 1959 novel, *The Crime*. Here, the original is restricted to a courtroom setting where prosecutor Abe Pedlock pursues the facts of a thinly-disguised Hall-Mills murder. Longstreet, who had been assigned to the factual case as a cub reporter, retains three of the principal characters only, and changes the setting to another American state. Nevertheless, his is the most faithful of the three factional versions.

FACTIONAL WORKS:

Anthony Abbott, *About the Murder of the Clergyman's Mistress* (New York: Covici Friede, [1931]). UK title: *The Crime of the Century*.

J. J. Connington, *The Twenty-One Clues* (London: Hodder & Stoughton, 1941).

Stephen Longstreet, *The Crime* (New York: Simon & Schuster, 1959).

FURTHER READING:

William M. Kunstler, *The Minister and the Choir Singer* (London: Victor Gollancz, 1964).

CARLYLE HARRIS USA 1892

Carlyle Harris, a medical student in New York, had secretly married fellow-student Helen Potter in 1890. Her uncle evidently had performed an abortion on Helen, and would later testify that Harris had done the same. Harris was a philanderer and was soon looking for a way out of his relationship with his secret wife. He frequently prescribed drugs for Helen when she was ill, and in February 1891, he gave her a box of six capsules supposedly containing quinine to aid her insomnia. She died after taking one of the capsules, and suspicion immediately fell on Harris.

He was arrested and tried in January 1892. The prosecution maintained that Harris had substituted morphine for quinine in the capsules, knowing full well that Helen had a weak heart and the dose would kill her. The prosecution also demonstrated that morphine had been found in her body, and they drew attention to the pin-point pupils that are a symptom of morphine poisoning. However, the defence put up a spirited fight and the outcome of the trial was in doubt. But Harris was found guilty, and was executed in February of that year. It was the first trial for morphine poisoning in New York, and inspired one other poisoner, Robert Buckanan, to try his luck with that method.

Algernon Blackwood had covered the Harris trial for the *New York Times*; he was in no doubt of Harris's guilt. In his short story, 'Max Hensig', published in the 1907 book *The Listener and Other Stories*, Harris/Hensig is seen as a vain and spiteful human being. Later, in his autobiography, Blackwood said of the Harris case, 'in a story, years later (Max Hensig), the facts were taken direct from life. It needed more than 15 years to dim their memory'. The major difference in Blackwood's tale is that Hensig is acquitted of the poisoning, and decides to use his skills on the reporter, Williams, who has castigated him in print throughout the trial. Williams, aware of Hensig's determination to kill him, succeeds in turning the tables on Hensig, and the executioner becomes the executed.

FACTIONAL WORKS:
Algernon Blackwood, 'Max Hensig', in *The Listener and Other Stories* (London: Nash, 1907).

FURTHER READING:
Charles Boswell and Lewis Thompson, *The Carlyle Harris Case* (New York: Collier, 1961).

WILL HARRIS USA 1906

Will Harris was a black ex-soldier with a record of burglary and arson. In November 1906, he came to Asheville, Carolina from nearby Charlotte. On the day of his arrival, a black porter, Tobey Johnson, found Harris in bed with his wife. After an argument, Harris shot at Johnson with his army rifle and missed. Johnson ran to the nearby police station, returning with a constable and police captain. Harris shot dead Constable Charles Blackstock as he entered the building, and wounded the captain. He then ran down the main street of the town, shooting people as he went. One man was wounded in the groin, another was killed as a bullet passed through the telegraph pole behind which we was hiding. After shooting at one person, Harris yelled, 'Nobody cares who I am. I am from Hell, and I don't care who sends me back'.

In all, Harris killed five people before he escaped to the local woods. He held out there for two more days against a posse of local police and townspeople. Finally, he was shot when his ammunition ran out. The body was returned to Asheville, where it was displayed in a local undertaker's.

Thomas Wolfe, the Asheville-born novelist, published his short story 'The Child By Tiger', in the *Saturday Post* in 1937. The story is told from the point of view of a few local boys who meet Dick Prosser, the fictional Harris. Prosser is a meticulous and religious person, who gains the admiration and respect of the boys. However, a hint of suppressed violence surfaces when the boys come across Prosser's army rifle, and he rounds on them angrily. The title of the story alludes to the duality of man and refers to Blake's poem, quoted at the end. Prosser is like Blake's tiger—proud and serene, but with a capacity for extreme passion and rage.

The details of the murders themselves follow the facts closely, although there are seven deaths in total, including the porter himself, who is given the real murderer's name. The major change in Wolfe's version is that the mob pursuing the murderer is violent and vengeful, breaking into a store to get arms for the manhunt. According to the news reports of the time, the real posse were calm and methodical in their pursuit of the murderer. In the story, Prosser is the calm one, quietly sitting down to take off his shoes before turning to face the mob when he meets his end. The story concludes with the boys remembering Prosser's Bible in his room—a final image emphasising the overall goodness of his nature.

Wolfe used the story again, as a chapter in his posthumously-published novel, *The Web and The Rock* (1939), which relates the story of George Webber and his progress from the Southern States through college to New York and a fortune of sorts. This semi-autobiographical work includes several incidents from Wolfe's life in Asheville, and from the town's history. Webber is now one of the children who befriend Prosser, but otherwise the chapter uses the events of the short story with little change.

FACTIONAL WORKS:

Thomas Wolfe, *The Web and the Rock* (New York: Harper & Bros., 1939).

Thomas Wolfe, 'The Child By Tiger', in *Complete Short Stories of Thomas Wolfe* (New York: C. Scribner's Sons, 1987).

FURTHER READING:

Floyd C. Watkins, *Thomas Wolfe's Characters* (Norman, Oklahoma: Oklahoma University Press, 1957).

WILLIAM HARRISON CASE GB 1660

On 16th August 1660, in the village of Chipping Campden, Gloucestershire, the Viscountess Campden's steward William Harrison disappeared while walking to a nearby village. John Perry, a servant, was sent to search for him. He did not return until the following day, looking unkempt and pale, saying he could find no trace of the steward. A search of the vicinity led to the discovery of Harrison's hat and comb, bloodstained and marked. Perry was questioned and told several conflicting stories. He named several murderers, who were all able to produce satisfactory alibis. Eventually, he confessed to the murder and named his mother Joan and elder brother Richard as his accomplices. He claimed the corpse was thrown into a local millpond; the pond was searched, without result.

Despite this, the three Perrys were charged with the murder and stood trial. The judge refused to admit the confession they all subsequently had made and threw out the case. But the Perrys were arrested again and stood trial before a second judge, who accepted the confessions, despite their subsequent retractions by the family. John, Joan and Richard Perry were found guilty of murder and executed.

Two years later, William Harrison reappeared in the village. He told an incredible story of being ambushed by two highwaymen, who kidnapped him and forced him aboard a ship at Deal. The ship sailed to Smyrna, where Harrison was sold as a slave. After eighteen months, his master died and Harrison managed to board a ship to England. Like the Elizabeth Canning case, Harrison's story was met with both derision and acceptance. The only certainty from the whole affair was that three innocent people had been unjustly hanged.

John Masefield's first short play on the Harrison affair, *The Campden Wonder*, was produced on the London stage in 1907 and published two years later. In Masefield's view, John Perry was a weak-willed drunk, whose mother berated him for not living up to his virtuous, hard-working brother. As a cruel vengeance on them, Perry implicates them in the supposed murder of Harrison. Harrison's widow scoffs at the idea, convinced that her ne'er-do-well husband will soon turn up. But she and the Perrys do not count on the zeal of the local parson to prosecute, and the drama follows its historical course, as the Perry family are sent to their deaths just before Harrison's untimely return.

Not content with ending the story there, Masefield returned to the case in a sequel, *Mrs Harrison*, published with *The Campden Wonder* in 1909. The short play shows Mrs Harrison confronting her husband with the deaths of the Perrys and asking for his explanation. Harrison admits that he was paid to keep in hiding and let the three accused hang. Mrs Harrison, overcome with horror at his actions, poisons herself, while her husband prays with the parson. In these two plays and many others, Masefield made popular the stage Gloucestershire dialect that was to be ridiculed so mercilessly in later years.

FACTIONAL WORKS:
John Masefield, 'The Campden Wonder' and 'Mrs Harrison', in *The Tragedy of Nan and Other Plays* (London: Grant Richards, 1909). (**P**)

FURTHER READING:
George Clark, ed., *The Campden Wonder* (London: Oxford University Press, 1959).

JOHN HATFIELD GB 1803

Hatfield (or Hadfield, as it is sometimes spelt) made a disreputable name for himself early in life. He married the illegitimate daughter of Lord Robert Manners, spent her £1,500 dowry in London, and left her and her three daughters—all before the age of twenty-three. He was thrown into the King's Bench prison for debt in 1782, but managed to free himself by appealing to the good nature of his father-in-law's kinsman, The Duke of Rutland. By this time, he had acquired the name of 'lying Hatfield' for his tales of high family connections and fictional wealth.

Over the next twenty years, Hatfield lived off his wits, using his persuasive tongue and sharp mind to worm his way into lucrative positions, and making off with what funds he could obtain. He was continually thrown into prison for debt, had been declared bankrupt, and had again married and again deserted his wife, all for financial gain. In 1802, he turned up in

Keswick in Cumberland, under the name of Lieutenant-Colonel Alexander Hope. Here, he courted and married Mary Robinson, a local belle who had been described in a contemporary travel book as 'the Beauty of Buttermere' and had been admired by the likes of Coleridge and De Quincey.

Unfortunately for Hatfield, the local magistrate knew the real Hope, and shortly after the wedding, Hatfield was once more on the run from the law. He was arrested near Swansea and tried in December 1802 for illegally franking letters—a privilege permitted MPs such as Hope, but an action that carried the death penalty for others. The jury took ten minutes to find Hatfield guilty and he was hanged a year later in Carlisle.

Melvyn Bragg, a native of the Lake District area where Hatfield attempted his last scam, fictionalised his final years in his 1987 passionate and romantic novel, *The Maid of Buttermere*. His 'Hope' (we never learn his true name until the end of the book) is a man torn between a life of crime and deception, and a desire for a settled existence. His love for Mary is seen as the one sincere act of his later life. For her part, Mary is attracted to him but wary of his intentions. She is already being courted by Richard Harrison, the man who she married in reality after Hatfield's death.

She eventually marries 'Hope' and they travel to Scotland on honeymoon; the bridegroom intending to show his bride the family estates. His deception brings on a breakdown, and after Hatfield's attempt at penance by spending a night out in a storm, he catches fever. The couple return to Buttermere, where Hatfield will eventually be exposed as a fraud.

Bragg's novel is rich with period detail, with genuine characters involved in the case. The author's love of his native Lakelands is evident throughout his novels, but nowhere more so than in this historical treatment. The writings and personal histories of the Romantic Poets are mentioned in passing, to provide a sense of the history unfolding alongside the principal plot.

The main fictional element of the work is the introduction of an accomplice for Hatfield, in the shape of the Machiavellian, enigmatic Newton. It is Newton who finally brings about Hatfield's doom, out of jealousy of his love for Mary (there are indications of a homosexual relationship between Newton and Hatfield prior to the novel's action), and Newton who offers to obtain Hatfield's freedom, on condition that they return to their fraudulent escapades. But Hatfield, who has finally confessed all to Mary and has acquired a new-found sense of honour in his life, accepts his fate.

Such a brief summary of the plot cannot suggest the breadth and imagination of this hugely enjoyable novel. For its attempt at psychological insight into a criminal mind, it stands in the forefront of crime faction. As the title suggests, Mary Robinson herself is as much the principal character as Hatfield, and Bragg does not overlook the irony of her position. A 'tourist attraction' from the age of fourteen, when Captain Budworth praised her beauty in his travel book, *A Fortnight's Ramble in the Lakes*, after Hatfield's arrest she is once more thrown grudgingly into the public eye. The story is as much concerned with Hatfield's betrayal of Mary as with his crimes against society.

FACTIONAL WORKS:
Melvyn Bragg, *The Maid of Buttermere* (London: Hodder & Stoughton, 1987).

FURTHER READING:
Jonathan Green, *The Directory of Infamy* (London: Mills & Boon, 1980).

BRUNO HAUPTMANN USA 1935

Charles Lindbergh had established fame and fortune with his astonishing non-stop flight from New York to Paris in 1927. In 1930, his wife gave birth to a son who was named after his famous father. On 1st March 1932, the baby was taken from the nursery of the Lindbergh's luxury mansion in New Jersey. A makeshift ladder was found on the grounds, and on the windowsill was a note written in broken English demanding a ransom of $50,000. Although the note instructed that the press and police not be notified, word had already spread, and the kidnapping became a major media event. Inevitably, crank calls and hoaxers plagued the authorities.

Dr John Condon of New York placed a letter in a local paper to volunteer his services as go-between for the kidnapper. He received a reply from a man called 'John' who promised to send the baby's night clothes to prove his veracity. A ransom drop was organised at which John collected the money (some of it in marked notes) and indicated where the baby could be found. Lindbergh rushed to the specified location, but could find no trace of his son. Then in May 1932, the body of Charles A. Lindbergh Jnr. was discovered in a makeshift grave not far from the Lindbergh home.

In September 1934, a garage attendant was given one of the marked notes by a customer, and took a note of his licence plate number. Bruno Richard Hauptmann was traced as the driver. Similar wood to that used in the makeshift ladder was discovered in the attic of his home, and over $11,000 was found hidden in his garage.

At his trial for murder in January 1935, handwriting experts linked Hauptmann's writing with that in the ransom note, and John Condon identified him as the mysterious 'John'. Hauptmann was found guilty and was executed on 3rd April 1936. There are still those who believe Hauptmann was an innocent victim of a police frame-up, which involved faked evidence and perjured witnesses.

Max Allan Collins tackled the crime in his fictional reconstruction, *Stolen Away* (1991). Nate Heller, a Chicago policeman who has already solved one kidnap attempt, is called in on the Lindbergh kidnapping by the distraught father. He finds himself visiting Al Capone in prison after the gangster indicates that he can get the child released in exchange for his own freedom. Heller follows up several other dead end leads before resigning from the enquiry because of Lindbergh's unorthodox methods. Four years later, as Bruno Hauptmann awaits the death penalty, Heller is called back on the case by Governor Hoffman of New York, who is convinced of Hauptmann's innocence. Heller is given three weeks to find some concrete evidence to confirm or quash Hauptmann's sentence.

The novel, which suggests gangland involvement in the kidnapping and the possible survival of the Lindbergh baby, combines the character of Heller and several other fictional characters with those directly involved in the case, and others on the side-lines, like detective Elliott Ness and gangsters Frank Nitti and Al Capone. The book is a heavily-researched work in which even the fictional players have some basis in fact; at 500 pages, it is definitely a weighty treatment.

FACTIONAL WORKS:
Max Allan Collins, *Stolen Away* (New York: Bantam, 1991).

FURTHER READING:
Ludovic Kennedy, *The Airman and the Carpenter* (London: Collins, 1985).

CATHERINE HAYES GB 1725

On 2nd March 1725, a human head was found on the banks of the Thames near Lambeth Bridge. The authorities set the head on a stake in the hope that it would be identified. Several people recognised it as the head of John Hayes, a local merchant and money lender. His wife, Catherine, initially refused to identify it, claiming that her husband had fled to Portugal following a duel in which he had killed a man. She was taken into custody, together with two lodgers, Thomas Billings and Thomas Wood.

Under interrogation, Wood broke down and confessed. Apparently, Catherine had bribed him to assist her in her husband's murder. John Hayes was plied with drink and brained with a hatchet. His head was severed to delay the corpse's identification; the body itself was disposed of in Marylebone. At their trial, all three were sentenced to death. Wood died in prison; Billings was hanged. Catherine, convicted of petty treason, as the murder of a husband was then classified, was sentenced to be throttled and burned. The executioner, however, botched the job and she was burned alive.

When William Makepeace Thackeray turned his attention to the Hayes case in 1839, it was in the wake of the popular 'Newgate fiction' of that period. Thackeray was disgusted by what he and many others considered to be a romantic portrayal of criminals. He intended *Catherine*, published first in *Fraser's Magazine* between May 1839 and February 1840, and in one volume in 1885, to satirise the genre. Although his plan was to make his villainess suitably loathsome and shocking, in the course of the work's initial ten-month serialisation, his sympathies shifted and he softened the narrative considerably.

Thackeray fictionalised much of Catherine's story: she falls in love with Count von Galgenstein and becomes his mistress, Tom Billings is actually their illegitimate son. When he eventually breaks from her, Catherine attempts to poison Galgenstein, but when he reappears in London, she murders Hayes to be free for him. When Galgenstein sees Hayes's head on the stake, he loses his reason, and Catherine is arrested and executed. The short novel was Thackeray's first attempt at sustained fiction, and paved the way for his more famous novels, including *Barry Lyndon* (see entry on 'Andrew Robinson Bowes').

FACTIONAL WORKS:
William Makepeace Thackeray, 'Catherine', in *Works*, vol. 20 (London: Smith, Elder & Co., 1885).

FURTHER READING:
G. T. Crook, ed., *The Complete Newgate Calendar* (London: Navarre Society, 1926).

NEVILLE HEATH GB 1946

In June 1946, the mutilated body of Margery Gardner was discovered in a bedroom of the Pembridge Court Hotel in Notting Hill, London. Police began searching for a 'Colonel' Heath who had booked the room the previous day. The parents of Yvonne Symonds were distressed to discover that the description of the wanted man matched that of their daughter's fiancée, Neville Heath. They instructed her to phone him and persuade him to go to the police. She did so, and fortunately for her, never saw him again. Instead of talking to the police as he had promised, Heath wrote a letter protesting his innocence which he sent to Scotland Yard. He then fled to Bournemouth, where he signed into a hotel under the name of Group Captain Rupert Brooke.

On 3rd July he met a girl named Doreen Marshall, who was staying at another hotel. They went for a walk together; Doreen was never seen alive again. Heath returned to his hotel with noticeable scratch marks on his neck. The battered body of Doreen Marshall was discovered three days later, just as Heath was being questioned by police about the murder of Margery Gardner. A cloakroom ticket in his jacket led detectives to a suitcase containing blood-stained clothes and a riding-switch which was similarly stained. He was arrested.

Heath's trial for the first murder was held at the Old Bailey in September 1946. His defence counsel tried to prove that he was 'morally insane'. He had a history of lying, bullying, theft and fraud; he had also been court-martialled three times. The murders and his actions in between suggested a psychopathic personality. The jury ruled out moral insanity and found him guilty of first-degree murder. Heath was hanged in October, having made no appeal against his sentence.

Playwright and novelist Patrick Hamilton had a fascination with real crimes and criminals (see entry for 'Leopold and Loeb'). The Heath case not only served this fascination but also paralleled Hamilton's own interest in sadomasochistic sex. Three years after Heath was executed, Hamilton created the murderer's fictional alter-ego, Ernest Ralph Gorse. Like Heath, Gorse is a psychopathic sadist whose insouciant charm and good looks fascinate his women victims. Unlike Heath, Gorse never actually commits murder. However, Hamilton did suggest that, had the series of books featuring Gorse progressed past the existing trilogy (*The West Pier, Mr Stimpson and Mr Gorse*, and *Unknown Assailant*), the character would have got his comeuppance. In the second novel, we are told '[Gorse] was to die painlessly and quickly. And he was not to do this in bed'.

The West Pier introduces us to Gorse as a cruel, bullying schoolboy who develops into a suave young man. He is intent on fleecing a working-girl, Esther Downes, of her small savings of £65. The description of pre-war Brighton is memorable; Hamilton had grown up (and wrote the novel itself) in the seaside town. Graham Greene, who had himself put Brighton on the literary map in a memorable crime novel, described Hamilton's book as 'the best novel written about [the town]'. *The West Pier* received unanimous praise on its publication in 1951.

In the 1953 sequel, *Mr Stimpson and Mr Gorse*, Gorse has moved on to Reading, where he is wheedling his way into the affections of a middle-aged, middle-class widow, Mrs Plumleigh-Bruce. Posing as a war veteran, Gorse sets his sights on the widow's money. He is rivalled by estate agent Donald Stimpson, but succeeds in parting Mrs Plumleigh-Bruce from her wealth in exchange for a marriage engagement. He flees the scene, leaving the widow suitably chastened, while Mr Stimpson rejects the foolish woman and marries her maid, Mary.

The final novel in the series, published in 1955, is a marked decline from its predecessors. Gorse's scam—to persuade barmaid Ivy Barton and her father to part with £200 supposedly to back a play—seems decidedly contrived. Gorse's sadistic sexual inclinations are described in more detail than in the previous books, but the violence below the surface that made the previous novels so chilling is dissipated.

Allan Prior adapted Hamilton's second Gorse novel for British television, under the title, *The Charmer*. The series proved so successful that Prior continued the story in a second series (which, in effect, bypasses Hamilton's third novel), to bring Gorse's career to a satisfying conclusion—at least for the audience. Prior's 1987 novel, *The Charmer*, adapts the plot of *Mr Stimpson and Mr Gorse* into a few chapters and adds a few more in which Donald Stimpson acts as Gorse's nemesis. Stimpson pursues Gorse to Brighton, where he is insinuating himself into the affections of Alison Warren, a war widow, while indulging his darker, sadistic sexual pleasures with Clarice Mannors, a young debutante. Two women meet their deaths before Ralph Gorse is finally brought to justice; the novel ends as his hands are pinioned behind his back prior to his execution.

In his thriller, *Murder at Midnight* (1962), Hugh Desmond presents a close fictional account of the Heath case. The story is told mainly from the viewpoint of Audrey Damar, who craves excitement away from her dominating parents. She falls for Captain William Streatham, a shallow but fascinating figure. When he disappears, Audrey learns that he is wanted in connection with a brutal murder. Streatham moves to Eastbourne under an assumed name and another murder takes place. But Audrey is still in danger from him, and only Detective Inspector Ronald Carson's efforts can save the girl, with whom he now has fallen in love. With the exception of the final section of the novel—where the murderer returns for a prospective third victim—the facts of the original are followed closely, with Audrey echoing Yvonne Symonds.

Where Desmond's novel is a straightforward thriller, Todd Mallanson's *Ladykiller* (1980) investigates the psychopathic personality of his Heath-like killer, Jimmy Armstrong. In the years following the Second World War, Armstrong glides through the upper social strata of Bournmouth life, his insouciant charm at odds with the horrific crimes he perpetrates. Mallanson provides an intriguing picture of a depressed period, and the desperate people looking for excitement—sometimes sexual and dangerous—to escape the monotony of their bored existences.

FACTIONAL WORKS:
Patrick Hamilton, *West Pier* (London: Constable & Co., 1951).
Patrick Hamilton, *Mr Stimpson and Mr Gorse* (London: Constable & Co., 1953).
Patrick Hamilton, *Unknown Assailant* (London: Constable & Co., 1955).
Hugh Desmond, *Murder at Midnight* (London: Wright & Brown, 1962).
Todd Mallanson, *Ladykiller* (London: Weidenfeld & Nicolson, 1980).
Allan Prior, *The Charmer* (London: Grafton, 1987).

FURTHER READING:
Paul Hill, *Portrait of a Sadist* (London: Spearman, 1960).

MARIE HERMANN GB 1894

Marie Hermann, an Austrian woman of forty-three, had at one time been a governess, but had fallen on hard times. She turned to prostitution to support her three children, one of whom was blind. She lodged in a house in Grafton Street, off Tottenham Court Road, in London. One evening in March 1894, her neighbours heard the sound of voices and a scuffle coming from her room. At one point during the evening, Marie was seen leaving the house and returning with a bottle of brandy. The next morning, Marie moved out of her lodgings, taking a large trunk with her. When blood was found in a communal sink, the police were called and apprehended Marie at her new address. The trunk was opened to reveal the body of an elderly man, who had been beaten to death.

Marie Hermann was charged with the murder of the man, who was identified as retired cab owner Henry Stephen. At her trial, she was defended by the young Edward Marshall Hall. It was his first major murder case, and he demonstrated the intuition and appeal to public sympathy that were to be his hallmarks. Marshall Hall established that Stephen had been a man of great strength and violent temper. From bruises found on his client's throat at the time of the murder, and from the position of the dead man's wounds, he put forward a strong case of self-defence. Witnesses for the prosecution had testified they had overheard Marie raising her voice in anger; Marshall Hall suggested that they were in fact her cries of despair.

He gave an emotional summing-up, emphasising Marie's devotion to her children and her reduced circumstances. The speech was greeted with applause from the public gallery. The judge also seemed swayed by the defence plea; he indicated that a verdict of manslaughter would be favourably accepted. This the jury delivered, with a recommendation for mercy. Marie Hermann was sentenced to six years' imprisonment.

In 1989, to coincide with his BBC television series, *Shadow of the Noose*, relating the career of Edward Marshall Hall, Richard Cooper published a novel of the same title. Unlike the TV series, which covered many of Marshall Hall's famous trials, the book concentrated on his tragic first marriage and his early career—including the Hermann trial. His wife had left him after a stormy, unconsummated relationship, had sunk into a life of squalor, and had died following a back-street abortion. Cooper suggests in the novel that Marshall Hall's impassioned commitment to the Hermann case was a direct result of the circumstances of his own loss. His feelings of guilt over his wife's death are assuaged by his efforts on behalf of Marie.

FACTIONAL WORKS:
Richard Cooper, *Shadow of the Noose* (London: Viking, 1989).

FURTHER READING:
Edward Marjoribanks, *Famous Trials of Marshall Hall* (Harmondsworth: Penguin, 1950).

HICKOCK AND SMITH USA 1960

Richard E. Hickock and Perry Smith were small-time crooks who had served prison sentences. Prior to the Clutter murders that were to bring them to the attention of author Truman Capote, Hickock had shared a prison cell in Kansas with Floyd Wells. Wells had once worked for Herbert Clutter, a wealthy wheat farmer, and Hickock questioned his cell-mate about the Clutter home and money. When Hickock and Smith were released from prison in November 1959, they headed straight to the Clutter farm in Holcomb. Here they tied the family up, cut the farmer's throat and killed his wife and two children with a shotgun.

They had been hoping to find ten thousand dollars; the money they took away with them was a meagre forty dollars. When news of the murders reached Kansas State Penitentiary, Wells informed the governor of his talks with Hickock. The two murderers were arrested in Las Vegas, and each promptly accused the other of the crime. At their trial, the defence relied heavily on psychiatric evidence. Hickock suffered from severe headaches following a 1950 motor accident; Smith showed signs of paranoia. The prosecution was out for blood, and urged the jurors not to be 'chicken-hearted'. The two were found guilty of four counts of murder. After several appeals, they were executed in 1965.

In 1959, when Truman Capote read of the murders in the *New York Times*, he travelled to Kansas with novelist Harper Lee, arriving in time for the family funeral. For the next six years, Capote interviewed everyone he could about the murders, including the killers themselves. He attended their executions in 1965; five months later, his 'non-fiction novel', *In Cold Blood*, made its first appearance, serialised in the pages of *The New Yorker* magazine. It was published in book form later the same year.

What can one say about a work of crime faction that is itself the prime source of information for its original? Some might argue against its inclusion in the present study. In four parts, Capote gives us the unblemished story of the Clutter murders. In the first section of the book, we see the family and criminals as their lives converge towards their meeting on 15th November 1959. The second section concerns the police investigation, while at the same time Capote follows the killers on their flight to Mexico and back. Part three concentrates on their capture and confession to the killings. Finally, the book concludes with the trial, the legal wrangles and the eventual executions.

How much of the story is fictional we will never know. Much of Hickock and Smith's autobiography in the work stems from conversations with Capote himself, who died in 1984. Although none of the talks were recorded, Capote claimed he had taught himself to transcribe conversation without the aid of a recorder with ninety-five-per-cent accuracy. Despite his claim that the book should be read as a novel, Capote insisted afterwards in several interviews that all the incidents reported were true. What cannot be argued, whether one accepts the book as fiction or not, is that Capote's descriptive style and attention to the smallest detail altered the shape of crime reportage completely. It also heralded a graphic realism in crime fiction itself that would reach its apogee in the work of such authors as James Ellroy.

FACTIONAL WORKS AND FURTHER READING:
Truman Capote, *In Cold Blood* (New York: Random House, 1965).

FILM ADAPTATIONS:
In Cold Blood, d. Richard Brooks. US: Columbia, 1967. Screenplay by Richard Brooks, based on the novel by Truman Capote.

H. H. HOLMES USA 1895

Born Herman Webster Mudgett, H. H. Holmes led a life of bigamy and fraud. He was employed as a chemist in a Chicago drugstore, which he took over when the owner mysteriously disappeared. On a plot of land adjoining the store, Holmes built a one-hundred room hotel. Its gothic design led to its christening as 'Holmes's Castle' by the locals. Many guests booked into the 'Castle', some remained there permanently.

In 1893, the year of the Chicago World Fair and a boom time for Holmes, the hotel was damaged by fire. Holmes's current girlfriend claimed that he had started the fire himself, and the insurance company refused to pay up. Subsequently, the girlfriend disappeared. Following the death of the hotel's architect, Holmes was wanted for embezzlement and went on the run. Police who searched the 'Castle' were horrified to discover that the building was a glorified torture-chamber. Some rooms had no windows, some were padded, others had gas-pipes and peep-holes concealed. In some, police found surgical instruments and chutes leading from upper storey rooms to the basement. Buried in the latter, the skeletons of several women were unearthed.

Finally captured, Holmes stood trial for the murder of his architect and was found guilty. While awaiting execution, he confessed to twenty-seven murders (although he later retracted his confession to all but two of these). He was hanged in 1896, following the dismissal of an appeal. If his original confession was true, he was America's first serial killer.

G. Gordon Gregg, protagonist of Robert Bloch's 1974 chiller, *American Gothic*, is a thinly-disguised version of Holmes. As Bloch notes in his 'Post-mortem': 'while certain liberties have been taken with contemporary events and his personal history, the basic facts remain. . . If anything, his private life-style was far more fantastic than this fictional account'. Bloch's fictional account presents the Holmes story as a nineteenth-century version of the Bluebeard fairytale.

Gregg's victims are seen as the embodiment of his warped sense of love and desire. All of them are young, attractive women. From his castle-like hotel in Chicago, Gregg selects his prey from the visitors to the World's Fair. One such visitor is a reporter named Crystal, who has become suspicious of the disappearances around the World's Fair. She discovers Gregg's sinister pastimes, endangering her own life. Ultimately, Gregg meets with a more poetic end than his real-life prototype.

FACTIONAL WORKS:
Robert Bloch, *American Gothic* (New York: Simon and Schuster, [1974]).

FURTHER READING:
Joseph H. Jackson, ed., *The Portable Murder Book* (New York: Viking, 1945).

FRANCES HOWARD GB 1615

Robert Carr, a favourite of James I, fell in love with Frances Howard, who was married to the Earl of Essex. Frances and Essex had never consummated their marriage, and after her affair with Carr began, Frances arranged for her servants to feed her husband drugs that would render him impotent. At one stage she even tried to poison Essex. When Carr was created the Earl of Somerset and Lord Treasurer, Frances's uncle, the Earl of Northampton, a political schemer, arranged for her divorce.

Sir Thomas Overbury, Carr's secretary (and possibly his lover) had helped his master in his lovemaking with the unhappy countess. However, with the prospect of their marriage, either fear of his loss of influence or sexual jealousy prompted him to malign Frances. She was not willing to stand idly by while he did so; she arranged for him to be thrown into the Tower on a trumped-up charge. The king lent his influence to keep his favourite happy, and Frances realised she must set into motion a plot to poison Overbury.

The prisoner was served poisoned food over a five-month period until he died in agony on 15th September 1613. Carr and Frances were then married. Shortly afterwards, Carr began to lose his influence with the king as George Villiers, the future Duke of Buckingham, usurped his place. One of the conspirators in the poisoning subsequently confessed on his death-bed. The king was informed and ordered an investigation.

Frances was tried, pleaded guilty and was sentenced to death. Carr, threatened with trial himself, warned the king that certain secrets would be made public if he were brought to court. At his trial, two men stood close to the prisoner ready to overpower him should he make any damning admissions. He was also sentenced to death. Both sentences were commuted by the king to imprisonment in the Tower. After six years they were released, and lived out the rest of their lives in retirement. The Countess died aged 39 in squalor and resentment.

The first faction based on the Overbury poisoning was Richard Savage's play, *The Tragedy of Sir Thomas Overbury*, produced at Drury Lane in 1723 and published the following year. Savage reduces the characters to a basic seven, and treats the facts freely. Among the factual characters, he places the fictional Isabella, ward of the Earl of Somerset, who falls in love with Overbury. In his version, the triangle is altered, as it is the Countess who harbours a passion for Overbury. Curiously, Savage himself was to be the subject of a later factional work, for his murder of James Sinclair.

In 1934, C. L. Stainer turned the case into a mock-Shakespearean tragedy in blank verse. Stainer's *Overbury* shows its title character to be scornful of Carr's reliance upon him. He foresees the end of his control over Carr when he hears of the impending marriage (a romantic jealousy is also implied). He threatens to spread rumours about Carr's previous lifestyle. It transpires that Overbury has heard of Frances's attempt on the life of Essex; this provides another motive for her hatred of him. Her uncle, Northampton, is concerned that Overbury will ruin the family's plans for advancement, and he is as responsible as Frances for Overbury's death (in fact Northampton's prominence in the plotting against Overbury is a key feature of Stainer's drama).

Mistress Turner, who supplies Frances with love philtres and other potions, persuades her that Overbury is dangerous if left alive. When Overbury refuses the offer of an ambassadorship to Russia, Frances persuades her uncle to give his own version of the refusal to the king, making it appear a personal affront to James. Thus Overbury is brought to the Tower. In all the plotting and poisoning, Carr is seen as a dupe, unaware of the murderous machinations progressing around him. The play ends with Overbury dying in his cell as the jailors debate what to do with the soon-to-be corpse.

In 1975, Jeremy Potter presented a different slant on the Overbury/Howard affair, viewing the events from the perspective of another ambitious climber at James's court. His novel, *Disgrace and Favour*, follows the fortunes of Robert Carey, cousin to Elizabeth I, who leaves the court after marrying without the Queen's consent, and takes on a minor post along the Scottish border. On a visit to the Queen, he travels with young Thomas Overbury, who is on his way to Oxford University. Carey tries to ingratiate himself with James of Scotland, promising to inform him as soon as the Queen dies, so that James can travel south and claim the throne before any doubts are raised. He is promised a position at court as reward, but the Howard family ensure that he loses the post to another. Carey has a friend, however, in James's queen, who appoints him to the staff of her youngest son, Charles.

Robert Carr, one of the hated Scottish Kerr clan, early rivals of Carey's, falls in love with Frances Howard. Essex, Carey and the Earl of Southampton all have reasons to detest the favoured Howards, and plan to bring them down, by rebellion if necessary. They groom young George Villiers to take Carr's place in the King's affections. Overbury, ambitious and overweening, is murdered in the Tower, and the Privy Council push for an investigation, despite the king's efforts at a cover-up. Carr and his wife are found guilty of murder and placed in the Tower.

After James's death, Charles rewards the faithful Carey with the earldom of Monmouth. But Carey's ambition has died along with his devoted wife, and he returns to the Border, where he makes his peace with the Kerrs. He meets Robert Carr, who has just been released from the Tower, who reveals that his hold over the old King was due to James's confession to the murder of the Earl of Gowrie and his brother in the Gowrie Plot of 1600. Also, Carr informs Carey that the King and Northampton had arranged the poisoning of Overbury, who had rejected Charles's passionate advances.

Potter's novel is the most successful of the Overbury treatments, not merely for the unique solution to the case, but also because of its strong sense of history: the Border rivalries, culminating in the hanging of the infamous Geordie Bourne; the death of the ageing Elizabeth I and James's succession; the death of James's oldest and most promising son, Henry; the imprisonment and release of Raleigh; and the rise and ultimate assassination of George Villiers, Duke of Buckingham. Potter paints an impressive and believable portrait of grasping and ambitious courtiers circling a weak and vacillating King.

FACTIONAL WORKS:
Richard Savage, *The Tragedy of Sir Thomas Overbury* (London: for Samuel Chapman, 1724). (**P**)

C. L. Stainer, *Overbury* (Oxford: Blackwell, 1934). (P)

Jeremy Potter, *Disgrace and Favour* (London: Constable & Co., 1975).

FURTHER READING:

Beatrice White, *Cast of Ravens* (London: John Murray, [1965]).

HULTEN AND JONES GB 1945

Karl Gustav Hulten, a deserter from the American army, met Elizabeth Jones in a cafe in London on 3rd October 1944. Jones (who was also known by her stage name, Georgina Grayson) was a small-time stripper with a florid imagination. When Hulten told her that he was a Chicago gangster, she immediately took on the role of his moll. For the next few nights, they toured London in a stolen army lorry, terrorising pedestrians. At one stage, they attacked a young lady with an iron bar and pushed her into the Thames; fortunately she survived.

On 7th October, they flagged down a private-hire taxi driven by George Heath. From the backseat, Hulten shot the driver. While Heath lay slumped in his seat dying, Jones ransacked his pockets. They drove the body to Staines where they dumped it, and took the car back to London. Police discovered Heath's body the following morning and traced the taxi to Hulten. He was arrested; Jones was picked up two days later.

The two stood trial at the Old Bailey in January 1945, the American government having waived the right to try Hulten as a serviceman. Found guilty of the 'Cleft Chin murder', as the press were calling it, they were sentenced to death, with a recommendation to mercy for eighteen-year-old Jones. Hulten was executed in March, two months before hostilities in Europe ended. Jones was reprieved, and left prison in 1954.

Austin Stone's 1949 novel, *Blood Stays Red*, manages to amalgamate details of the Hulten and Jones case with those of the earlier Patrick Mahon murder trial of 1924 (see relevant entry). Nicholas Dearden, a philandering salesman, has promised to run away with his pregnant girlfriend. Luring her to a deserted cottage, he murders her with a poker and proceeds to dismember her in the style of Mahon. Then, reluctant to share the house alone with a corpse (like Mahon before him), he invites another girl to stay the night with him, with the body locked in an adjacent room.

The girl, Margot Hunter, is a bored, thrill-seeking secretary who has led a life of abuse and neglect. When the police close in on Dearden, she takes him in and proposes that they form a team to revenge themselves on an uncaring world. On the run, they hitch a lift and murder the driver. He turns out to be a fence, with a flat full of money and stolen goods. Soon, the murderous duo find themselves on the run from the police and the fence's associates, and forcibly involved in yet another murder plan. Stone admits the two sources of his tale in his afterword, but the plot follows his own literary invention after the driver's death.

In 1989, the story of Hulten and Jones was filmed as *Chicago Joe and the Showgirl*. David Yallop's script was adapted as a novel by M. Gaynor under the same title. Both film and novel show Hulten's influence on the bored and insensitive Jones. She is the one who incites Hulten to murder. Their fantasy life as gangster and moll are seen as an escape route from the depressing reality of end-of-war London. As they leave the court and face a barrage of journalists at the end of the novel (and film), fantasy takes over completely for Jones; in a scene reminiscent of Sunset Boulevard, she imagines herself to be a Hollywood star facing her grateful fans and photographers. The epilogue to Gaynor's book, stating the true facts of the case, returns the reader to the bleak reality.

FACTIONAL WORKS:
Austin Stone, *Blood Stays Red* (London: John Gifford, [1949]).
M. Gaynor, *Chicago Joe and the Showgirl* (London: New English Library, 1990).

FURTHER READING:
Gordon Honeycombe, *The Murders of the Black Museum, 1870–1970* (London: Hutchinson, 1982).

FILM ADAPTATIONS:
Chicago Joe and the Showgirl, d. Bernard Rose. GB: Palace/New Line, 1989. Screenplay by David Yallop, novelised by M. Gaynor.

ABE HUMMEL USA 1907

William F. Howe and Abe Hummel were two of the most unscrupulous 'shyster' lawyers in American history. After his career as a doctor was finished following a prison sentence for performing an abortion, Howe emigrated from England. He started a law firm in New York and proved to be an adept and suitably theatrical defence lawyer. In the 1860s, Abe Hummel joined the firm and soon became a partner. Abe's speciality was finding loopholes in the law that Bill could use in his arguments to the jury. Usually, Hummel's loopholes relied heavily on the semantics of the laws passed by the State.

A typical case was that of Harry Carlton who murdered a policeman in 1888. Found guilty with no recommendation for mercy, Carlton's obvious sentence at that time was death. However, New York State had abolished hanging in June of that year to make way for the electric chair, to be used for executions after January 1889. The new law outlining this change was ambiguously worded, stating that 'electrocution should apply to all convictions punishable by death on or after January 1st'. Howe argued that since Carlton's murder had been committed before June, the verdict should be hanging, which had been abolished; and that therefore since his client had been sentenced to death with no recommendation for mercy (thus forfeiting a prison sentence), he should be set free!

The judge was so perplexed by this tack that he passed the decision on to the Supreme Court. Howe and Hummel lost the argument (Carlton was hanged two days after Christmas), but for a while the papers carried the story that they had managed to make murder legal. The corrupt pair were not above bribing juries to get their clients off, and naturally their office became swamped with a preponderance of guilty rather than innocent clients, who relied on the unscrupulous duo as a last resort.

In 1907, a year after Howe died, Hummel was accused of presenting a thousand-dollar bribe to win a divorce action. He was sentenced to two years in prison. On his release, he emigrated to England, where prior to his death in 1926, he was a regular visitor to the public gallery of the Old Bailey.

Howe and Hummel were reincarnated in fiction as Gottlieb and Quibble in Arthur Train's novel, *The Confessions of Artemus Quibble* (1911). At the beginning of the novel, Massachusetts-born Quibble is studying at Harvard. When his father dies, he is disappointed that he does not receive an inheritance. He reasons that since the law has robbed him of his money, it is by the law that he will earn his keep. He leaves Harvard to escape creditors and arrives in New York, eventually setting up business with Abraham Gottlieb, who has established a reputation for defending clients on the flimsiest of legal arguments, and winning. Established close to the Tombs prison, the firm accepts clients on the ability to pay, and bribes police to push more business in their direction. Soon, however, the two shyster lawyers find themselves on trial for perjury. They are sentenced to two years in Sing Sing.

FACTIONAL WORKS:
Arthur C. Train, *The Confessions of Artemus* Quibble (New York: C. Scribner's Sons, 1911).

FURTHER READING:
Richard H. Revere, *Howe and Hummel: Their True and Scandalous History* (New York: Farrar, Straus & Giroux Inc., 1947).

ROBERT IRWIN USA 1938

On 28th March 1937, Easter Sunday, Joseph Gedeon, his daughter Ethel and her husband arrived at the New York apartment that Mary, Joseph's estranged wife, shared with their other daughter, Veronica and a lodger, Frank Byrnes. When they received no answer, Joseph went up to the apartment and discovered the bodies of Mary, Veronica and Byrnes. The women had been strangled, the lodger stabbed to death. No valuables were missing and there was no evidence of a sexual motive for the killings. As Veronica had been a model, the tabloids splashed her picture over the front covers.

Joseph Gedeon was suspected. Although the police gave him a thorough interrogation, no charges were made, except for illegal possession of a firearm. Stephen Butter, the last person to see Veronica alive, was their next candidate but he was able to provide an alibi. Then police discovered an uncollected suitcase at Grand Central Station containing a sculptor's knife and concluded that it was the same instrument used to stab Byrnes. The case belonged to Robert Irwin, a former tenant of Gedeon's. Police issued a warrant for Irwin's arrest. In Chicago, Irwin himself contacted the local newspaper, the *Herald-Examiner,* to sell his story. They published his photo on their front page before he turned himself in.

Irwin's trial for the triple murders began in November 1938. He had a past record of psychiatric disorders, including religious mania (inherited from his mother) and attempted self-mutilation. According to Irwin, Veronica had tried to seduce him and when he balked at her advances, she spread rumours of his homosexuality. After a failed attempt at theological college (he was expelled), he decided to kill Veronica and them himself. However, her mother and their lodger were at the apartment when he arrived, so he murdered them first and waited for Veronica to return. Irwin was lucky to be defended by Samuel Leibowitz, who saved him from the electric chair. Instead, he was jailed for 39 years. He died of cancer in 1975.

Curtis Gathje, the nephew of Stephen Butter, heard the basic facts of the case from his uncle over a Thanksgiving meal years later. His 'true fiction', *A Model Crime* (1995), tells the story from many angles, a style favoured by Truman Capote. Principally it covers the story through its newspaper coverage. Sprinkled with cuttings from the tabloid press, Gathje's novel shows how the press dictated the course of the investigations. 'The comic-strip rendering of Ronnie Gedeon's murder' is his subject, as he admits in his preface, 'a story of newspapers and consequences'. One consequence was that innocent people like Joseph Gedeon and Stephen Butter were at the mercy of the reporters in their search for a good story. Another consequence, mentioned ironically by Gathje, is the way the yellow press turned Irwin into a celebrity before his ultimate incarceration.

FACTIONAL WORKS:
Curtis Gathje, *A Model Crime* (New York: Donald I. Fine, 1995).

FURTHER READING:
Jay Robert Nash, *World Encyclopedia of Twentieth-Century Murder* (New York: Marlowe & Co., 1994).

JACK THE RIPPER GB 1888

Probably the most infamous murderer in English criminal history, the character who called himself Jack the Ripper is still officially unidentified. Over a period of three months, five prostitutes were murdered in the Whitechapel district of London. In each case, they were stabbed to death and horribly mutilated. Sometimes organs were removed from the bodies. Four of the murders took place in the streets and alleys of Whitechapel; the fifth and most violent was committed indoors.

The first murder occurred on 31st August 1888. After a second was committed on September 8th, the press received a letter signed 'Jack the Ripper'. The author of the letter was clearly familiar with the murders and promised more deaths to come. The police were at a total loss, although the accuracy of the incisions suggested a medical practitioner. The first victim had been seen escorting a soldier, although a later witness spoke of a man with a moustache and a foreign complexion and another had spotted a man with a shiny black bag. After the last murder on 9th November, the killings stopped as suddenly as they had begun.

Most theorists on the case—in fact and fiction—have dwelt on the possible identity of the Ripper. The medical profession seems a likely source, as does the butcher's trade (a leather apron was discovered close to one of the bodies). Other prominent captured murderers have been put forward as candidates (see entry on 'Thomas Neill Cream'). Writers have mused on the failure of the police, suggesting government collusion in covering up a scandal of untold proportions—even royalty have been suspected. The recently discovered 'diary' of the Ripper, if genuine, identifies him as James Maybrick, whose wife Florence was found guilty of his murder in 1889! Whatever effect the case may have had in the field of criminology, it proved a godsend to the publishing trade.

As befits the most famous killer of all time, the Ripper has spawned more factional treatments than any other criminal—at least twenty-three to date, of which three are collections of short stories devoted to the case. Jack also made a guest appearance in Frank Wedekind's play *Die Büchse der Pandora* (*Pandora's Box*), first published in 1904 and translated into English ten years later. The second of Wedekind's two dramas concerning Lulu, an innocent who exudes sexuality and falls victim to ruthless men, the play traces Lulu's descent from respectability to prostitution. In the final scene, Lulu and her friend, the Countess Geshwitz, are brutally stabbed to death by the Ripper.

Marie Belloc Lowndes's novel, *The Lodger*, is probably the most famous Ripper treatment and indisputably a classic in the faction genre. Originally composed as a short story for *McClure's Magazine* in January 1911, it was expanded into a novel for publication in the UK and America two years later. The story tells of Mrs Bunting, who comes to believe that her solitary, morose lodger, Mr Sleuth, might be the Avenger, a multiple murderer terrorising London. He pays the landlady extra money not to take in other lodgers, he turns the paintings of women in his room to the wall, he exhibits signs of religious mania.

Although the atmosphere of the novel strikes the modern reader as incredibly cosy and quaint, the mounting tension as Mrs Bunting finds her fears justified is still effective. The motive of religious mania is as believable as many of the theories in non-fiction studies of the case. Lowndes was inspired by the success of her novel to write further factional treatments of famous cases.

Hugh Brooke's 1932 novel, *Man Made Angry*, favours the theory of the

Ripper as butcher. Clovis Dell, a provincial butcher's son, comes into a small fortune and moves to London. There, he mingles with a different class of people who look down on his inferior upbringing and parochial habits. This rejection leads him to seek revenge with the two butcher's knives he has brought with him. Brooke's story is a good psychological horror yarn and an early fictional portrayal of alienation in the modern city.

Edward Hale Bierstadt not only employed the Ripper case but also the Crippen and Borden murders in his 1935 American novel, *Satan Was a Man*. Carroll Lindsay, a writer, lives at home with his mother and sister Dorothy. Carroll loves a waitress named Lucile Wynne, but his domineering, drunken mother disapproves. Researching criminal psychology for a book, Carroll finds himself drawn into the criminal careers of three murderers. In his dreams he relives the trials of Lizzie Borden and Harvey Crippen, as well as the last murder of Jack the Ripper. His dreams become reality when he commits a series of murders.

Gaunt, the Lindsay family servant who is also a retired professor of applied psychology, has watched Carroll closely and suspects him of murder. In the end, Gaunt persuades Carroll to commit suicide while he is dreaming about the Ripper murder. The Ripper scenes are based on Leonard Maltin's theory as expounded in his 1929 study, *The Mystery of Jack the Ripper*, that the murderer was a doctor whose son had died of venereal disease contracted from one of the Ripper's eventual victims.

Hugh Desmond's 1956 novel, *Death Let Loose*, moves the story forward to London in the 1890s, where the Slasher is at work knifing prostitutes in the East End; a surprising and far-fetched murderer is unmasked. John Brooks Barry's novel, *The Michaelmas Girls* (1975), is the diary of a young social worker in Whitechapel in the 1880s. He becomes involved in the murders, developing his own theory on the Ripper's identity and how he has escaped capture.

The Ripper File, written by Elwyn Jones and John Lloyd, brought a twist to the story, by placing Jones's television policemen, Detective Chief Superintendents Charlie Barlow and John Watt, on the case of the Ripper. Published in 1975, the book is a curious hybrid: the fictional scenes of Barlow and Watt sifting through the evidence are interspersed with a factual investigation of the crime. It was originally written as one of a series of BBC films in which the fictional duo tackled true cases, but it was the only one to be novelised.

In 1974, Ron Pember's and Denis de Marne's musical play *Jack the Ripper* was staged in London. Presenting an investigation of the crimes in a music-hall setting, the drama juxtaposes pseudo-Victorian songs and variety acts with reconstructions of the murders. Several possible candidates are suggested before the final scene reveals Montague Druitt to be the murderer. Druitt, one of the most acceptable candidates in non-fiction studies, took his life at the time the murders ceased.

1976 saw the appearance of two novellas by Patrice Chaplin, daughter-in-law of the London-born comedian, on the Ripper theme. *By Flower and*

Dean Street & The Love Apple presents tales of two different people in modern London who find themselves possessed by characters involved in the Ripper murders. The author describes perfectly the mundane existence of modern-day suburbia and the horror of encroaching insanity.

Karl Alexander's science fiction novel, *Time After Time* (1979), posits the possibility of the Ripper as time traveller, a theme already examined by several short-story writers (see below). Alexander's coup is to have Jack travel into the future in a time machine invented by H.G. Wells. When the murderer escapes into modern-day America, Wells is forced to follow him and bring him to justice. The author makes much of Jack's ready acceptance of modern-day life with its violence and lack of morality, in comparison to the straight-laced Wells.

Richard Gordon, author of the best-selling *Doctor* series, brings a physician's view to the case in his 1980 novel, *The Private Life of Jack the Ripper*. His protagonist, Bertie Randolph, is a rich young doctor and a procurer for a brothel, run by the infamous Adelaide Bartlett. Other doctors are also seen sampling the dubious pleasures of Whitechapel. Gordon presents a fictional suspect as the Ripper, but a feasible motive and method.

Robert Bloch's 1984 novel, *The Night of the Ripper*, follows a young American doctor named Mark Robinson, as he assists Inspector Abberline, the genuine policeman on the Ripper case, in his hunt for the murderer. The novel introduces an assortment of historical characters—George Bernard Shaw, Arthur Conan Doyle, Oscar Wilde, the Duke of Clarence, even John Merrick, the Elephant Man. Bloch chooses an historical suspect as his Ripper candidate, together with a surprising accomplice. Despite the gruesome facts of the case, the truly horrific details in Bloch's novel are those in historical references to torture and murder quoted at the head of each chapter.

Yours Truly, Jack the Ripper, a 1987 novel by American author Pamela West, presents the diary of Inspector John West, a policeman assigned to the Ripper case. In this well-researched novel West follows a royal connection to discover the killer's identity. More unusual is Iain Sinclair's *White Chappell, Scarlet Tracings* (1987), a prose mosaic combining the search of modern-day antiquarian booksellers combing the country for stock with musings on the characters and events of 1888 Whitechapel.

Mark Daniel's *Jack the Ripper*, published in the centenary year of the murders, is based on a television film. Sergeant George Godley, assistant to Inspector Abberline tells the story of the investigation and solution of the case. The story is interspersed with Daniels's comments on established theories and facts. While Abberline proceeds with his detective work, a reporter from the radical paper, *The Star*, tries to arouse dissatisfaction and riot among the Whitechapel populace. Abberline is presented as an honest policeman, at odds with his politically-motivated and masonically-connected peers. Four endings are given in the novel, with four Ripper candidates from which to choose. Only one of these endings was used for the television adaptation.

In a refreshing change of angle, Paul West's *The Women of Whitechapel and Jack the Ripper* (1991) concentrates on the lives and actions of the murderer's victims. The murders themselves are seen as a vicious adjunct to their frequently violent trade. The events are viewed from the standpoint of the sympathetic painter, Walter Sickert, who strides the worlds of respectability and degradation. Sickert is both drawn to and repelled by the female inhabitants of Whitechapel, and looks on in horror as the events of late 1888 unfold. Once more a connection is drawn between the Ripper and the royals.

Hilary Bailey's *The Cry From Street to Street* (1992) is told by a fictional Mary Kelly (also the name of the Ripper's last victim). Bailey's Mary Kelly had escaped from Whitechapel to Canada prior to 1888, and has made her fortune as a brothel-keeper. In that fateful year, she returns to London to look for her two sisters, one of whom is living in poverty in Whitechapel. Eventually, she finds the Ripper himself, and a solution to the historical mystery, as well as that presented by Bailey: what association does this Mary Kelly have with the Ripper's victim of the same name?

Another novel of 1992, Edmund McCoy's intriguing thriller, *Blood of the Fathers*, seeks to give the Ripper tale a modern frisson, offering a fascinating connection between the Ripper murders and the IRA. Sorting through his mother's possessions after her mysterious death, an editor named Phillip Tarpin discovers a trail of murder in his family that stretches back to 1888, and the events of 9th November in a room in Whitechapel. The trail continues and Tarpin subsequently finds his own life in danger.

Richard Laymon's novel, *Savage* (1993) presents a sequel to the Ripper's London crimes. Fifteen-year-old Trevor Bentley, whose uncle is a policeman working on the case, finds himself hiding under Mary Kelly's bed on the night that she is murdered. Trevor vows to bring the Ripper to justice, and pursues the serial-killer across England and America, to a final showdown in the still-untamed West. Laymon's attempt at a turn-of-the-century adventure story (Mark Twain's *Huckleberry Finn* is mentioned often by the teenage narrator) sits uneasily with the graphic descriptions of violence he presents.

Since Sherlock Holmes, the most famous fictional detective of all time, made his debut a year before the Ripper murders, it was inevitable that he should be called in to investigate the case. Conan Doyle himself never envisaged a meeting between his creation and the famous murderer, but later authors rose to the challenge. The first was Ellery Queen, who with both his own eponymous sleuth and Sherlock Holmes, tackled the Whitechapel murders in the novel, *A Study in Terror* (1966; the UK title was *Sherlock Holmes versus Jack the Ripper*). Taking the script of a 1965 film by Donald and Derek Forde as its basis, the novel follows Sherlock Holmes tackling the Ripper case, while contemporary detective Ellery Queen reads Watson's manuscript description of this historic encounter. The story-within-a-story suggests that the Ripper is an aristocrat, avenging a death in his family.

However, in the end Queen suggests that Holmes had not given Watson all the facts, and presents his own solution.

According to Allen J. Hubin's authoritative *Crime Fiction 1749-1980* (1984), the Queen sequences in *A Study in Terror* were written by Frederic Dannay and Manfred B. Lee (the two cousins who used 'Ellery Queen' as their pseudonym) while the Holmes section was the work of Paul W. Fairman, with contributions by Dannay and Lee.

Michael Dibdin, who was later to achieve success with his own detective, Aurelio Zen, also presents another recently-discovered manuscript of John Watson's in *The Last Sherlock Holmes Story* (1978). In this work, Dibdin comes up with the most fantastic fictional Ripper candidate to date. Robert Weverka's *Murder by Decree* (1979) is a novelisation of a screenplay by John Hopkins for the film of the same title. The story, which concerns Holmes's discovery of a Masonic plot to protect the British throne, draws its inspiration from Stephen Knight's factual study, *Jack the Ripper: The Final Solution* (1976), as inaccurate a title as that of Dibdin's novel.

Ray Walsh's *The Mycroft Memoranda* (1984) provides us with another fictional Ripper, as extraordinary as that proposed by Dibdin. Walsh, however, makes the mistake of taking his pastiche too seriously, and the novel is followed by a 'retrospection' which pedantically places the Ripper investigation within the framework of Holmesian chronology. Also, the Ripper is unmasked with little of the Holmesian deduction prevalent in Conan Doyle's work, and the denouement is hurried and unexciting. The only clever conceit is the introduction of Lord John Roxton, one of the heroes of Conan Doyle's classic fantasy adventure, *The Lost World* (1912).

Edward B. Hanna's mammoth novel, *The Whitechapel Horrors* (1992), also plays seriously with the Holmesian elements of his story—there are 120 notes in the text giving links between Hanna's plot and the Holmes canon. The story itself is never dull: in the course of his sleuthing Holmes meets Sir Randolph Churchill, Oscar Wilde and George Bernard Shaw. In one humorous scene, the Great Detective even gives Shaw the idea for his play *Pygmalion*. The facts of the Ripper case are closely followed, and the theory of the royal connection is once more employed. Hanna ends his novel with a summary of the theories on the Ripper's identity.

In addition to the many novels based on the Ripper murders, a large number of short stories have taken the case as their theme. The best and most famous of these are collected in three anthologies—Allan Barnard's *The Harlot Killer* (1953), Michel Parry's *Jack the Knife* (1975) and Susan Casper's and Gardner Dozois's *Jack the Ripper* (1988). Four stories in particular should be mentioned in detail here.

Marie Belloc Lowndes's short version of 'The Lodger', first published in 1911, demonstrates the ideas that she was to expand to novel form. The short story has a tone similar to that of the novel, and all the main characters and events are still present. Thomas Burke's 'The Hands of Mr Ottermole', first published in 1931, presents the murderer as a strangler. The plot provides an intriguing solution to the question of how the real murderer may have escaped detection. Burke's story has been much anthologised, often cited as a Ripper faction, and has lost none of its impact over the years.

Mention should also be made of Robert Bloch's first factional Ripper treatment, 'Yours Truly, Jack the Ripper', published in 1945. Bloch was one of the first authors to place the Ripper in a science fiction setting.

Finally, Hilary Bailey brought a new twist to the genre of Holmes-Ripper confrontations when she pitted the Ripper not against Sherlock but his sister Charlotte. In her series of interlinked short stories, *The Strange Adventures of Charlotte Holmes* (1994), Bailey presents 'An Adventure in Whitechapel' in which Charlotte discovers the common link between the Ripper's victims and a house in Flower and Dean Street. She corners the murderer, a fictional candidate, with the assistance of her famous brother. Bailey's collection also provides an alternative solution to the Baskerville Hound case, and sees Charlotte making love to Inspector Lestrade. It is doubtful Holmes would have approved.

FACTIONAL WORKS:

Marie Belloc Lowndes, 'The Lodger', in *McClure's Magazine*, January 1911.

Marie Belloc Lowndes, *The Lodger* (London: Methuen, 1913).

Frank Wedekind, *Pandora's Box* (New York: A. & C. Boni, 1914). First published in German as *Die Büchse der Pandora*, 1904. (P)

Thomas Burke, 'The Hands of Mr Ottermole', in *The Pleasantries of Old Quong* (London: Constable & Co., 1931).

Hugh Brooke, *Man Made Angry* (London: Longmans, 1932).

Edward Hale Bierstadt, *Satan Was a Man* (New York: Doubleday, 1935).

Robert Bloch, 'Yours Truly, Jack the Ripper', in *Opener of the Way* (Sauk City: Arkham House, 1945).

Allan Barnard, ed., *The Harlot Killer* (New York: Dodd Mead & Co., 1953).

Hugh Desmond, *Death Let Loose* (London: Wright & Brown, 1956).

Ellery Queen, *A Study in Terror* (New York: Lancer, [1966]).

John Brooks Barry, *The Michaelmas Girls* (London: Andre Deutsch, 1975).

Elwyn Jones and John Lloyd, *The Ripper File* (London: Arthur Barker, 1975).

Michel Parry, ed., *Jack the Knife* (Frogmore: MayXower, 1975).

Patrice Chaplin, *By Flower and Dean Street & The Love Apple* (London: Duckworth, 1976).

Denis de Marne and Ron Pember, *Jack the Ripper* (London: Samuel French Ltd., 1976). (P)

Michael Dibdin, *The Last Sherlock Holmes Story* (London: Jonathan Cape, [1978]).

Karl Alexander, *Time after Time* (New York: Delacorte Press, 1979).

Robert Weverka, *Murder by Decree* (New York: Ballantyne, 1979).

Richard Gordon, *The Private Life of Jack the Ripper* (London: William Heinemann, 1980).

Robert Bloch, *The Night of the Ripper* (New York: Doubleday, 1984).

Ray Walsh, *The Mycroft Memoranda* (London: Andre Deutsch, 1984).

Iain Sinclair, *White Chappell, Scarlet Tracings* (London: Goldmark, 1987).

Pamela West, *Yours Truly, Jack the Ripper* (New York: St. Martin's Press, 1987).

Susan Casper and Gardner Dozois, eds., *Jack the Ripper* (London: Futura, 1988).

Mark Daniel, *Jack the Ripper* (London: Penguin/Thames, 1988).

Paul West, *The Women of Whitechapel and Jack the Ripper* (New York: Random House, 1991).

Hilary Bailey, *The Cry from Street to Street* (London: Constable & Co., 1992).

Edward B. Hanna, *The Whitechapel Horrors* (New York: Carroll & Graf, 1992).

Edmund McCoy, *Blood of the Fathers* (London: Orion, 1992).

Richard Laymon, *Savage* (Terra Alta, W. V.: Headline Books, 1993).

Hilary Bailey, 'An Adventure in Whitechapel', in *The Strange Adventures of Charlotte Holmes* (London: Constable & Co., 1994).

FURTHER READING:
Donald Rumbelow, *The Complete Jack the Ripper* (London: W. H. Allen & Co. Ltd., 1975).

FILM ADAPTATIONS:
Pandora's Box, d. G. W. Pabst. Germany: Nero Film, 1929. Silent. Screenplay by G. W. Pabst, based on the play by Frank Wedekind.
The Lodger, d. John Brahm. US: TCF, 1944. Screenplay by Barre Lyndon, based on the novel by Marie Belloc Lowndes.*
A Study in Terror, d. James Hill. GB: Compton-Tekli, 1965. Screenplay by Donald & Derek Ford, novelised by Ellery Queen.
Murder by Decree, d. Bob Clark. GB/Canada: Avco/Decree Productions, 1978. Screenplay by John Hopkins, novelised by Robert Weverka.
Time After Time, d. Nicholas Meyer. US: Warner/Orion, 1979. Screenplay by Nicholas Meyer, based on the novel by Karl Alexander.

JIM JONES GUYANA 1978

The son of an alcoholic Klansman, Jones discovered religion and was preaching sermons by the age of fourteen. He made a reasonable fortune by importing exotic animals, and opened the People's Temple in Indianapolis in 1957, where he preached racial integration and brotherly love. He was ordained a minister in 1964 and shortly afterwards transferred his Temple to San Francisco. His community work won him the approval of the local authorities, and his wealth and number of followers both began to accumulate.

Soon rumours were reaching the press that all was not right at the People's Temple. Defectors spoke of physical and mental coercion. There were tales of bizarre rituals and of Jones's sexual promiscuity, even though he preached abstinence. Aware of the criticism, Jones moved his cult of 1,000 followers to Guyana. Here his megalomania reached epic proportions; he began to believe he was a living god.

Californian congressman Leo Ryan persuaded the authorities to let him visit the Temple to investigate the worrying rumours. He arrived in November 1978 with an entourage of journalists and photographers. Several of Jones's followers confessed to the senator that they wanted to leave the Temple. When they reached the airport to return to the States, a group of gunmen from the Temple opened fire, killing the senator and four others. Jones meanwhile prepared his followers for a mass suicide. Large vats of Kool-Aid laced with cyanide were produced, and parents doled out the lethal concoction to their children. The adults then began to drink it themselves. Those who showed any hesitation were shot. Jones took his own life with a bullet through the head. 913 corpses were discovered by the Guyanese authorities.

In 1980, Anthony Burgess published his mammoth novel, *Earthly Powers*, which examined the role of the Catholic church—in particular, the Pope—

in the modern world. Burgess was disappointed by the stance taken by Pope John XXIII, whose Pelagian views (basically, a denial of the doctrine of original sin) were seen by the author as fundamentally harmful to the church. *Earthly Powers* follows a turbulent fifty-year period and the reign of a fictional Pope, Gregory XVII, firmly based on John XXIII. The novel is narrated by Kenneth Toomey, a playwright and novelist who has known the Pope when he was Carlo Campanati, a dedicated priest.

One of the many plots in this complex novel concerns Godfrey Manning, miraculously healed by Campanati when doctors had diagnosed terminal tubercular meningitis. Like Jones, Manning was brought up in Indiana, established a church in his home state and is eventually driven out by local Klansmen. He moves his sect, the Children of God, to the Mohave Desert in California. Known as 'God' Manning, his charitable works keep the authorities in check, until rumours of coercion and violence within the sect begin to circulate.

When a senator's daughter joins the sect, her father invokes the Mann Act, which states that the transportation of young girls over a state border for immoral purposes can lead to prosecution. The senator visits the Place of Prayer (as Manning's compound is known) with FBI agents and is murdered along with several officers. Manning leads his followers in a mass suicide (ironically, the weapon of death is not a poisonous drink, but 'the body of Christ administered as a cyanide tablet'). Some of the children refuse to take their 'medicine' and Manning is forced to kill them with his own hands. Unlike Jones, Manning escapes from the compound with some of his ill-gotten gains, but horrified by what he has seen and done, he turns himself in to the police. His story ends as psychiatrists determine whether he is sane enough to stand trial.

Jonestown (1996), a fascinating novel by Wilson Harris, takes an unusual stance in its investigation of the actions and motives of Jim Jones. The novel is presented as the 'Dream book' of the fictional Bone, sole survivor of the Jonestown massacre. Haunted by images of the last hours of Jones and his followers, Bone uses his book to confront and heal the trauma he has suffered. Jonah Jones, as he calls the leader of the People's Temple, is presented in all his megalomania and charisma—a frightening and alluring personality. At the same time, the fictional Bone (and, by extension, the author himself) posits a comparison between the modern conflagration in Jonestown, and the unknown causes for the destruction and disappearance of the pre-Columbian civilisations of South America. Could they, he suggests, have gone the same way, as victims of a rigid, inflexible religious regime?

FACTIONAL WORKS:
Anthony Burgess, *Earthly Powers* (London: Hutchinson & Co., 1980).
Wilson Harris, *Jonestown* (London: Faber & Faber, 1996).

FURTHER READING:
Ethan Feinsod, *Awake in a Nightmare* (New York: W. W. Norton, 1981).

JOHN KELLO GB 1570

Kello was the first minister to be appointed to the village of Spott following the reformation of the Kirk of Scotland in 1560. Being an ambitious man, he invested what little money he had, successfully at first. Eventually he came to grief with his speculations, and decided that without his wife Margaret, he could marry again into wealth. To prepare the ground, he spread rumours that Margaret was unbalanced and might one day take her own life.

He tried poisoning her, but her constitution proved too resilient. On 24th September 1570, while his wife was praying, Reverend Kello strangled her with a towel, hanging the corpse from the ceiling of her bedroom. He locked the front door from the inside and left through the back door of his study, which was by custom also locked. He then went off to church and preached a sermon.

On his return home, Kello made sure that neighbours accompanied him as he 'discovered' his wife's hanging body. He played the part of the grieving husband to the hilt, even going as far as to deny the existence of a stern God who would refuse his self-murdered wife eternal salvation. Kello overstepped the mark, however, when he continued discussions of his wife's 'suicide' with a colleague, Reverend Andrew Simpson of Dunbar. Something aroused Simpson's suspicion and he pleaded with Kello that if he were responsible for his wife's death he should confess. The Reverend literally put the fear of God into Kello; the parson of Spott finally acknowledged that he was a murderer and he was taken to Edinburgh to make his confession in a court of law. He was condemned to death by hanging and his body was burned.

Scottish author John Ferguson presented a heavily fictionalised version of the Spott murder in his 1924 novel, *Mr Kello*. He combined the tale with elements of contemporary Scottish witchcraft. In Ferguson's book, Kello is a pious and fervent man with a mission to rid his small parish of witches. To this end, he persecutes the women of the parish. However, one of them threatens him with a secret from his past. Kello intends to accuse her of witchcraft and bury the secret with her, but his determination falters.

His wife becomes caught up in the zeal of her husband's mission and looks for signs of the Devil in all things out of the ordinary. When she notices his hesitation in bringing to the stake the woman who shares his secret, she suspects him of being possessed and threatens to denounce him at the Kirk Session. Kello murders her and preaches an eloquent and moving sermon over her corpse. The novel ends with the people of the village, his accomplices in so many witch-hunts, turning on their parson when they learn the truth and executing justice in the manner he has taught them.

FACTIONAL WORKS:
John Ferguson, *Mr Kello* (London: G. G. Harrap & Co., 1924).

FURTHER READING:
William Roughead, *Twelve Scots Trials* (Edinburgh: William Green & Sons, 1913).

CONSTANCE KENT GB 1865

In 1860, the body of four-year-old Francis Savile Kent was discovered in an outside toilet on the grounds of his parents' home in Road, Wiltshire. He had been taken from his cot while the family was asleep and his throat had been cut, although suffocation was believed to have been the ultimate cause of death. There were no signs of a break-in, so the murderer was believed to be one of the family or servants; one of the housemaids was actually arrested but was later freed. After further fruitless enquiries by local police, Scotland Yard was called in. Inspector Whicher of the Yard promptly arrested Constance Kent, Francis's twenty-one-year-old step-sister. Much was made of the fact that three of Constance's night-dresses had disappeared, and a bloodstained garment was found on the premises, although this item was later lost by the police.

However, the evidence against Constance was insufficient to warrant a trial and she was released. When the family moved to Wales, Constance went to a convent in France. However, after she returned to England in 1865, Constance finally confessed to the murder; her only motive was a long-concealed hatred for her stepmother. She was tried and sentenced to death, but the sentence was commuted to life imprisonment. Released in 1885, she lived to the age of ninety-nine. Some modern criminologists have cast doubt on her confession, believing that she was covering up for her father, who might have committed the murder because his son had seen him making love to a servant girl.

Even before her return to England in 1865, a character resembling Constance Kent featured in Margarete Houston's *Such Things Are* (1862) as a suspected murderess. Elements of both the Madeleine Smith case and the murder of young Francis Kent were brought into Houston's fictional story of two sisters-in-law who have past secrets. One, who is being blackmailed on the eve of her marriage, poisons her erstwhile lover; while the other finds her husband has discovered that she was the prime suspect in the Bogden (Kent) murder. The novel drew a stream of protest from a *Quarterly Review* writer (see entry on 'Madeleine Smith').

Another major factional treatment which borrowed details from the Kent Murder was Wilkie Collins's *The Moonstone* (1868), first published in Charles Dickens's magazine, *All the Year Round*. Like Dickens's own *Bleak House*, *The Moonstone* featured a fictional portrait of a well-known Scotland Yard detective; Collins's inspiration for the character of Sergeant Cuff was Inspector Whicher. The author had previously written about Whicher in a series of articles for an earlier Dickens magazine, *Household Words*.

On first examination, the diamond theft which is the subject of *The Moonstone*, bears little relationship to the Constance Kent case. However, like Whicher, Cuff is removed from the case when he is seen to be pursuing the wrong leads; he is later proven right in his conclusions. The novel also uses the feature of a night-dress which disappears from the scene of the crime. The inspector shows much of the persistence and acumen—and the free use of flippant, enigmatic statements—that were later to distinguish Arthur Conan Doyle's Sherlock Holmes.

In fact, Collins's novel has its own unique position in the history of detective fiction. T. S. Eliot referred to *The Moonstone* as 'the first, the longest and the best of modern English detective novels'. Nine years after the book's publication, it was dramatised by the author and staged at the Olympic Theatre, where it ran for nine weeks. The play was privately printed by Charles Dickens's son. The action of the novel was compressed into one day, and the opium addiction that was such a principal feature of the novel was removed. Several characters also disappeared, but the Constance Kent allusions were retained.

Alan Brock's *The Browns of the Yard* (1952) tells of four generations of policemen as they pursue on particular case. Inspector William Brown finds himself investigating the Street End House murder (young Neville Duke has been killed in circumstances duplicating those of Francis Kent's death). Brown believes Neville's step-sister, Margaret, to be the perpetrator, but dies disgraced before he can solve the case. His son John joins the force and takes up the investigation, but is killed in a Fenian bomb explosion (Margaret is also connected with this atrocity). William's grandson is assigned to the Mersham Tunnel murder (a genuine case, committed by Percy Lefroy), and sees the hand of Margaret in this new crime. But it is left to the fourth generation of the family, Jack Brown, to finally solve the original case from a photograph of the crime scene.

Elbur Ford's *Such Bitter Business* (1953) gives a distinct twist to the Kent family mystery. Ford pictures Constance as a female Hamlet, using Francis's murder to avenge herself on her detested step-mother, whom she holds responsible for her own mother's death. Unfortunately, this intriguing notion is ruined by repetition and cliché. Whicher's first interrogation of Constance is suitably dramatic, but the characters as a whole are inadequate and the tension is dissipated.

More successful is Francis King's novel, *Act of Darkness* (1983), which transfers the case and characters to India between the two world wars. When young Peter Thompson's body is discovered in an outside lavatory, stabbed and smothered, the murder is believed to be the work of local Dacoits. Helen Thompson, Peter's step-sister, returns to England to live with her aunt, and there confesses to the murder. King suggests an interesting new motive for the murder, involving a lesbian relationship between Helen and her step-brother's governess.

FACTIONAL WORKS:
[Margarete Houston], *Such Things Are* (London: Saunder, Otley & Co., 1862).
Wilkie Collins, *The Moonstone* (London: Tinsley Brothers, 1868).
Wilkie Collins, *The Moonstone* (London: Charles Dickens & Evans, 1877). (**P**)
Alan Brock, *The Browns of the Yard* (London: G. G. Harrap & Co., 1952).
Elbur Ford, *Such Bitter Business* (London: William Heinemann, 1953).

Francis King, *Act of Darkness* (London: Hutchinson & Co., 1983).

FURTHER READING:
Bernard Taylor, *Cruelly Murdered* (London: Souvenir Press, 1979).

FILM ADAPTATIONS:
The Moonstone, d. Reginald Barker. US: Monogram, 1934. Screenplay by Adele Buffington, based on the novel by Wilkie Collins.*

DOT KING MURDER USA 1923

Dot King was born Anna Marie Keenan. She changed her name for her career as a model, before becoming a hostess at a speakeasy in New York. There she attracted the attention of a rich businessman and became his mistress. On 15th March 1923, her body was discovered in her apartment, lying on the bed next to an empty bottle of chloroform. Suicide was ruled out when it was found that her arm had been twisted behind her back.

The immediate suspects were Dot's two lovers—the mysterious sugar-daddy known only as 'Mr Marshall'; and a young gigolo, Alberto Santos Guimares, whom Dot had showered with gifts and money. Guimares had an alibi—he had been in the company of a prominent belle on the night of the murder. 'Mr Marshall' was finally identified as J. Kearsley Mitchell, son-in-law of a Philadelphia millionaire. The police accepted his denial of any link with the murder.

One theory was that Dot had been murdered by robbers, who had used the chloroform to overpower her. This was given credence when another girl was found dead in the vicinity a year later, in similar circumstances. She had apparently answered the door to two men who claimed to have a parcel for her. Whatever the motive for Dot King's murder, it remains unsolved.

In S. S. Van Dine's second novel (and second factional work—see the entry on the 'Elwell Murder'), amateur detective Philo Vance investigates *The Canary Murder Case* (1927), which involves a famous Broadway singer who is found strangled in her apartment. The police and Vance have to choose between four suspects, all of whom are known to be in love with Margaret Odell, 'the Canary'. One of the original suspects is also murdered before Van Dine solves the crime. The fictional treatment of the case is presented in the style of a classic detective story, the culprit's identity undisclosed until the final chapters.

FACTIONAL WORKS:
S. S. Van Dine, *The Canary Murder Case* (New York: C. Scribner's Sons, 1927).

FURTHER READING:
George P. Lebrun and Edward Radin, *It's Time to Tell* (New York: Morrow, 1962).

FILM ADAPTATIONS:
The Canary Murder Case, d. Frank Tuttle. US: Paramount, 1929. Screenplay by Florence Ryerson and Albert LeVino, based on the novel by S. S. Van Dine.

MOLL KING GB 1718

Material relating to Moll King's life is scarce. Her criminal career was pieced together by Gerald Howson, while researching his biography of Jonathan Wild. Her real name appears to have been Mary Godson, although she used the aliases of Bird and King, and it was under the latter name that her infamy spread. She was arrested for stealing a gold watch from a lady in St. Anne's Church, Soho in October 1718, and was sentenced to transportation. A pregnancy may have prevented the sentence from being carried out, as she was not transported until January 1720. She soon returned to England and was again arrested and committed to Newgate in June 1721.

By then she was known as 'one of the most notorious Pickpockets of the Town'. In July she was tried for robbing a house in Little Russell Street, and also for returning from transportation. Acquitted of the first offence, she was found guilty and condemned to death for the second. She impeached another criminal, Richard Grantham and was reprieved, only to be transported again in January 1722. Amazingly, she returned to England once more and was again sent to Newgate in September of that year. Prosecuted in March 1723, she was returned to America in September.

Several articles on Moll King have been attributed to Daniel Defoe. One from *Appleby's Original Weekly Journal* of July 1720 purports to be a letter from a girl called 'Moll of Rag Fair', and describes her apparent blackmail for returning from transportation. Another attributed article, from *The Weekly Journal* of September 1722, also concerns the notorious pickpocket.

Defoe was obviously aware of Moll's existence and reputation, and Howson gives a convincing case that Defoe actually had met Moll frequently in Newgate while he was visiting Nathaniel Mist, editor of *The Weekly Journal*, who was in prison at the end of 1721.

In January 1722, two days after King's second transportation, Defoe published his novel *The Fortunes and Misfortunes of the Famous Moll Flanders*. Several points link the fictional and factual Moll. Like her real counterpart, she is a notorious pickpocket—her training includes 'taking off Gold Watches from Ladies' Sides', the very offence for which Moll King was first transported. Moll Flanders was also taken to America and returned to England. The incident for which the fictional Moll was arrested, the robbery of 'a private Dwelling-House', is similar to the offence for which Moll King was acquitted in 1721. What other aspects of the plot are based on Moll King's true life story we will never know. However, both Moll King and her fictional counterpart did achieve a fame of sorts through the writings of Defoe.

FACTIONAL WORKS:

Daniel Defoe, *The Fortunes and Misfortunes of the Famous Moll Flanders* (London: for W. Chetwood, 1721 [1722]).

FURTHER READING:

Gerald Howson, 'Who Was Moll Flanders?', *The Times Literary Supplement* (18 January 1968).

FILM ADAPTATIONS:
  The Amorous Adventures of Moll Flanders, d. Terence Young. GB: Paramount/Winchester, 1965.
    Screenplay by Dennis Cannan, based on the novel *The Fortunes and Misfortunes of the Famous Moll Flanders* by Daniel Defoe.*

IVAR KREUGER SWEDEN 1932

Kreuger was born in 1880, the son of an owner of several match factories. Ivar studied as an engineer and worked in America for a time, before returning to Sweden. There he established a construction firm employing American methods, and soon had several firms throughout the world which dealt in both construction and materials. In 1913, he took over a number of match factories from his father and combined these with other manufacturers to form the United Swedish Match Factories (which was later known as the Swedish Match Company). By the end of the First World War, Kreuger was referred to as the 'Swedish Match King'.

He set up a holding company called Kreuger and Toll, which was basically a front for his shady dealings on the stock market. He intended to extend his empire by taking over the entire European match production industry. To this end, he floated Kreuger stock on the American market, created an American firm (International Match) and loaned money to various countries in exchange for their state match monopolies.

Then in 1929 the Wall Street Crash occurred, signalling the beginning of the end for Kreuger. He moved what money he had from bank to bank throughout the world, drawing more millions on the strength of his name alone. However, more and more financiers were beginning to question the strength of the Match King's financial foundation. In 1931, Kreuger began to forge share certificates and bonds to keep his empire afloat.

Finally, after attempting to raise two million pounds at the Swedish National Bank, he learned that they were to investigate his books. On 12th March 1932, Kreuger shot himself through the heart in a Paris hotel. A search of his offices revealed forged bonds and huge discrepancies in his finances. Kreuger and Toll was declared insolvent, with debts exceeding two hundred and thirty-four million pounds—a sum that exceeded the Swedish National Debt. Kreuger's empire, built on forgery, fraud and deceit, collapsed with the suicide of its enigmatic founder.

In March 1933, Graham Greene reviewed a biography of Ivar Kreuger for the *Spectator* magazine. Four months later, he noted in his diary: 'Almost decided on going to Stockholm next month as Kreuger will probably be the model for one of the principal characters in next novel.' In August 1933 he did in fact travel to Sweden and in November of that year began work on his novel, *England Made Me*, which was eventually published in 1935.

Tony Farrant is one of life's drifters, in and out of various jobs. His sister Kate, mistress of Erik Krogh, gets him employment as Krogh's bodyguard, but the feckless Tony is ill at ease with his new-found security. He befriends Minty, a down-at-heel English journalist and a kindred spirit. Disgusted by Krogh's business methods, Tony leaks a piece of confidential information to Minty and resigns his job. But he knows too much about Krogh's shady deals and tragedy ensues.

The relationship between Tony and Kate, with its strong incestuous overtones, is the centre of Greene's narrative, but the author is also fascinated by the domineering figure of Krogh, a powerful but emotionally impotent man, with many of Kreuger's characteristics. Greene makes one direct reference to his source when he indicates Krogh's determination to provide his own solution for his problems: 'Kreuger, lying shot in the Paris hotel, was his example.'

Ayn Rand, the American social critic and novelist, published her first work in 1936, a year after Greene's novel appeared. Her play, *The Night of January 16th*, was first staged in Hollywood as *The Woman on Trial*. Karen Andre is accused of murdering her employer and lover, millionaire industrialist Bjorne Faulkner, found shot after falling from the balcony of his penthouse suite. While the prosecution suggest that Andre committed the killing, her defence put forward the case for Faukner's suicide. Faulkner, who is involved in illicit deals worth millions of dollars, was on the point of being investigated.

It transpires that Faulkner has faked his death, the mangled body was a decoy. However, on the way to South America where Andre was to join him, Faulkner dies in a plane crash. Evidently, members of the audience became the jury, and their decision dictated the ending of the play.

FACTIONAL WORKS:
Graham Greene, *England Made Me* (London: William Heinemann, 1935).
Ayn Rand, *The Night of January 16th* (New York: Longmans, [1936]). (P)

FURTHER READING:
Allen Churchill, *The Incredible Ivar Kreuger* (London: Weidenfeld & Nicolson, 1957).

FILM ADAPTATIONS:
England Made Me, d. Peter Duffell. GB: Hemdale/Atlantic, 1972. Screenplay by Desmond Cory and Peter Duffell, based on the novel by Graham Greene.

PETER KÜRTEN GERMANY 1931

Kürten was the son of a sadistic drunkard who regularly sexually abused his children. From an early age, Peter tortured animals and gained sexual fulfilment from starting fires and witnessing road accidents. He half-choked his girlfriend at the age of fourteen and fantasised about creating mass destruction and death. He committed his first murder when he was thirty, strangling and stabbing thirteen-year-old Khristine Klein in her bedroom. For a time, Khristine's father was suspected of the killing.

Kürten's murderous career began in earnest in 1929, when a wave of killings alerted the people of Düsseldorf that a mass murderer was in their midst. Women and young girls were his chosen victims, ranging in age from five to twenty-six. The police sent out 'decoys' to try and trap the 'Beast of Düsseldorf', as the tabloid press labelled him, with no success. He was finally caught when he released the half-strangled Maria Budlick, convinced that she had forgotten his address. Unfortunately for Kürten, she hadn't.

When Maria led the police to his flat, he fled. Meeting up with his wife shortly after, he confessed his double life to her and persuaded her to turn him in to collect the reward. Arrested in May 1930, Kürten was interviewed over several months by psychiatrist Karl Berg, who wrote *The Sadist*, a classic study in psychopathology based on the case. Tried in April 1931, Kürten offered no excuse for his crimes. He was found guilty. Sentenced to be guillotined, his last wish was that he would hear the sound of the blood gushing from his neck when he was executed.

The year of his trial saw the release of Fritz Lang's film, *M*, based on the Düsseldorf murders. The script, by Lang and his wife Thea von Harbou, was translated into English and published in 1968. Taking the newspaper reports of the killings as its source, the film captures the mood of panic in Düsseldorf at the time. The authorities are powerless to catch the psychopath who is murdering young girls; and members of the underworld, crippled by the heavy police presence on the streets, become determined to capture the elusive murderer themselves (his actions brand him an outsider, even to other criminals). The juxtaposition of the efficient criminals and the impotent law forms an ironic commentary throughout the film.

The murderer is spotted in the streets and his shoulder is marked with a chalked 'M'. He is pursued and eventually captured by the underworld. They hold a kangaroo court, their chief witness a blind man who has recognised the murderer from the tune he whistles. The killer, Hans Beckert, confesses to the slayings, admitting his compulsive tendencies. He pleads for mercy (Peter Lorre's performance as Beckert makes this plea both moving and chilling). The police arrive before the court can carry out its sentence.

Colin Wilson's novel, *The Killer*, was published in 1970 (the American edition was entitled *Lingard*). Arthur Lingard is a composite portrait based on Kürten, the American murderer William Heirens, and the Dutch psychopath Hans van Zon. Wilson's aim was to remedy what he saw as Truman Capote's unsuccessful attempt at a 'non-fictional novel' with *In Cold Blood* (see entry on 'Hickcock and Smith'). With *The Sadist*, Wilson felt that '[Karl] Berg has shown the way. . . His book about Kürten is as compelling as a novel; but it also has a clinical realism that gives it a brutal impact far beyond the range of fiction'. Wilson was determined that his novel would 'capture the impact of Berg's book on Kürten'.

The Killer follows prison psychiatrist Samuel Kahn as he investigates the life, crimes and motives of Lingard, one of his patients. Lingard is serving the last few years of an eight-year sentence for manslaughter. Subject to fits of catatonia and plagued by nightmares, the prisoner opens up to the doctor.

Kahn discovers that his patient is a multiple murderer and psychopath responsible for several gruesome killings. Kahn pieces together the killer's life from interviews with Lingard, his relatives and acquaintances, discovering in the process the events that have helped to shape his warped character. Faced with this knowledge and with the desire to know more about Lingard, the doctor becomes concerned that the authorities, unaware of his mental state, might release him shortly. Before he is forced to act (and thereby lose Lingard's confidence), his patient is transferred to Broadmoor following an attack on a guard, and there is murdered by a fellow inmate.

Wilson admits that Lingard's childhood is strongly based on that of Kürten. He succeeds in giving his story the 'brutal impact' of Berg's book in his claustrophobic and chilling portrayal of Lingard's sexual and criminal depravities. While one reviewer condemned *The Killer* as 'closer to pornography than to a novel', Wilson must have felt he had accomplished his goal when another reviewer commented: 'it may be a novel, but it has something of the classic case study about it'.

FACTIONAL WORKS:
Fritz Lang [with Thea von Harbou, Paul Falkenberg, Adolf Jansen and Karl Vash], *M* (London: Lorrimar, 1968). (**P**)
Colin Wilson, *The Killer* (London: New English Library, 1970). US title: *Lingard*.

FURTHER READING:
Karl Berg, *The Sadist* (London: Acorn Press, 1938).

FILM ADAPTATIONS:
M, d. Fritz Lang. Germany: Nero Film, 1931. Screenplay by Thea von Harbou, Paul Falkenberg, Adolf Jansen and Karl Vash.*

HENRI LANDRU FRANCE 1922

Prior to the First World War, Landru led a life of small-time crime and fraud. Even before his career as a murderer began, he was wanted by the police in connection with various financial swindles. It was during the War, however, that Landru hit upon the *modus operandi* that was to make him infamous: he would marry lonely French women and then kill them for their fortunes. Sometimes he advertised in newspapers for a spouse, often he simply relied on casual acquaintance. Between 1915 and 1919, Landru murdered ten women and one boy, the son of his first victim.

The bodies were never recovered, although splinters of bone were discovered in the fireplace of his villa at Gambais. The possessions of his victims were still in his villa, however, and his meticulously-kept journals recording his conquests helped to convict him. He was tried in 1921, two years after his arrest. He was found guilty and executed, although he refused to confess to his crimes.

In 1964, French author Rene Masson's novel, *Les Roses de Gambais*, was translated into English as *Number One*. Masson provides a striking portrait of Landru, adhering closely to the records of the case and giving a fresh psychological insight into his character. The reader sees Landru developing his technique after the first murder, which is almost accidental. After this, he refines his method until his pride and his compulsion lead to his arrest and condemnation.

More ambitious in scope is William Wiser's 1980 novel, *Disappearances*, which not only concentrates on the Landru case, but also paints a colourful portrait of French high society of the period. An American journalist in Paris with his father covers the French Bluebeard's trial in 1922. The details of Landru's sexual and homicidal career as revealed in court are ironically juxtaposed with scenes of the young American's own carnal pursuits. In the course of the book, the narrator makes the acquaintance of many of the fashionable people in Paris, including Gertrude Stein and her entourage.

FACTIONAL WORKS:

Rene Masson, *Number One* (London: Hutchinson & Co., 1964). First published in French as *Les Roses de Gambais*, 1962.
William Wiser, *Disappearances* (New York: Atheneum, 1980).

FURTHER READING:
Dennis Bardens, *The Ladykiller* (London: Peter Davies, 1972).

LEOPOLD AND LOEB USA 1924

In May 1924, fourteen-year-old Bobbie Franks failed to return to his Chicago home. His mother received an anonymous phone call, saying that the boy had been kidnapped and to expect a ransom demand. The following day, Mr Franks received a note demanding ten thousand dollars for the release of his son. The ransom was never paid—later that day, police discovered the boy's body in a drainpipe. An important piece of evidence was a pair of spectacles found near the scene.

Police traced the owner of the spectacles, a college student named Nathan Leopold Jr., who claimed to have dropped the glasses while birdwatching. Leopold was brought in for questioning with his friend Richard Loeb, as they claimed they had been together at the time of the murder and far from the scene of the crime. Under interrogation, Loeb confessed to the murder. He and Leopold were fascinated by Nietzschean philosophy, with its dictum that certain people were above the law. With this in mind, the two had attempted the 'perfect crime'. The ransom was a hoax; both Leopold and Loeb came from extremely wealthy families. Their sole purpose was to kill young Franks—and get away with it.

They were defended by the famed American attorney, Clarence Darrow, who stressed their abnormal psychological makeup and pleaded for a sentence of life imprisonment. In a hostile atmosphere that favoured their execution, Darrow's impassioned closing speech (which lasted two days) won the two murderers their life sentences. Loeb was stabbed to death in 1936, in a prison brawl; Leopold was released in 1958 and died in 1971, a seemingly reformed character.

Patrick Hamilton used the characters and beliefs of the two Chicago students in his 1929 play, *Rope*. Like Leopold and Loeb, Wyndham Brandon and Charles Granillo are convinced of their mental superiority; like their American counterparts, the two British youths plan the perfect murder to prove it. They strangle a fellow-student, Ronald Kentley, and hide his body in a trunk in their house, then hold a party in the room where the corpse is stored.

Among the guests is Rupert Cadell, their sardonic, unprincipled friend who has himself discussed the superiority of the cultured mind and the possibility of a perfect murder. The evening turns into a mental sparring-match between Cadell and the two murderers, in which he is finally forced to face his own moral scruples and lack of genuine cynicism.

The most successful factional treatment based on the Leopold-Loeb case and one of the classics of the genre is Meyer Levin's *Compulsion* (1956). In the story of Artie Strauss and Judd Steiner, and their murder of Paulie Kessler, Levin gives a close rendition of the famous Chicago murder of the twenties. The author attempts a psychoanalytical approach to the subject, delving into the thoughts and feelings of the two would-be *Übermenchen*. A good deal more Freudian insight is provided by a fictional fellow student, Willie Weiss, who is studying psychiatry at the college.

The final chapters of the novel are a reconstruction of the trial, as Jonathan Wilk (Clarence Darrow) tries to save the youths from a death sentence. Levin gives a close pastiche of Darrow's summation, complete with the quotes from A. E. Houseman and Omar Khayyám that the famous lawyer used to support his argument against capital punishment. Levin was a contemporary of Leopold and Loeb at the University of Chicago, and the novel is narrated by his fictional alter ego, Sid Silver, a cub reporter for a local paper. Silver's recollections are made thirty years after the events, following a request by an editor that he interview Judd Steiner, who is eligible for parole.

It is no coincidence that at the time Levin was writing his novel, Nathan Leopold was indeed applying for a parole hearing. Leopold attempted to prevent publication of the novel on the grounds that it would adversely affect his case, but he failed. Two years later, he did in fact win his parole.

In 1959, Levin adapted his novel for the New York stage. The published version of the play was never produced on Broadway—it was drastically altered by the producers and was a dismal failure at the box-office. In Levin's original version, Sid Silver visits Judd Steiner in prison (a meeting that never occurs in the novel, although Sid considers the possibility). He urges Steiner to mentally confront his crime and admit his guilt; Judd wants only to 'grow away from it' and start a new life. But since he knows that the interview may affect his chances of parole, he reluctantly agrees, and the action of the novel occurs in flashback, beginning with Paulie Kessler's murder and ending with Jonathan Wilk's plea for the defence. The play concludes with Sid and Judd shaking hands—Judd has faced up to the enormity of his deeds, Sid better understands the horrific actions of his old acquaintance.

James Yaffe's 1957 novel, *Nothing but the Night*, published a year after *Compulsion*, was bound to suffer by comparison. A freer version of the case, Yaffe's narrative concentrates strongly on the home life of the killers and the inability of their parents to understand their spoilt, wayward children. Yaffe is intrigued, as Levin was, by the mental hold that extrovert Richard Loeb had over the introverted Leopold. The title of the novel was taken from the words of an A. E. Houseman poem that Clarence Darrow quoted in his defence summary.

FACTIONAL WORKS:
Patrick Hamilton, *Rope* (London: Constable & Co., 1929). (P)
Meyer Levin, *Compulsion* (New York: Simon & Schuster, 1956).
James Yaffe, *Nothing but the Night* (Boston: Little, Brown, [1957]).
Meyer Levin, *Compulsion* (New York: Simon & Schuster, 1959). (P)

FURTHER READING:
Hal Higden, *The Crime of the Century* (New York: G. P. Putnam's Sons, 1975).

FILM ADAPTATIONS:
Rope, d. Alfred Hitchcock. US: Transatlantic, 1948. Screenplay by by Arthur Laurents, based on the play by Patrick Hamilton.
Compulsion, d. Richard Fleischer. US: TCF/Darryl F. Zanuck Productions, 1959. Screenplay by Richard Murphy, based on the novel by Meter Levin.

RACHEL LEVERSON GB 1868

Although Rachel Leverson was not involved in her trial at the time that Wilkie Collins was placing her in a fictional context, she was already a figure of notoriety. She was born around 1806 in Northern England. Married twice (her first husband died at sea), she began respectably enough as a second-hand clothes dealer, before amassing sufficient funds to open her beauty emporium at 47A New Bond Street. A sign hanging over the door held out the promise: 'Beautiful for Ever'. Inside, ladies were persuaded to part with enormous sums for fake remedies such as Arabian Baths and Precious Jordan Water.

But there was a second entrance to the establishment, where the real money changed hands. Here the customers could meet with admirers—most of them procured by Leverson herself. She was not above using blackmail to advance her interests. In 1868, she was charged with obtaining money by false pretences and conspiracy to defraud. Her victim was Mrs Mary Borradaile, who was arrested for debt after she had been cheated by

Leverson and her solicitor, James Haynes. In the guise of go-between for Mrs Borradaile and a certain Lord Ranelagh, Leverson had taken £3,000 of the lady's money.

The jury could not agree, as Mrs Borradaile seemed a self-deluding, pathetic creature in the witness-box, and it took a second trial before Leverson was found guilty and sentenced to five years imprisonment. After her sentence was served, Leverson returned to her establishment and continued her felonious pursuits, until another trial led to a further prison sentence. She died in Woking Prison before her term was up.

The complex, tortuous plot of Wilkie Collins's 1866 work, *Armadale*, centres on attempts to inherit the estate of Allan Armadale, and a confusion of identities. At one time in the novel, there are five characters going under the name of Allan Armadale—all interrelated in some way. One of the strongest characters in the book is the scheming adulteress and poisoner, Lydia Gwilt, who intends to obtain a share of the Armadale estate. As a child, Lydia had been sold to Mrs Oldershaw, who used her to advertise beauty products.

Oldershaw is a beauty consultant and procurer who bears a great resemblance to Rachel Leverson. Like Leverson's establishment, Oldershaw's Lady's Toilette Repository in Pimlico has two entrances, the second for her more nefarious occupation. She is first introduced through her unctuous letters to Lydia in which she admits that she has 'twenty years' experience among our charming sex in making up battered old faces and worn-out figures to look like new'.

The trade is obviously lucrative: she has 'made fifty guineas today by putting [the bloom of youth] on the spotted shoulders of a woman old enough to be your mother'. Oldershaw backs Lydia's attempts to marry one of the Armadales, intent on poisoning him and inheriting his money. When their plans go awry, she escapes and is last seen preaching on the 'Pomps and Vanities of the World by A Sinner Who Has Served Them' to an audience of her elderly ex-customers.

Collins adapted the novel for the stage as he did with *The Moonstone* and *The Woman in White*—an easy way for an author to protect his dramatic copyright. His publishers, Smith, Elder ran off twenty-five copies for Collins. The adaptation never made it to the stage, but Collins revised it in 1875, as *Miss Gwylt*. Though the latter version concentrated on the principal *femme fatale*, the character of Mrs Oldershaw disappeared from the plot.

In the year of Leverson's trial, Frederick Hay's one-act farce, *Beautiful for Ever*, was staged at the Prince of Wales Theatre, Liverpool, and was published in London. A married couple have been taking bogus beauty treatments without each other's knowledge, and are both being blackmailed for full payment of the exorbitant bill. The character of Rachel Paynter, fake beautician and blackmailer, obviously had her origins in the London procurer who was even then serving her prison sentence as the Liverpool audiences were laughing at the gullibility of her victims.

FACTIONAL WORKS:

Wilkie Collins, *Armadale* (London: Smith, Elder & Co., 1866).

Wilkie Collins, *Armadale* (London: for the author by Smith, Elder & Co., 1866). (P)

Frederick Hay, *Beautiful for Ever* (London: T. H. Lacy, [1868]). (P)

FURTHER READING:

Elizabeth Jenkins, *Six Criminal Women* (London: Sampson Low, 1949).

RONALD LIGHT CASE GB 1920

In 1919, the corpse of young Annie Bella Wright was discovered on a country lane in Leicestershire. She had been shot through the head; a bullet was found nearby. The police had few leads to follow, although witnesses recalled a man on a green bicycle talking with Bella shortly before her death. In February 1920, a green bicycle was discovered in a canal close to the scene of the crime. The serial number led the police to Ronald Light, a teacher who lived with his invalid mother.

Light was tried for the murder of Bella Wright in June 1920. He had the good fortune to be defended by Sir Edward Marshall Hall, who made much of the fact that the evidence was largely circumstantial. Marshall Hall also emphasised the unusually small size of the deceased girl's head wound, suggesting that the bullet might have been fired at a distance and struck the girl accidentally. Light was placed in the witness box and admitted dumping the bicycle in the canal in order to spare his mother any anxiety should he be questioned in relation to the crime. He proved an excellent witness, and the jury acquitted him. The 'Green Bicycle' case remains officially unsolved.

It did provide the inspiration for two short stories. H. Trueman Humphries wrote 'The Green Bicycle Case', published in *The Strand* in February 1922. It warranted a mention in Edward Marjoribanks's 1929 biography of Sir Edward Marshall Hall for its intriguing solution to the mystery. Humphries concentrates on a curious aspect of the case—the discovery of a dead raven in a field near the scene of the crime. It was suggested at the time that the bird had gorged itself to death on the girl's blood. Humphries, however, suggests that a youth with a rifle had stalked and shot the raven; the bullet, having passed through its body, had struck the girl as she went by. The author had investigated the area of the murder before writing his version. Marshall Hall reputedly dismissed these fanciful suggestions.

In 1944, Vincent Starrett's short story, 'The Raven's Claw', appeared in the collection, *The Casebook of Jimmy Valentine*. John Hamilton Carter is Starrett's Ronald Light, accused of the murder of Barbara Stagg, whose body is discovered at the edge of a golf course in a Chicago suburb. As in the Light case, there is a green bicycle and a bird gorged with blood. Barbara, however, had been riding a horse when she was shot, and an attempt had been made to disguise the death as an accidental trampling by the frightened horse. Starrett's detective, Jimmy Lavender, after finding Carter's bicycle and tracing it to its owner, provides a solution that has its origin in the fictional location of the golf course rather than in the facts of the actual case.

FACTIONAL WORKS:
H. Trueman Humphreys, 'The Green Bicycle Case', in *Strand Magazine*, February 1922.
Vincent Starrett, 'The Raven's Claw', in *The Casebook of Jimmy Valentine* (New York: Gold Label, 1944).

FURTHER READING:
John Rowland, *Murder Mistaken* (London: John Long, 1963).

CAROLINE LUARD MURDER GB 1908

Major-General Charles Edward Luard and his wife Caroline lived at Ightham in Kent. In August 1908, the major-general found his wife's body in the summerhouse close to their home, Ightham Knoll. She had been shot through the head, and her purse and jewellery were missing. The time of death was ascertained from witnesses who had heard the shots. Two inquests followed. In each case, it was emphasised that General Luard had an alibi, as he had been identified in locations far from the scene of crime.

The general opinion was that the murder had been committed by an itinerant worker in the vicinity—the district was a popular site for hop-pickers from London. Despite this, General Luard became the victim of a slander campaign, receiving several poison-pen letters. Shortly after the second inquest, the General threw himself under a train. In a note to a friend he had written, 'I have gone to her I loved'. The murder remains officially unsolved.

Osbert Sitwell uses the Luard case as the starting-point for his short story 'The Greeting', published in 1924 in the collection, *Triple Fugue*. The wife of a retired army man is killed in a summerhouse hidden in the woods; a vagrant is suspected. To this point, Sitwell follows the facts of the 1908 murder. However, the victim in his version has been bludgeoned to death and is an invalid with a nurse (thus providing a love interest for the husband, and therefore a motive). A pet parrot accidentally reveals the murderer.

Closer to the case is Alan Brock's novel, *After the Fact* (1935), which presents the Luard murder in the form of a whodunit. Brook identifies the factual base for his novel in his foreword, adding that 'the murderer paid the penalty for another and later crime'. This intriguing statement suggests that Brook was aware of and believed the theory that the Luard murderer was John Alexander Dickman, hanged in 1910 for the killing of John Nisbet. Dickman was believed to have been associated with Mrs Luard via a plea for financial help that he had placed in the *Times*.

FACTIONAL WORKS:
Osbert Sitwell, 'The Greeting', in *Triple Fugue* (London: Grant Richards, 1924).
Alan Brock, *After the Fact* (London: Nicholson & Watson, 1935).

FURTHER READING:
Bernard Taylor and Stephen Knight, *Perfect Murder* (London: Grafton, 1987).

THE LYONS MAIL ROBBERY FRANCE 1796

In 1796 a regular mail-coach service was run between Paris and Lyons. On 27th April of that year, the coach leaving Paris carried seven million francs in paper currency bound for Napoleon's troops in Italy. When the coach failed to arrive at the village of Melun, a search was made. The abandoned vehicle was discovered on a side road; the courier and the post-boy had been killed and the money was gone. Four horsemen had been seen following the coach. Police arrested Etienne Couriol, who had stabled horses in Paris that matched the description of the mounts. Couriol also had a large amount of money in his possession that he could not account for.

Two of his fellow-lodgers, Charles Guenot and Joseph Lesurques, called at the Palais de Justice where Couriol was being held. All three were identi-fied as having been in the vicinity of the robbery. These three, along with several others who had also been arrested, were charged with the robbery and murders. The case against Lesurques was the weakest. When he was pronounced guilty along with the rest, Couriol admitted his own guilt but supported Lesurques's plea that he was innocent.

In jail, Couriol confessed that Lesurques had been mistaken for Jean-Guillaume Dubosq, who had murdered the courier. Dubosq was the same height as Lesurques, and although Lesurques was fair-haired while Dubosq was dark, Couriol claimed that Dubosq had worn a blond wig. Several prominent people believed Couriol's confession and appeals were made. They were rejected, however, and Lesurques was executed with the rest.

The authorities still pursued Dubosq, a known criminal, and he was finally arrested in 1800. His trial turned into a posthumous retrial for Lesurques, as the authorities now also claimed that Lesurques had been mistaken for Dubosq. The original witnesses could not agree that Dubosq, even with a blond wig, was the man they had seen four years ago. However, there was sufficient evidence to convict him as an accessory to the robbery, and he was duly found guilty and executed. Whether Lesurques was guilty or innocent is still a matter of debate.

The facts of the case were revived nearly sixty years later when the French dramatists Moreau, Siraudin and Delacour collaborated to produce the melodrama, *Le Courier de Lyons*. Their play was to provide the basis for three English dramas and a novel. In the French original, Lesurques and Dubosq were understood to be almost identical in appearance. Also, the ending was alternated on different nights. At one performance, the efforts of Lesurques's children and Dubosq's mistress would result in the unmasking of Dubosq as the villain, just as Lesurques is being led to the guillotine. At another, the inno-cent man would go to his death.

The principal feature of the play, which drew three of England's finest Victorian actors to it, was that Lesurques and Dubosq were played by the same performer. By the judicious exit of one character before the entrance of the other, the play provided an ambitious actor with two diverging performances in one drama. The three English versions—by Ben Webster in 1851, Edward Stirling in 1852 and Charles Reade in 1854 remained faithful to the action of the French original.

Reade's adaptation, *The Courier of Lyons*, originally with Charles Kean in the dual role, proved the most enduring. It was revised by the author for Henry Irving in 1877 as *The Lyons Mail*. This version also served for veteran Victorian actor Sir John Martin-Harvey, when he played the roles in 1930. Martin-Harvey's version found its way onto film in the same year, and the script was adapted as a novel entitled *The Mystery of the Lyons Mail* by crime writer Grant Edwards.

FACTIONAL WORKS:
[Charles Reade], *The Courier of Lyons* (London: T. H. Lacy, [1854]). (P)
Edward Stirling, *The Courier of Lyons* (London: S. G. Fairbrother, 1854). (P)
Ben Webster, *The Courier of Lyons* (London: John Dicks, [1897]). (P)
Grant Edwards, *The Mystery of the Lyons Mail* (London: Collins, [1930]).

FURTHER READING:
Rayner Heppenstall, *French Crime in the Romantic Age* (London: Hamish Hamilton, 1970).

FILM ADAPTATIONS:
The Lyons Mail, d. Arthur Maude. GB: Twickenham, 1930. Screenplay by H. Fowler Mear, based on the play by Charles Reade. Novelised by Grant Edwards as *The Mystery of the Lyons Mail*.*

A. M. CASE GERMANY? DATE UNKNOWN

This fascinating attempted crime, which inspired at least two works of fiction, was cited in Hans Gross's popular text-book, *Criminal Investigation*. Although not a criminal case *per se*, it was an obvious attempt at fraud and could have resulted in the death of an innocent person. 'A. M.' (Gross's name for the 'victim'), a grain merchant, was found shot through the head on the middle of a bridge over a stream. Police discovered that he had been previously drinking at an inn and had repeatedly displayed his full wallet.

Police arrested a vagrant who had also been there, although he denied all knowledge of the deed. Fortunately for him, the policeman in charge of the case spotted a mark on the wooden parapet of the bridge, close to where the body was found. He suspected that the mark was connected with A. M.'s death and ordered the stream to be dragged. A gun was discovered tied to one end of a cord; at the other end was a stone weight.

Further investigation showed that A. M. was in financial difficulties and that he had recently insured his life for a substantial amount. The investigating officer concluded that A. M. had committed suicide. He had shot himself while the stone weight hung over the bridge parapet. After his death, his fingers released the gun, the weight pulled it over the parapet (striking it as it went) and into the stream. Murder would be suspected, and the insurance company would have had to pay up.

Sherlock Holmes solved a fictional version of the A. M. case in 'The Problem of Thor Bridge', first published in the *Strand Magazine* in 1922, and later in *The Case-Book of Sherlock Holmes* (1927). Holmes investigates what appears to be the murder of the wife of an American gold-mining magnate at his estate, Thor Place. She had been found shot through the head, holding a note from her husband's secretary. The note contained details of a meeting on the bridge where she had been found. Like the policeman in the A. M. case, Holmes rescues the innocent secretary from a possible miscarriage of justice. Here the motive of the suicide is revenge rather than fraud.

Arthur Conan Doyle made no reference to the inspiration for his short story, although S. S. Van Dine credits the source for his 1928 novel, *The Greene Murder Case*. His detective, Philo Vance, is called in to investigate the case of Julia Greene's murder and the wounding of her younger daughter. The shootings seem to be the work of an interrupted burglar. Three more deaths ensue before Vance solves the mystery, after seeing a copy of Gross's book in the Greene family library. The murderer has used the book as a virtual manual, relying particularly on a skilful adaptation of the A. M. case.

FACTIONAL WORKS:
Arthur Conan Doyle, 'The Problem of Thor Bridge', in *The Case-Book of Sherlock Holmes* (London: John Murray, 1927).
S. S. Van Dine, *The Greene Murder Case* (New York: C. Scribner's Sons, 1928).

FURTHER READING:
Hans Gross, *Criminal Investigation* (London: Sweet & Maxwell, rev. ed. 1924).

JESSIE M'LACHLAN GB 1862

The Sandyford Mystery, as it is sometimes known, began on 7th July 1862. On that day, an accountant named John Fleming returned to his house in prosperous Sandyford Place in Glasgow. He was met at the door by his father, James, instead of the servant-girl, Jessie M'Pherson. His father told him that Jessie had not been seen in four days and that the door to her room was locked. After unlocking her door, the men found Jessie's body lying by her bed. She had been attacked with a butcher's cleaver. Bloody footprints were found around the room.

At first, James Fleming was taken into custody, but six days later police arrested Jessie M'Lachlan, another servant who had attempted to pawn some of the family silver. The bloody footprints were hers. At her trial for murder in September, Jessie was found guilty mostly on circumstantial evidence. James Fleming testified for the prosecution, and despite several suspicious and conflicting statements, was treated favourably by the judge.

Jessie's defence was 'that the murder alleged in the indictment was committed by James Fleming'. As the accused was not allowed to give evidence in those days, Jessie made a concluding statement that she had visited M'Pherson on Friday evening and discovered her wounded on the floor of her bedroom. M'Pherson had told her that Fleming Senior had tried to seduce her a few days before and that earlier that day he had quarrelled with her and struck her. Jessie M'Lachlan had tended the girl's wounds and when she had attempted to go for help, Fleming had killed M'Pherson. Jessie had been sworn to secrecy, the old man saying that he would disguise the murder as a break-in.

The judge treated M'Lachlan's statement with contempt, and sentenced her to death. However, many Glaswegians were struck by the cool demeanour of the accused, the poor showing of James Fleming in the witness-box, and the judge's obvious bias towards the latter. An inquiry was held into the findings of the court, and in November Jessie's death sentence was commuted to life imprisonment. In 1877, she was released from prison and emigrated to America, where she died in 1899.

Two novels have been based on the Sandyford Mystery. D. Erskine Muir's *In Muffled Night* (1933) is a close reconstruction, apart from the transfer of the action to contemporary Highgate in London. Muir's hero, Detective-Inspector Woods, pursues the murder case against Mary Spens (the fictional Jessie M'Lachlan), solving it after she gives her last statement in court.

The Dear Old Gentleman, a 1936 novel by George Goodchild and Bechofer Roberts, returns to the Scottish location while retaining a contemporary setting. Margaret Sampson is on trial for the murder of Bessie McIntosh; one witness is the 'dear old gentleman', Angus Aitken. The trial ends in a 'not proven' verdict, unique to Scotland (see MADELEINE SMITH). Local newspaper editor, Mr Wilberforce, with the aid of his staff, pursues the case after this unsatisfactory conclusion and learns the 'dear old gentleman's' secret.

FACTIONAL WORKS:
D. Erskine Muir, *In Muffled Night* (London: Methuen, 1933).
George Goodchild and Bechofer Roberts, *The Dear Old Gentleman* (London: Jarrolds, 1936).

FURTHER READING:
Christianna Brand, *Heaven Knows Who* (London: Michael Joseph, 1960).

PATRICK MAHON GB 1924

Patrick Mahon was an habitual criminal with a record of fraud, embezzlement and robbery. Although married with one child, he was having an affair with a typist, Evelyn Kaye. They shared a cottage along the stretch of Sussex coast known as the Crumbles. Emily believed that Mahon intended to leave his wife and go to South Africa with her. On April 12th 1924, Mahon drove down to the Crumbles to meet Emily; she was never seen alive again.

Mrs Mahon, suspicious of her husband's disappearances, found a cloakroom ticket in his jacket pocket and sent a friend along to Waterloo Station to collect whatever was being kept there. She found a gladstone bag containing a bloodstained knife and women's clothing. The police were informed and Mahon was arrested as he went to collect the bag. He claimed that the clothing belonged to Emily Kaye, whose body would be found in the cottage at the Crumbles. Sure enough, police discovered her dismembered body there.

At his trial for the murder of Emily Kaye, Mahon's defence was that he had argued with her, and during a struggle she had fallen and struck her head on a coal-skuttle. Discovering that she was dead, Mahon had dismembered the body with a saw in order to dispose of it. Prosecution pointed out that the coal-skuttle was undamaged, and that Mahon had bought the saw and knife used to dismember the body shortly before her death—thus proving premeditation. Mahon was found guilty and hanged in September 1924. An interesting coda which arose from the case was that due to problems with the recovery of the body, the 'Murder Bag' was introduced. It is still used by police to carry forensic instruments to the scene of a crime.

Established crime writer and criminologist, Marie Belloc Lowndes, used the Mahon case as the basis of her short story, 'Her Last Adventure', published in the 1928 collection, *Great Short Stories of Detection, Mystery and Horror*, edited by Dorothy L. Sayers. The tale is told by Eva Bude, who meets James Malton on a train. An affair begins and Malton takes Eva to his seaside cottage, 'The Folly', where they spend three days. During their stay, one room of the cottage remains locked. Eva returns to London, after deciding to marry another admirer. There she is informed that Malton had murdered his wife and hidden her body in the locked room at the cottage. Apart from the victim's relationship with the murderer, the plot mirrors the experience of Ethel Duncan, who had spent three nights with Patrick Mahon at his cottage, while the corpse of Emily Kaye was hidden in an adjacent room.

Austin Stone managed to bring the facts of the Mahon case together with those of the Hulten and Jones 'Cleft Chin' murder in his 1949 novel, *Blood Stays Red* (see relevant entry).

FACTIONAL WORKS:
Marie Belloc Lowndes, 'Her Last Adventure', in Dorothy L. Sayers, ed., *Great Short Stories of Detection, Mystery and Horror, Part 1* (London: Victor Gollancz, 1928).
Austin Stone, *Blood Stays Red* (London: John Gifford, [1949]).

FURTHER READING:
Gordon Honeycombe, *The Murders of the Black Museum, 1870–1970* (London: Hutchinson, 1982).

MARIA MANNING GB 1849

Maria Manning, a Swiss-born lady's maid, lived in Bermondsey with her husband Frederick. There she renewed her acquaintance with Patrick O'Connor, an Irish money-lender with whom she had lived on and off since 1846 (even after her marriage in 1847). In August 1849, O'Connor disappeared, after receiving a dinner invitation from Maria. Police questioned her about

O'Connor and left. When they returned later, Maria and Frederick had fled. The house was searched, and an excavation of the kitchen floor resulted in the discovery of O'Connor's body.

Maria was arrested in Edinburgh; her husband was finally apprehended in Jersey. At their trial in October 1849, each sought to throw suspicion on the other. It appeared that Maria had shot O'Connor through the head and Frederick had battered him with a chisel. They had then taken money, bonds and jewellery from his home. When they were sentenced to death, Maria stated, 'there is no justice and no right for a foreign subject in this country' (her foreign origins had resulted in a good deal of prejudice against her). The Mannings were executed in November before a large crowd. The fact that Maria wore black satin to the gallows made the material unfashionable for many years after.

Among the 50,000 spectators at the Manning execution was Charles Dickens, who was so horrified by the spectacle that he wrote a letter to *The Times* protesting at the barbaric nature of public hangings. It is generally accepted that Maria Manning served as the model for the character of Hortense in *Bleak House*, which he began writing two years to the month after the Mannings were hanged. The novel was serialised from March 1852 to September 1853, and was published in its entirety in 1853.

Certainly Maria's imperious demeanour informed that of Lady Dedlock's French maid in the novel. Hortense murders the lawyer Tulkinghorn, after he refuses her demands to find her new employment upon her departure from Bleak House, the Dedlock residence. Hortense's proud manner is demonstrated early in the novel. After Lady Dedlock takes the carriage home during a storm, 'without the least discomposure of countenance, [Hortense] slipped off her shoes, left them on the ground, and walked deliberately in the same direction [of her ladyship's coach], through the wettest of the wet grass'. Watching her go, one of the servants points out that 'she's mortal high and passionate'; when asked why she should walk barefoot through the rain water, he says prophetically that perhaps 'she fancies it's blood. She'd as soon walk through that as anything else, I think, when her own's up!'

FACTIONAL WORKS:
Charles Dickens, *Bleak House* (London: Bradbury & Evans, 1853).

FURTHER READING:
Albert Borowitz, *The Woman Who Murdered Black Satin* (Columbus: Ohio University Press, 1981).

MASSIE CASE USA 1932

A classic example of political intrigue affecting a trial, the Massie case created racial tensions in Hawaii that lingered for years, particularly between native Hawaiians and the large contingent of Navy personnel on the island. In 1931, after leaving a party by herself, Thalia Massie, the young wife of a Navy lieutenant was discovered dishevelled and bruised. Taken to a nearby hospital, she claimed to have been raped by a gang of two Hawaiians, two Japanese and one Chinese boy. The next morning, following arrests of several youths, she identified four of her assailants; a fifth youth was arrested shortly after. At the subsequent rape trial, the jury could not reach a verdict and the boys were freed.

Six days later Lieutenant Massie, together with two sailors and his mother-in-law, the socialite Grace Fortescue, kidnapped one of the Hawaiian youths, Joseph Kahahawai, to extract a confession from him. When police learned of the kidnapping, they apprehended a car seen at the site of Kahahawai's disappearance. Inside were the four abductors and the body of the Hawaiian.

At the subsequent murder trial, defence lawyer Clarence Darrow put in a plea of temporary insanity for Massie, who admitted to firing the fatal shot. A mixed jury handed down a verdict of manslaughter, and the four were each sentenced to ten years' imprisonment. This may have satisfied native Hawaiians, but servicemen and congressmen were furious. Demands for a presidential pardon were raised, and President Hoover phoned the Governor of Hawaii to discuss the situation. Finally, the four were held in custody for one hour in the court and then released; a sentence that did little to appease Hawaiians. The Massies were persuaded to leave the island. They divorced two years later.

Norman Katkov's novel, *Blood and Orchids* (1983), provides a new version of the case. Hester Murdoch, wife of navy lieutenant Gerald, is beaten by her lover, Lieutenant Bryce Partridge when he discovers she is pregnant. She is taken to hospital by four Hawaiian youths, where her mother, a wealthy pillar of the Hawaiian community named Doris Ashley, persuades her to accuse the four boys of rape to avoid the greater scandal.

The trial of the Hawaiians results in a hung jury and Murdoch kidnaps and murders one of the youths, Joe Liliuohe. Curt Maddox, the policeman in charge of the Murdoch case, is incensed when the Navy take Murdoch and his accomplices into protective custody. In the meantime, Bryce Partridge has been arrested in a drunken brawl, and Maddox notices a resemblance between the wounds of his assailant and those of Mrs Murdoch. As the tensions on the island increase, veteran lawyer Walter Bergman is assigned to Murdoch's defence and Maddox begins an affair with Bergman's young wife.

Hester collapses during the second trial and confesses the truth to naval officials. Partridge is thrown out of the navy, and the trial is brought to an abrupt end as the defendants are retained in custody for an hour. Murdoch, now aware of his wife's infidelity, commits suicide, and Maddox is left wondering whether Bergman's wife will leave the island with her husband.

Katkov is successful in his portrayal of Bergman, giving his fictional lawyer many of the traits and legal tricks associated with Darrow. Also successful is the sympathetic portrayal of Princess Luahine, last member of native Hawaiian royalty, who becomes involved in the defence of the four

Hawaiians. But the author provides every minor character with an overly detailed biography, padding out the story and thus dissipating the tension.

FACTIONAL WORKS:
Norman Katkov, *Blood and Orchids* (New York: St. Martin's Press, 1983).

FURTHER READING:
Theon Wright, *Rape in Paradise* (New York: Tower Books, 1966).

FLORENCE MAYBRICK GB 1889

Florence Chandler was born in Alabama. She married James Maybrick, an English cotton merchant, in 1881. They settled in Liverpool, where they raised two children. James was a hypochondriac and frequently took doses of arsenic as an aphrodisiac. He had a mistress, but when Florence reciprocated by taking a lover, they quarrelled violently and Florence was beaten. Shortly after, Maybrick's health deteriorated. He suffered violent bouts of sickness and diarrhoea and he died on 11th May 1889. His relatives, who had never been fond of Florence, virtually held her prisoner in her own house. She was arrested for murder when two large doses of arsenic were found in Maybrick's stomach.

At her trial in July 1889, the prosecution made much of Florence's purchase of flypaper; she maintained that the arsenic in the paper was used to prepare cosmetics. Her defence stressed Maybrick's hypochondria and the amount of drugs he took, suggesting that he had accidentally exceeded a dose. Unfortunately, Judge Fitzjames Stephens was not only fanatically puritan but was also showing the first signs of mental illness that would shortly send him to an asylum. He condemned Florence on moral grounds, and she was found guilty and sentenced to death. However, the sentence was commuted to life imprisonment and after fifteen years in jail, she returned to America. She died there in poverty in 1941. More recently, the Maybrick case has gained renewed interest with the discovery of Jack the Ripper's 'diary', which, if authentic, identifies James as the Ripper.

In 1926, Anthony Berkeley placed the Maybrick murder in a contemporary setting in the second of his Roger Sheringham detective novels, *The Wychford Poisoning Case*. In one of his first attempts at a psychological detective story (he was later to perfect the technique in his books written as Francis Iles. See entry on 'Herbert Armstrong'), Berkeley sets amateur sleuth Sheringham the task of proving the innocence of the attractive Mrs Bentley. She is accused of murdering her husband by arsenic poisoning. Other similarities to the Maybrick case lead one critic to call the book 'a clever reconstruction of a classic riddle'.

News of Florence Maybrick's death in 1941 attracted the attention of historical novelist Margaret Gabrielle Long. Under the pseudonym of Joseph Shearing, she reconstructed the case in her 1943 novel, *Airing in a*

Closed Carriage. The author acknowledges in a foreword that 'the theme, the central characters and incidents, [and] some parts of the legal speeches' are taken from the 1889 original. 'For the psychology that is at once the core of the story and the solution of the mystery' Shearing presents her own interpretation. As usual with Shearing's work, it is the psychological insight into the role of women in Victorian England that raises the novel above the level of much of her historical fiction.

May Tyler, the fictional Mrs Maybrick, is another cold, calculating 'heroine' in the mould of Laura Sarelle (see entry on 'John Donellan') and Lucille Clery (see entry on 'Duc de Praslin'). The short-lived mayfly that bears her name and appears symbolically throughout the novel suggests her wish for freedom, however brief. Prey to the whims of her elderly invalid husband and his vindictive brother, May yearns for happiness in the dreary confines of nineteenth-century Manchester. Unlike many of Shearing's major female characters, she is innocent of the charges brought against her, but she is found guilty. After the death sentence is commuted, she must suffer an extension of her closeted existence within her prison cell. Upon her release, she lives the remainder of her life in seclusion and abject poverty, as did her factual counterpart.

FACTIONAL WORKS:
[Anthony Berkeley], *The Wychford Poisoning Case* (London: Collins, [1926]).
Joseph Shearing, *Airing in a Closed Carriage* (London: Hutchinson & Co., [1943]).

FURTHER READING:
Bernard Ryan and Sir Michael Havers, *The Poisoned Life of Mrs. Maybrick* (London: Kimber, 1977).

FILM ADAPTATIONS:
The Mark of Cain, d. Brian Desmond Hurst. GB: GFD/Two Cities, 1947. Screenplay by Francis Crowdy, Christianna Brand and W. P. Lipscomb, based on the novel *Airing in a Closed Carriage* by Joseph Shearing.

EUPHRASIE MERCIER FRANCE 1886

In 1882, Edolie Menetret, a rich Parisian lady in her forties, made the acquaintance of Euphrasie Mercier, a shoe-shop proprietor. The following year, Mme. Menetret invited Mercier to become her housekeeper and companion, unaware of her friend's varied life prior to her appointment. The sixty-year-old Mercier came from a strict religious family. Three of her sisters suffered from mental disorders verging on religious mania. Euphrasie and her sisters had travelled the country in search of work and accommodation, but Euphrasie's eccentricity and her sisters' mental illness had always resulted in temporary situations.

In 1883, Euphrasie moved into Mme. Menetret's home, while her sisters stayed in apartments in Paris. Previously kind to her companion, Mercier suddenly became unsympathetic and overbearing. Mme. Menetret told a neighbour that her housekeeper was frightening her. She had asked Mercier to leave but the woman had refused. Shortly afterward, Menetret disappeared. Mercier announced that her employer had entered a convent, producing a scrawled note from Menetret stating that Mercier was to supervise her affairs from then on.

Mercier brought her sisters to the house, and by 1885, Mercier's niece and the illegitimate son of one of her sisters were also in residence. The two cousins fell in love and ran away, but not before they informed local authorities that they suspected foul play at the house. The garden was searched and the remains of Edolie Menetret were discovered in a dahlia-bed. Euphrasie Mercier was tried for murder in 1886. Due to the strong circumstantial evidence and her evasive replies, she was found guilty and sentenced to twenty years imprisonment, a life sentence considering her age.

Edward Percy and Reginald Denham transferred the Mercier case to the Thames marshes in their 1940 play, *Ladies in Retirement*. Ellen Creed, the housekeeper of retired actress Leonora Fiske, asks her employer's permission to invite her sisters to stay for a week. The sisters prove to be unbalanced and when they outstay their welcome, Miss Fiske orders them from the house. Creed strangles her mistress and conceals the body in a disused baking oven. When Albert Feather, Ellen's nephew, shows interest in the disappearance, events come to a head. Percy and Denham manage to create a modicum of sympathy for Ellen Creed, as she attempts to find a refuge for her eccentric family in an unsympathetic world.

Elbur Ford's novel, *The Bed Disturbed* (1951), is a more straightforward retelling of the case, restored to its French setting and the original names. Euphrasie, through her experiences in life, has developed a deep-seated hatred of men; and the irony of her destruction by her flamboyant, handsome nephew is not lost on the reader. Ford is the pseudonym of Eleanor Burford Hibbert, who also wrote as Victoria Holt and Jean Plaidy.

FACTIONAL WORKS:
Edward Percy and Reginald Denham, *Ladies in Retirement* (London: English Theatre Guild, [1940]). (**P**)
Elbur Ford, *The Bed Disturbed* (London: Werner Laurie, [1951]).

FURTHER READING:
H. B. Irving, *Studies of French Criminals* (London: William Heinemann, 1901).

FILM ADAPTATIONS:
Ladies in Retirement, d. Charles Vidor. US: Columbia, 1941. Screenplay by Edward Percy and Reginald Denham, based on their play.*

ANNETTE MEYER GB 1847

Meyer was a domestic servant working in Paddington. She suspected her lover, Henry Tucker of the Coldstream Guards, of having other affairs. In February 1847, she bought a gun from a shop in Regent Street, ostensibly to put down a vicious dog. The following day, she met Tucker as he was strolling along Birdcage Walk and shot him in the head. She was captured before she could escape. Tried at the Central Criminal Court, she was found guilty, but the jury recommended her to mercy. Their recommendation was not acted upon, however, and Annette Meyer was executed later that year.

From the bare bones of this case, Kathleen Kellow (one of the many pseudonyms of Eleanor Hibbert) fashioned a tale of rejection, blackmail and murder. *It Began in Vauxhall Gardens* (1955) tells the life story of Melisande St. Martin, the bastard daughter of a Cornish nobleman. Her father fetches her from the French convent which has been her early home, to England where she is to be companion to his legitimate daughter. Melisande is admired by the daughter's fiancé, who even after his marriage continues to pursue her. She falls instead for an exiled Frenchman; however, when his young charge is killed in a suspicious boating accident, she rejects him. Her father sends her to work in a London salon, but after her brother-in-law follows her, she quits her job and becomes maid to an overbearing old lady.

She meets a soldier who proposes to her. However, after he learns her father's identity and the circumstances of her birth, he threatens to blackmail the old Cornishman. Melisande kills the soldier with her employer's pistol and is arrested and tried for murder. Sentenced to death, she is reprieved by the efforts of the four people who had failed her previously: her father, her brother-in-law, the French exile and the owner of the salon.

Despite an interesting plot and plenty of opportunity for psychological insight, Kellow's style is poor. Unlike the novels of Joseph Shearing, there is no feel for historical period and little attention to detail (although the mid-nineteenth century setting, the location of the murder and the occupation of the two protagonists confirm the factual basis of the story).

FACTIONAL WORKS:
Kathleen Kellow, *It Began in Vauxhall Gardens* (London: Robert Hale, 1955).

FURTHER READING:
David Cargill and Julian Holland, *Scenes of Murder* (London: William Heinemann, 1964).

GILES MOMPESSON GB 1584–1651?

Mompesson was born in 1584. He married into the family of the powerful George Villiers, Duke of Buckingham. Elected to Parliament in 1614, he proposed a scheme to license inns and became one of the commissioners. He used his office to line his pockets, charging exorbitant fees and offering new licences to closed premises in return for large bribes. He was assisted in his enterprise by his crony, Sir Francis Michell. Despite his illegal dealings, Mompesson was knighted in 1616.

In 1621, a committee was set up to investigate the licensing procedures. Sir Giles was censured for his corrupt actions and placed under arrest. He escaped and fled to France. Although branded an outlaw, he managed to return to England and retire to Wiltshire, where he was known to be living as late as 1651.

Robert Ball, in the work quoted below, investigated the career of Giles Mompesson and his fictional counterpart, Sir Giles Overreach. Overreach appeared in Philip Massinger's 1633 play, *A New Way to Pay Old Debts*. Massinger's Mompesson is reduced to a usurer, although still attended by his Michell-like accomplice, here called Justice Greedy Woodcock. Overreach plots to get his nephew Frank Welborne into his debt, in the meantime using his wiles on his neighbours to steal their land from them. Welborne, however, turns the tables on his uncle and frees himself from Overreach's clutches. The final blow comes when Overreach's plans to marry his daughter into money are foiled by her love for Alworth, a page. With this, the comic villain goes mad.

There are further links between Mompesson and Overreach. Massinger's play, although published in the 1630s, appears to have been written around 1622–5, shortly after Mompesson's trial *in absentia*. Therefore, Mompesson must have been in the news at the time of the play's composition. We learn in Act II that Overreach is a criminal of sorts; one character asserts that he 'breaks through all law-nets, made to curb ill men, as they were cobwebs'. But it is in Overreach's dealings with the innkeeper, Tapwell that the principal link between the fictional and factual villain lies. Tapwell runs his inn as a brothel; Overreach uses his influence to allow it to stay open, presumably well-paid by Tapwell for his magnanimity—just as Mompesson was by other such corrupt innkeepers.

FACTIONAL WORKS:
Philip Massinger, *A New Way to Pay Old Debts* (London: E. P. for Henry Seyle, 1633). (P)

FURTHER READING:
Robert H. Ball, *The Amazing Career of Sir Giles Overreach* (London: Oxford University Press, 1939).

A. J. MONSON CASE GB 1893

Monson, a private tutor, made the acquaintance of Major Hamborough in 1890, when his seventeen-year-old son, Cecil needed tuition before joining the army. Hamborough had estates in various parts of the country, but had borrowed heavily on them and was on the point of bankruptcy. Monson took over Cecil's education, in the meantime wheedling his way into the major's property by trying to buy the interest in the estates. He insured Cecil's life for £20,000, borrowing the deposit from Cecil himself, and took him to Ardlamont, one of Hamborough's Scottish properties.

One day in August 1893, Monson and Cecil went boating. They returned from the outing soaking wet, the boat having overturned. The next day

Monson and a friend of his called Scott took his charge shooting. Monson and Scott returned alone, claiming that Cecil had accidentally shot and killed himself. Monson immediately put in a claim for the insurance, arousing the company's suspicions. Scott mysteriously disappeared and Monson was arrested and tried for both the attempted murder (the boating accident) and the actual murder of Cecil Hamborough.

At the trial in Edinburgh, the prosecution presented a weak case. The complex financial situation baffled the jury and the judge summed up favourably for Monson. The verdict was 'not proven' (see entry on 'Madeleine Smith'). In a curious epilogue, Monson brought an action for libel against Madame Tussaud's in London for displaying his wax effigy in the Chamber of Horrors, implying that he was guilty of the murder charge. He won the case but was awarded one farthing. Obviously the jury, while conceding the legal point, were expressing their own doubts on the verdict of Monson's original murder trial.

John Drummond's 1956 novel, *Proof Positive*, provides a contemporary version of the case. Francis is left as trustee to his nephew Adrian's fortune. Adrian's uncle and aunt, Jack and Lorna Macdonald Smith, invite him to a lonely island off the Scottish coast, not far from Ardlamont. It appears that Uncle Jack, Adrian's next-of-kin, intends to duplicate the suspected actions of Monson. The plot is not so much a whodunit as a will-they-get-away-with-it, with a neat ending worthy of detective fiction.

FACTIONAL WORKS:
John Drummond, *Proof Positive* (London: Duckworth, 1956).

FURTHER READING:
John Gray Wilson, *Not Proven* (London: Secker & Warburg, 1960).

WILMA MONTESI DEATH ITALY 1953

The body of young Wilma Montesi was discovered at the Tor Vaianica, along the coast south of Rome, in April 1953. The autopsy indicated that she had drowned. Italian newspapers from both the right and left suggested the possibility of a political scandal and murder. In 1954, right-wing editor Silvano Muto claimed in his newspaper that Montesi had died at a party in a nearby hunting lodge owned by the Marquis of San Bartolomeo, Ugo Montagna. The Foreign Minister, Attilio Piccioni, was said to be involved. When Muto was tried for libel, he revealed his source: Anna Maria Caglio, Montagna's former mistress.

Caglio, who was dubbed 'The Black Swan' by the press, told a story of political corruption on a high scale, involving drug-trafficking, bribery and murder. She said that Montagna was the head of a drug ring, and that the parties at his lodge had been orgies, at which drugs were freely circulated. She suggested that Piccioni had been responsible for Wilma's death.

On the basis of Caglio's testimony, Piccioni was tried three years later for 'culpable homicide' (criminal negligence) resulting in the death of Wilma Montesi. Montagna was tried for complicity, as was Saverio Polito, the Chief of Police in Rome. Caglio repeated her accusations in court, but Piccioni provided an alibi that he had been in Amalfi at the time of Montesi's death. Film actress Alida Valli came forward to support Piccioni, giving evidence that they had been together at the villa of film producer Carlo Ponti that night. It also transpired that Wilma Montesi had died a virgin, which threw doubt on the orgiastic parties she supposedly attended. Piccioni, Montagna and Polito were acquitted. The court's findings supported a verdict of accidental death, but as in the Starr Faithfull case, some still suspected an official cover-up.

In M. E. Chaber's 1956 novel, *A Lonely Walk*, his series detective, insurance investigator Milo March, flies to Italy to check on the supposedly accidental death of a girl on a beach. One character notes that the death 'has all the earmarks of another Wilma Montesi case', and the similarities multiply as March digs deeper. In addition to the political ramifications of the original case, the fictional investigation involves a possible fraud. The dead girl, Anna Maria Pericoloso, has been heavily insured and the policy includes a double indemnity clause. In the time-honoured tradition of the realistic crime novel, the hero comes in for some rough treatment before he finally solves the case, which does involve murder.

FACTIONAL WORKS:
M. E. Chaber, *A Lonely Walk* (New York: Holt Rinehart, 1956).

FURTHER READING:
Wayland Young, *The Montesi Scandal* (London: Faber & Faber, 1957).

ED MORRELL USA 1871–1946

It was not the criminal deeds of Ed Morrell that brought him to the attention of Jack London, but in effect the crimes committed against him in Fulsom Prison and San Quentin. Morrell was born in Pennsylvania but moved to California in 1891. There the situation was tantamount to civil war, as hired gunmen working for the railroad murdered settlers and the settlers themselves organised their own vigilante groups. Morrell belonged to one such gang, the California Outlaws. They would rob the railroad of its funds, making a point of leaving the passengers and mail untouched.

Spying between the two camps was common, and Morrell was soon working among the railroad gangs getting information for the Outlaws. When the head of the Outlaws, Chris Evans, was arrested, Morrell found himself assigned by his railroad 'employers' to help Evans in a fake escape, during which he would be shot. Morrell decided to help his leader to escape unharmed. They were betrayed; Evans was sentenced to life imprisonment, while Morrell, who would normally have received a few years for aiding an escapee, was framed for stealing the police chief's revolver and was also sentenced to life. He was moved to Fulsom Prison, where unknown to the authorities, the warden was on the railroad payroll.

Morrell was subjected to all manner of cruelties, including the infamous 'Fulsom Derrick', where the prisoner was hung with his arms behind his back and his feet barely touching the floor. Another mode of torture was the lime cell. The prisoner was placed in a recently hosed cell covered with a layer of lime. The chloride produced by the lime and water burned the throat and mouth of the inmate. Transferred to San Quentin, Morrell suffered long periods of solitary confinement and San Quentin's own refined torture, the 'overcoat'. This was a long sheet of thick canvas which was bound tightly around a prisoner, resulting in excruciating numbness and pain.

Fortunately for Morrell, the corrupt warden of San Quentin was replaced in 1903 by a more humane administrator. In 1908 Morrell received a pardon and left prison. He became a prison reformer, while lecturing and writing his autobiography, *The 25th Man*. He died in 1946, having seen the implementation of many of the reforms he had recommended and the elimination of many of the tortures he had endured.

One of Morrell's methods of withstanding torture, especially the 'overcoat', was a form of self-hypnosis in which he mentally left his body and dreamed of travelling through space and time. Meeting Jack London in 1912, he told the novelist of this technique. London, who wanted his fiction to 'put across a staggering punch against the whole damnable, rotten American Jail System', incorporated Morrell's experiences in his 1915 novel, *The Jacket* (British title. The later US edition was called *The Star Rover*).

Darrell Standing is the fictional Morrell, convicted of murder and implicated in a prison break. He undergoes similar tortures and learns to project himself through time and space. Much of the novel is taken up with his astral travels, although ample space is given to London's 'staggering punch' against the corrupt prison system. Although Standing can be seen as London's fictional Morrell, Morrell himself features as another character in the novel, together with his real-life fellow-convict, Jake Oppenheimer. London shows the two using the 'knuckle talk' (a form of coded rapping on walls and bars) that they had actually invented in prison years earlier.

FACTIONAL WORKS:
Jack London, *The Jacket* (London: Mills & Boon, [1915]). US title: *The Star Rover*.

FURTHER READING:
Carl Sifakis, *The Encyclopedia of American Crime* (New York: Facts on File Inc., 1982).

Rosemarie Nitribitt was born in 1933 in Dusseldorf. Early in her childhood, she was placed in care and lived in welfare houses until 1950, when she moved to Frankfurt. There she became a prostitute and moved up the social ladder, her clients the rich industrialists and politicians of the Rhineland. She earned around £1,000 a month, enough to buy a flat on the elegant Stift-strasse. She was praised by her clients, and was famous enough to be satirised by night-club comedians and singers. However, those who knew her well were amazed by her miserliness and her haughty airs, and believed her to be essentially a lonely person.

In the summer of 1957, Rosemarie developed what appeared to be a perse-cution complex; she believed she was being followed. She devised a pass-word when receiving phone calls and had a spy-hole, a hidden camera and a tape recorder installed in her flat. She also bought a gun, convinced that someone would try to kill her. On 1st November, her charwoman rang the doorbell and received no reply, apart from the barking of Rosemarie's poodle. The police were called. They broke down the door and found her corpse; she had been bludgeoned and strangled. Nothing had been stolen from the apartment except the film from the hidden camera and the tape from the recorder. It appeared that there had been no forced entry, which suggested that the murderer was someone well-known and trusted by the victim.

The police discovered Rosemarie's list of clients, which contained initials only, and began to scour the upper classes as well as the underworld for suspects. Shock waves ran through the rich, male business population of Frankfurt. Eleven men in high positions claimed that they had been black-mailed by Rosemarie. With no solution in sight, the press began to talk of a political cover-up. Heinz Pohlmann, a commercial salesman who had been friendly with Rosemarie, was the chief suspect for some time, and in 1960 was charged with the murder. However, he was acquitted at a subsequent trial. The case remains unsolved.

A year after the murder, Erich Kuby wrote the screenplay for a film about the case, which proved to be a *succès de scandale*. It was abhorred by the establishment in Germany, who tried exhaustively to prevent the film from being made. Despite attempts by the German Foreign Office to have it removed from the programme, it won the Italian Critics Prize at the Venice Film Festival. Kuby turned his script into a novel the same year, which was translated into English in 1959.

Rosemarie begins with a discussion amongst a group of businessmen, known as the Insulation Batting Cartel, over the progress of a secret rearma-ment deal specifically involving the design of a missile. One of their number, Hartog, picks up a prostitute, the eponymous Rosemarie. Soon he has her installed in a flat and is visiting her regularly. Rosemarie still continues to entertain other clients and makes the acquaintance of another Cartel member, Bruster. He is less perturbed by her professional pursuits than

Hartog—in fact, he helps Rosemarie streamline the running of her 'business' (one of the successes of Kuby's novel is his ironic comparison of Rosemarie's success with German post-war economic growth and affluence).

Soon Rosemarie is keeping detailed ledgers of her clients. A third Cartel member, Schmitt, persuades her to provide a service for his company's clients (who will use a secret password) and to install a tape recorder so that his firm can spy on them. Rosemarie's income increases with this new project, but she comes under pressure by the secret police to install a second listening device. It transpires that without her knowledge, her phone is also being tapped.

Rosemarie's life is becoming complicated. She tries to blackmail Hartog into marrying her, although his devoted sister attempts to warn her off. She has loaned money to an old client, and has to threaten him with legal action to reclaim her stake. It is then that Schmitt discovers the second listening device in her flat. The novel ends with the discovery of Rosemarie's body. Although there is no indication of the murderer's identity, several tempting clues are provided as to possible suspects.

FACTIONAL WORKS:
Erich Kuby, *Rosemarie* (London: Weidenfeld & Nicholson, 1959). First published in German, 1958.

FURTHER READING:
John Godwin, *Killers Unknown* (London: Herbert Jenkins, 1960).

FILM ADAPTATIONS:
The Girl Rosemarie, d. Rolf Thiele. Germany: Roxy, 1958. Screenplay by Erich Kuby, Rolf Thiele, Joe Herbst and Rolf Ulrich. Novelised by Erich Kuby as *Rosemarie*.

ROBERT NIXON USA 1938

Robert Nixon, a black Chicago youth with a history of criminal convictions, was arrested in 1938 for the murder of Florence Johnson. Police assumed that Florence had been killed after disturbing an assailant attempting to rob her home. They were intrigued by the similarity between her murder and a 1936 homicide in which the same weapon, a brick, had been used to bludgeon a woman. In the case of the earlier murder, the killer had used lipstick to scrawl 'Black Legion Game', the name of a right-wing racist group in Detroit, on a mirror found at the scene.

The Los Angeles police were also interested in the case. Several murders had been committed there between 1936 and 1938 by a brick-wielding assailant. During that period Nixon had been living in Los Angeles under the name of Thomas Crosby. He had been arrested several times for petty crime, and his fingerprints were still on file. These bore a similarity to those taken at the scene of the two Chicago murders.

Nixon stood trial in Chicago on one count of murder, although Los Angeles police had attempted to extradite him on a similar charge. He was originally to be defended by Joseph Roth of the International Labor Defense, but the National Negro Congress supplied a black lawyer for his trial. He was found guilty, and after several appeals was executed in 1939.

Nixon's case was in the news while Richard Wright was preparing the first draft of his masterpiece, *Native Son*. Intrigued by the details, Wright asked his friend Margaret Walker to send him newscuttings of the trial (this she did—'enough to spread all over his nine by twelve bedroom floor'). He later travelled to Chicago to do some personal research and to get a sense of the city's atmosphere for his novel. He incorporated features of the case and the trail into his developing plot, including the inquest reports, trial speeches and the racist press coverage (Nixon had been dubbed the 'Brick Moron' by the yellow press). His novel was published in 1940 to universal acclaim.

Native Son tells the story of Bigger Thomas, an underprivileged black man living in Chicago. He is given a job as a chauffeur to a rich white family, the Daltons, whose liberal-minded daughter, Mary and her Communist boyfriend Jan, patronise him insufferably. One night, while returning the drunken Mary to her house, he accidentally smothers her with a pillow to prevent being heard in her room. Bigger goes on the run after confessing to his girlfriend Peggy what he has done. When he realises that she might betray his trust he murders her too. He is tracked down, tried for Mary's murder and sentenced to death. Bigger concludes as he awaits his execution that the constraints, the bigotry and the poverty he has endured all his life are the principal reasons for his predicament'.

Wright adapted several specific incidents from the Nixon case. After the first murder, Bigger scribbles the word 'Red' on a mirror with a hammer and sickle under it. Also, Bigger's defence lawyer is Max (a fictional Joseph Roth), assigned by the Labor Defenders. He gives Bigger's plea a political and economic stance, leaving Bigger himself (and the incidents in his short life as described in the novel) to present the arguments of racism and bigotry in his defence.

The novel was successful enough for Wright and Paul Green to turn it into a play, staged and published the following year. The drama's ten scenes cover Bigger's appointment as a chauffeur, his accidental murder of Mary, his arrest during a gunfight with the police in which his girlfriend is killed, his trial and sentence. Wright was later to transfer the story to the screen— he starred himself as Bigger Thomas.

FACTIONAL WORKS:
Richard Wright, *Native Son* (New York: Harper & Bros., 1940).
Paul Green and Richard Wright, *Native Son* (New York: Harper & Bros., 1941). (P)

FURTHER READING:
Jay Robert Nash, *World Encyclopedia of 20th Century Murder* (New York: Marlowe & Co., 1994).

FILM ADAPTATIONS:
Native Son, d. Pierre Chenal. Argentina: ASF International, 1950. Screenplay by Pierre Chenal and Richard Wright, based on the novel by Richard Wright.

KATHERINE OGILVY GB 1765

Katherine Nairn married Thomas Ogilvy (sometimes spelled Ogilvie) in 1765, although her father, a prominent knight, felt his daughter had married beneath her. She moved to Ogilvy's house in Forfar, Scotland. Already in residence were Ogilvy's mother, his brother Patrick, who was a lieutenant in a regiment of foot, and three servants. They were soon joined by Anne Clark, a cousin of Thomas's who had been a prostitute and had once had an affair with Thomas's brother Alexander. An enmity developed between Katherine and Anne, and soon the cousin was spreading malicious rumours about Katherine's supposed adultery with Patrick.

After a family quarrel, Thomas ordered Patrick out of the house. Shortly after this, Katherine wrote to Patrick; she later claimed that she had asked him to send her some laudanum for her insomnia. Andrew Stewart, a brother-in-law, delivered the parcel from Patrick. Although he suspected that it contained poison, he did nothing apart from informing his mother of his suspicions. Thomas was taken ill and died two days later, exactly four months after his marriage. Before his death, he declared that he had been poisoned by his wife. Alexander then arrived from Edinburgh and accused Katherine and Patrick of incest and murder.

They were arrested and held in Forfar prison, prior to their trial in Edinburgh. In the meantime, Alexander and Anne Clark took possession of the property, selling some cattle under a false authority from Patrick. In court, the two accused were found guilty of the charges, despite the fact that the poisoning was never medically established. Patrick Ogilvy was executed in November 1765 (at the first attempt, he fell through the noose, and had to be hauled back up to complete the job). Katherine's execution was postponed until March of the following year, due to her pregnancy. She gave birth to a daughter in January. Shortly before the date of her execution, she escaped from the Tolbooth prison in Edinburgh and made her way to the continent. She was never re-apprehended.

There is still some debate as to the guilt of Katherine and Patrick, some writers suggesting a murder plot between Anne Clark and Alexander Ogilvy. Both factional treatments make Katherine the principal character. Winifred Duke, as in all her factional works, concentrates on the subsequent life of the accused murderer rather than on the deed itself. In her 1925 novel, *The Laird*, she focuses on Katherine Ogilvy's existence on the continent after her escape from Tolbooth prison. In Duke's version, Katherine is innocent of the murder and a new solution is provided to the case.

Jean Stubbs's 1970 novel, *The Case of Kitty Ogilvie*, is based on research carried out by Theodora Benson, who had intended to produce a non-fiction account of the case. Stubbs utilises Benson's work to provide a new theory and motive for the murder. She describes vividly the Ogilvy's squalid existence in the family's decaying manor house. To show the research that contributed to the novel, the reader is provided with a plan of the scene of the crime.

FACTIONAL WORKS:
Winifred Duke, *The Laird* (London: John Long, [1925]).
Jean Stubbs, *The Case of Kitty Ogilvie* (London: Macmillan, 1970).

FURTHER READING:
William Roughead, *Classic Crimes* (London: Cassell & Co., 1951).

WILLIAM PALMER GB 1856

Palmer was born and lived in Rugeley, Staffordshire. After obtaining his medical qualifications at St. Bartholemew's Hospital in London, he returned to his home town to set up as a doctor. He married, established a steady practice and inherited a small fortune from his father. However, his fortunate position gave him leave to satisfy his taste for gambling. Soon, members of his family began to die under mysterious circumstances. Five of his young children, including one of his many illegitimate offspring, his wife Annie, his mother-in-law and his brother all died within a short period of time. It transpired that the deceased were either Palmer's creditors or people insured by him, from whose deaths he would benefit. Amazingly, the doctor did not come under suspicion until the death of a man named John Cook.

In November 1855, Palmer attended Shrewsbury Races with Cook, a young friend who owned a horse called Polestar. The horse was entered in one race and won. Cook and Palmer had a drink to celebrate, during which Cook became violently ill. Palmer arranged to collect Cook's winnings and promptly used the money to settle some of his own debts. After buying strychnine and prussic acid, the doctor visited his sick friend and prescribed some pills. Cook died in agony. The young man's father-in-law became suspicious, and the police were called in.

In addition to an autopsy on John Cook, Palmer's wife and brother were exhumed, and surprisingly Palmer was allowed to attend their subsequent autopsies. Palmer was arrested for murder by poisoning. His trial was transferred to the Old Bailey, due to the local hostility toward him in Rugeley. He was found guilty on the overwhelming circumstantial evidence and returned to Stafford to be executed in June 1856.

One hundred years after the doctor's execution, the poet and novelist Robert Graves wrote a fictional defence of the Rugeley doctor. His novel, *They Hanged My Saintly Billy* (1957) set out to prove that Palmer, although a rogue and a thief, was not a murderer.

Graves suggests that the medical evidence against Palmer was of little use and the circumstantial evidence was in conflict. The novel takes the form of a series of interviews with the doctor's acquaintances and those involved in the case, interspersed with scenes from the trial. Graves believed that the Lord Chief Justice and the Attorney-General, both of whom were involved directly in the trial, were determined to obtain a conviction regardless of the facts. The author suggests that Palmer's wife committed suicide so that her insurance policy could save her family from debt.

Agreeable and engaging as the novel is, illustrated with contemporary engravings and containing a sizeable bibliography to demonstrate Graves's reliance on the facts, his case in defence of Palmer is still tenuous. One finishes the book with admiration for a well-constructed apologia, but still with a great deal of scepticism.

REFERENCE:
Robert Graves, *They Hanged My Saintly Billy* (London: Cassell & Co., [1957]).

FURTHER READING:
Giles St. Aubyn, *Infamous Victorians* (London: Constable & Co., 1971).

LEA AND CHRISTINE PAPIN FRANCE 1933

Lea and Christine Papin were born in Le Mans and educated at the Good Shepherd convent. Christine, the elder sister, had been abused by her alcoholic father at an early age. She had subsequently turned to her simple younger sister for affection, even sexual gratification. The sisters were inseparable, in fact they displayed worrying changes of mood if they were apart for any length of time. In 1926, they went into domestic service together. They were employed as maids to a solicitor, M. Lancelin, and his wife and daughter.

For seven years, the Papin sisters waited on the Lancelins. It later transpired that Mme. and Mlle. Lancelin were very fastidious and the girls had a difficult time pleasing them. On 2nd February 1933, while the solicitor was away from home, Lea and Christine turned on their tormentors and bludgeoned the mother and daughter to death. They then retired to their room, where they were apprehended by the police.

The sisters were tried in October of that year. Christine was sentenced to death, Lea to ten years hard labour. Christine's sentence was commuted to imprisonment, but she was declared insane shortly afterwards and moved to an asylum where she died within a year. Lea was paroled in 1942.

Jean Genet utilised the facts of the case in his play, *Les Bonnes*, staged and published in 1947. It went through two revisions before an English translation, *The Maids*, was published in 1956.

The drama concerns two sisters, Solange and Claire, maids to an employer referred to throughout the play only as Madame, whom they detest. They act out their intentions to murder her, each girl taking it in turn to play Madame, as the other assumes the role of her own sister. When Madame returns home, they put an overdose of tranquillisers in her tea, but she leaves to meet her lover without drinking it. Rather than be thwarted in their revenge, Claire—in the character of Madame—drinks the poisoned tea, thus ritualistically killing her employer.

Despite the misdirected murder, the plot has obvious parallels with the

Papin case. Like the Papins, the fictional maids are treated contemptuously by their employer and develop a hatred that moves toward homicide. Solange and Claire, like their factual counterparts, are involved in an incestuous lesbian relationship. At one stage, Solange expresses her desire to marry Claire. This echoes a statement made by Christine: 'I am convinced that in another life I ought to be the husband of my sister'.

A closer adaptation of the case can be found in Wendy Kesselman's play, *My Sister in This House*, staged in 1981. The plot follows Lea and Christine Lutton, maids to Mme. Danzard and her daughter Isabella. The sisters have been placed in service by their mother to keep her in money. Mme. Danzard's establishment is oppressive in the extreme—their employer is paranoid about the cleanliness of her home, following the maids' efforts with a rigorous inspection.

At first, Lea is the subservient sister, a simple teenager dependent on the dominant Christine. But as Christine becomes afraid that Isabella will take Lea away with her when she marries, the relationship between the sisters changes subtly. As with the Papins, there is a strong suggestion of incest. Christine's concern over Lea's possible departure is partly jealousy. After their roles are reversed, and Christine comes to depend on Lea, their work noticeably declines. When an iron blows a fuse, Christine has to protect her sister from the incensed Mme. Danzard. After years of oppression, they murder their two employers. The play ends with the result of their trial—Lea sentenced to imprisonment, Christine to death. Kesselman's drama was filmed in 1994, under the title *Sister, My Sister*.

FACTIONAL WORKS:
Jean Genet, *The Maids* (New York: Grove Press, [1956]). First published in French as *Les Bonnes*, 1947. (**P**)
Wendy Kesselman, 'My Sister in This House', in Gillian Hanna, ed. *Monstrous Regiment* (London: Nick Hern, 1991). (**P**)

FURTHER READING:
Raymond Rudorff, *Monsters* (London: Spearman, 1968).

FILM ADAPTATIONS:
The Maids, d. Christopher Miles. GB: Ely Landau/Cinevision, 1974. Screenplay by Robert Enders and Christopher Miles, based on the play by Jean Genet.
Sister, My Sister, d. Nancy Mecker. GB: Film Four International, 1994. Screenplay by Wendy Kesselman, based on her play *My Sister in This House*.

CHARLES PEACE GB 1879

Charles Peace had the perfect physique for his chosen profession of cat-burglar. His powerful, compact body was ideal for crawling through small spaces, his rubber features helped him in his disguises to escape the police. He settled in Darnall, near Sheffield in the 1870s, posing as a respectable picture-framer. In 1876, he shot and killed a policeman during a robbery;

two other men were charged with the murder, one of them sentenced to death for the crime.

Later in 1876, Peace killed his neighbour, Arthur Dyson. Peace had been having an affair with Dyson's wife, and when the husband objected, the burglar began to persecute the family. After murdering Dyson in a struggle, Peace fled to London, where he continued his criminal career. In 1878, during another break-in, he was caught after wounding a policeman. He was charged under a false name with attempted murder and placed in Pentonville Prison. While he was there, his true identity was discovered.

On the train back to Sheffield to stand trial for Dyson's murder, Peace managed to escape police guards by jumping through a window. He hit his head in the fall and was found unconscious by the track. Patched up by a police doctor, Peace had his preliminary hearing in his cell. His trial in February 1879 resulted in a verdict of guilty. Before his execution, Peace made a full confession, not only to Dyson's murder but also to the shooting of the policeman in 1876. The men who had been arrested in his place were pardoned.

Edgar Wallace used Peace's name and reputation, if little else, for his 1931 novel *The Devil Man*. Wallace's Charles Peace, an employee of a band of foreign criminals, has been assigned to steal the formula for a new kind of metal. His nemesis is Alan Mainford, who first rescues a nurse from Peace's clutches and finally brings Peace to justice at Leeds Assizes in 1879. The last few chapters in the novel, including Peace's escape from the train, his trial and execution, adhere most closely to the facts. *The Devil Man* was reprinted in 1932 under the title *The Life and Death of Charles Peace*, to cash in on its supposed basis in truth.

More authentic is John Cashman's novel, *Kid Glove Charlie* (1978). In his foreword, Cashman states that the story 'is based on facts, legends and half-truths'. He attempts a sympathetic portrayal of the criminal, the murders he commits are seen as accidental homicides. All the relevant details are given, including Peace's attempted escape from the train. The well-researched novel concludes with a glossary of slang terms used by criminals of the period and an appendix discussing aspects of Peace's genuine life story.

FACTIONAL WORKS:

Edgar Wallace, *The Devil Man* (London: Collins, [1931]). Reprinted as *The Life and Death of Charles Peace*, 1932.

John Cashman, *Kid Glove Charlie* (New York: Harper & Row, 1978).

FURTHER READING:

David Ward, *King of the Lags* (London: Elek, 1963).

SERAFINO PELIZZIONI CASE GB 1866

On Boxing Day 1865, a fight broke out in the Golden Anchor public house on Great Saffron Hill in London, between some of the local Italian community and a group of English customers. After a brief scuffle in the tap room, Michael Harrington was found stabbed through the stomach. An Italian picture-framer named Serafino Pelizzioni was apprehended. He was taken to the hospital where Harrington lay dying, and placed in a makeshift identity parade in which the wounded man identified Pelizzioni as his assailant. But Harrington refused to sign a document to that effect and died shortly afterwards. Nevertheless, Pelizzioni was arrested for murder.

At his trial in February 1866, the defence rested on Pelizzioni's claim that he had been mistaken for another Italian, and that the knife found in the taproom belonged to Gregorio Mogni, who was known to have participated in the fight. Witnesses for the defence stated that the accused had actually been called from another public house in order to stop the fight. After fifteen minutes' deliberation, the English jury found the Italian guilty.

A local businessman named Henry Negretti was convinced a miscarriage of justice had occurred. He traced Gregorio Mogni, who confessed to the murder, but the police would not act. Negretti hit on a unique method of reopening the case, by taking out a private prosecution against Mogni for the murder of Harrington. At Mogni's trial, the charge was reduced from murder to manslaughter, as Mogni claimed he had acted in self-defence. A sensation was caused when Pelizzioni, still under sentence of death, was called as a witness. Mogni was found guilty of manslaughter, with a recommendation for mercy, and was sentenced to five years' imprisonment.

The Home Secretary announced that Pelizzioni had won a stay of execution. A fortnight later, however, it was decided that he should stand trial a second time for the murder. By then not only were the sympathies of the court with the picture-framer, but also discrepancies in prosecution testimony at the first trial became apparent. This time, Mogni gave evidence in Pelizzioni's defence and the jury brought in a verdict of not guilty. After three appearances in a murder trial and almost two months in the condemned cell, Serafino Pelizzioni walked free.

When Anthony Berkeley's novel, *Trial and Error*, was published in 1937, certain reviewers took him to task over his interpretation of British law. In a subsequent edition, Berkeley stated that his basic premise had been devised from the Pelizzioni case. Berkeley's protagonist, Laurence Todhunter, is diagnosed by his doctor as having only a few months to live. He decides that his last act should be to murder the most repellent person he can find, 'in the service of humanity'. He selects Jean Norwood, a vitriolic actress, as the ideal victim and performs the deed without being suspected. However, when someone else is arrested for the crime, Todhunter persuades a colleague to take out a private prosecution against him for Jean Norwood's murder. In his story, Berkeley has used only the barest of details from the Pelizzioni case; the twists at the end of his novel are not founded in the true facts.

FACTIONAL WORKS:

Anthony Berkeley, *Trial and Error* (London: Hodder & Stoughton, 1937).

FURTHER READING:
Richard S. Lambert, *When Justice Faltered* (London: Methuen, 1935).

ARMAND AND LEON PELTZER BELGIUM 1882

The three Peltzer brothers—Leon, James and Armand—were born in Germany but were naturalised as Belgian citizens. Armand, the eldest, had several business concerns in South America; Leon and James were exporters based in Antwerp. In 1873, their export business hit financial difficulties. They were rescued with the help of Armand and his lawyer friend Guillaume Bernays. In the meantime, Armand had fallen in love with Bernays's wife, Julie, but was warned off by the lawyer himself. He called on Leon to help him resolve the situation and together the brothers planned what they thought would be a perfect murder.

In January 1882, an Englishman named Henry Vaughan met Bernays to discuss a business venture. Bernays's body was later discovered in a flat in Antwerp; he had been shot. The police received a letter from Vaughan stating that the lawyer had accidentally killed himself. Although a reward was posted for Vaughan, the police also investigated Bernays's colleagues. They became suspicious of the Peltzer brothers when it was noticed that there were similarities between Leon's handwriting and that of the mysterious 'Vaughan'. Armand and Leon were arrested.

Leon accepted his fate and confessed to the murder. Both brothers were found guilty and sentenced to death, although this was commuted to life imprisonment. Armand died in prison within three years, while Leon was released in 1912. Ten years later, he threw himself into the sea at Ostend. It is said that the carpet from the Antwerp flat in which Bernays had been killed was sold following the murder, found its way to the house of a farmer near Ostend, and was subsequently used to cover Leon's drowned body.

In Kathleen Kellow's novel, *The Call of the Blood* (1956), the murder is seen as the direct consequence of a strong filial bond between Hansi and Emil Kritchner. Hansi is haunted by an incident in his childhood, when he was set upon by a group of bullying children and almost beaten to death. His brother, Emil came to his rescue. From that moment, Hansi worshipped Emil and swore to help him in his time of need. When Emil falls for Corinne Fernard, he persuades his younger brother to help him dispose of Corinne's husband. Even at their trial, Hansi tries to except full blame for the murder. Emil dies in prison and Hansi, on his release, commits suicide to be reunited with him.

FACTIONAL WORKS:
Kathleen Kellow, *Call of the Blood* (London: Robert Hale, 1956).

FURTHER READING:
Leonard Gribble, *Famous Feats of Detection and Deduction* (London: G. G. Harrap & Co., 1933).

VINCENZO PERUGGIA FRANCE 1911

On 21st August 1911, the Louvre was closed for cleaning. The following morning, a guard noticed that the *Mona Lisa* was not in its position in the Salon Carré. He assumed that it had been taken away for photographing. When the picture still had not returned in the afternoon, he reported it as missing. Police searched the museum and discovered the painting's frame on a staircase; the painting itself had disappeared. The newspapers had numerous theories: it was a practical joke, the work of a madman, an attempt to blackmail the government, a theft by a discontented employee.

The Sûreté was flooded with sightings of the missing picture. The director of national museums was dismissed, as was the chief attendant at the Louvre, and several guards were disciplined. The poet Guillaume Apollinaire was arrested in connection with the robbery (he had been indirectly involved in the theft and return of two statuettes stolen from the Louvre in 1907) but was soon released. Then in November 1913, an Italian art dealer named Alfredo Geri, received a letter from Paris. The correspondent, referred to only as 'Leonard', offered Geri an opportunity to buy the *Mona Lisa* for 500,000 lira. As Geri met Leonard in Florence and was shown the painting, the police arrived and Leonard was arrested. It transpired his real name was Vincenzo Peruggia, an Italian who had worked as a contractor at the Louvre. He claimed that he had stolen the painting solely for patriotic reasons: to return it to Italy.

In fact, the French police had questioned Peruggia at the time of the theft, but had not taken his fingerprints. Had they done so, the two-year search for the missing painting could have been avoided. Peruggia was tried in Florence for the theft of the *Mona Lisa*. He was sentenced to a year's imprisonment, but a month later his lawyers appealed on medical grounds. The judge reduced the sentence to seven months—the period Peruggia had spent in prison since his initial arrest. He was released and returned to the room at the hotel where he had met Geri. In the meantime, the establishment had changed its name—to *La Gioconda!*

Martin Page's 1984 novel, *Set a Thief*, suggests a more intricate story behind the theft. In Page's version, the robbery is the brainchild of American millionaire J. Pierpont Morgan, who persuades master-thief Adam Worth (a genuine, if obscure, character) to steal the painting for a fee of five million dollars. The novel follows Worth's painstaking methods in planning and executing the crime. Vincenzo Peruggia himself eventually appears to take credit for the crime, for the same reason as he did in reality—to be considered a hero in his native country. Page provides a twist in the end when the painting is restored to the Louvre—or is it?

Three years after Page's book was published, Wolf Mankowitz produced his version of the case, *Gioconda*. Like Page, Mankowitz mixes real and fictional characters and events. Among the likes of Peruggia, Picasso, Apollinaire, Proust and Freud, the author places Daniel Lavine, an imaginary

British art dealer who acquires the painting shortly after its theft. Lavine's travels with the *Mona Lisa* are interspersed with both factual and fictional events associated with the painting's disappearance. Once again, the novel ends with the suggestion that the original was never returned to the Louvre.

FACTIONAL WORKS:

Martin Page, *Set a Thief* (London: Bodley Head, 1984). US title: *The Man Who Stole the Mona Lisa.*

Wolf Mankowitz, *Gioconda* (London: W. H. Allen, 1987).

FURTHER READING:

Milton Estrow, *The Art Stealers* (London: Millington, 1975).

WILLIAM PIERCE GB 1857

In 1854, William Pierce, a disreputable character with a criminal record, was working as a clerk in a betting shop. It was during the Crimean War, when shipments of gold were regularly sent to the continent. Pierce, who had formerly worked as a ticket printer for the South Eastern Railway, hit on the idea of robbing one such shipment. He brought three more men into the scheme—Edward Agar, a safecracker and acquaintance of 'Jim the Penman' (see entry on 'James Saward'), and Tester and Burgess, two employees of the South Eastern Railway. The accomplices knew that the gold passed from London to Folkestone by train in the guard's van and that two keys were needed to open the safe.

They started to watch the route and wait for their opportunity. It is an indication of their thorough planning and patience that their surveillance lasted one year before the robbery itself took place. Ironically, when two of the keys were lost, the authorities decided to change the locks, and one of the newly-prepared keys found its way into Tester's hands long enough for Agar to make a copy. The second key was copied during a slack period at the Folkestone booking office. When the clerk was absent, Pierce took the key from its cupboard and passed it to Agar, who took an impression; the two crooks disappeared before the clerk returned.

Agar managed to travel down in the guard's van with Burgess, the guard on the route, to test the rough copies and file them until they opened the safe smoothly. They were now ready for the robbery. Having estimated the largest amount of gold they could carry, the team prepared bags of lead shot to the appropriate weight and had them taken into the guard's van at London. Agar slipped into the van and opened the safe while the train was speeding towards Folkestone. Gold and shot were swapped, and the bags of gold were passed to Tester who was waiting at Redhill station.

During the rest of the journey to Folkestone, other valuables were stolen and replaced with lead shot. The 'gold shipment' was taken out at Folke-stone while the robbers hid in a corner of the van. They then travelled to

Dover and left the train with their bags of swag. The theft was not discovered until the cases were weighed at Paris and the lead shot was discovered.

The robbers would never have been apprehended if Agar had not been arrested for passing a forged cheque. To help him out of his predicament, his mistress Fanny Kay went to Pierce for Agar's share of the money. However Pierce, through greed or suspicion, refused to part with it. Kay went to the authorities with her story. When Agar heard of Pierce's treachery, he did the same. Pierce, Burgess and Tester were arrested and tried at the Old Bailey in January 1857, eight months after the robbery. Tester and Burgess were found guilty of theft from their employer and were transported for fourteen years. Because he was not an employee of the railway, Pierce received the lesser sentence of two years for larceny; the judge insisted, however, that three months should be spent in solitary confinement.

American novelist Michael Crichton dressed up the facts for his 1975 novel, *The Great Train Robbery* (the subsequent film and paperback edition were called *The First Great Train Robbery* in the UK to distinguish it from the notorious 1963 heist). In Crichton's version, Pierce is a more mysterious and affluent villain than his factual counterpart, moving in high circles frequented by ministers and bankers. The fictional robbers in this instance need to find four keys to open the one safe—two in a cupboard at London Bridge Station, one in the possession of the senior partner of the bank responsible for the shipment, and the fourth around the neck of the general manager of the bank.

To obtain the first two keys, Pierce has to break a cat-burglar, Clean Willy Williams, out of Newgate. For the other keys, he must tempt the two guardians through gaming and women. As for the robbery itself, Agar must hide in a coffin to travel in the guard's van, as the authorities will allow no passengers. Pierce has to clamber along the roof of the speeding train from his compartment to help Agar open the safe and throw the gold out to their waiting accomplice.

All this makes for an enjoyable, if far-fetched, romp. Crichton employs genuine Victorian criminal slang, credible scenes of the sporting and sexual lowlife of the period—including a stomach-churning description of a ratting match and an amusing seduction at a brothel—and a sardonic view of corrupt gentility. The author relies heavily on Kellow Chesney's fascinating history, *The Victorian Underworld* (1970), which contains much of the criminal minutiae found in the novel. Crichton scripted and directed a film version of his book, which loses none of the exhilaration of the original.

FACTIONAL WORKS:
Michael Crichton, *The Great Train Robbery* (New York, A. A. Knopf, 1975).
UK paperback title: *The First Great Train Robbery*.

FURTHER READING:
George Dilnot, ed., *The Trial of Jim the Penman* (London: Geoffrey Bles, 1930). Also contains the trial of Pierce and his associates.

FILM ADAPTATIONS:

The First Great Train Robbery, d. Michael Crichton. GB: UA/Starling, 1978. Screenplay by Michael Crichton, based on his novel.

DUC DE PRASLIN FRANCE 1847

In 1824, Charles-Louis-Theobold, Marquis (later Duc) de Praslin, married Alatrice-Rosalla-Fanny Sebastini, daughter of a Napoleonic general. In 1841, to help with their growing family (they eventually had nine children), they appointed a governess named Henriette Deluzy-Desportes. She was the illegitimate granddaughter of a baron and the daughter of a soldier. Her introduction into the Praslin household was to create tensions in the already disintegrating marriage.

The Duke was intent on distancing his wife from her children (there had been rumours of the Duchesse's lesbian affairs) and Henriette became a second mother to them. Whether she was ever the Duc's mistress remains unknown, but he definitely spent more time with her and the children than with his wife. The first four years of Henriette's employment were fraught with accusations and tantrums from the Duchesse. In 1846 the situation seemed to be resolved when she extended the hand of friendship to her governess.

However, the next year, Henriette was advised by the Duchesse's confessor to leave the family, or the Duchesse would instigate divorce proceedings. The Duc was also warned; if the Duchesse won her divorce, she would almost certainly receive custody of the children. So Henriette left on 17th July to take up a post at a school. The next week the Duc visited her with two of the children—it was to be their last encounter.

In the early hours of 18th August, the Duc entered his wife's bedroom with a rope, a pistol and a knife. He had prepared the ground by removing the bolts to the door leading from his wife's chambers to his own and securing all other entrances. When he left the room, the Duchesse was dead: she had thirty stab wounds in her body and had been bludgeoned with the pistol butt and a brass candlestick. However, her screams had aroused the household.

The Duc was quickly taken into custody and questioned. A commission of peers was set up for his trail, but before they could commence, he swallowed a dose of arsenic. He lingered on for six days and died on the day of his wife's funeral. Henriette Deluzy-Desportes was herself arrested and interrogated, but after three months was discharged. In 1849, she married a Presbyterian minister, Reverend Henry Field and left France for America. She died in 1875, aged sixty-three.

In 1932, the prolific novelist Joseph Shearing produced a fictional account of the case in *Forget-Me-Not*; the U. S. title was *Lucille Cléry*. The novel begins as the unscrupulous Lucille, the illegitimate daughter of a Frenchwoman, is rejected by her English lover. She drowns her sorrows in laudanum and flicks through the book of sketches entitled *Forget-Me-Not* that her lover has left her. She changes her name to Mademoiselle Debelleyme to take up a post as governess to the children of the Duchesse du Boccage. On meeting the Duc, she is shocked by his resemblance to her former lover. He gives her *carte blanche* in the running of the household, and a trust soon develops between them.

The Duchesse is nervous and hysterical. She is prone to suicide attempts; following one such incident in which the Duc is injured, he declares his love for Lucille. The jealous Duchesse has the governess dismissed, after which Lucille tries to persuade the Duc to divorce his wife. As he is a staunch Catholic, he refuses. However, he proposes a permanent method of disposing of his wife. After the Duc commits the murder, Lucille is arrested as an accomplice; she is released following the Duc's suicide. She leaves France in the company of an unexciting American pastor Nathaniel Meadows, just as the ruling House of Orleans whom she detests flees the country. In America, her tedious hours are spent compiling a book of Parisian sketches; her husband suggests that they be published under the title of *Forget-Me-Not*.

As in her other novels, Shearing paints a convincing portrait of an ambitious, vindictive woman whose plans affect all around her. The details of ninteenth-century France are credible, particularly her description of the corrupt and indolent House of Orleans.

Shearing's interpretation of Henriette's character could not be more different from another treatment of the Praslin story. Rachel Field was already a distinguished children's author and historical novelist when she published her 1938 novel, *All This And Heaven Too*. The book was an immediate best-seller, prompting an equally successful film version two years later. The author bases her novel on her family: grandfather Matthew, who with his brother Cyrus laid the first transatlantic cable; great-grandfather David, an author and Congregational minister; great-uncle Henry, writer, editor and Presbyterian minister. But chiefly the novel concerns great-aunt Henriette, who as Mlle. Deluzy-Desportes featured so prominently in a French *cause célèbre*.

This fictional biography of Henriette traces her life from 1817, as a headstrong girl making her way through post-Napoleonic France, through her involvement in the Praslin case, to her death in New York in 1875. The portrait is much idealised, with Henriette seen as the innocent party in the murder of the Duchesse de Praslin. The Duchesse is the real villain of the piece—hysterical, half-insane with jealousy and making her stoical husband's life a misery.

The success of the French scenes overshadows the second half of the novel, when the action moves to America. However, the author populates both parts with factual characters apart from her relatives, including the French House of Orleans and the English House of Hanover and American celebrities such as Harriet Beecher Stowe, Ralph Waldo Emerson and Samuel Morse. Some of the facts of the case were obtained directly from her Aunt Claire, who had been raised by Henriette herself.

FACTIONAL WORKS:
Joseph Shearing, *Forget-Me-Not* (London: William Heinemann, 1932). US title: *Lucile Cléry*.
Rachel Field, *All This and Heaven Too* (New York: Macmillan, 1938).

FURTHER READING:
Stanley Loomis, *A Crime of Passion* (New York: Lippincott, 1967).

FILM ADAPTATIONS:
All This and Heaven Too, d. Anatole Litvak. US: Warner, 1940. Screenplay by Casey Robinson, based on the novel by Rachel Field.

EDWARD WILLIAM PRITCHARD GB 1865

Pritchard was born in 1825. Following his medical studies, he progressed from naval surgeon to a doctor with a private practice in Yorkshire. In 1850, he married a young Scottish lady, Mary Taylor and in 1860 they moved to Glasgow. A liar and a braggart, Pritchard alienated his medical colleagues. In 1863, his house was partially destroyed in a fire in which a servant girl died. The insurance company had their suspicions, but were forced to meet his claim. In 1864, Pritchard's wife discovered that the doctor had had an affair with another servant-girl, made her pregnant and performed an abortion.

In November of that year, Mary Pritchard became ill. She left for her family in Edinburgh where made a recovery, but as soon as she returned to Glasgow her sickness resumed. Her mother arrived to nurse her daughter, but was soon suffering herself from bouts of sickness. The mother died in February 1865. A Dr Patterson was called on to provide a death certificate, but refused to do so; Pritchard signed it himself, giving the cause of death as apoplexy. Then Mary died in March of that year. Again, Pritchard supplied the death certificate, giving the cause as gastric fever. His hypocrisy knew no bounds—he had the lid of his wife's coffin removed so he could kiss the corpse.

While Pritchard was in Edinburgh organising Mary's funeral, the Glasgow police received an anonymous letter accusing the doctor of murder. He was arrested on his return and the bodies of Mrs Pritchard and Mrs Taylor were exhumed. Antimony and aconite were discovered in the corpses. Pritchard stood trial for murder in July 1865. His defence lawyers tried to shift the blame for the deaths onto the servant-girl whom Pritchard had seduced. However, the jury found the doctor guilty. Pritchard was hanged in Glasgow after confessing to the murders—the last public hanging in Scotland.

Sarah Campion transferred the details of the Pritchard murders to Australia for her 1946 novel, *Dr. Golightly*. Golightly has escaped to Australia after committing a murder in London. He, his wife and her mother take on two sisters, Rachel and Bella, as servants. Bella soon dies in circumstances reminiscent of the death of Pritchard's servant in 1863. A third sister, Catherine, arrives to comfort Rachel, who has become an alcoholic. She proceeds to exact revenge on the doctor by poisoning his wife and mother-in-law. The doctor is suspected; two more murders occur and Golightly returns to England before the intricate mystery is eventually resolved.

The story of Pritchard also appealed to Glaswegian playwright, James Bridie. In his play, *Dr. Angelus* (1949), Bridie focuses on young Dr Johnson who becomes the partner of the elderly doctor of the title. When Angelus's mother-in-law falls ill, the attending specialist warns Johnson to be wary of the old doctor. The woman dies and Angelus persuades Johnson to sign the death certificate, giving cause of death as gastritis. After one of Angelus's patients also tells Johnson of her suspicions, he begins to also suspect his partner.

When Mrs Angelus eventually becomes ill, Angelus plies Johnson with whiskey to prevent him from saving her. While he is drunk, Mrs Angelus dies. Before Johnson can go to the police, they arrive to investigate Angelus's insurance claim on his mother-in-law. Angelus breaks down and confesses. Johnson fears that he will be arrested as an accessory, but the police realise that he has been duped by the older man.

Elbur Ford's 1950 novel, *The Flesh and the Devil*, is a more straightforward re-telling of the Pritchard case. The author's preface confirms the basis of the plot, and the narrative contains no derivations. Ford's main concern is the character of the hypocritical, self-obsessed, murdering doctor.

FACTIONAL WORKS:
Sarah Campion, *Dr. Golightly* (London: Peter Davies, 1946).
James Bridie, 'Dr. Angelus', in *John Knox and Other Plays* (London: Constable & Co., 1949). (**P**)
Elbur Ford, *The Flesh and the Devil* (London: Werner Laurie, 1950).

FURTHER READING:
Richard T. Altick, *Victorian Studies in Scarlet* (London: J. M. Dent & Sons Ltd., 1972).

ETHEL PROUDLOCK KUALA LUMPUR 1911

On the night of 23rd April 1911, Kuala Lumpur police were called to the house of a teacher named William Proudlock. There on the veranda they found the body of William Steward, a tin-mine manager; he had been killed with six shots from a Welsley revolver. Mr Proudlock's wife, Ethel, claimed that Steward had called at the house while her husband was absent and tried to rape her. She had shot him in self-defence.

Ethel Proudlock was tried for murder in Singapore. She still maintained that Steward had tried to rape her, although the prosecution insinuated that Steward was Ethel's lover and that she had killed him in a fit of jealousy over his Chinese mistress. They made much of the fact that she had pulled the trigger not once, but six times. Ethel was found guilty of murder and sentenced to death. Local residents sent petitions to Britain in an attempt to procure a reprieve. She received a free pardon and left Kuala Lumpur to return to England. Unfortunately, the weeks of the trial had taken their toll and she died in an asylum.

William Somerset Maugham heard of the case from a local lawyer,

Courtenay Dickerson, and adapted it in his short story, 'The Letter' (collected in a 1926 publication and subsequently produced as a play the next year). Maugham added to the facts the device of a letter written by Leslie Crosbie (the Ethel Proudlock character), inviting Hammond to her house on the night of the murder. Joyce, Leslie's lawyer, is persuaded to buy the letter from Hammond's Chinese mistress to prevent it being used as evidence in the trial. Her husband supplies the money for the letter's purchase, although he isn't aware of its contents or of his wife's infidelity. Neither Crosbie nor Joyce know until the end that Leslie had killed Hammond in cold blood and not in self-defence.

In Maugham's version, Leslie is found not guilty. There is a justice of sorts, as she intends to stay with her forgiving husband in a loveless marriage, still in love with the man she killed. Evidently, Maugham took many of Joyce's characteristics from Dickerson, and sent a copy of the story to Dickerson's wife acknowledging the fact. The subsequent play, although faithful to the action of the short story, changes the focus from Joyce to Leslie herself; she accompanies Joyce to meet Hammond's Chinese mistress in one of the principal scenes—the purchase of the letter. This no doubt reflects the fact that the legendary Gladys Cooper played Leslie in the original production. Cooper's performance ensured that *The Letter* ran for over three hundred performances.

A final point of interest: the 1940 film version of the play ends with Leslie, played by Bette Davis, being murdered by Hammond's Chinese mistress. Hollywood could not allow a proven adulteress to get away scot-free.

FACTIONAL WORKS:

W. Somerset Maugham, 'The Letter', in *The Casuarina Tree* (London: William Heinemann, 1926).

W. Somerset Maugham, *The Letter* (London: : William Heinemann, [1927]). (P)

FURTHER READING:

Ted Morgan, *Somerset Maugham* (London: Jonathan Cape, 1980).

FILM ADAPTATIONS:

The Letter, d. William Wyler. US: Warner, 1940. Screenplay by Howard Koch, based on the play by W. Somerset Maugham.

SØREN QUIST DENMARK 1625

Søren Jensen Quist was born in Aalso. He studied for the clergy and became parson of the town of Vejlbye around 1600. Although reasonably popular there, the parson made an enemy of Jens Mikkelsen, an old man whose proposal to marry Quist's daughter was met with scorn and derision by the Quist family. In 1607, Quist's wife, Irene travelled to the fair at the nearby town of Grenaa, taking with her a pair of oxen driven by herdsman Jep Skade and Jesper Hovsgaard. The latter was not only one of the parson's servants but also Mikkelsen's uncle. After completing her business, Mrs Quist could not find Hovsgaard and made her own way home. The servant was never seen again.

Soon after, rumours began circulating around Vjelbye that Parson Quist had murdered Hovsgaard. One source of these rumours was Jep Skade apparently encouraged by Mikkelsen himself. He was pressed to make an official accusation, but when the matter came to court in 1612, he swore that he knew nothing of Hovsgaard's disappearance and exonerated the accused parson.

There the matter rested until 1622, when workmen digging in a field belonging to Quist unearthed some human bones. Quist had the hole filled, but again the rumours began. Mikkelsen once more demanded an enquiry and in 1625 Søren Quist found himself arrested for murder. The principal witness for the prosecution was Jep Skade, who contrary to his evidence in court thirteen years ago, now related another story.

According to his new account, Jesper Hovsgaard did return home with Mrs Quist late at night. The parson had flown into a rage at the lateness of their arrival, had struck the servant with a pewter mug behind the ear and continued to batter him until Hovsgaard died from his wounds. Parson Quist and his brother had buried the body in the field. Other evidence appeared that seemed to support the story and Quist was found guilty. He was executed in 1626, nineteen years after Hovsgaard's disappearance.

In 1829, the Danish poet and short story writer, Steen Steensen Blicher, published his novella, *Praesten i Vejlbye* (translated in 1928 by Hanna A. Larsen as *The Parson of Vejlbye* and included in her 1945 anthology of Blicher's work, *Twelve Stories*). Blicher's tale, characteristically Nordic in its pathos and stoicism, is narrated in two parts. The first comprises the diary of a young judge in the district who falls for Quist's daughter and is accepted despite the machinations of an older man for the girl's hand. After the disappearance of the servant, the rumours and the discovery of the body, the judge finds himself having to try his future father-in-law for murder.

In a novel twist, Blicher has Quist, overwhelmed by the evidence against him, convincing himself that he must have committed the murder in a somnambulistic state and confessing to the crime. Quist hears the death sentence from his daughter's fiancée. The story then moves forward twenty years, and is taken up by the new parson of Vejlbye. He is visited by a vagrant who identifies himself as the supposed victim of Quist's murderous wrath. He tells the narrator of the scheme by which he and his brother had Quist accused of murder; circumstantial evidence seals his fate. Blicher's novella ends as the vagrant's body is discovered by the parson's grave.

Although Blicher's novella was not translated into English until eighteen years after Mark Twain's death, it is possible that Twain could have heard the story from Anna Hegermann-Lindencrone, the wife of the Danish ambassador to the United States from 1872-80. It provided him with the inspiration for his novella, *Tom Sawyer, Detective*, originally published in *Harper's Magazine* from August to September 1896. Twain admitted that the details came 'from an old-time Swedish [sic] criminal trial', but the similarities to Blicher's adaptation of the true story are inescapable. Huckleberry Finn narrates the story of Tom Sawyer's defence of his Uncle Silas. Silas's daughter has been courted by Brace Dunlap, whom Silas has rejected. When Dunlap's brother Jubiter disappears, Silas is suspected of murder. At his trial, Silas foolishly pleads guilty, until Tom explains that Jubiter is in the courtroom in disguise. It transpires that Jubiter's twin brother had been murdered and Jubiter dressed the corpse in his own clothes to incriminate Tom's uncle. The ending is happier than that of the genuine Quist case.

In Janet Lewis's 1947 novel, *The Trial of Søren Quist*, a beggar appears in the village of Aalso years after Søren Quist's death. He claims to be Niels, the brother of Marten Bruus and heir to his fortune. He tells of the day his master Søren Quist struck him severely; afterwards his brother persuaded him to leave the village, letting people believe that Quist had killed him. As part of their plan, they dig up a newly-buried suicide, dress him in Niels's clothes and bury him in the pastor's garden.

Lewis gives Quist a history of violent, angry outbursts. The frequent beatings he inflicts on Niels are in retribution for Marten's designs on Quist's daughter. He is ashamed of his angry outbursts but will not let Niels go, convinced that God is testing him and that he must overcome his choler. The irony is that Quist's piety leads to his ultimate destruction. He accepts his execution readily, believing that Niels must have died after their last argument.

FACTIONAL WORKS:

Mark Twain, 'Tom Sawyer, Detective', in *Tom Sawyer Abroad, Tom Sawyer, Detective and Other Stories* (New York: Harper & Bros., 1896).

Steen Steensen Blicher, 'The Parson of Vejlbye', in *Twelve Stories* (New York: Princeton University Press, 1945). First published in Danish as 'Praesten I Vejlbye', 1829.

Janet Lewis, *The Trial of Søren Quist* (New York: Doubleday, 1947).

FURTHER READING:

J. Christian Bay, 'Tom Sawyer Detective, the Origin of the Plot', in *Essays Offered to Herbert Putnam*, edited by W. W. Bishop and A. Keogh (New Haven, Conn.: Yale University Press, 1929).

GILLES DE RAIS FRANCE 1440

De Rais was born in 1404. He became Marshal of France during the Hundred Years War, fought alongside Joan of Arc and officiated at the coronation of Charles VII. At the siege of Paris, he and Joan were in the thick of the fighting. De Rais had many large, wealthy estates throughout France and he eventually retired to these to live in splendour. A darker side of the marshal's character then began to emerge.

If the transcription of his trial is to be believed, he was a sadistic pederast who kidnapped, tortured and murdered young children for his own sexual pleasure. Later in life he took an interest in alchemy, and under the tutelage of an unfrocked priest, Francesco Prelati, found a purpose for his murderous activities in the practice of black magic and ritual sacrifice.

His downfall was through his rejection of the established church. Arrested in 1440 for beating a priest, he was accused of sexual perversion and murder. De Rais was charged with one hundred and forty homicides after more than fifty bodies were apparently discovered in his castle at Machecoul. Although threatened with torture, the marshal was contemptuous of his accusers. He finally broke down and confessed only after he had been formally excommunicated and his appeal rejected. He was hanged and burned in October 1440.

Gilles de Rais is often cited as the original for Barbe-bleu (Bluebeard) in Charles Perrault's 1697 story of the same name. Like de Rais, Bluebeard is a murderer; however, his victims are his former wives, whose bodies he keeps locked away from the sight of his present wife. Once she has discovered their existence, Bluebeard has no choice but to murder her as well. However, her brothers rescue her just in time and kill Bluebeard. Although de Rais was himself known as Bluebeard, the *Brewer's Dictionary of Phrase and Fable* states that Perrault's story 'is of an internationally widespread and ancient type and it is unprofitable to regard Gilles de Rais. . . as the historical Bluebeard'.

It was another French author, Joris-Karl Huysmans, who first introduced the genuine crimes of de Rais into a fictional setting. His 1891 novel, *Là-bas* (translated in 1924 as *Down There*), pursues three plot strands. The principal story concerns a writer named Durtal and his relationship with the satanist Madame de Chantelouve. Durtal is working on a life of Gilles de Rais, and it is this study, recounted with relish, that forms the second strand of the plot. It has been suggested that Huysmans had originally intended a serious documentary book on de Rais, but in the course of his research into contemporary mysticism and Satanism, realised that there was sufficient material for a full-length novel. Thus, a third plot strand is introduced as Durtal is drawn into the murky world of spiritualism and black magic.

The sections of the novel relating to de Rais are fictionalised to a certain extent, and Huysmans is obviously fascinated with de Rais's involvement in alchemy and Satanism. The passages were factual enough, however, for Huysmans to extract them and publish them separately as a pamphlet entitled *Sorcellerie en Poitou* (*Sorcery in Poitou*). The author turned from the black arts to embrace Catholicism later in life; even his character Durtal does so in a later novel.

More recently, the de Rais case has featured in three contemporary novels. In 1983, Michel Tournier's masterly *Gilles et Jeanne* appeared (it was translated into English in 1987). Tournier sees the appearance of Joan of Arc at the French court as the turning point in de Rais's life. Unlike the other courtiers, who regard her as a necessary evil, de Rais is impressed by her purity and recognises her as a true saint. When she is caught and tried, he attempts to rescue her. He reaches Rouen in disguise, only to join other spectators as she is burned at the stake. As he had pledged to follow her to Heaven or Hell, and she has been burned as a heretic, de Rais feels duty-bound to follow her to Hell through his crimes and his forays into black magic.

James Havoc's *Raism* (1988) is not so much a novel, as a kaleidoscope of scatological and sadistic images, based loosely on de Rais's murderous activities. The writing is heavy in alliteration and graphic in its lurid description.

Robert Nye's 1990 novel, *The Life and Death of My Lord Gilles de Rais* is an altogether more complex work. The narrator is Gilles's priest, Dom Eustache Blanchet, who is dying of leprosy in an Italian monastery. As he writes his reminiscences, Blanchet looks back to a time when his own interest and affection for Joan of Arc led him to seek out Gilles de Rais. He offers his services to the marshal, but becomes aware early on that all is not right in de Rais's household. De Rais is distant and enigmatic, his companions are sinister and depraved and there are rumours of mysterious disappearances. Blanchet learns that de Rais has indulged in sadistic acts in the past, but later submitted himself totally to Joan's mission. Blanchet suggests that de Rais was aware that his great deeds in her service were in spite of his true nature.

When Joan is executed, de Rais becomes distraught: 'the world is mad, where truth and purity are burned at the stake in the market-place, and evil triumphs'. After this, de Rais returns to his estates and makes a pact; he will create beautiful things not to enjoy their beauty but to contaminate it. The pact that de Rais makes, he tells Blanchet enigmatically, is not with the Devil but with God. The conflict between de Rais and an all-seeing but pitiless God is reminiscent of the plays of Peter Shaffer, in which similar metaphysical battles are enacted. Nye's thought-provoking, atmospheric and well-researched novel describes fully de Rais's horrific acts. However, this sense of unmitigated evil is even more oppressive when contrasted with the character and deeds of the pure Joan of Arc.

FACTIONAL WORKS:

Joris-Karl Huysmans, *Down There* (New York: Albert & Charles Boni Inc., 1924). First published in French as *Là-bas*, 1891.

Michel Tournier, *Gilles and Jeanne* (London: Methuen, 1987). First published in French as *Gilles et Jeanne*, 1983.

James Havoc, *Raism* (London: Creation Books, 1988).

Robert Nye, *The Life and Death of My Lord Gilles de Rais* (London: Hamish Hamilton, 1990).

FURTHER READING:

Jean Benedetti, *Gilles de Rais: the authentic Bluebeard* (London: Peter Davies, 1971).

RATTENBURY AND STONER GB 1935

Like the Thompson and Bywaters case thirteen years before, the Rattenbury and Stoner case involved a *ménage à trois* in which a murder was committed. Both cases proved fatal for the married couples involved, although in the latter crime, not for the lover.

Francis and Alma Rattenbury lived in the Villa Madeira in Bournemouth. Francis was a sixty-seven-year-old retired architect. Alma, who was twenty-nine years his junior, had been a lyricist. In 1935, their household also included Irene Riggs, Alma's devoted companion, and George Stoner, the nineteen-year-old chauffeur. Stoner had been appointed a year before and he and Alma had soon become lovers.

On the night of 24th March 1935, Stoner attacked Francis Rattenbury with a mallet. When the police arrived at the scene, Alma was hysterical and insisted that she had committed the crime. Rattenbury died of his injuries four days later, and Stoner confessed. Both Stoner and Alma were charged with the murder.

Their trial began that May at the Old Bailey. The prosecution attempted to prove that they had planned the murder together. In the witness-box, Alma admitted that Stoner was jealous of the possibility of further sexual relations between her and her husband. He had only told her of the attack after he had struck Rattenbury.

Stoner himself took full responsibility for the deed. The jury found Alma not guilty; Stoner was sentenced to death. Three days after her acquittal, Alma Rattenbury committed suicide. Stoner's sentence was subsequently commuted to life imprisonment.

In 1940 John Van Druten's play, *Leave Her To Heaven*, premiered in New York. It tells the story of Madge Monckton, the wife of an older man, who has an affair with her young chauffeur, Robert Ewen. Ewen murders Madge's husband with a mallet in a fit of jealousy. At Ewen's subsequent trial, Madge tries to shield her lover, but he is found guilty and she commits suicide. Van Druten had a passion for murder cases; two of his plays were based on true crimes (see entry on 'Robert Wood Case').

In 1977 the Rattenbury-Stoner case was once again adapted for the stage. Terence Rattigan's *Cause Célèbre* is similar to his early play *The Winslow Boy* in that it concentrates not only on the participants in the trial, but also on peripheral characters. Rattigan's fictional juror, Edith Davenport, has no sympathy for Alma Rattenbury. Her pity extends only to George Wood (Stoner had by this time been released from prison, hence the change of name), who is the same age as her son. She sees Alma as a cruel *femme fatale*, who has seduced and influenced the young chauffeur.

Scenes of Alma and George's relationship are contrasted with those between Edith Davenport and her son, Tony. Her fierce moral beliefs force Tony to rebel; he sleeps with a prostitute from whom he contracts syphilis. Heavily involved in the trial, Mrs Davenport equates Alma's actions with those of the prostitute who has corrupted her son. In the meantime, Alma is pressed by her defence counsel to tell the truth and not risk her own life defending her lover.

Realising she is biased against Alma, Mrs Davenport tries to remove herself from the jury, but is refused. In the meantime, her oppressive moral-ity drives Tony to attempt suicide and her estranged husband arrives to take

Tony away. When Alma finally takes the stand, Mrs Davenport is struck by her demeanour and realises she has misjudged her. The play ends with Mrs Davenport drowning her sorrows, while Alma commits suicide.

Simon Gray's play *Molly*, based on his television drama *Death of a Teddy Bear*, opened in London the same year as *Cause Célèbre*. The passionate Molly is trapped in a loveless marriage with the embittered, sadistic Teddy. Her only companion is Eve, until young Oliver joins the household as gardener and chauffeur. Molly and Oliver begin an affair, but Teddy finds out and dismisses him, humiliating the young man in front of his lover.Oliver stabs Teddy to death with a pair of garden shears. Convinced of her culpability in the murder, Molly decides to divert suspicion from Oliver, but is dissuaded by Eve. Gray's play is finally as much a study of the friendship between the two women as it is of the eternal triangle of Teddy, Molly and Oliver.

FACTIONAL WORKS:
John Van Druten, *Leave Her to Heaven* (New York: Samuel French Inc., 1941). (P)
Terence Rattigan, *Cause Celebre* (London: Hamish Hamilton, 1978). (P)
Simon Gray, *Molly* (London: Samuel French Ltd., 1979). (P)

FURTHER READING:
Sir David Napley, *Murder at the Villa Madeira* (London: Weidenfeld & Nicholson, 1988).

HORACE GEORGE RAYNER GB 1907

William Whiteley, the founder of the first department store in Britain, was shot dead in January 1907. Whiteley, the self-styled 'Universal Provider', was believed to be a conscientious, morally-upright old gentleman; his motto had been 'Add Conscience to your Capital'. The public felt revulsion and hatred towards his murderer, Horace Rayner. However, at Rayner's trial, another side of Whiteley was revealed.

Rayner was born in 1888. His father George refused to accept him as his son. As a result, Horace believed that he was in fact the illegitimate child of William Whiteley.

Rayner had lived in poverty most of his life and finally appealed to Whiteley for support. However, his efforts were in vain. He decided to visit the 'Great Provider' at his office that day in January to plead with him one last time. Rejected, he pulled a gun out of his pocket and shot the old man twice in the head. He then turned the gun on himself, shooting out one eye. After he had recovered, he stood trial for Whiteley's murder in March 1907. Rayner's defence was one of temporary insanity. The facts about his supposed paternity won him support, and it was established at the trial that Whiteley had indeed fathered a child by Rayner's aunt, Louise Turner. However, the judge summed up heavily against him, dismissing the plea of insanity.

The jury found him guilty and the death sentence was pronounced. The Home Secretary, however, swayed by a sizeable petition for a reprieve, commuted the death sentence to one of life imprisonment. After two suicide attempts while in prison, Rayner was released in 1919.

George Bernard Shaw added the facts of the Rayner case to the intricate plot of his play, *Misalliance*, first staged in 1910 and published four years later. One weekend a number of eccentric characters invade the home of millionaire businessman John Tarleton. Among them is Julius Baker, a clerk whose mother had been seduced by Tarleton years ago. Although he is disdainful of calling Tarleton his father, Baker plans to shoot the millionaire and take his own life. In the preface to his play, entitled 'Parents and Children', Shaw makes it clear where his interest in the detailed plot of his comedy lies. Fortunately, both Tarleton and Baker escape the fates of their factual counterparts—Baker is disarmed and dissuaded from continuing his vendetta.

FACTIONAL WORKS:
George Bernard Shaw, 'Misalliance', in *Misalliance, The Dark Lady of the Sonnets, and Fanny's First Play* (London: Constable & Co., 1914). (**P**)

FURTHER READING:
Richard Lambert, *The Universal Provider* (London: G. G. Harrap & Co., 1938).

RICHARD P. ROBINSON CASE USA 1836

Helen Jewett was a popular and infamous prostitute in New York at the time of her death. Among her many customers was Richard P. Robinson, a young and profligate socialite. For some of the time he knew Helen, Robinson employed the alias 'Frank Rivers'. He was intensely jealous of her other clients, but would not go as far as 'making an honest woman' of her. In fact, he married someone of his own social standing shortly before Helen's murder.

On 10th April 1836, Robinson was seen entering the brothel where Helen worked. Later that day, Helen's bludgeoned body was discovered; she had been battered to death with a hatchet. Robinson was an obvious suspect, but the police showed a reluctance to arrest him because of his social position and Helen's shameful profession. Eventually they were forced to take action, and Robinson was charged with murder.

Immediately, the sanctimonious yellow press went into action, disgusted that an upstanding citizen should be jailed for ridding New York of a social menace. Young men paraded the streets shouting 'no man should hang for the murder of a whore'. Robinson's trial was a fiasco. After five days—during which time a juror was bribed, a fake alibi was presented and witnesses for the prosecution began to forget important details—the accused was acquitted. Robinson returned home in triumph, to the disgust of the *New York*

Herald, which despaired of 'events that must make philosophy pause, religion stand aghast, morals weep in the dust, and female virtue droop her head in sorrow'.

Manuel Komroff's 1932 novel, *A New York Tempest* (entitled *A Human Tempest* in the U.K.) reconstructs the Jewett murder, providing a justice of sorts that the real murderer escaped. Oliver Benson is the fictional Robinson, who stabs a prostitute named Jane Holden to death because she knows something from his past. Benson's rich uncle hires the best legal minds to save his nephew's life. The trial divides New York society along class lines—the well-to-do support Benson, the working class sympathise with the murdered girl. Komroff charts the effects of the trial on those involved: defence lawyer John Hopkinson, who sees the case as a way back into local politics; grocer Henry Boole, who commits perjury to be in the limelight; actress Polly March, a friend of Jane's who uses her stage act to influence the populace against Benson. The final third of the book investigates the effect of Benson's acquittal on these various characters, primarily on the guilt-ridden Benson himself.

In Raymond Paul's 1982 novel, *The Thomas Street Horror*, the Robinson case is presented as a detective story. Lon Quincannon, Paul's series detective, is convinced of Robinson's innocence and manages to persuade cub reporter David Cordor of his convictions. Cordor had spent several nights with Helen Jewett. He has also made the acquaintance of Robinson, whom he finds arrogant but not a likely candidate for a murderer. Lawyer Quincannon agrees to defend Robinson, while the local press use the murder as a springboard for a campaign against prostitution. Quincannon himself, much to Cordor's disgust, uses his influence with one paper to support Robinson. Meanwhile, Cordor falls in love with Robinson's girlfriend, Sophia Willett, who knows that Robinson is innocent. A prime suspect is murdered before Quincannon brings the case to a successful solution in the courtroom.

FACTIONAL WORKS:
Manuel Komroff, *A New York Tempest* (New York: Coward & McCann, 1932). UK title, *A Human Tempest*.
Raymond Paul, *The Thomas Street Horror* (New York: Viking, 1982).

FURTHER READING:
Russell Crouse, *Murder Won't Out* (New York: Doubleday, Dorann, 1932).

AMY ROBSART DEATH GB 1560

In 1550 Lord Robert Dudley married seventeen-year-old Amy Robsart, the daughter of a Norfolk knight. She continued to support her husband after he and his three brothers were imprisoned in the Tower of London following the beheading of Lady Jane Grey. After his release, he attracted the attention of Elizabeth Tudor, who on her ascension to the throne appointed him Master of the Horse. While Robert ministered to the Queen's wishes at court, Amy stayed with relatives.

Elizabeth showered her favourite courtier with gifts, including £12,000 for his expenses. She made him Knight of the Garter and installed him in rooms next to hers in Whitehall. Rumours abounded that the Queen intended to marry Dudley, that she had had an illegitimate child by him and that Dudley would get his wife out of the way by poisoning her.

On 8th September 1560, Amy's body was discovered at the foot of a flight of stone steps at Cumnor Hall; her neck was broken. Her attendants had been sent to a local fair and in their absence, two of her husband's servants had come to see her. Only a few days earlier, the Spanish ambassador, Alvaro de la Quedra, had been told by William Cecil that Amy 'would take very good care they did not poison her'. It looked as if Dudley had found another way to rid himself of his wife. Rumours spread throughout the country that Dudley, with or without the Queen's blessing, had murdered his poor spouse.

The case had the makings of a major scandal. Elizabeth, in fear of her position, sent Dudley away from court temporarily. An inquiry was held into Amy's death which reached a verdict of accidental death, but this did not silence the gossip-mongers. Eventually Dudley resurfaced and was created Earl of Leicester in 1564. However, he never again held as high a position in the Queen's affection as he had prior to Amy's death.

Although modern forensic opinion favours the findings of the court of inquiry, this has not prevented novelists and dramatists from following a murder conspiracy theory. Sir Walter Scott was the first to take up the case in his 1821 novel, *Kenilworth*, based on the Elizabethan ballads which reflected rumour rather than official report. In his book *The Laird of Abbotsford*, A. N. Wilson argued that after 1820, Scott began 'to abandon the novelistic techniques which he had perfected and to go back to writing narrative poetry'. This is definitely reflected in the characters of *Kenilworth*, who bear more relation to the stereotypical characters of early ballads than the more robust *dramatis personae*, for example, in *The Heart of Midlothian* (see entry on 'Isobel Walker').

In Scott's version, Amy's secret marriage to Dudley is alluded to in the Queen's presence by Edmund Tressilian, who is himself in love with Amy and wishes her to return to her family. To pacify the Queen, Dudley's servant, Sir Richard Varney, claims that Amy is in fact his wife. The Queen insists that Amy be present at the revels to be held in Kenilworth Castle. Varney, afraid that Amy will reveal the truth, drugs her to prevent her from attending. However, Amy manages to meet with the Queen, but this time Varney persuades Elizabeth that she is mad and cannot be believed. To convince Dudley that he must rid himself of his wife, Varney plays Iago and leads his master to believe that Amy is in love with Tressilian.

At Cumnor Hall, Amy is forcibly kept from her husband. She is enticed to the landing by a secret signal Dudley often uses to announce his arrival. Only this time it is Varney, who has planted a trap. Amy falls to her death through a secret door to the staircase below. Meanwhile, Dudley has confessed everything to the Queen, and she dispatches Tressilian and Sir Walter Raleigh to save Amy. They arrive too late, but arrest Varney, who eventually poisons himself in prison. Informed of Varney's deceit and his wife's innocence, Dudley is temporarily exiled from court.

Scott's melodramatic novel proved a powerful magnet to dramatists of the day. In the year of its publication alone, eight stage versions were produced. Of these, only one, ascribed to Alfred Bunn, appears to have been published and was performed at Covent Garden. The play concentrated on Amy and Dudley's relationship. It altered Scott's ending, so that it is Varney who falls to his death through the trapdoor. In 1822, E. B. Impey's *Cumnor* was published, although it was never staged. The author concentrated the action into one day, thus losing much of the peripheral action of the novel. Impey's version has Tressilian also dying, in the hope of being reunited with Amy in death.

Two anonymous plays were published in 1823 and 1824 respectively, which appear to have been more faithful to Scott's novel. S. Heath's 1843 version of Scott's work, *The Earl of Leicester*, plays on the parallels between the novel and Shakespeare's *Othello*; Heath's drama is even presented in blank verse. Once more, the ending is 'improved upon', with Varney poisoning Amy, who dies in front of her husband, and then stabbing himself to death.

Andrew Halliday and F. Lawrence made a burlesque of the tale in their 1858 version, *Kenilworth; or, Ye Queene, Ye Earle and Ye Maydenne*. To the then-familiar plot—which sees Amy saved from death and forgiving Varney, and the Queen comically courted by most of her followers—the authors add many topical references. Thus mention is made of Rowland Hill's postal service and the Atlantic cable, and comic songs are sung to black spiritual tunes of the period.

The final stage version of *Kenilworth* to appear in print appears to have been J. A. Coupland's *Leicester*, published around 1883. Once more the author finds similarities with *Othello*, particularly in the character of Amy's father, Sir Hugh Robsart (killed early in the play) who takes on the role of Brabantio. Again, the Shakespearean tone is accentuated with a five-act structure and blank verse.

FACTIONAL WORKS:

Sir Walter Scott, *Kenilworth* (Edinburgh: for Archibald Constable, 1821).

Alfred Bunn, *Kenilworth* (London: J. Duncombe, [1821]). (**P**)

Elijah B. Impey, *Cumnor; or, The Bugle Horn* (London: Longman, Hurst Rees, Orme & Brown, 1822). (**P**)

Anon., *Kenilworth* (Edinburgh: for J. L. Huie, 1823). (**P**)

Anon., *Kenilworth* (London: Simpkin and Marshall, 1824). (**P**)

S. Heath, *The Earl of Leicester* (London: Saunders & Otley, 1843). (**P**)

Andrew Halliday and F. Lawrence, *Kenilworth; or, Ye Earle and Ye Maydenne* (London: T. H. Lacy, [1859]). (**P**)

J. A. Coupland, *Leicester* (London: John Dicks, [1883]). (**P**)

FURTHER READING:
Derek Wilson, *Sweet Robin* (London: Hamish Hamilton, 1981).

MARY ROGERS DEATH USA 1841

Mary Rogers worked as a cigar-girl in a tobacco store in New York. The shop was frequented by some of the great American authors of the time, including James Fenimore Cooper, Washington Irving and Edgar Allan Poe. Mary was something of a local beauty, and when her body was discovered in the Hudson River in July 1841, the press coverage was extensive.

The coroner who presided over the autopsy claimed later that some of the findings had been incorrect. As the true facts of her death were thus obscured, a spate of theories followed. At first, the press suggested that she had been abducted and strangled by several sailors. A later suspect was a young man who had made advances to an unidentified girl on Staten Island and was rejected. It was thought at first that the girl may have been Mary Rogers, but the woman in question fortunately came forward and confirmed the man's alibi. Then in 1842, a Mrs Loss made a death-bed confession that Mary had died as a result of an abortion at her house and her body had been dumped in the river. Although Mrs Loss's version is generally accepted today, the case is still officially unsolved.

In 1842, when Edgar Allen Poe was planning a sequel to his detective story 'The Murders in the Rue Morgue', he decided to adapt the facts of the Rogers mystery. At this time, the abortion theory had not been raised, and Poe's tale, 'The Mystery of Marie Roget', conceived the deed as murder. Serialised in *Snowden's Ladies Companion* between November 1842 and February 1843, the action takes place in Paris, where Poe's detective, Chevalier C. Auguste Dupin, investigates the mysterious death of a young *grisette*.

Marie is the sole child of a widow, Estelle. She has attracted the attention of Le Blanc, who persuades her to become an assistant in his a perfume shop. When her body is discovered in the Seine, Dupin, after examining the newspaper reports (adapted by Poe from the New York articles on the genuine case), proves the fallacy of the various journalists' solutions and identifies the murderer.

Many contemporary reviewers agreed that Poe had provided an acceptable solution to the true crime. He at least presented logical arguments against the popular theory of a gang-murder, pointing out that Mary could only have been killed by a single assailant. When the abortion story came out, Poe adapted his story for the 1845 book edition, so that both possibilities were deduced by Dupin. The notes to this edition, however, implied that the author adhered to his own solution. What Poe had definitely succeeded in doing was to produce the first factional detective story in which a true crime is solved in fictional form purely by detection, not by fate or chance.

FACTIONAL WORKS:
Edgar Allan Poe, 'The Mystery of Marie Roget', in *Tales* (New York: Wiley & Putnam, 1845).

FURTHER READING:
John Walsh, *Poe the Detective* (New Brunswick, N. J.: Rutgers University Press, [1968]).

FILM ADAPTATIONS:
The Mystery of Marie Roget, d. Phil Rosen. US: Universal, 1942. Screenplay by Michael Jacoby, based on the story by Edgar Allan Poe.*

ALFRED ARTHUR ROUSE GB 1931

Rouse was a commercial traveller with a voracious sexual appetite. Although he was married in 1914, he had a string of lovers around the country, many illegitimate children and another wife from a bigamous marriage in 1924. With numerous maintenance orders against him and his finances dwindling, Rouse decided to extricate himself from what seemed an impossible position.

On 6th November 1930 in Hardingstone, Northamptonshire, two men out walking saw a fire in the distance. They spotted a smartly-dressed man approaching them and asked the cause of the blaze; he replied that someone was having a bonfire. The men walked on and found the true source of the fire, a blazing Morris Minor with a charred corpse in the front seat. The car's number plate was still identifiable.

Police called to the scene discovered that the owner of the car was one Alfred Rouse. Their first impression was that Rouse had died in his car. However, the description of the man seen by the two walkers matched that of the commercial traveller and his name was released to the press. One month after the fire, Rouse gave himself up to the police. He claimed that he had given a lift to a hitch-hiker and had stopped to fill up his tank. While relieving himself, the car caught fire. He panicked and ran off. Despite his story, he was charged with murder.

At his subsequent trial, the prosecution suggested that Rouse had killed the passenger and faked his own death in the blaze to escape his financial and personal difficulties. Rouse was found guilty of murder and his appeal was rejected. After his execution, his confession was published in the *Daily Sketch*. He had strangled the passenger and set fire to the car. To this day, the hitch-hiker's identity remains unknown.

In Alan Brock's novel, *Earth to Ashes* (1939), George Brooks, alias Joseph Strange, is a travelling salesman who shares Rouse's duplicity. Married under the name of Strange, he has also taken lodgings under the name of Brooks with a girl called Maude Ash. Ash's husband, Richard, has a weak heart and is not expected to live long. George romances Maude and extracts a promise of marriage. When Richard dies, George's alter-ego, Mr Strange, also dies in a car fire. However, murder is suspected. Inspector Kennedy and his astute assistant, Constable Vine, investigate a complex web of relationships and solve the case, which although it involves many factors of the Rouse murder, is based on a far more elaborate premise.

FACTIONAL WORKS:
Alan Brock, *Earth to Ashes* (London: Nicholson & Watson, 1939).

FURTHER READING:
Douglas G. Browne and E. V. Tullett, *Bernard Spilsbury: His Life and Cases* (London: George G. Harrap & Co., 1951).

JAMES BLOMFIELD RUSH GB 1849

Rush was a tenant farmer on a Norfolk property held by Isaac Jermy. Rush lived at Potash Farm with his mistress, Emily Sandford, who had been governess to the Jermy family. Jermy himself lived at Stanfield Hall with his wife, son and servants. There was ill-feeling between the two men—Rush maintained that he was the true owner of the land and property owned by Jermy, including the Hall. Furthermore, he was in debt to his master. He was suspected of radical tendencies, having assisted in setting free several farm-workers accused of destroying threshing machines and persuading poorer claimants to Jermy's land to take him to court. All of these actions did little to endear him to the local conservative squirearchy. By November 1848, Rush was on the point of bankruptcy, with a loan from Jermy due for payment at the end of the month.

On the night of the 28th, Isaac Jermy heard a sound in the grounds of Stanfield Hall. When he went to investigate, he was shot dead. His son, his wife and a servant, who had all followed behind him, were wounded. The police immediately suspected the troublesome tenant farmer. When they arrived at Potash Farm, Emily Sandford claimed that she had spent the night with Rush—a claim she later withdrew.

After they discovered a cloak and wig at the farm, the police arrested Rush for the murder of Jermy and his son, who had since died of his wounds. At his trial in March 1849, Rush put in a plea of not guilty and conducted his own defence. He mentioned that he had left the farm for ten minutes only on the night of the crime; Sandford, who had become the chief prosecution witness, refuted this. Also, the wounded maid identified Rush by his build, although she claimed he had been heavily disguised in a long cloak and wig, such as those found at Potash Farm. Rush's over-pious, bullying defence worked against him; he was found guilty and hanged.

The prolific crime-faction writer, Joseph Shearing, used the Rush case as the basis for the 1939 novel, *Blanche Fury*. Clere Hall is the setting for the story of Philip Strangeways, the illegitimate son of Adam Fury. Strangeways is steward of the hall, now the property of Simon Fury and the family of Adam's second wife. Simon's niece, Blanche comes to stay and falls in love with the recalcitrant steward. She resents the family's treatment of Philip, who considers the hall and estates to be his rightful property.

Together, they hatch a plot to return the property to him. Simon, his son and daughter-in-law are shot, apparently by an intruder. However, Blanche is consumed with guilt when Lavinia, the youngest member of the family and Blanche's confidant, is also mortally wounded. The seemingly perfect murder begins to fall apart. Into this intricate plot, Shearing introduces the fictional legend of Fury's ape, the ghost of a former owner's pet, which is supposed to watch over the family's fortunes and avenge their wrongs.

FACTIONAL WORKS:

Joseph Shearing, *Blanche Fury* (London: William Heinemann, [1939]).

FURTHER READING:
Richard D. Altick, *Victorian Studies in Scarlet* (London: J. M. Dent & Sons Ltd., 1972).

FILM ADAPTATIONS:
Blanche Fury, d. Marc Allégret. GB: GFD/Cineguild, 1948. Screenplay by Audrey Erskine Lindop, Hugh Mills and Cecil McGivern, based on the novel by Joseph Shearing.

SACCO AND VANZETTI USA 1921

Many criminal trials in the United States have helped blacken the name of American justice (see the entry on the 'Scottsboro Boys'), but none more so than that of Sacco and Vanzetti in the 1920s. Non-fiction accounts of the case are frequently published, and the debate over the guilt or innocence of the two Italians is still hotly pursued. Often such debates overlook the essential points of the case. Firstly, the ballistic evidence that helped convict the men was extremely suspect. Secondly, the judge demonstrated that he was heavily biased against the defendants. Finally, Sacco and Vanzetti were convicted principally on their acknowledged anarchist beliefs (in this respect, the case echoes that of Steinie Morrison in England). Accept these points, and one must also accept that the trial was a travesty of justice.

In April 1920, the payroll of the Slater and Merrill Shoe Factory in South Braintree, Massachusetts was robbed. In the process, two employees were killed. Police arrested Nicola Sacco, a shoemaker and Bartolomeo Vanzetti, a fishmonger, because they had been seen in a car similar to that used in the robbery. The two Italians were self-confessed anarchists, but denied involvement in the crime. They were found to be carrying pistols, and the police claimed one of these as the murder weapon.

Their trial in the summer of 1921 was pursued in an atmosphere of reactionary fervour. Police guards were positioned around the court house to prevent any anarchist reprisal. Judge Thayer made prejudiced statements in public, referring to the defendants as 'dagos', 'sons of bitches' and 'anarchist bastards'; his final summing-up was also intolerant and biased. The 'expert' evidence on Sacco's pistol was later proven to be inaccurate and possibly perjurous. Unsurprisingly, Sacco and Vanzetti were found guilty of murder.

For the next seven years, a series of appeals were lodged, while the world's press focused on the deliberations over the case. Finally in 1927, a special commission was set up to investigate the findings of the trial. The commission concluded that there were no grounds for a mistrial, although they criticised Judge Thayer's 'grave breach of official decorum'. Demonstrations were held around the world for the two Italians, but on 23rd August 1927, Sacco and Vanzetti went to the electric chair. Fifty years later, their names were cleared in a special proclamation by the then governor of Massachusetts, Michael Dukakis.

The legend of Sacco and Vanzetti was taken to heart by American socialist writers. In the year following the execution, Maxwell Anderson and Harold Hickerson presented the case in their play, *Gods of the Lightning*. Sacco and Vanzetti become Macready and Caprari, who are tried for the murder of a payroll messenger. Macready is guilty of nothing more than leading a strike; Caprari is a passionate but pacifist anarchist. Framed for the murder, they are sent to their deaths, their comrades gloomily reading of their execution in the official bulletins.

Maxwell Anderson was to return to the Sacco-Vanzetti legend in a later and more successful play, *Winterset*, published in 1935. The case is covered obliquely through the story of Mio Romagna, whose radical father was wrongfully executed for murder. Mio has evidence enough to have the real murderer, Trock Estrella, brought to justice; in the light of his father's pacifist beliefs, he decides not to do so. Estrella, however, is convinced that Mio will want revenge and tracks him down with the intention of killing him. Among the play's other characters is Judge Gaunt, who sent Mio's father to his death, and is wracked by guilt over the miscarriage of justice to which he contributed (evidently, Anderson had heard that Judge Thayer had been tormented by remorse, which is highly unlikely, given his views). *Winterset* was written principally in blank verse, giving a tragic and mythical quality to the story.

Upton Sinclair's 1928 novel, *Boston*, tells the story of Cornelia Thornwell, a rich, respectable widow who turns her back on her wealth and position. Leaving her former life, she takes lodgings with a poor Italian family. She befriends a fellow-lodger, Bartolomeo Vanzetti. Five years later, Cornelia and her grand-daughter, Betty, find themselves heavily involved in the defence of her former acquaintance. The novel mixes factual and fictional characters and events, although Sinclair admitted that the character of Cornelia was based on a woman he had met while working for the reprieve of Sacco and Vanzetti. When the novel was published in England, the *Times Literary Supplement* described it as 'the fullest account yet published in this country of the Sacco-Vanzetti case in all its aspects'.

Nathan Asch's 1930 novel, *Payday*, takes a bleak, ironic view of the day of Sacco and Vanzetti's execution. The central character is Jim, a clerk whose social life revolves around payday. While Jim tours the speakeasies and jazz clubs of New York, newspaper boys call out the latest news on the approaching execution. Jim's friends discuss the pros and cons of the case. Asch cleverly encapsulates the anguish of Sacco and Vanzetti by juxtaposing their last hours with the ongoing amusements of everyday life around them.

John Dos Passos was one of the many left-wing intellectuals such as Upton Sinclair who had been heavily involved in the struggle to free Sacco and Vanzetti. In the year of their execution, he had written a non-fiction account of the case, *Facing the Chair*. In a letter published in *The Nation*, he had condemned the review committee of the trial as judicial murderers. He also attended a protest march in Boston and was arrested. He returned to the case once again in a travel book, *In All Countries* (1934).

Given his interest in the case, it was inevitable that Dos Passos would eventually draw on it in *The Big Money* (1936), the third volume of his *USA* trilogy. *The Big Money* follows the stories of several characters affected by political events of the period. Among these is Mary French, a reporter and union worker who assists the Sacco and Vanzetti defence committee. Their eventual execution, coupled with problems in her personal life, lead her to abandon her union work. However, by the end of the novel, she returns to her true vocation.

Ruth McKenney's 1943 novel, *Jake Home*, follows the eponymous labour leader from his birth in a Pennsylvania mining community, through his career as a miner and union worker, to his eventual marriage to a wealthy woman. He finds himself at odds with his wife's social environment and eventually returns to his occupation as a union organiser. The novel ends with Jake attending a workers' parade in New York in 1932, confirmed in his old beliefs. In one lengthy sequence of the book, Jake becomes his party's representative on the Sacco-Vanzetti defence campaign, and takes part in a cross-country tour on their behalf.

A later factional work concerning the two anarchists more directly is Howard Fast's *The Passion of Sacco and Vanzetti* (1953). The action takes place on the day of Sacco and Vanzetti's execution, as several characters directly and indirectly connected with the case reflect on their part in the events leading up to their deaths. Fast presents the story almost as a morality play (hence the title), with characters identified by their positions in life—the Warden, the Judge, the President and the Dictator (a fictional Mussolini). Only the prisoners themselves, and the real murderer (whom Fast identifies) are named.

FACTIONAL WORKS:

Maxwell Anderson and Harold Hickerson, 'Gods of the Lightning', in *Gods of the Lightning, Outside Looking In* (New York: Longmans, Green & Co., 1928). (P)
Upton Sinclair, *Boston* (New York: Albert & Charles Boni Inc., 1928).
Nathan Asch, *Pay Day* (New York: Brewer & Warren Inc., 1930).
Maxwell Anderson, *Winterset* (Washington: Anderson House, 1935). (P)
John Dos Passos, *The Big Money* (New York: Harcourt, Brace & Co., 1936).

Ruth McKenney, *Jake Home* (New York: Harcourt, Brace & Co., [1943]).
Howard Fast, *The Passion of Sacco and Vanzetti* (New York: Blue Heron Press, [1953]).

FURTHER READING:
Katharine Anne Porter, *The Never-Ending Wrong* (London: Secker & Warburg, 1977).

FILM ADAPTATIONS:
Winterset, d. Alfred Santell. US: RKO, 1936. Screenplay by Anthony Veiller, based on the play by
   Maxwell Anderson.

JOHN SADLEIR GB 1856

John Sadleir was the son of the owner of a Tipperary bank. He studied law, subsidised by loans from his father. He came of age during the railway expansion; and in his new-found position of parliamentary agent, cashed in on the boom by pushing bills through Parliament to develop the railway network in Ireland. Elected Member of Parliament for Carlow, he succeeded his father as owner of the Tipperary Joint Stock Bank. After this, his career took off—he was appointed chairman of the Royal Swedish Railway Company, director of the East Kent Railway Company and chairman of the London and County Bank.

In 1853, Sadleir became a junior Lord of the Treasury under Lord Aberdeen (at this period, ministers could still hold directorships and other positions in business). By now he owned property in Ireland and England, including a house in Gloucester Square in London. He entertained lavishly and was wildly extravagant. To pay his way, he drew heavily on the Tipperary bank; his brother, a complaisant manager, assumed he was investing the money elsewhere. In addition, he resorted to forging land deeds and selling worthless railway stock.

He counted on his position in the government to provide him with both inside information on the stock market and a means of covering his dealings. However, Sadleir overreached himself. Several of his colleagues at the Treasury brought their suspicions to the Prime Minister. Sadleir was forced to resign from the government. Although his creditors grew more vociferous, for a while he managed to maintain the situation. However, by 1855 his debt with the London and County Bank had reached £200,000.

On 16th February 1856, he attempted to raise a substantial loan on some forged land deeds, but the stockbrokers involved decided to check them out. Convinced that he would be exposed, Sadleir wrote letters of confession to various associates, then headed to Hampstead Heath. His body was discovered on the Heath next morning. Extravagant to the last, he had taken prussic acid from a silver cream jug.

Charles Dickens's use of the Sadleir case demonstrates how the author employed topical events in his novels, which usually appeared first serialised in magazines. Dickens had already begun writing *Little Dorrit* while abroad in Europe. On his return to England in February 1856, he read of

Sadleir's suicide and the subsequent scandal concerning his shady dealings. He realised the details would be pertinent to his novel, which dealt with corruption and greed in contemporary Britain. As the author admitted, 'I had the general idea of the Society business before the Sadleir affair, but I shaped Merdle himself out of that previous rascality'.

Mr Merdle, a scheming banker, is courted by high society, Parliament and the nouveau riche, the latter represented by the Dorrits. William Dorritt, the head of the family, has been recently released from the Marshalsea debtor's prison. The collapse of Merdle's empire and his subsequent suicide brings about the financial ruin of many of the novel's principal characters, including the Dorrits and Dickens's hero, Arthur Clenham. Arthur and Amy Dorrit (the 'Little Dorrit' of the title) are brought together in their shared calamity, and eventually admit their love for each other.

Charles Lever, a friend of Dickens's and probably the most popular Irish novelist of the nineteenth century, wrote entertaining exposés of Irish life and society. They sold well in England, but were condemned by Irish intellectuals because of their lack of realism. After the potato famine of 1845, however, readers found a new nationalism and accompanying realism in Lever's work, and a pessimism toward English politics and politicians.

In *Davenport Dunn* (1859)—one of the few Lever novels set outside his native land—the title character, an Irish-born millionaire, profits from the gullibility of his countrymen before transferring his corrupt enterprise to England. During the Crimean War, Dunn establishes a limited liability company supposedly promoting Anglo-French relations. He is courted by the rich and powerful, and plays the role of confidant to politicians and nobility. He intends finally to marry into the aristocracy. However, his schemes collapse, his criminal dealings are revealed, and as he attempts to escape on his private train, he is beaten to death in a scuffle with one of his henchmen, 'Grog' Davis.

A third popular Victorian novelist also found inspiration in the Sadleir legend. Anthony Trollope's longest novel, *The Way We Live Now*, was serialised in monthly instalments between 1874 and 1875, culminating in publication as a book. The author was inspired to write 'by what [he] conceived to be the commercial profligacy of the age'. Nowhere was this notion more abundantly expressed in Trollope's book than through the character of the mysterious Augustus Melmotte, who suddenly appears in London and bluffs society into accepting him as a powerful financier.

The aristocracy fawn on him, the bankers and bureaucrats of the capital throw money into his grandiose schemes. He gains a seat in Parliament, despite rumours that all is not well with his financial dealings. A second strand of the novel follows Melmotte's attempts to arrange a respectable and influential marriage for his daughter, Marie. She, however, steals from her father and elopes with the rakish Sir Francis Carbury. Carbury eventually leaves her and gambles her money away, while her father, who is ruined, makes a final, drunken appearance in Parliament, then takes his own life.

FACTIONAL WORKS:
Charles Dickens, *Little Dorrit* (London: Bradbury & Evans, 1857).
Charles Lever, *Davenport Dunn* (London: Chapman & Hall, 1859).
Anthony Trollope, *The Way We Live Now* (London: Chapman & Hall, 1875).

FURTHER READING:
A. F. L. Deeson, *Great Swindlers* (London: W. Foulsham & Co. Ltd., 1971).

FILM ADAPTATIONS:
Little Dorrit, d. Christine Edzard. GB: Sands/Cannon, 1987. Screenplay by Christine Edzard, based on the novel by Charles Dickens.*

RICHARD SAVAGE GB 1727

Savage's origins are obscure. According to his own account, he was the bastard son of the Countess of Macclesfield and her lover, Richard Savage, Earl Rivers, whose name the boy took for himself. He claimed to have written the play, *Woman's a Riddle*, which was staged in 1716, but another author, Christopher Bullock accused him of plagiarism. He did write *Love in a Veil* (staged in 1719) and one play which finds its way into the present survey, *Sir Thomas Overbury* (see entry on 'Frances Howard'). The latter work established him as an author of note and coupled with his widely-known life story, won him influential friends.

In 1727 Savage got into an argument with James Sinclair at Robinson's Coffee House in London. Savage's fierce temper got the better of him, and he ran the unarmed man through with his sword. Sinclair named his assailant before he died and Savage was arrested. Although he conducted his own defence at his trial, he was sentenced to death. His powerful friends petitioned the king, who pardoned him.

After his release, Savage wrote his most famous work, the autobiographical poem *The Bastard* (1728). He continued to write poetry and earn a living of sorts, but his vile temper constantly plagued him. He lost many acquaintances and died a pauper in 1743.

Between 1841 and 1842, Charles Whitehead produced a fictionalised biographical novel entitled *Richard Savage*, whose narrator is Savage himself. According to Whitehead, the Countess of Macclesfield's mother had passed the infant Richard to a servant named Ludlow, and instructed him to rid the family of the child. Ludlow gives the boy to his sister, who raises him as her own. When he learns the truth about his parentage, Savage visits his natural mother, but she will have nothing to do with him. She arranges to have him abducted and murdered, but he escapes. She then pressures Ludlow's wife into signing a document proving she is Savage's mother. This persecution causes Ludlow to go mad, and he eventually dies.

Savage falls for Elizabeth Wilfred, the illegitimate daughter of Sir Richard Steele. He has a rival for her hand in Sinclair, an old schoolfriend. The Countess of Macclesfield arranges a forced marriage between Elizabeth and Sinclair, but Richard rescues her and later kills Sinclair at a coffee house. He is tried and pardoned. A free man, he meets Elizabeth again and tries to seduce her in a drunken stupor. They are reconciled at Ludlow's grave, shortly before Savage is thrown into prison for debt. The last section of the novel is in the form of a letter from a prison guard to Samuel Johnson. He tells of Elizabeth's visit to Savage on his prison deathbed, her death shortly after and their burial together.

Whitehead's novel was serialised in *Bentley's Magazine*, the source of many Newgate novels of the period, before its publication as a book in 1842. The author takes liberties with the facts and gives Savage a valid motive for Sinclair's murder. However, he retains the details of Savage's violent temper and his descent into poverty and alcoholism. The novel has all the intrigue, daring escapes and intricate plotting indicative of contemporary imitators of Sir Walter Scott.

More recently, Keith Heller turned the murder into a whodunit in his detective novel, *Man's Loving Family* (1986). After a prediction of his death is placed in a newspaper, James Sinclair hires a bodyguard named George Man. Man is a member of the London Parish Watch and a friend of Richard Savage. When Sinclair is indeed murdered before Man's own eyes and the killer appears to be Savage, the watchman suspects that Savage has been framed and he investigates. Heller introduces factual characters such as George Psalmanazar, the 'Formosan' fraud and the novelist-to-be Henry Fielding, fresh from the country and pursuing a career as a watchman himself. The Sinclair family, a tight-knit and incestuous group, hold the key to the mystery.

FACTIONAL WORKS:
Charles Whitehead, *Richard Savage* (London: Bentley, 1842).
Keith Heller, *Man's Loving Family* (London: Collins, 1986).

FURTHER READING:
Clarence Tracy, *The Artificial Bastard* (Cambridge, Mass.: Harvard University Press, 1953).

JAMES TOWNSEND SAWARD GB 1857

Saward began his working life as a barrister, called to the bar in 1840. Even then, he was into criminal activities. As a receiver of stolen goods, he dealt with some of the proceeds from the 1855 Great Bullion Robbery (see entry on 'William Pierce'). His speciality was forging cheques and letters of credit. He always ensured that he was not himself responsible for cashing the forgeries; there were several intermediaries between himself and the cashier. Although he was suspected by the police, a search of his premises revealed nothing. Shortly after he disappeared from his offices. A year or two later, a Captain Bevan bought a letter of credit for £2,000 in New York. The letter of credit was cashed after Bevan had changed the amount to read £20,000. It was the work of Saward. Subsequently, forged circular notes were retrieved from all parts of the globe to the total amount of £43,000, all cashed by Saward, or 'Jim the Penman' as he was to be known.

He finally retired from his career of forgery with £80,000. He settled in a villa in Britain. His previous criminal acquaintances, however, discovered his whereabouts and he was forced to pay them off to keep his alias intact. One such character made the mistake of opening an account under an assumed name and cashing a cheque under his real name. Subsequent enquiries resulted in the arrest of Saward on forgery charges. Incriminating documents were found in his villa. He was found guilty at his trial in 1857 and was sentenced to transportation.

Sir Charles Young's drama, *Jim the Penman*, opened in 1886 at the Theatre Royal, Haymarket. It was published around 1912. Young's Saward is James Ralston, a talented forger who works with a criminal gang. He is well established, with a son who is an army officer and a daughter betrothed to one of the nobility. He himself is elected as a Liberal candidate, but is more concerned with using his talent for criminal purposes. At one stage, he uses his forging gifts to separate a woman whom he loves from an ardent admirer. He eventually dies of a heart attack while struggling with one of his partners in crime. Not surprisingly, in a decade that saw the emergence of Sherlock Holmes, Jim the Penman is pursued through the play by an amateur detective.

Dick Donovan's novel, *Jim the Penman* (1901), is a highly fictionalised version of Saward's life story. He is referred throughout the novel as Captain Bevan. Bevan is recruited by Argave, a well-to-do villain, and his associates to discover a means of forging bills without possible detection. Argave intends to be the brains of the organisation, but when Bevan discovers the secret of near-perfect forgery, he ensures that Argave is removed to the sidelines. When Bevan retires and Argave attempts blackmail, the Penman has his persecutor interred in a private asylum. However, Argave escapes and puts the police onto Bevan. The two are arrested and transported to Australia. There, Argave kills Bevan in a penal colony and is then killed himself while escaping.

The Saward plot runs parallel to the love story of Bevan's daughter, Marie. She is worshipped by Wilfred Leonard, a protege of an Italian countess. However, Marie discovers her father's criminal deeds and refuses to marry Leonard. She takes an assumed name and begins a career in the theatre. Years later, they meet again. In the meantime Leonard has discovered a criminal secret in his own parents' past. He proposes again and the two are finally re-united by their parents' crimes.

FACTIONAL WORKS:
Dick Donovan, *Jim the Penman* (London: Newnes, 1901).
Sir Charles Young, *Jim The Penman* (London: Samuel French Ltd., [1912]). (**P**)

FURTHER READING:
George Dilnot, ed., *The Trial of Jim the Penman* (London: Geoffrey Bles, 1930).

JOHN SCANLAN IRELAND 1820

Since the death of her mother, Ellen Hanley had been raised by her uncle. They lived in the village of Ballycahane in County Limerick. On 29th June 1819, the fifteen-year-old girl left her uncle's house and disappeared. Just over two months later, her body was dragged out of the River Shannon many miles from her home; she had been trussed up with rope and bludgeoned to death. It transpired that she had last been seen with Lieutenant John Scanlan and his boatman, Stephen Sullivan, on Carrig Island.

The authorities made out warrants for the arrest of the two men, who had vanished completely. Scanlan was the first to be found, hiding in a pile of straw in Ballycahane Castle (he had jumped out when a suspicious soldier stuck his lance into the straw). He was tried in Limerick in 1820 and was defended by the great Irish orator, Daniel O'Connell. However, he was found guilty. Still protesting his innocence on the gallows, Scanlan was hanged.

Meanwhile, the authorities found Sullivan, who was already in jail in Tralee under an assumed name. Like Scanlan, he declared his innocence throughout his trial, but he made a confession on the gallows. He admitted that Scanlan had been in love with Ellen, and had persuaded Sullivan to masquerade as a priest and marry them in a mock ceremony. However, he soon tired of her and got Sullivan to take her onto the Shannon and kill her.

As a young man, Irish writer Gerald Griffin had been a reporter at both trials. He used the case for the climax of his 1829 novel, *The Collegians*, a work of social criticism and one of the founding novels of Anglo-Irish literature. Transferring the location to Killarney and the period to the late-eighteenth century, Griffin tells the story of well-to-do Hardress Cregan, who has recently returned to his native town of Garryowen from Trinity College. Eily O'Connor, the beautiful daughter of the local rope-maker, catches his eye. He marries her secretly, aided by his servant, Danny Mann. His mother, however, intends him to make a wealthy marriage and encourages him to court Ann Chute, the heiress of Castle Chute. Intent on marrying the woman his mother favours, Cregan presses Danny Mann to get Eily out of Garryowen. But Mann misunderstands his master's meaning and kills the girl instead. Both men are arrested. Danny Mann is hanged and Cregan is transported for life. He dies of a broken heart as his convict ship leaves the shores of Ireland.

Griffin created a minor comic character in the shape of the dubious horse-trader, Myles Murphy, better known as Myles-na-Coppaleen. When Irish dramatist Dion de Boucicault adapted Griffin's novel for the New York stage in 1860, Myles became a vital part of the unfolding drama. *The Colleen Bawn; or, The Brides of Garryowen* follows the climax of Griffin's novel closely, apart from one detail. Myles is also secretly in love with Eily. When Danny Mann attempts to drown her, Myles shoots Danny dead and dives into the river to rescue the girl. Boucicault himself played Myles in the original production and in subsequent revivals, recreating his famous dive when he was into his sixties.

Twentieth-century Irish dramatists would take Boucicault to task for his portrayal of Myles as a sentimental rogue, cheat and poacher. They suggested that he was perpetuating the stereotype of the Irish wastrel on stage. However, the play proved immensely popular in the late-nineteenth century and established Boucicault's reputation. It prompted at least one imitation—Henry J. Byron's 1861 burlesque, *Miss Eily O'Connor*. Where Boucicault managed to retain a dramatic edge to his tale, Byron's play was a broad farce, with some excrutiating puns ('You flung me off a rock—a dreadful thing/But you were young, and youth will have its fling.').

FACTIONAL WORKS:
[Gerald Griffin], *The Collegians* (London: Saunders & Otley, 1829).
Henry J. Byron, *Miss Eily O'Connor* (London: T. H. Lacy, [1862]). (**P**)
Dion de Boucicault, *The Colleen Bawn* (London: T. H. Lacy, [1865]). (**P**)

FURTHER READING:
W. Mac Lysaght, *Death Sails the Shannon* (Tralee: The Kerryman Ltd., 1953).

SCOPES MONKEY TRIAL USA 1925

In March 1925, an Anti-Evolution bill was passed as law in the state of Tennessee. It was part of a strong Fundamentalist movement in America's Bible Belt, principally aimed against Darwin's theory of evolution. With the passing of the bill, any teacher using textbooks supporting Darwin's theory would be in violation of the law and subject to fine and imprisonment.

A group of Tennessee liberals, opposed to what they saw as an attack on their liberties, persuaded a teacher named John T. Scopes to stand as a test case in the hopes of embarrassing the Fundamentalists and removing the law from the statute books. Scopes was arrested for teaching Darwin to his class and sent for trial in Dayton. The defence acquired the services of the free-thinking lawyer Clarence Darrow, who was then sixty-eight years old and approaching the end of a distinguished career (see entries on 'Leopold and Loeb' and the 'Massie Case'). The prosecution was headed by William Jennings Bryan, former Secretary of State under Woodrow Wilson, who was firm in his principles and rigid in his belief in Fundamentalist values.

These two oratorical giants each made convincing opening statements. Bryan insisted that any attack on the bill was an attack on the very foundation of Christianity. Darrow argued that the prosecution were trying to promote religious bigotry and a return to the religious persecutions of the Middle Ages. The prosecution won a major tactical point when testimony on behalf of Darwin's theory was excluded by the judge as irrelevant.

Darrow, who was deeply committed to the cause of the defendant, at one stage was cited for contempt. The turning point came when Darrow, in a unique legal manoeuvre, asked Bryan to testify as an expert on the Bible. Under Darrow's cross-questioning, Bryan came across as a narrow-minded religious fanatic with no knowledge of other religions, Darwinism or, for that matter, the Bible itself. At one point, he admitted that the Creation may not have literally taken days but 'might have continued for millions of years'. His fellow prosecution counsel objected that, as a co-operative witness called by the defence, Bryan should not be subjected to Darrow's argumentative questioning. Eventually, the judge terminated the heated exchanges and ruled all of Bryan's evidence as inadmissible. Darrow promptly asked the jury to return a verdict of guilty, so that he could appeal. As he had hoped, the Supreme Court overturned the verdict on a legal technicality. The defence had won a major victory. Although the law remained on the statute books, schools returned to teaching Darwinism and the Fundamentalist movement received a sizeable blow. Bryan died shortly after the trial, from 'a busted belly', according to the irascible Darrow.

Playwrights Jerome Lawrence and Robert E. Lee saw the dramatic potential in the case, which had received wide media coverage at the time. Their 1955 play, *Inherit The Wind*, restages the legal battle in the fictional town of Hillsboro. Bertram Cates, a local schoolteacher, takes on the legal and religious establishments because of his own experience of bigotry and his belief in freedom of thought. During the trial he recounts the story of a student's funeral. The boy who had died was not baptised and had been condemned to hellfire by the local preacher. The conflict is heightened for Cates by his love for Rachel, the preacher's daughter.

The two dominant figures in the play, as in the historical trial, are the principal lawyers. The free-thinking, homely, shabby Henry Drummond is an accurate fictional representation of Darrow. He is opposed by his former friend, the ambitious, narrow-minded Matthew Harrison Brady. The acerbic columnist and critic, H. L. Mencken, who attended the trial, is represented by the equally-vitriolic E. K. Hornbeck. The trial is a close facsimile of the original proceedings, as Drummond triumphs over Brady's posturings and bigotry.

Both the judge and the mayor, aware of the negative media coverage and Brady's poor showing, let Cates off with a fine of one hundred dollars. As Drummond indicates that they will appeal, Brady, horrified that his glorious battle has ended so disastrously, launches into a tirade that brings on a fatal heart attack. As Cates and Rachel prepare to leave Hillsboro, Hornbeck honours Brady with an ironic epitaph from Proverbs 11, a quotation that Brady himself had used earlier: 'He that troubleth his own house shall inherit the wind, and the fool shall be servant to the wise in heart'.

FACTIONAL WORKS:
Jerome Lawrence and Robert E. Lee, *Inherit the Wind* (New York: Random House, [1955]). (**P**)

FURTHER READING:
Irving Stone, *Clarence Darrow for the Defence* (Garden City, N.Y.: Doubleday, 1941).

FILM ADAPTATIONS:
Inherit the Wind, d. Stanley Kramer. US: UA/Lomitas, 1960. Screenplay by Nathan E. Douglas and Harold Jacob Smith, based on the play by Jerome Lawrence and Robert E. Lee.

SCOTTSBORO BOYS USA 1931

In the case of the Scottsboro Boys, the alleged crime they committed was as shocking as the crime inflicted on them by the bigoted South. In 1931 a freight train, travelling through Alabama to Memphis, Tennessee, was halted after a group of white youths claimed that they had been thrown off by a gang of black teenagers. Two white girls, Victoria Price and Ruby Bates, claimed that they had been raped by a dozen black men, three of whom had jumped from the train. In total, nine black youths were taken from the train and into custody in Scottsboro, where they were charged with rape.

They were tried within twelve days amidst an atmosphere of racial tension and threats of lynch-law. The National Guard were called out to protect the court house. The girls who had been raped were held up as examples of Southern womanhood; they were in fact prostitutes who had brought the accusations to escape a charge of vagrancy. Against the medical evidence, all the youths, including their supposed ringleader, Haywood Patterson, were sentenced to death, except for the youngest, who was sentenced to life imprisonment.

This was only the beginning of the scandal. In 1932, the Supreme Court overruled the original verdict due to inadequate counsel for the defence. New York lawyer Samuel S. Leibowitz was brought in to defend the boys in a series of trials and retrials. Ruby Bates finally denied that any rape had taken place, but this did not dampen the prejudice of Southern juries. Despite some advances, Patterson himself was still given a seventy-five-year prison sentence.

However, by this time international protest was making an impression on the case. Leibowitz managed to get charges against four of the boys dropped, after the Supreme Court declared that the exclusion of blacks from juries was unconstitutional—probably the most important victory to be won in the course of this scandal. Subsequently, the other youths were paroled except for Patterson, who after escaping from jail in 1948, was convicted of manslaughter in Michigan. He died in prison in 1952. In 1976, Clarence Norris, the last surviving Scottsboro Boy, was granted a pardon by Alabama governor George Wallace. In 1977, after receiving a hero's welcome on his return to his home state, Norris was finally awarded ten thousand dollars in compensation.

They Shall Not Die, John Wexley's play based on the Scottsboro case, was staged in New York in 1934 and published the same year. Although the author insisted that the plot was fictional, its basis in fact is obvious. Nine black youths are taken from a train in Cooksville, charged with the rape of two white girls, Virginia Ross and Lucy Wells. Sheriff Trent is convinced the girls are prostitutes but he and Mason, a local solicitor, see a chance of gaining political mileage from a rape case against the boys. They persuade the girls to commit perjury. They try the same tactics on a white boy named Collins, who had also been on the train, but he refuses to be part of any conspiracy. The police beat two of the youths into making a confession. A third boy, Heywood Parsons, refuses to be intimidated.

At the trial they are all found guilty and sentenced to death. The boys follow the advice of Joe Rokoff of the National Labor Defense, who suggests that it is possible the death sentence might be commuted to life if there is a retrial. Lucy Wells runs away before the second trial can begin and Collins then comes forward, as a witness for the defence. He confesses that he had made love to Lucy on the train, thus destroying the prosecution's strong medical evidence of rape.

Despite Collins's testimony and their new-found confidence, the defence still seem to be losing the case. It is then that Lucy Wells appears and admits her perjury. The prosecution's summing-up is more an anti-unionist and anti-Semitic lambast against the NLD and their lawyer, Nathan J. Rubin, than a reasoned argument. Even as the play ends, the jury is out and the verdict is still in doubt. As Rubin waits in court, he hears laughter from the jury room and rises furiously. He had warned Rokoff against dragging politics into the case; he finally sees it is inevitable. 'There are hundreds of thousands of men and women meeting in a thousand cities of the world in mass protest,' he storms at the off-stage jury, '. . . and over them you have no jurisdiction. . . these boys, they shall not die!'

FACTIONAL WORKS:
John Wexley, *They Shall Not Die* (New York: A. A. Knopf, 1934). (P)

FURTHER READING:
Haywood Patterson, *Scottsboro Boy* (New York: Doubleday, 1950).

FREDERICK H. SEDDON GB 1912

In 1910, Miss Eliza Barrow became a lodger at the Islington house of an insurance agent named Frederick Seddon. Seddon was a grasping, miserly man obsessed with money and profit. Miss Barrow transferred her assets, which consisted of £1,600 in shares and the leasehold of an inn and a barber's shop, to Seddon in return for an annuity and rent-free accommodation. On 14th September 1911, Eliza Barrow died; the cause of death was given as epidemic diarrhoea. Seddon arranged a pauper's funeral, haggling over the cost.

Miss Barrow's relatives were unaware of her death until a week later, when her cousin, Frank Vonderahe, called at Seddon's house. When Vonderahe heard that Seddon now owned his cousin's property, he called in the police. Miss Barrow's body was exhumed and found to contain large traces of arsenic. Seddon was arrested and charged with her murder. He was defended at the Old Bailey in 1912 by Edward Marshall Hall. In contrast to his usual stance, Hall felt no sympathy at all for his client: 'the blackest case I have ever been in' was how the advocate summed it up to a friend.

Upon hearing the verdict of guilty, Seddon made a masonic sign to the judge (who was also a mason) and declared himself innocent of the charge 'before the Great Architect of the Universe'. The judge returned the sentence of death. Seddon was hanged in April 1912.

The character of the miserly insurance man appeared twice on the English stage. E. H. W. Meyerstein's *Heddon* (1921) recast him as an assistant manager of a chemist's firm, but his thinly-disguised surname, his standing as a freemason and the murder of his paying guest, Miss Marrow, confirm his model. Mrs Heddon and her teenage daughter, Alice, are forced to ingratiate themselves to the overbearing and wilful Miss Marrow. Heddon, a loving father and husband, is afraid that her threatened departure will lower his standing with his employers and in the community, where her meagre wealth reflects well on him. Rather than lose his position and her money, he poisons her. Ironically, this cowardly act elevates him in the eyes of his wife, who sees the murder as an indication of his love for his family. She foresees that he will be caught eventually, and urges him to proclaim his innocence to the judge and jury, so that his children will retain their respect for him.

Seddon reappeared as Frederick Dyson, the protagonist in Rodney Ackland's drama, *A Dead Secret* (staged in 1957, published a year later). Dyson is a spendthrift and greedy character who rules his family with an iron will. He persuades his lodger, Miss Lummins, to turn over her property to him in exchange for an annuity. When she dies from arsenic poisoning, there are several possibilities: she could have overdosed on the drugs she frequently used, or it could have been the fault of Henrietta Spicer, the imbecilic parlour-maid. Or it could have been Dyson, the new owner of her property.

Sir Arthur Lovecraft must decide whether he believes Dyson or, more to the point, whether he is willing to defend him. Ackland stresses the whodunit aspect of his play. Before he provides a solution to the murder, he paints a believable portrait of a petty domestic tyrant, thoroughly repellent, like his factual prototype.

FACTIONAL WORKS:
E. H. W. Meyerstein, *Heddon* (Oxford: Blackwell Ltd., 1921). (P)
Rodney Ackland, *A Dead Secret* (London: Samuel French Ltd., 1958). (P)

FURTHER READING:
Gordon Honeycombe, *Murders of the Black Museum, 1870-1970* (London: Hutchinson & Co., 1982).

JACK SHEPPARD GB 1724

Jack Sheppard must rate second only to Dick Turpin as England's best-known criminal of the eighteenth century. However, Turpin had to wait until the nineteenth century to find fame again in fiction and drama, whereas Sheppard's factional popularity was established in his own century.

John Sheppard was born in the Spitalfields district of London in 1702, the son of a carpenter. He was eventually apprenticed to another in the trade, Owen Wood, from whom he learned the locksmith's art that was to stand him in good stead later in life. He was soon in trouble, thieving whilst out on the job, and mixing with other petty criminals. He made the acquaintance of Elizabeth Lyon, known as 'Edgeworth Bess', a prostitute and pickpocket. Quarrels ensued with the Wood family and Jack left his job. He and his brother Thomas joined forces as burglars. Thomas was eventually caught and transported to America. He named Jack as his accomplice.

Jack was arrested and committed to St. Giles Roundhouse, but on his first night there he escaped through the roof. A few weeks later he was once more captured and this time taken to St. Ann's Roundhouse. He again attempted to escape, this time with the help of Edgeworth Bess. They were caught and taken to Clerkenwell's new prison. Friends managed to smuggle tools into their cell, and on 24th May 1724, he and Bess escaped over the walls by means of a makeshift rope. Returning to burglary, Jack and his colleague, Joseph 'Blueskin' Blake, robbed a former master of his and also took part in several highway robberies.

By this time, Jack's activities had come to the attention of Jonathan Wild, the self-styled 'Thief-Taker General'. Wild's men arrested Sheppard and this time he was interred in Newgate Prison. At his trial that August, he was sentenced to death. In the condemned cell, Jack was visited by Edgeworth Bess and a prostitute friend, Poll Maggot. He filed through his chains and was hauled through the bars of his cell by the two women.

On the loose, Sheppard found he had become a celebrity. He hid in Finchley Common, only to be taken by a gang of turnkeys. Sheppard was flung once more into the condemned cell at Newgate, before being transferred to the Castle, considered to be the most secure room in the prison. Chained to the floor and manacled, he managed to break free and leave the Castle up a chimney flue, through a locked room, into the chapel, out onto the roof, back to the Castle to get a blanket, across the roof of a house adjoining the prison and into the streets and freedom. He made this amazing escape on 15th October 1724.

Jack was now the talk of the country. Ballads were sung in his praise, letters purporting to be from him were published in the press, sightings of him were made throughout England. However, his fame made him careless and he was arrested while casually strolling through the streets dressed in ornaments he had recently stolen. He was returned to Newgate, where he was heavily manacled and constantly under guard. There he was visited by celebrities of the day, including the King's painter, Sir John Thornhill, the poet John Gay and the artist William Hogarth. He finally went to the gallows in November 1724.

Twelve days after his death, the Theatre Royal, Drury Lane, staged John Thurmond's *Harlequin Sheppard*, which was published the same year. In ten scenes, the author concentrates on Jack's escape from Newgate and his subsequent adventures. Despite its topicality, the play was not popular and failed at the box-office ('dismissed with a universal hiss', according to one contemporary critic). Perhaps for this reason, a second anonymous play, *The Prison Breaker*, destined for production the following year, was never staged, although it was published. According to a later source, John Gay probably borrowed heavily from this latter farce for his own version of Sheppard's story.

Gay's musical drama, *The Beggar's Opera*, was staged at Lincoln's Inn Fields in January 1728 and published the same year. It was an immediate success and has remained a staple of English theatre. The poet was obviously fascinated by the criminal fraternity of the period; an earlier poem, 'Newgate's Garland', concerns an attempt on Jonathan Wild's life by Blueskin Blake at his trial in 1724. The poem had been included in John Thurmond's published version of *Harlequin Sheppard*. Gay had even spent a night with Wild at an inn, where he gained much of his knowledge of criminal London. Whatever his source, there is little doubt that in *The Beggar's Opera*, an altered version of Wild appears in the character of Peachum and Macheath is a more heroic visualisation of Sheppard himself.

Like Wild, Peachum is a receiver of stolen goods and a police spy, hence his name, 'impeach them'. His daughter Polly is in love with the highwayman Macheath. Peachum decides that Polly should marry Macheath and then turn him in, thus making her fortune as a widow. Polly warns her lover but he admires Peachum's business acumen, and decides to go along with the double-cross. He is thrown into Newgate.

He effects his escape by wooing Lucy Lockit, the jailer's daughter. Peachum recaptures Macheath at a brothel, followed by Polly and Lucy. Confronted by the two rivals for his love, Macheath goes willingly to the Old Bailey. He waits in the condemned cell for his imminent execution. But the Beggar, who has introduced the play, returns in the end, persuaded to give his 'hero' a reprieve.

The Beggar's Opera provides a good fictional account of the clash between Wild and Sheppard, and in the character of Macheath attempts to demonstrate Sheppard's immortality in the eyes of the contemporary criminal world. The success of Gay's drama persuaded Thomas Walker to construct a musical version of the anonymous 1725 play, *The Prison Breaker*. Walker added five new characters, several new incidents and many songs to his farce. Drawing an obvious parallel to Gay's play, which was staged and published the same year, Walker named his version *The Quaker's Opera*.

The Sheppard legend languished for over a century before it was resurrected in an extremely popular novel. William Harrison Ainsworth had told the story of Dick Turpin in his first novel, *Rookwood*, published in 1834. Five years later he turned again to eighteenth-century crime for inspiration. *Jack Sheppard*, which appeared first as a serialisation, proved as huge a success as *Rookwood*, prompting a flood of pastiches and stage adaptations.

As one of the instigators of the notorious Newgate novels, which were seen to romanticise criminal life, Ainsworth came in for much harsh criticism. His situation was aggravated by the confession of Francois Courvoisier, a Swiss-born valet, who in 1840 murdered his master, Lord William Russell. He claimed that he was inspired by Ainsworth's novel and a stage version of the tale. The confession was to have a far-reaching impact on stage censorship in Victorian England.

Jack Sheppard was a heavily fictionalised version of the criminal's life. It introduced the fictional character Thames Darrell, so called because of his rescue from the river as a baby. Although Sheppard and Darrell are brought up together as apprentices to carpenter Wood, they could not be more different; Darrell is virtuous while Jack is an idle reprobate and a thief. Jack's single virtue is his love for his mother, the sister of Sir John Trenchard. Trenchard and Jonathan Wild are attempting to prevent Thames, the son of nobility, from coming into his inheritance.

However, the two schemers fall out, and Wild murders Trenchard and tries to get his hands on his fortune by marrying his sister. But his intended bride commits suicide. In the meantime, Jack, having performed his great escape from Newgate Prison, is arrested again at his mother's graveside. At Tyburn, he is cut down from the gallows by the rampaging mob, but a bullet fired into the crowd hits him through the heart. He is buried next to his mother, while Thames discovers his true identity and inherits his fortune.

The novel is well served by George Cruikshank's evocative and dramatic illustrations, influenced in some cases by the work of contemporary artists such as Thornhill and Hogarth. In fact, Ainsworth saw his book as 'a sort of Hogarthian novel' and the allusions to the artist's engraving sequence, 'The Idle Apprentice' are unmistakable. Apart from a fictional breakout from Willesden gaol, Jack's prison escapes are factual, although the rest of the novel is greatly romanticised. With its abundance of action and its florid, melodramatic language, the novel was a natural for theatrical adaptation.

The serialisation of the novel was not completed until October of 1839; however, during that year, no fewer than eight stage versions appeared. Of these, only two appear to have survived in print. Thomas Greenwood's dramatisation, produced at Sadlers Wells Theatre (and published probably a year later) is notable for the fact it was staged on a multiple set, whereby several rooms could be viewed at the same time. This fashion in set design had been popularised by the play, *The Gamblers* (see entry on 'Thurtell and Hunt'), and usually consisted of four rooms, two on the ground floor and two above. Greenwood's designer went one better, creating a third level to represent the roof of Newgate, with the cells through which Sheppard escaped below.

The most popular stage version of the novel, however, was J. B. Buckstone's *Jack Sheppard*, which opened at the Adelphi in October and ran until Christmas (it was probably published the following year). Adhering closely to the novel, it won the approval of the *Times* reviewer who stated that it gained the 'almost unequivocal approbation of an overflowing audience'.

Jack was played by a woman, Mrs Keeley, who would nightly collapse offstage after the exertions of the Newgate escape scene. The play's main deviation from Ainsworth's tale was in Wild's demise; he is burnt to death in his own house, while a crowd mocks him. Jack, who has yet to meet his own end, is given the opportunity to gloat.

Buckstone's play retained its popularity and was revived repeatedly in the provinces, but was not restaged in London until 1852. The popularity of Newgate dramas had aroused the ire of such journalists as Thackeray and John Forster (who later became Dickens's biographer). Their attacks on the genre opened a debate on the adverse influence of drama on an audience—not unlike the current controversy concerning the effects of television and film violence on viewers. With Courvoisier's confession, the Lord Chamberlain felt obliged to act and, although no formal prohibition was announced, future playwrights found it difficult to get a license for any play based on Sheppard's life or Ainsworth's novel.

Some dramatists simply changed the characters' names. Thus, when Newgate drama again achieved popularity in the 1870s—probably due to the rise of the sensation novels of Wilkie Collins and others—all references to Jack and his accomplices were deleted, although the dramas still adhered to either the actual facts of the case or to Ainsworth's novel. Buckstone's play of 1839 was adapted and staged in 1873 by Ben Webster under a new title, *The Stone Jug*. In Webster's version, the character of Jack became Robert Chance and Wild became Sampson Savage.

Even so, the Lord Chamberlain's office put sufficient pressure on Webster to necessitate a complete refashioning of the play. The burning of Wild's (Savage's) house was retained, but the march to Tyburn deleted. Also, the characters of Edgeworth Bess and Poll Maggot, although they had been renamed, were also removed. Once these changes has been made, the Examiner's only argument with Webster was that he continued to advertise the play as a revision of *Jack Sheppard*. Although the reviewers were quick to condemn the work as morally objectionable, the public had already lost their taste for Newgate drama, and the play ran for only thirteen performances.

Also staged at this time was *Old London*, adapted from a French dramatisation of Ainsworth's novel, *Les Chevaliers du Brouillard*. The original had been performed in Paris in 1857, unintentionally reducing Ainsworth to tears of laughter when he saw it. *Old London* was published in 1880 under the title, *London Bridge, 150 Years Ago*. Although it again changed the names of the principal characters, it did manage to faithfully recreate the major scenes of the novel, including an escape from a Thames flood by rope ladder on London Bridge. The main alteration was in the ending, with the Sheppard and Wild characters led off to their execution together.

Sheppard's next factional appearance was in Joseph Hatton's 1899 novel, *When Rogues Fall Out*. Although the work had been based on Hatton's 1898 play, *Jack Sheppard* (evidently by the 1890s, Jack's name was no longer anathema on stage) the dramatised version was never published, probably because it was as unsuccessful as Webster's version. Again, Ainsworth's novel formed the basis of the plot, with a few changes of name (Sir Patrick Brent replaced Ainsworth's Roland Trenchard and Eric Beryl replaced Thames Darrell). Hatton's novel ends as Wild is thrown into Sheppard's former cell, and Jack goes singing to his execution. The novel's stage origins are obvious—each chapter is set in a single location and plot exposition takes the place of any fluid action. Hatton's one original touch was to add historical foootnotes, thus placing the action within its factual framework.

Philip Lindsay added to the factional Sheppard treatments with his well-researched but much fictionalised 1943 novel, *Jack Laughs at Locksmiths*. Lindsay's forte was placing genuine crimes and criminals in the framework of an original story. In this instance he creates a fictional friend of Sheppard's named William Page, and follows his amorous pursuit of a pretty barmaid.

By the 1960s, Sheppard had been eclipsed by Dick Turpin in the public's interest. Sheppard's most recent appearance was in the 1969 film, *Where's Jack?* The screenplay was faithfully novelised by David Newhouse in the same year. The story concentrates on a duel of wits between Sheppard and Jonathan Wild. While trying to save his brother from being sent to prison on Wild's orders, Sheppard falls into Wild's clutches. He agrees to become a housebreaker for the thief-taker general. But when Wild reneges on their agreement and Jack's brother is transported, Sheppard steals from Wild and is thrown into St. Giles prison. He escapes, but when Edgeworth Bess is arrested, Jack once more surrenders himself to Wild.

Following his great escape from Newgate, Jack's notoriety (as a highwayman in this version) grows. He is tempted by the King's wager that he cannot steal the Lord Chamberlain's chain of office. The wager is a trap, and Jack is soon on his way to the gallows. Following a riot at Tyburn Hill, he is snatched from the rope by the crowd and secretly resuscitated. While the authorities bury his weighted coffin, Jack is reunited with Bess. Adequate as Newhouse's novel is, it is fascinating to consider how the director James Clavell, himself a best-selling novelist, could have told the story.

FACTIONAL WORKS:

John Thurmond, *Harlequin Sheppard* (London: J. Rogers and A. Dodd, 1724). (P)

Anon., *The Prison-Breaker; or, The Adventures of John Sheppard* (London: for A. Moore, 1725). (P)

John Gay, *The Beggar's Opera* (London: John Watts, 1728). (P)

[Thomas Walker], *The Quaker's Opera* (London: for J. W., 1728). (P)

William Harrison Ainsworth, *Jack Sheppard* (London: Bentley, 1839).

J. B. Buckstone, *Jack Sheppard* (London: Chapman & Hall, [1840]). (P)

Thomas Greenwood, *Jack Sheppard* (London: J. Cumberland, [1840]). (P)

J. B. Buckstone [and Ben Webster], *The Stone Jug* (London: John Dicks, [1873]). (P)

Anon., *London Bridge, 150 Years Ago* (London: Samuel French Ltd., [1880]). (P)

Joseph Hatton, *When Rogues Fall Out* (London: C. Arthur Pearson, 1899).

Philip Lindsay, *Jack Laughs at Locksmiths* (London: Hutchinson & Co., [1943]).

David Newhouse, *Where's Jack?* (London: Sphere Books, 1969).

FURTHER READING:
Christopher Hibbert, *The Road to Tyburn* (London: Longmans, 1957).

FILM ADAPTATIONS:
The Beggar's Opera, d. Peter Brook. GB: British Lion/Imperadio, 1952. Screenplay by Dennis Cannan and Christopher Fry, based on the play by John Gay.
Where's Jack?, d. James Clavell. GB: Paramount/Oakhurse, 1968. Screenplay by Rafe and David Newhouse, novelised by David Newhouse.

GEORGE SHOTTON GB 1920

George Shotton married an ex-chorus girl named Mamie Stuart in 1918. In the next year the couple moved to a villa near Swansea, called Ty-Llanwydd ('The Abode of Peace'). From there Mamie wrote to her parents, but when they replied, their letter was returned marked 'House Closed'. They received a Christmas telegram, allegedly from Mamie, but nothing more.

At the time of their marriage, Mamie didn't realise that Shotton already had a wife. In May 1920, he was arrested for bigamy. By then police had cause to suspect him of another crime, as Mamie had disappeared. A case containing her torn clothing had been discovered in a Swansea hotel and a leather handbag containing her ration card, a vital document in post-war Britain, was discovered at the deserted Ty-Llanwydd. Shotton had been located a few miles from Swansea living with his first wife. At his bigamy trial, he denied his marriage to Mamie Stuart, saying he had lived with her until they had quarrelled and she had then left. Found guilty, he was sentenced to eighteen months' hard labour.

In 1961, a human skeleton was discovered by potholers in a disused mine shaft along the Welsh coast. Fragments of clothing were identified as Mamie Stuart's, and the size and shape of the skeleton matched the missing woman's. At a Coroner's inquest, an ex-postman remembered having met Shotton around the time of Mamie's disappearance, as he was leaving Ty-Llanwydd carrying a large sack. 'Oh God,' Shotton had exclaimed in horror, 'for a minute I thought you were a policeman'. The inquest jury decided that Mamie Stuart had been murdered by her 'husband'. However, George Shotton escaped justice—he had died three years earlier.

The factional novel based on the Mamie Stuart case placed the facts within the genre of a police procedural. Bernard Picton's *The Thread of Evidence* (1965) begins as a skeleton covered with remains of clothing is found in an unused lead mine. Local gossip suggests that these are the remains of Mavis Hewitt, who disappeared in 1929. Her husband, Roland, had left for Canada to escape the possible scandal after Mavis vanished, but had returned to the village five years ago. The police pursue a case against Hewitt, after superimposing a photo of his wife over one of the uncovered skull to establish a match—a method actually used in the Shotton case. Hewitt's guilt seems to be established, until two new pieces of evidence come to light and the case takes off in a new direction. The second half of

Picton's story is completely fictional, but no less ingenious than the conclusion of the Shotton case.

FACTIONAL WORKS:
Bernard Picton, *The Thread of Evidence* (London: Robert Hale, 1965).

FURTHER READING:
Brian Lane, ed., *The Murder Guide to South-West England and Wales* (London: Harrap, 1989).

OSCAR SLATER CASE GB 1909

Marion Gilchrist, a wealthy octogenarian, lived in a flat in Queen's Terrace, Glasgow. On 21st December 1908, she sent her servant, Helen Lambie, to fetch a newspaper. On her return, Lambie was informed by a neighbour, Arthur Adams, of a commotion in the Gilchrist flat. As she entered the flat, a man sped by and ran out into the street, almost knocking down a fourteen-year-old girl named Mary Barrowman. Lambie discovered her mistress had been beaten to death in the flat. Despite her wealth, only one thing was missing: a diamond brooch.

Police discovered that a German Jew named Oscar Slater had recently sold such a brooch; however, they disregarded the fact that the sale had taken place a month before the murder. In addition, Slater had sailed from Liverpool to America five days after the murder. He was nevertheless extradited and taken to Edinburgh to stand trial. The proceedings began in May 1909. Lambie, Borrowman and Adams—who had all been sent to America to identify Slater—testified for the prosecution, although Barrowman admitted she had been shown a photograph of Slater before she had identified him. Despite this—and the fact that Adams would only say that Slater 'closely resembled the murderer'—Slater was found guilty and sentenced to death. However, at the last minute, the sentence was commuted to life imprisonment.

The dubious and conflicting evidence aroused great concern. Many prominent figures, including Arthur Conan Doyle, Edgar Wallace, lawyer Edward Marshall Hall and criminologist William Roughead, campaigned for an enquiry into the case. Nineteen years later, Slater was finally released, and was awarded £6,000 in compensation. He died in 1948.

The Slater case was transferred to Chicago in Vincent Starrett's short story, 'Too Many Sleuths' , which was collected in his 1930 volume, *The Blue Door*. Helen Lambert, a descendant of the Gilchrist family, is murdered in her locked apartment. Her maid and a neighbour see a man leave the building. Twelve others come forward who have seen a man waiting outside the house; a thirteenth, who is a pawnbroker, has also received a brooch similar to that owned by Miss Lambert. Oscar Slaney is identified by all the witnesses. The solution to the mystery 'violates the historical facts', as Barzun and Taylor have pointed out, but is nevertheless an intriguing one.

In a *Sunday Times* review of Dorothy Erskine Muir's 1934 novel, *Five to Five*, criminology expert Dorothy L. Sayers identified the Slater case as its inspiration. The facts of the initial murder have been used as the springboard for a fictional story. The novel begins as an elderly man is murdered in his apartment. A stranger is seen leaving the room and is spotted outside by another witness. From here, however, the story diverges strongly from the facts, and a second murder is committed before the case can finally be solved.

FACTIONAL WORKS:
Vincent Starrett, 'Too Many Sleuths', in *The Blue Door* (New York: Doubleday, 1930).
D. Erskine Muir, *Five to Five* (London: Blackie & Sons, 1934).

FURTHER READING:
Peter Hunt, *Oscar Slater* (London: Carroll & Nicolson, 1951).

GEORGE JOSEPH SMITH GB 1915

Smith was born in 1872. By the age of sixteen, he had already spent eight years behind bars in a reformatory. Including a two-year sentence for receiving stolen goods, he was in and out of prison until 1902. It was then that he turned to a new line of embezzlement. Smith began to prey on single women whom he married and then deserted, taking their savings with him. In fact he had originally married in 1898 but was separated from his wife; thus his later marriages were all bigamous.

In 1912, Smith added murder to his list of previous crimes. With his new wife, Bessie Mundy, he leased a house in Herne Bay. The house had no bath, so Smith had one installed to his liking. Soon after he took his wife to a doctor, claiming she had suffered a fit. The doctor prescribed some medicine and husband and wife returned home. Subsequently, the doctor was called to their house, where Smith explained that Bessie had suffered another fit, this time in the bath, and had drowned. The doctor supplied a death certificate accordingly.

Smith had been living in Herne Bay under an alias. He collected his wife's inheritance and then disappeared. The next year, Smith resurfaced in Swansea and married Alice Burnham. They moved to Blackpool, where in December 1913, Alice drowned in her bath; Smith collected £600 and left. A year later, under the name Lloyd, he married Margaret Lofty. The couple moved to Highgate, where the next day, Mrs Lloyd was discovered dead in the bath of her new home; the verdict, once more, was misadventure.

This time, however, a relative of Miss Burnham wrote to the police, remarking on the similarity between Margaret's death and that of Alice. So did the landlady in whose house Alice had died. In January 1915, Smith was arrested. His trial took place in June. Although Smith was only accused of the murder of Bessie Mundy, the prosecution won an important point when evidence of the two other deaths was admitted to establish method. Pathologist Bernard Spilsbury stated that the baths were too short for the deaths to be accidental; he claimed that the victims had been dragged under the water by their legs and their heads had been held down. The police experimented by using a policewoman; the shock of the water entering her nose and mouth rendered her unconscious and there were a few anxious moments before she was revived. Smith was found guilty and sentenced to death. The 'Brides in the Bath' murderer, as the press called him, was executed in August 1915.

Marie Belloc Lowndes used the Smith case as the basis for her short story, 'An Unrecorded Instance', which was written in 1924 and published in 1931. Jack Grantham is the Smith-like murderer who marries Hetty Mingle, who is reasonably well-off. He and his young bride move to a bungalow in Sussex. There he installs a new bath, and subsequently takes his wife to the local doctor to complain about her health. A few days later, Hetty sees a newspaper article about a young bride who had drowned in her bath. By the end of the story, Hetty still remains blissfully unaware of her husband's murderous activities, but has inadvertently given him a nasty shock.

American author Marjorie Carlton provided two more substantial versions of the case in her 1944 play, *The Bride Regrets*, and her 1950 novel of the same name. The action is transferred to America, where a husband and his new wife check into a hotel. His plan to drown her in the bath is thwarted by a heroic young man, who has fallen in love with her. Both the play and the novel end as the husband's other murders are revealed and he goes to his execution.

Peter Lovesey's version of the 'Brides in the Bath' case is detailed in his 1973 short story, 'The Bathroom'. In a contemporary setting, a recently-married woman named Melanie Lloyd decides to have a bath, against her husband's wishes. While soaking in the tub, she reads a crime book based on the Smith case and begins to notice certain similarities between her present position and that of Smith's victims. The story ends with a twist which is at odds with the original but entirely in keeping with Lovesey's usual elaborate plotting.

FACTIONAL WORKS:

Marie Belloc Lowndes, 'An Unrecorded Instance', in Dorothy L. Sayers, ed., *Great Stories of Detection, Mystery and Horror, Part 3* (London: Victor Gollancz, 1931).

Marjorie Carlton, *The Bride Regrets* (Boston, Mass.: Baker, [1944]). (P)

Marjorie Carlton, *The Bride Regrets* (New York: Morrow, 1950).

Peter Lovesey, 'The Bathroom', in Virginia Whittaker, ed., *Winter's Crimes, 5* (London: Macmillan, 1973).

FURTHER READING:

Arthur La Bern, *The Life and Death of a Ladykiller* (London: Frewin, 1967).

MADELEINE SMITH CASE GB 1857

Madeleine Smith was the daughter of a prominent architect in Glasgow. In 1855, she fell in love with a French office clerk named Pierre L'Angelier and began a passionate affair with him. They met in secret and Madeleine wrote intense letters to her lover—letters that would later almost cause her downfall. Soon Madeleine's feelings towards L'Angelier cooled. She did not appear displeased when her father began to prepare her engagement to William Minnoch, a merchant. When L'Angelier heard of this, he threatened to blackmail Madeleine with her letters. After Madeleine met with him to discuss the situation, L'Angelier returned home ill. Following a week confined to bed, he left his lodgings late at night and on his return, collapsed and died. An autopsy revealed a large quantity of arsenic.

When Madeleine's letters were discovered, she was arrested and charged with L'Angelier's murder. At her trial in 1857, her defence lawyers suggested that the Frenchman had poisoned himself after their break-up. The prosecution tried to prejudice Madeleine's by producing her passionate letters and also evidence of several visits to the chemist to purchase arsenic. Madeleine stated in her final declaration that the arsenic was for cosmetic purposes—a common practice in Victorian times.

The Scottish jury reached the verdict of 'Not Proven' and Madeleine walked free. She moved to London, where she married an artist. She eventually emigrated to America, and married again, before her death in 1928.

A *cause célèbre* such as the Smith case was certain to be promoted in fiction and drama. In fact, five years after her trial, Madeleine made a veiled appearance in Margarete Houston's novel, *Such Things Are*, as the sister-in-law of a character based on Constance Kent (see entry). Two old friends become engaged to a pair of brothers. They each have secrets in their past. One of them is blackmailed on the eve of her wedding by her ex-lover, who threatens to show her passionate letters to her fiancé. She poisons him with strychnine and the marriage takes place.

A critic for the *Quarterly Review* of 1863 was scandalised by the use of recent factual murders as the basis for fiction, and commented: 'Everybody knows that the crimes as described were not really committed by the persons to whom they are attributed in the story, but by very different persons and under very different circumstances; and the whole moral is at once destroyed by the glaring untruthfulness and incongruity of the story. A book of this sort is simply a chamber of horrors without even the merit of giving a correct likeness of the criminals exhibited. To think of pointing a moral by stimulants of this kind is like holding a religious service in a gin-palace'.

William D. Lyell incorporated aspects of the Smith mystery into a Wilkie Collins-style sensation novel entitled *The House in Queen Anne's Square* (1920). As in many of Collins's classic novels, Lyell tells a story of deception, drug-addiction and murder in the voices of several narrators. A Scottish setting, arsenic poisoning and incriminating letters are elements of the Madeleine Smith case which Lyell incorporates into a fictional plot which relies on another unique feature of Scottish law.

Winifred Duke took time off from writing crime novels to adapt the Madeleine Smith case for the stage in 1928. In her two-act play, *Madeleine Smith*, the court appearance is not shown. The first act takes place at a soirée on the day that L'Angelier, dies in agony; the second act sees Madeleine arriving home from her trial. In these sombre settings, Duke provides strong psychological insight into the Glasgow poisoning affair.

Marie Belloc Lowndes admitted that the two principal characters in her 1931 novel *Letty Lynton* 'were suggested by a famous Scottish trial'. However, she casts the story in a contemporary setting. Letty is the headstrong daughter of a rich chemical manufacturer. She has already concluded one affair with Noel MacLean, when she launches into an even more passionate liaison with a Swede, Axel Ekebon. Having shocked her parents the first time, she intends to keep this second affair secret. However, when her father is knighted, she finds herself moving in a higher social circle. She becomes engaged to Lord Tintagel.

The existence of her incriminating love letters to Ekebon remains a worry, and she contemplates poisoning her ex-lover. When Ekebon dies suddenly, the inquest virtually turns into a murder trial for murder, with Letty as the accused. However, the jury return a verdict of murder by person or persons unknown, reflecting the 'Not Proven' verdict of the original case. Having escaped with her life, Letty faces the prospect of a forced, loveless marriage to her former lover, MacLean, with no chance that poison might free her a second time.

Hugh Desmond's 1962 novel, *Stay of Execution*, also brings the Smith story up-to-date. Anne Strangeways, the daughter of Sir Gervase, falls for Pierre de Chatelet. When her father proves he is nothing but a shallow and scheming wastrel, Anne severs the relationship and becomes engaged to the Earl of Harrington. De Chatelet threatens blackmail with Anne's love letters and is subsequently found poisoned. Anne faces the noose, but the jury cannot agree a verdict. While Anne awaits a retrial, Sir Gervase hires private investigator Alan Fraser to prove his daughter's innocence. The murderer he reveals is more in keeping with the fictional elements of Desmond's novel than the factual details of the Smith case.

Norah Loft's *Lovers All Untrue* (1970) returns the case to the Victorian period but in an English setting. Marion Draper, the daughter of a Victorian businessman, falls for a French chemist's assistant, Jean de Brissac. They meet secretly at Marion's house, where she regularly supplies her lover with a glass of brandy. Marion becomes pregnant, but during a staged seaside accident, engineered to introduce de Brissac to her father in a heroic light, she loses the child.

De Brissac supplies Marion with arsenic, ostensibly for her complexion, although he truly believes she intends to murder her father. However, when she becomes engaged to another man and de Brissac threatens to reveal the contents of her love letters, Marion uses the arsenic to poison his brandy. After his death, his landlady discovers the letters and turns them over to Marion's father. Faced with the evidence of her affair, Marion has a nervous breakdown. The final chapter of the book finds her in a nursing home, mentally unstable.

The first half of Loft's novel is a close rendition of the Smith affair. The irony of de Brissac supplying the means for his own death is effective, as is the suggestion of the boredom and claustrophobia that comprise a Victorian woman's existence. However, Loft's narrative gradually becomes melodramatic and meandering, and even the novelty of Marion's symbolic 'sentence of death' in the nursing home cannot save the story.

Two other factional treatments of the Smith case appeared before a definitive representation of Madeleine in fiction. Lane Kaufmann's 1973 *Villain of the Piece* concentrated on a New York writer involved in researching a book about the Smith case who becomes drawn deeply into the events of over a century ago. The novel establishes an ironic contrast between the mundane existence of the author and his family with the passion and the life-and-death struggle of Madeleine and her French lover. Mary Anne Ashe's *Alas For Her That Met Me!* (1976) is a close rendition of the affair which adds an important character in Madeleine's sister, thus raising a possible motive of jealous rivalry.

Finally, 1983 saw the publication of Pamela West's novel, *Madeleine*. Like her later factional treatment of the Ripper, the novel is a closely researched and highly atmospheric examination of the period and the events. West uses the trial as the framework in which to describes Madeleine's life, from childhood to eventual acquittal, and afterwards. The author finds Madeleine guilty of not one but two murders, and uses her actual letters to L'Angelier to form a constant counterpoint to the staid proceedings of the trial.

FACTIONAL WORKS:
[Margarete Houston], *Such Things Are* (London: Saunder, Otley & Co., 1862).
William Darling Lyell, *The House in Queen Anne's Square* (London: W. Blackwood, 1920).
Winifred Duke, *Madeleine Smith* (Edinburgh: Hodge & Co., 1928). (P)
Marie Belloc Lowndes, *Letty Lynton* (London: William Heinemann, 1931).
Hugh Desmond, *Stay of Execution* (London: Wright & Brown, 1962).
Norah Lofts, *Lovers All Untrue* (London: Hodder & Stoughton, [1970]).
Lane Kaufmann, *Villain of the Piece* (New York: Milton House, 1973).
Mary Anne Ashe, *Alas for Her that Met Me!* (London: Star, 1976).
Pamela West, *Madeleine* (New York: St. Martin's Press, [1983]).

FURTHER READING:
Henry Blyth, *Madeleine Smith* (London: Duckworth, 1975).

FILM ADAPTATIONS:
Letty Lynton, d. Clarence Brown. US: MGM, 1932. Screenplay by John Meehan and Wanda Tuchock, based on the novel by Marie Belloc Lowndes.

SIDNEY SMITH GB 1882

In May 1880, the *Cutty Sark* set sail from London. The chief mate on board was thirty-one-year-old John Anderson, alias Sidney Smith. One night in August, shortly after the ship had rounded the Cape, Smith found himself in command of the watch. The crew were hauling the sail around and a black able seaman, John Francis, was given the job of letting go the fore lazy tack. Francis dropped the end overboard, and Smith accused him of doing so out of spite. An argument ensued, and Smith wrestled a capstan bar from Francis's grasp and struck him over the head with it. Francis died the following day from his injuries.

As the *Cutty Sark* sailed on to Anger, Smith was assisted by the captain in his escape overboard. The ship continued on to Singapore, but en route the captain disposed of the capstan bar and then committed suicide by jumping into the sea. Smith was arrested in London and tried at the Old Bailey in August 1882. Witnesses gave evidence of Smith's previous good conduct and testified that Francis had threatened Smith's life several times. The judge directed the jury to return a verdict of manslaughter, for which Smith was sentenced to seven years imprisonment.

Out of the bare bones of this case, Joseph Conrad crafted one of his most compelling stories of mystery set at sea. 'The Secret Sharer', published in 1912, is narrated by an anonymous young captain on his first command, alone and feeling rejected by his crew. One night, a young man named Leggatt swims from another vessel and asks for his help. He has killed a sailor who was mutinous and threatening the safety of their ship. The captain is struck by the likeness between the fugitive and himself, and hides him in his cabin, dressed in his own clothes.

The captain decides to bring his vessel perilously close to a rocky island so that Leggatt can swim ashore to safety. By doing so, not only does he aid his friend, but also wins the admiration of his own crew. From a lonely, nervous leader of men, he has proven his worth to himself and others, attaining 'the perfect communion of a seaman with his first command'. The story ends on a note of irony, as the captain, in saving the life of one who was concerned about the safety of his crew, has also risked the lives of his own men.

FACTIONAL WORKS AND FURTHER READING:

Joseph Conrad, 'The Secret Sharer', in *'Twixt Land and Sea, Tales* (London: J. M. Dent & Sons, 1912).

Joseph Conrad, *'Typhoon' and Other Tales* (Oxford: Oxford University Press, 1986). This edition includes the *Times* report of the trial.

FILM ADAPTATIONS:

Face to Face, d. John Brahm, Bretaigne Windust. US: RKO/Huntington Hartford, 1952. Screenplay by Aeneas Mackenzie and James Agee, based on the story 'The Secret Sharer' by Joseph Conrad.

THE SNEAD-WARDLAW CASE USA 1911

On 29th November 1909, Virginia Wardlaw called a doctor to a run-down house in New Jersey. There he found the body of her niece, twenty-four-year-old Oceana Snead lying in a bathtub, her head beneath the water. In the corner of the bathroom was a suicide note which read that Oceana, being 'prostrate with illness' and missing 'near and dear ones' had gone 'to join them in heaven'. The doctor became suspicious: the house was completely empty apart from one furnished room; and Oceana's body was emaciated (in fact, she weighed less than six stone). He called the police.

Investigations led to an address in Brooklyn, the home of Virginia's sisters, Mary Snead and Caroline Martin. Caroline was Oceana's mother and Mary, apart from being the girl's aunt, was also her mother-in-law, as Oceana had married her first cousin, Fletcher Snead (who had subsequently left her). Police discovered other 'suicide notes' in Caroline's possession and an insurance policy for twenty-four thousand dollars in Oceana's name. They suspected a murder plot similar to the 1877 Staunton case in Britain. The three sisters were arrested.

Before their trial for murder came to court, Virginia Wardlaw went on a hunger strike and died in custody. Caroline Martin's subsequent plea of insanity was not accepted, and she changed her plea to guilty of manslaughter. She was sentenced to seven years in jail and was eventually transferred to an asylum, where she died two years later. Since there was no such crime as accessory to manslaughter in those days, Mary Snead was released.

Mary Allerton's 1940 novel, *The Shadow and the Web*, transfers details of the case to Virginia. Miss Morphew, the head of a girls' school, dominates her two younger sisters and keeps her rebellious niece under control by the use of drugs. The claustrophobic family are finally torn apart by blackmail, petty theft and religious frenzy. The author acknowledged her use of the case as a starting point for her novel, but apart from speculating that religious frenzy may have been a contributing cause, gives no further insights into the original crime.

FACTIONAL WORKS:
Mary Allerton, *The Shadow and the Web* (New York: Bobbs-Merrill Co., 1940).

FURTHER READING:
Richard and Molly Whittington-Egan, *The Bedside Book of Murder* (Newton Abbot: David & Charles, 1988).

SNYDER AND GRAY USA 1927

Ruth Snyder was married to Albert, an art editor on a New York magazine, who was thirteen years her senior. Ruth met Judd Gray, a corset salesman, in 1925 and they became lovers. Ruth told Gray a hard-luck story of life with a penny-pinching, dull husband. She had, by her own account, made several attempts on her husband's life. She then persuaded the besotted Judd that he must help her. On 20th March 1927, Gray hid in the Snyder house. When the Snyders returned home, Gray and Ruth together attacked Albert with a window-sash weight, finishing the job with chloroform and choking him with picture wire.

The following morning, Ruth was found bound and gagged in the same room as her husband's dead body. She told police that a foreign-looking attacker had broken in and ransacked the house. They were doubtful, as Ruth showed few signs that she had been assaulted. Gray's name was later discovered in an address book. On a hunch, the police told Ruth that Gray had confessed; she fell for the ruse and informed them of the entire murder plan. Gray was arrested and the couple stood trial in April 1927. They were found guilty and sent to Sing Sing to the electric chair. An enterprising reporter even managed to take a photo with a concealed camera at the moment of Ruth Snyder's death.

Sophie Treadwell's play, *Machinal*, was staged and published in 1929. Although critics claimed it was a dramatisation of the Snyder-Gray case, the author herself denied it. She was right to do so, as her unflattering portrayal of Albert Snyder would not have pleased his surviving family. The play is structured as an allegory: a character referred to only as the Young Woman, marries her mundane boss. An appalling honeymoon is followed by a difficult childbirth. Eventually, in a speakeasy she meets a young man who showers her with flattery. They become lovers.

The action of the play then jumps forward in time to her trial for murder. She tells of two men who broke into her home and killed her husband. However, when the prosecution lawyer reads a letter from her lover, she breaks down and confesses—she murdered her husband 'to be free'. The play ends with a stylised representation of her execution.

The emphasis on the Young Woman's dull existence is stressed by the used of sound in the play. The hum of the office, the sounds from a building-site outside her hospital room (where she is recovering from her child's birth), a couple arguing in the speakeasy, the repetitive business conversations of her husband, the droning of the lawyers at her trial, all give the impression of the monotony of modern industrial life.

T. S. Matthews' 1931 novel, *To The Gallows I Must Go*, tells the story from Judd Gray's perspective. The novel is written in the form of Todd Lorimer's confession. Lorimer, a travelling salesman, has a loveless life with a cold wife and compensates with alcohol and casual sex. His latest mistress enthrals him, and he finds himself drawn into a plot to murder her husband. The novel ends with Lorimer's arrest and confession.

FACTIONAL WORKS:

Sophie Treadwell, 'Machinal' [abridged text], in Burns Mantle, ed., *Best Plays of 1928-29* (New York: Dodd Mead & Co., 1929). (P)

Thomas Stanley Matthews, *To The Gallows I Must Go* (New York: A. A. Knopf, 1931).

FURTHER READING:

Jonathan Goodman, ed., *The Pleasures of Murder* (London: Allison & Busby, 1983).

ISAAC 'IKEY' SOLOMONS GB 1827

Isaac Solomons was born around 1785. By 1810 he was married with two children and had already established a reputation as a pickpocket of note. In that year, he was arrested for theft and sentenced to transportation, but served out his time on the prison hulks in the Thames. He was released six years later, and began a lucrative career fencing stolen goods. He was almost caught again in 1826, when a search of his house revealed his wares, but he managed to escape. In 1827, he was again arrested and held in Newgate. Durring his application for bail, he escaped from the court and fled the country.

Solomons travelled to Van Diemen's Land to join his wife, who was already serving a sentence for receiving stolen goods. He was arrested there as an escaped felon and returned to England to stand trial. In 1831, he was sentenced to transportation, returning to Van Diemen's Land as a convict. He became a ticket-of-leave man and joined his family again. In 1835, he and his wife were arrested for drunkenness and afterwards parted company. Solomons was pardoned in 1840 and died ten years later in poverty.

Was Ikey Solomons the original model for Charles Dickens's Fagin? Solomons was definitely in the news as Dickens was writing *Oliver Twist*, which was serialised in *Bentley's Magazine* between 1837 and 1839. Like Fagin, Solomons was an accomplished pickpocket and a fence. Unlike Fagin, however, Solomons had no gang of adolescent thieves and he was in his forties when he finally left England, whereas Dickens's Fagin was an old, wizened character. The theory of a Solomons-Fagin connection was first suggested in 1926, and has come to be accepted as fact. However, Solomons's biographer, J. J. Tobias, is of the opinion that Dickens created an entirely fictional character, although he admits that the truth will never be known. One certainty is that Dickens's friend Thackeray was familiar enough with Solomons's reputation to use his name as a pseudonym for his Newgate novel, *Catherine* (see entry on 'Catherine Hayes').

FACTIONAL WORKS:
Charles Dickens, *Oliver Twist* (London: Bentley, 1838).

FURTHER READING:
J. J. Tobias, *Prince of Fences* (London: Vallentine, Mitchell, 1974).

FILM ADAPTATIONS:
Oliver Twist, d. David Lean. GB: GFD/Cineguild, 1948. Screenplay by David Lean, based on the novel by Charles Dickens.*

BATHSHEBA SPOONER USA 1778

Bathsheba Ruggles was the daughter of a staunch Tory who supported British rule in the American colonies. She married Joseph Spooner in 1766. The marriage was a disaster; Spooner was much older than Bathsheba, and with the coming of the 1775 War of Independence, he sided with the rebels. Bathsheba appears to have taken many lovers, including a young soldier in the American army, Ezra Ross. In 1778, Bathsheba persuaded Ross to murder her husband. Ross twice failed to go through with the deed, until Bathsheba gave lodging to two British soldiers who had escaped from prison. They agreed to assist Ross in the murder of her husband, who was away at the time. For a fortnight after his return, she hid them on the Spooner estate as they made their plans.

On 1st March 1778, the three men struck; Spooner was accosted as he returned from a tavern, knocked to the ground, half-strangled and thrown down a well. The trio took his watch and clothes (plus a sizeable award from Bathsheba), and set off for a nearby town. Bathsheba made a pretence of searching for her husband, whose body was soon found. The three murderers were apprehended easily and confessed readily to the murder. At their trial, however—the first capital trial under new American law—the men changed their plea to not guilty, and Bathsheba's lawyer tried to obtain a verdict of insanity for his client. However, all four were found guilty as charged and were hanged.

Esther Forbes's 1938 novel, *The General's Lady*, adapts some facts of the Spooner case. The story is told chiefly from the perspective of Dilly Lavender, maid to Morganna Milroy. Morganna falls in love with a British deserter, Alan Brann, whom she persuades to murder her husband. In Forbes's version, Morganna feels morally responsible for her actions and pleads guilty to the murder. She is hanged, while Brann is returned to the British forces. Although the novel contains some attractive scenic description and period detail, the plot is unbelievable and there is a racist characterisation of Morganna's black maid, Phillis, which mars the narrative.

FACTIONAL WORKS:
Esther Forbes, *The General's Lady* (New York: Harcourt, Brace & Co. 1938).

FURTHER READING:
Jay Robert Nash, *Murder, America* (New York: Simon & Schuster, 1980).

THE STAUNTONS GB 1877

Louis Staunton was an auction clerk, who married an heiress named Harriet Richardson in 1875. Harriet was a simple-minded girl who readily consented to sign over her fortune to her husband. They settled in Brixton, where Harriet's mother visited once and was discouraged from calling again. In 1876, they moved to Staunton's house in Kent. There Staunton's brother, Patrick kept an eye on Harriet, while her husband lived at a nearby farm with his mistress, Alice Rhodes. Rhodes was the sister of Patrick's wife, Elizabeth.

In London, Rhodes was spotted by Harriet's mother wearing her daughter's jewels. When Mrs Richardson tried to visit her daughter, she was driven away by the brothers. Harriet had recently given birth to a child and in April 1877, the boy was left at a London hospital, where he died of malnutrition a in a matter of hours. Four days later, Harriet was moved to a house in Southeast London, where she died on 13th April. She was found in a dirty condition, weighing just over five stone. The doctor called to the house gave the cause of death as 'cerebral disease and apoplexy'. By an amazing coincidence, a brother-in-law of Harriet's overheard a conversation which mentioned her death and called the police. The three Stauntons and Alice Rhodes were arrested for murder.

At their trial in September 1877, Patrick Staunton's defence lawyer suggested that Harriet had died of tuberculosis; he was backed up by several medical witnesses. The pathologists who had examined the body, however, gave the cause of death as starvation due to neglect. The jury agreed with their findings. All four were found guilty of murder and sentenced to death. However, the medical profession placed their weight behind the defence witnesses' conclusions and seven hundred doctors signed a petition for reprieve. The Home Office commuted the death sentences on the three Stauntons to prison sentences of various lengths; Alice Rhodes was released.

Elizabeth Jenkins's novel, *Harriet* (1934), is a psychological study of the perpetrators of this horrifying crime: Patrick and Lewis Oman and two sisters, Elizabeth and Alice Hoppner. Harriet's money arouses their greed and they keep her a virtual prisoner. They treat their prisoner well (Harriet even falls in love with Lewis) until she gives birth to a son. The story then follows the sinister details of the genuine case, through the trial and subsequent prison sentences. In an ironic final chapter, Elizabeth is brought news of the death of her husband, Patrick. She shows no interest. Her sole concern is that her regular meal should be delivered to her in her prison cell: 'the sure knowledge that at certain hours it would come was the support of her existence'.

FACTIONAL WORKS:
Elizabeth Jenkins, *Harriet* (London: Victor Gollancz, 1934).

FURTHER READING:
Edgar Lustgarten, *The Woman in the Case* (London: Andre Deutsch, 1955).

JAMES STEWART GB 1752

After the failure of the 1745 Jacobite Rebellion in Scotland, those who fought for the Stuart cause were forced to live under the supremacy of clans loyal to the House of Hanover. In Appin country, on the west coast of Scotland, this meant that the Campbells held sway over the lives and lands of the Camerons and Stewarts. Accordingly, on 14th May 1752, Colin Campbell of Glenure set off with a small party to evict some undesirable tenants from their farms. As the group rode through Lettermore Wood, a shot rang out and the Red Fox (as Campbell was known) fell from his horse. He died later.

James Stewart (James of the Glen) was the senior member of the local Appin Stewarts and served as Campbell's assistant factor. Although relations were generally good between them, Stewart was known to have threatened his master after a drunken argument. Stewart was also a close friend of Alan Breck, a Jacobite soldier and spy who had been spotted in Appin shortly before the incident. Stewart was charged as an accessory to the murder of Colin Campbell. He was arrested and held at Fort William, while the Campbells set about preparing their case. The court sat in September of that year, with the Duke of Argyll—not only Lord Justice-General of Scotland, but also the most important member of the Campbell clan—as presiding judge. Eleven of the fifteen jurymen were also Campbells. The prosecution's case was that Alan Breck was the chief instigator, and as he had fled to France, would be tried *in absentia*. The charge against Stewart was therefore unlawful; in Scots law an accessory to a crime could not be tried prior to the principal suspect. Nonetheless, Stewart was found guilty and was hanged soon after.

Historians ever since have debated the verdict: were Stewart and Breck guilty? Novelist Robert Louis Stevenson addressed the question in two of his novels, *Kidnapped* (1886) and *Catriona* (1893). In the first novel, Alan Breck joins the fictional David Balfour on his trek across Scotland to return to his rightful estates, which have been seized by his uncle. Stevenson places Balfour with Campbell at the scene of the murder. Although Balfour suspects Breck of the deed, Breck swears his innocence. They continue on their perilous journey as far as Edinburgh, where they part company— Balfour to claim his rightful inheritance and Breck to await a ship for France.

The first part of the sequel, *Catriona*, follows the trial of James Stewart for the murder of Colin Campbell. David Balfour comes forward as a witness for the defence, but Argyll is not impressed by Balfour's honesty, and an attempt is made to scare him off. While Balfour tries unsuccessfully to save James of the Glens from the gallows, he is meanwhile falling in love with Catriona. She is the daughter of James More Drummond, who commits perjury at the trial. The second part of the novel follows Balfour's flight to Europe with Catriona. There, Alan Breck is instrumental in bringing about their marriage. Stevenson's source for both works was a copy of *The Trial of James of the Glen*, which his father had bought him in 1881.

FACTIONAL WORKS:
Robert Louis Stevenson, *Kidnapped* (London: Cassell & Co., 1886).
Robert Louis Stevenson, *Catriona* (London: Cassell & Co., 1893).

FURTHER READING:
George Malcolm Thomas, *A Kind of Justice* (London: Hutchinson & Co., 1970).

FILM ADAPTATIONS:
Kidnapped, d. Delbert Mann. GB: Omnibus, 1971. Screenplay by Jack Pulman, based on the novel by Robert Louis Stevenson.*

HARRY THAW USA 1907

On 25th June 1906, architect Stanford White was watching a show at the rooftop dinner theatre of Madison Square Garden in New York. In the audience was millionaire Harry Thaw and his wife, an ex-chorus girl named Evelyn Nesbit. During the performance, Thaw stood up and walked towards White. He pulled out a revolver and shot the architect twice through the head, and once again as he fell to the floor. Emptying his revolver, Thaw stood quietly until police arrived to take him away.

The trial for murder opened in January 1907. Thaw's lawyer had prepared the ground by spreading tales of White's reputation as a seducer of innocent women, including Evelyn. She testified that prior to her marriage, she had been drugged and then raped by White. The defence claimed that Thaw, who was intensely jealous, had beaten the story out of his wife. He had avenged her disgrace by murdering her seducer. The prosecution suggested that the tale of rape and drugging was a lie and that Thaw was naturally sadistic in his treatment of women. As the defence plea was temporary insanity, the prosecution produced psychiatrists to pronounce Thaw legally sane. The jury could not agree on a verdict. In 1908, a second trial was held. Thaw was found not guilty on the grounds of insanity, and was committed to an institution for the criminally insane. However, in 1913 he escaped to Canada. His mother's wealth obtained him a hearing in 1915, in which he was declared sane. He was released, but returned to an asylum the following year after kidnapping and whipping a teenage boy. In 1922 he was again released and travelled the world, running through his fortune. He died in 1947, aged seventy-six.

Thaw becomes a minor character in E. L. Doctorow's novel, *Ragtime* (1975), a mosaic of American life in the years prior to the First World War. As the novel opens, White's murder has already occurred and Thaw is in Tombs prison awaiting trial. Evelyn Nesbit, the catalyst in the case, is very much to the fore in the first part of Doctorow's story, as she prepares her testimony for the forthcoming trial of her brutal husband. In the meantime, she has an affair with the famous anarchist Emma Goldmann. Thaw also meets a personality from the period—Harry Houdini, who is in the cell opposite, attempting a much-publicised escape. The novel is filled with appearances from other notable figures, such as Pierpont Morgan, Sigmund Freud and Henry Ford, whom Doctorow places in fictional situations. The Thaw trial is just one of several plot strands Doctorow pursues in his complex work.

FACTIONAL WORKS:
E. L. Doctorow *Ragtime* (New York: Random House, [1975]).

FURTHER READING:
Michael Macdonald Mooney, *Evelyn Nesbit and Stanford White* (New York: Morrow, 1976).

FILM ADAPTATIONS:
Ragtime, d. Milos Forman. US: Ragtime/Sunley, 1981. Screenplay by Michael Weller, based on the novel by E. L. Doctorow.

THOMPSON AND BYWATERS GB 1922

Edith Thompson married in 1915. Her husband Percy worked as a shipping clerk and was a staid, quiet man. By contrast, Edith was lively and passionate, and possessed a vivid imagination. In 1920 the couple moved to Ilford. There, they met Frederick Bywaters, a sailor with the P&O Line, who was seeing Edith's sister. Soon, Bywaters and Edith found themselves attracted to each other. Percy, unaware of the developing relationship, invited Frederick to become their lodger. However, in August 1921, Frederick argued with Percy over his treatment of Edith, and the young sailor was asked to leave. In September, Bywaters sailed for the Far East.

He and Edith wrote to each other frequently. Edith's florid letters gave scope to her romantic dreams of a different life with Frederick. She fantasised of clearing a path for her lover by getting rid of her husband. However, Edith never went beyond these fantasies; although she wrote of putting ground glass in her husband's food, the coroner's report at her subsequent trial gave no evidence of such an attempt. When Frederick finally returned to England in October 1921, the two lovers tried to persuade Percy to give Edith a separation. When Percy refused, they simply resumed their affair.

On 3rd October 1922, Bywaters met the Thompsons as they returned from the theatre and pulled a knife on Percy. They struggled, and Bywaters stabbed his rival several times. When Percy died of his injuries, Edith eventually named her lover as his murderer. The Thompson and Bywaters trial opened at the Old Bailey in December. Frederick was accused of murder, Edith of murder and conspiracy and incitement to murder. The young man made no attempt to deny his guilt but insisted that Edith was innocent. The major evidence against her was the batch of letters that Frederick had kept. The prosecution insisted that these proved incitement to murder and indicated that they described previous attempts on Percy's life.

The judge was shocked at the passionate nature of the correspondence, and summed up heavily against Edith. In a climate of moral outrage, she was portrayed as the prime instigator in the murder. The jury agreed and the couple were sentenced to death. Petitions were raised to gain a reprieve, but these and various appeals were unsuccessful. On 9th January 1923, Frederick Bywaters was led to his death at Pentonville prison. At the same time, Edith Thompson, drugged and in a state of collapse, was carried from the condemned cell in Holloway to her execution.

A year later, E. M. Delafield published her novel, *Messalina of the Suburbs*. The story centres on seventeen-year-old Elsie Palmer, who marries a wealthy older man and finds herself trapped in a stultifying relationship. She falls in love with her sister's boyfriend, thus instigating the events which will lead to her trial for murder. Elsie is portrayed as a victim of circumstance, an innocent in a cruel world. Delafield appears to have taken her title from the tabloid reports of the trial, in which Edith was referred to as 'the Messalina of Ilford'.

In 1928 A. E. W. Mason used some aspects of the Thompson-Bywaters case for his otherwise totally fictional Inspector Hanaud novel, *The Prisoner in the Opal*. The case against Edith Thompson rested heavily on her incriminating letters to Bywaters, but on his instructions, she had destroyed his letters to her. Mason explored the idea that although her letters were certainly provocative, Bywater's side of the correspondence might have contained a more accurate picture of the events and incriminated the genuine culprit.

The most faithful representation of Edith Thompson's tragic story is F. Tennyson Jesse's 1934 novel, *A Pin to See the Peepshow*. It is a work of powerful psychological insight and one of the masterpieces of the crime faction genre. Although the author's disclaimer states that 'no reference whatever is intended to any living person', the character of Julia Almond strongly echoes Edith Thompson.

The novel begins with a description of Julia as a young girl. She conjures a fantasy world of her own creation from a crude home-made peepshow box containing cotton wool and card images. Thus the author establishes a character whose ripe imagination and strong reliance on self-delusion will later provide an escape from her life of servility and boredom.

Julia marries Herbert Starling, but her husband proves to be stolid, brutish and dull. In the meantime, she falls for Leonard Carr and takes him as her lover. While Carr is at sea, Julia enters into a passionate and inventive correspondence with him that will soon bring about her own death. The murder of her husband and the subsequent trial are reconstructed faithfully from the facts of the original case. Jesse was well-versed in her subject; as a noted criminologist, she had attended the Thompson-Bywaters trial and had been responsible for editing the trial transcript of the similar Rattenbury and Stoner case for the *Notable British Trials* series.

With its sympathetic portrayal of an innocent woman condemned to death by a predominantly male establishment, the novel has held a significant place in feminist fiction (it has recently been reprinted in Britain by Virago Press). Jesse and her husband, H. M. Harwood, subsequently dramatised the novel, but encountered problems when Thompson's brother persuaded the Lord Chamberlain's office to prevent its staging. They were initially forced to present the play exclusively in private clubs. When it finally reached the West End in 1948, it ran for only three weeks and the Broadway opening was also a failure. The play was never published.

FACTIONAL WORKS:

E. M. Delafield, *Messalina of the Suburbs* (London: Hutchinson & Co., 1924).

A. E. W. Mason, *The Prisoner in the Opal* (London: Hodder & Stoughton, 1928]).

F. Tennyson Jesse, *A Pin to See the Peepshow* (London: William Heinemann, 1934).

FURTHER READING:

Rene Weiss, *Criminal Justice* (London: Hamish Hamilton, 1988).

ABRAHAM THORNTON CASE GB 1817

The Mary Ashford affair holds a particular interest for criminologists, on two points of ancient law that were invoked at the subsequent trials. On 26th May 1817, Mary Ashford and her friend, Hannah Cox went to a dance at the Tyburn House, Erdington (now a suburb of Birmingham). There, Mary met a local bricklayer named Abraham Thornton and subsequently left with him. She later called at Hannah's house to change her clothes before setting off for home. Early the following morning, her body was found in a water-filled pit. There were footprints and signs of a struggle at the edge of the pit.

The authorities suspected that Mary had been raped and murdered. Thornton was arrested for the crime. The defence relied on timing and alibi to prove his innocence: witnesses gave evidence that Thornton was far from the scene of the crime when it was believed to have occurred. Thornton did admit that he had had sex with Mary earlier, but denied the charge of rape and murder. He was found not guilty and discharged, although public opinion was very much against him. Mary's younger brother, William was persuaded to invoke an ancient legal procedure known as 'appeal of murder', by which the closest relative of a murder victim could appeal against the acquittal of the accused.

Thus, Thornton found himself in the dock again, faced with the same murder charge. He managed to turn the tables on William by claiming the ancient right to 'trial by combat' against the frail young boy to prove his innocence. William was advised to refuse the challenge and the case was dismissed. Thornton emigrated to America, and the points of 'appeal of murder' and 'trial by combat' were eventually removed from the statute books.

Opinion is still divided as to how Mary Ashford met her death. Suggestions such as suicide, accidental death and murder by persons unknown have been put forward. As he was in his day, Thornton has remained the favoured suspect. Recent feminist writers have seen the case as a classic example of male oppression and the acceptance of sexual violence in a male-dominated society.

In the same year as the murder itself, the case was dramatised by a local writer, Geoge Ludlam. *The Mysterious Murder, or, What's the Clock?* is a three-act melodrama which thinly disguises the facts and accuses Thornton of the crime. In the play, Maria Ashfield is portrayed as a virtuous woman, whereas Thorntree is a scheming seducer. He has already decided to murder Maria before he commits the rape. After the deed, his own father is the first to suspect him. However, his lawyer Quibble, in the case solely for the money, manages to win a 'not guilty' verdict. Still, Thorntree is plagued by guilt and dreams of his murderous actions. The play ends with a tableau in which Maria's spirit ascends to heaven. Ludlam's play was popular enough to run to several editions, and can be seen as a precursor of the Red Barn plays (see entry on 'William Corder'), based on a similar murder trial.

Ludlam's play was followed in 1819 by a lesser work, *The Murdered Maid, or, The Clock Struck Four* (the author of which was known only by the initials 'S.N.E.'). Although the setting is France, and the characters are called Marie and Thornville, there is no doubt as to the source or the guilt of the accused. The author states in a preface that 'every disgusting circumstance is carefully omitted' from the retelling. The author obviously felt that the murderer's freedom was one such 'disgusting circumstance', since the play concludes with Thornville's suicide.

Although its connection with the Thornton case is indeed tenuous, one other drama that should be mentioned is William Barrymore's *Trial by Battle*. It was staged a year after Mary Ashford's death, although it may not have been published until 1831. Several theatre historians have suggested that Barrymore was given the idea by Thornton's request to 'trial by combat'. However, Barrymore's story bears no relationship to the facts of the case. Two unrelated but nevertheless interesting facts are that Barrymore was an ancestor of the famous American theatre family, and that the play was the first to appear at the Coburg Theatre, which eventually became the Old Vic.

FACTIONAL WORKS:
[George Ludlam], *The Mysterious Murder; or, What's the Clock* (Birmingham: the Author, [1817]). (P)

S. N. E., *The Murdered Maid; or, The Clock Struck Four* (Warwick: Heathcote & Foden, 1819). (P)

William Barrymore, *Trial by Battle* (London: J. Duncombe, [1831]). (P)

FURTHER READING:
J. P. Lethbridge, *Murder in the Midlands* (London: Robert Hale, 1989).

THURTELL AND HUNT GB 1824

John Thurtell was the son of a Norwich merchant who joined the Royal Marines at the end of the Napoleonic Wars. From there he drifted into the sporting underworld of Regency London, known as the 'fancy'. He became well-known in these circles as a trainer and promoter of prize fighters, as well as a gambler and a spendthrift. By 1823, he was heavily in debt. After losing a game of billiards to another gambler named William Weare, Thurtell decided his only recourse was to rob his opponent. He enlisted the services of two other members of the fancy, Joseph Hunt and William Probert.

On 25th October, Weare and Thurtell set out in a gig towards Probert's cottage in Gill Hill Lane, near Elstree. As they neared the cottage, Thurtell shot at Weare with his pistol. Weare, who was only wounded, managed to jump from the cart, crying for help. Thurtell turned his weapon into a cudgel, beating Weare about the head with it. To complete the task, he cut Weare's throat with a penknife. The body was taken to the cottage, where it was thrown into a nearby pond.

The murderer and his accomplices returned to the scene of the crime the following day, to look for the penknife which Thurtell had dropped in the scuffle. They ran off when they spotted some labourers eyeing them curiously. The labourers searched the area and found the bloody weapon. Bow Street Runners questioned Probert, who turned King's evidence. Soon Thurtell and Hunt were under arrest. The subsequent trial excited much interest at the time. Journalists and sightseers flocked to the scene of the crime and the town of Hertford where the trial was held. Thurtell complained justifiably that his case was being prejudged by the tabloid press and the judge had much to say regarding their intrusion in his court. The verdict, however, was never in doubt. Both men were found guilty; Thurtell was hanged two days later, while Hunt was eventually transported to Australia.

In 1823, while the Thurtell trial was still *sub judice*, the owner of the Surrey Theatre in London decided to cash in on the public's interest. He approached dramatist Edward Fitzball with the suggestion that he write a play concerning the murder. Fitzball had already adapted works of Sir Walter Scott for the stage and was later to dramatise the Jonathan Bradford case. In this instance, however, he was horrified at the manager's proposal and turned him down. The manager simply turned to a lesser-known playwright with fewer scruples, and set him to work adapting the facts of the case.

The product of his commission, *The Gamblers*, was staged later that year. It advertised that actual props involved in the case were featured, including the fatal gig itself. Thurtell's counsel obtained an injunction against the play, and it was removed six weeks before the trial began. But as soon as the verdict was reached and Thurtell went to the gallows, the Surrey Theatre resurrected *The Gamblers*, with enormous financial success.

The drama concerns a young man who loses money at a gaming table. When his colleagues hatch a plot to retrieve his money by foul means, he refuses to serve as an accomplice. The play ends as he denounces the murderers to the authorities. It was published the following year and proved popular enough for Hannah Jones to produce a novelisation in 1824 entitled *The Gamblers; or, The Treacherous Friend*. To distance it from any charge of sensationalism, the author added the subtitle: 'a moral fable founded on recent facts'.

Four years later, Edward Bulwer Lytton used the case in *Pelham*, the first of his four crime faction novels. The murder itself forms the latter part of the novel and sits uneasily with the author's predominantly light-hearted tone. Tom Thornton, a sportsman and gambler, owes two thousand pounds to Sir John Tyrrell. As they travel together on an isolated country road, Thornton cuts Tyrrell's throat, washes his hands and, to avoid detection later, drinks the bloody water. However, the author suggests that Tyrrell, like Weare, is no more than a common gambler himself and that the murder is simply a falling-out among thieves.

The novel's eponymous hero brings Thornton to justice by infiltrating his gang and persuading Dawson (an amalgamation of Probert and Hunt) to turn King's evidence. Although the murderer and the deed are clearly based on the Thurtell case, Bulwer Lytton appears to have derived the names of killer and victim from two earlier sources. Sir John Tyrrell recalls Barnabas Tyrrel, the murder victim in William Godwin's 1794 crime novel, *Caleb Williams*, while Thornton is the surname of another notorious suspected murderer (see entry on 'Abraham Thornton Case').

The scholar and erstwhile gypsy, George Borrow, claimed that Thurtell had taught him how to box. Borrow included a character who is not named but who resembles Thurtell in his fictionalised autobiography, *Lavengro* (1851). When Borrow knew Thurtell he had yet to commit the murder, but the powerful description of him in Borrow's book gives an indication that Thurtell left an impression on those who crossed his path.

Lavengro (the fictional Borrow) describes meeting Thurtell first at a gypsy camp and later, as the promoter tries to persuade a magistrate to lease his field for a prize fight. When the magistrate refuses, the promoter stages the fight outside a nearby town instead. Lavengro attends with a gypsy friend, Petulengro. The fight is brought to a close by a thunderstorm, during which Petulengro notices a cloud looking 'something like a stream of blood', a portend of tragedy. When Lavengro asks for whom, his friend points at 'the sporting gentleman of my acquaintance'. How much of this encounter is genuine remains a mystery, but it is an intriguing story.

In Borrow's *Romany Rye* (1857), a sequel to *Lavengro*, the scholar-gypsy is told a story by a jockey concerning a sportsman who loaned him two hundred pounds. The sportsman jokes that he is to come and see him hanged in lieu of payment. Later, the jockey sees the very man on his way to the gallows, and greets him as he is led to his death.

Crime novelist Dick Donovan liberally adapted the facts of the murder for the fanciful plot of his 1906 novel, *Thurtell's Crime*. Donovan's version features a kidnapping in which Thurtell and a fellow-gambler hold a young couple prisoner. The book also introduces Thurtell's lover, Dora Melfont, who following Thurtell's execution, throws herself into the same pond which had concealed Weare's body.

Thomas Burke's *Murder at Elstree* (1936) is a more successful and accurate portrayal of Thurtell's crime. The novel begins at the scene of the prize fight witnessed by Borrow and Petulengro. Thurtell then goes to London, where he makes the acquaintance of Weare and subsequently loses his money in a fixed card game. Burke follows the facts of the killing, the police investigations and the arrests. The novel ends as Borrow, rather than the jockey, greets Thurtell at his execution.

For added authenticity, Pierce Egan, the contemporary reporter and writer on boxing, appears several times in Burke's novel. Egan plays an even larger role in Philip Lindsay's 1955 novel, *The Swell Yokel*. There, he is given the task of breaking the news of Thurtell's death to his lover, Anne Noyes, who is also Probert's sister-in-law. Her relationship with Thurtell is one of Lindsay's few embellishments. As with most of the adaptations, Lindsay sees Thurtell as a born murderer, who would probably have killed again if not convicted for Weare's death. What little capacity he has for affection is reserved for Anne. It transpires that they had married in secret and she is carrying his child at the end of the novel.

FACTIONAL WORKS:

Anon., *The Gamblers* (London: J. Lowndes, [1824]). (**P**)

Hannah Jones, *The Gamblers* (London: E. Livermore, 1824)

Edward Bulwer Lytton, *Pelham* (London: Henry Colburn, 1828).

George Borrow, *Lavengro* (London: John Murray, 1851).

George Borrow, *The Romany Rye* (London: John Murray, 1857).

Dick Donovan, *Thurtell's Crime* (London: Werner Laurie, 1906).

Thomas Burke, *Murder at Elstree* (London: Longmans, 1936).

Philip Lindsay, *The Swell Yokel* (London: Hutchinson & Co., [1955]).

FURTHER READING:

Albert Borowitz, *The Thurtell and Hunt Murder Case* (Baton Rouge: Louisiana State University Press, 1987).

TICHBOURNE CLAIMANT GB 1871–72

This classic case of imposture resulted in a double trial that occupied the courts for a total of 290 days. The story began in 1853, when *The Bella*, a ship sailing bound for New York from Rio de Janeiro, was lost at sea. Among those presumed dead was Sir Roger Charles Doughty Tichbourne, heir to a sizeable estate in England. His mother, the Dowager Lady Tichbourne, refused to believe her son had died and advertised in the world press for news of him.

In 1863 word arrived from Wagga-Wagga, Australia that a butcher named Thomas Castro was claiming to be the long-lost heir to the Tichbourne fortunes. Lady Tichbourne contacted Castro and sent Sir Roger's retainers to identify him. Castro was brought to meet Lady Tichbourne in person. Sir Roger had spoken fluent French, unlike Castro, who also could not recall his mother's maiden name. Despite these shortcomings, he managed to convince Lady Tichbourne that he was indeed her son. He rallied sufficient support to enable him to begin proceedings in the British courts for the recovery of Sir Roger's estates.

Five years preparation finally resulted in a trial which lasted one hundred and two days, during which a veritable army of witnesses gave testimony in support of the so-called Claimant. Despite this, Castro's bumbling court appearances resulted in a verdict against him. He was arrested for perjury. At his subsequent trial, the prosecution insisted that he was really Arthur Orton, a butcher from Wapping who had moved to Australia via South America. The prosecution implied that Orton could have met Sir Roger while still in South America and could have supplemented their conversations with information gleaned from press reports of his disappearance. After a further one hundred and eighty-eight days, Castro was found guilty of perjury and sent to prison. He was released in 1884 and toured for a while as the Tichbourne Claimant, finally dying in obscurity in 1898.

The Tichbourne trials were unfolding as Marcus Clarke's novel, *His Natural Life*, was being serialised in the *Australian Journal*. The full version was published in Australia in 1874, and was later revised under the title, *For The Term of His Natural Life*. Another in the popular series of novels dealing with convict life, heavily influenced by Hugo's *Les Miserables*, Clarke's sprawling epic centres on Richard Devine. The natural son of Lady Devine, he is thrown out by her husband and arrested for robbery. After taking the name Rufus Dawes, he is transported to Australia, along with another convict named John Rex.

While they are imprisoned in the infamous Port Arthur penal colony, Rex escapes and returns to England, where he impersonates Divine in an attempt to inherit the family fortune. It transpires that Rex is in fact Richard's half-brother, who has killed their mutual father. Rex suffers a massive stroke which renders him totally incapacitated. Meanwhile, Richard and his lover Sylvia Vickers, escape from a penitentiary at Norfolk Island, only to be drowned at sea in a cyclone.

In his ground-breaking novel, probably the most influential work of nineteenth-century Australian fiction, Clarke obviously adapted the facts of the Tichbourne case. A more faithful rendition was Robin Maugham's 1969 novel, *The Link*. Maugham was carrying on a family fascination with true crime—his uncle, W. Somerset Maugham, had used the Ethel Proudlock case as inspiration for one of his short stories and his father had written a factual account of the Tichbourne Claimant.

Maugham's atmospheric novel begins with the reminiscences of James Steede, heir to the Steede estates. He recounts his early life and homosexual encounters at Eton, and his subsequent career at Cambridge, where his search for male companionship leads to confusion and rejection. His one heterosexual relationship is thwarted by his domineering mother, and Steede leaves for South America. There, he boards a ship to Australia, unaware that the crew have decided to execute a fraud by reporting the ship and its passengers as missing at sea. Steede settles in Australia as a horse-breaker, content to live a life of drunkenness, promiscuity and obscurity.

Meanwhile, in England a claimant has appeared insisting that he is James. As with the Tichbourne impostor, the Steede Claimant can recount essential facts about James's life but is ignorant of others. Nevertheless, he is accepted by James's mother and the girl he almost married. His opposition is Steede's sister, whose indolent husband and young son will loose their position if the Claimant's case is accepted. It is only in the third part of the novel that the Claimant's true identity and his motives are discovered.

Many aspects of the Tichbourne case are recalled: the claimant is a butcher's son from London, there is a South American and Australian connection, a ship is lost at sea.. Maugham's contribution is a believable explanation for the heir's wish for obscurity, and a family connection between the heir and the Claimant. In all, *The Link* is an acceptable solution to a case that still intrigues.

FACTIONAL WORKS:
Marcus Clarke, *His Natural Life* (London: Bentley, 1875).
Robin Maugham, *The Link* (London: William Heinemann, 1969).

FURTHER READING:
Michael Gilbert, *The Claimant* (London: Constable & Co., 1957).

EMMETT TILL MURDER USA 1955

Emmett Till, a black teenager from the outskirts of Chicago, was sent to stay with his great-uncle in Leflore County, Mississippi in August 1955. Emmett noticed a difference in the way he was treated by white Southerners. Indeed, his mother had warned him to be cautious.

One day, he and several black friends visited Bryant's Grocery Store in the town of Money. At that time Ron Bryant's wife, Carolyn and her sister-in-law, Juanita Milam were behind the counter.

Some of the boys dared Emmett to talk to Carolyn. He walked into the store, bought some gum and shouted 'bye, baby' as he left. It was claimed he had also whistled at her. Four days later, Ron Bryant and J. W. Milam drove to the house of Emmett's great-uncle, Mose Wright and took the boy by force. He never returned. The two men were later arrested for kidnapping, although they were also suspected of murder.

As feared, a few days after Emmett's disappearance, his naked body was fished out of the Tallahachie River. He had been badly beaten and shot through the head; Mose Wright could only identify the corpse from an inscription on the boy's ring. His mother had Emmett's body returned to Chicago for burial and placed in an open coffin so that 'the world could see what they did to my boy'. The body lay in state for four days, attracting thousands of mourners, and the subsequent funeral was attended by thousands more.

The trial of Bryant and Milam took place less than a fortnight later, amidst intense media coverage. There was some doubt as to whether any of Emmett's black friends would give evidence, but Mose Wright identified the two men as the kidnappers and two other witnesses placed them at the possible scene of the murder. However, the all-white jury found the accused not guilty and they left court to a jubilant reception from the local white community. The black press and the liberal-minded Northern papers condemned the verdict. In November, another all-white jury dropped the charges of kidnapping against Bryant and Milam. The following month, they confessed to journalist William Bradford Huie that they had murdered Emmett because he refused to apologise for having 'insulted' Bryant's wife. They received four thousand dollars for their story.

The Emmett Till murder became one of the catalysts of the Civil Rights movement in America. Protest rallies took place throughout the States, and the martyrdom of young Emmett and the courage of his great-uncle in giving evidence against fierce prejudice fired the imagination of many young activists. Among these was the novelist and playwright, James Baldwin. His dramatic indictment, *Blues for Mister Charlie* (1964), takes a scathing look not only at Southern racism, but also at white complacency and conformity, and black reliance on religion. In a preface to the published text, Baldwin locates the action in the fictional Plaguetown—'the plague is race, the plague is our concept of Christianity'—although it is given no name in the play itself. He presents two communities, divided by mistrust and fear, into whose midst walks Richard Henry, son of the local black minister, Meridian Henry. Richard has made it big up North in entertainment, although drugs have destroyed his self-esteem. Back home, he falls in love and begins to recapture his sense of respect.

His attitude causes friction, as he is unwilling to bow to the local white ideal of black subservience. Lyle Britten, a local store-owner once accused of murdering a black man, clashes with Richard. The boy's social, sexual and financial freedom rankles with the white bigot. He kills Richard and is brought to trial. Chief among the witnesses is Parnell Thomas, editor and friend of the local black community. When Britten's wife commits perjury by accusing Richard of assault, Thomas cannot bring himself to call her a liar. Thus the murderer goes free because Southern 'morality' and 'honour' is stronger than commitment to multi-racial equality.

FACTIONAL WORKS:
James Baldwin, *Blues for Mr Charlie* (New York: Dial Press, 1964). (P)

FURTHER READING:
Sanford Weaver, *The Civil Rights Movement: an Eyewitness History* (New York: Facts on File Inc., 1993).

DICK TURPIN GB 1739

Richard Turpin was born in 1705, the son of an innkeeper and butcher. He had a reasonable education for the period, and became a butcher's apprentice. He soon owned his own shop, but when it became known that the meat he sold was often stolen, he fled the area. He became a smuggler and housebreaker, often in league with the Essex (or Gregory) gang, a brutal bunch who terrorised Essex, Middlesex and Kent. When a reward of one hundred pounds was posted for the gang's capture, two of its members were caught at a tavern in Westminster; Turpin escaped by jumping through a window. Most of the gang were eventually brought to justice, except Turpin, who began his career as a highwayman.

At first, he worked with the pewtersmith, Thomas Rowden, but eventually he teamed up with Tom King; legend has it that they first met when Turpin held up his future partner. They operated from a cave in Epping Forest. By this time, the ex-butcher was notorious enough to be mentioned in the 1737 *Country Journal* as 'the famous Dick Turpin'. After he murdered an Epping Forest keeper who tried to arrest him, the reward for his capture was raised to two hundred pounds. In another scuffle, Turpin accidentally shot and killed Tom King. He then decided London had become too dangerous and moved to Yorkshire, posing as a horse dealer; in actuality he was a horse thief.

Finally, it was a minor incident that led to Turpin's arrest. He shot and killed a gamecock belonging to a tavern owner, and when he threatened to shoot the owner too, he was arrested. Under his assumed name of 'John Palmer' he was lodged in York Castle. His deceit was exposed when a letter to his brother was confiscated. Tried as a highwayman and murderer, Turpin was eventually hanged in York on 7th April 1739.

William Harrison Ainsworth was solely responsible for the mythology that now surrounds Dick Turpin, including his heroic ride to York on his trusty steed, Black Bess. In Ainsworth's hugely successful 1834 novel, *Rookwood*, Turpin is a minor character in the story of Luke Bradley and his efforts to claim his inheritance. Turpin first appears at Rookwood Hall, disguised as Mr Palmer, wagering that Dick Turpin will never be caught. He is shown throughout in an heroic light, although Ainsworth describes his criminal activities and his violence when roused.

The latter part of the novel focuses on Turpin's ride to York to escape arrest after the accidental shooting of Tom King. In a preface to his novel, Ainsworth claimed that this episode was written 'in one day and one night . . . My pen literally scoured the pages. So thoroughly did I identify myself with the flying highwayman that, once started I found it impossible to halt'. In the course of nine chapters, Turpin makes his escape on Black Bess, vaulting over the Hornsey toll-gate, dodging gunfire from the guard on the York Mail and finally collapsing within sight of York. He prepares to make his stand over the dead body of his faithful mare but is persuaded to flee. A postscript describes Turpin's eventual death on the gallows at York.

Rookwood was one of the most successful of the many Newgate novels which created a furore in early Victorian literature. The novel inspired several stage adaptations, but only the most popular appears to have survived in print. H. M. Milner's *Turpin's Ride to York* ran at the famous Astley's Amphitheatre from Whit Monday 1836. The arena was used mainly for equestrian events, so the emphasis of the piece was on Turpin's ride on Black Bess, who plays a principal role in the drama. There was plenty of spectacle, including the leap over Hornsey toll-gate. The play concludes with Bess's death and Turpin holding off the law, who throughout the tale are portrayed as bumbling fools. The published version did not appear until the 1880s.

W. E. Suter's melodrama, *The Adventures of Dick Turpin and Tom King*, published around 1859, tells an original story about the two highwaymen. In the village of Greenfield, a disguised Tom King is preparing for a robbery. Meanwhile, Dick Turpin, also in disguise, takes leave of Mary Watson, daughter of the local squire. Turpin and King meet, and after trying to rob one another, decide to join forces. However, Mary declares her undying love to Turpin and he promises to go straight after one last job. Turpin and King are interrupted while robbing the home of Squire Whimsey, and Turpin accidentally wounds King. He escapes with Mary, followed by Squire Watson and his men. Mary is killed after she comes between Turpin and their pursuers. A distraught Turpin is prevented from taking his own life, only to be led off to the gallows.

FACTIONAL WORKS:
William Harrison Ainsworth, *Rookwood* (London: Bentley, 1834).
W. E. Suter, *The Adventures of Dick Turpin and Tom King* (London: T. H. Lacy, [1859]). (P)
Henry M. Milner, *Turpin's Ride to York; or, Bonny Black Bess* (London: John Dicks, [1885]). (P)

FURTHER READING:
Derek Barlow, *Dick Turpin and the Gregory Gang* (London: Phillimore, 1973).

LEON URIS LIBEL CASE GB 1964

It is not unusual for an author to fictionalise a trial that he or she has attended, but it is rare to find a novel based on the author's trial experiences as the accused. In 1959, Uris published his best-selling novel, *Exodus*, a fictionalised history of the founding of the modern state of Israel. One sentence in the novel referred to the concentration camp at Auschwitz in Poland, and Uris stated that a certain Dr Dehring 'performed 17,000 experiments in surgery without anaesthetics'. Upon the book's publication in England, Dr Alexander Dering, a Polish physician who had moved to the UK after the war (at the same time dropping the 'h' in his name), brought an action for libel against Uris and his publishers.

Dering did not deny his presence as a surgeon at Auschwitz. Nor did he deny performing 17,000 operations, although he refuted the charge that they were 'experimental'. He maintained that they were necessary operations on suffering human beings, and in all cases an anaesthetic was used. The defence, led by Gerald Gardiner QC, conceded that some of the operations did employ anaesthetic, although he maintained that in most instances this consisted of a single spinal injection. As a result, the patients were still conscious during the proceedings and suffered terribly. Defence also conceded that only 130 operations were 'not ordinary operations', which could be categorised as the 'experiments' referred to in Uris's novel.

Dering impressed the jury with his medical record. He had worked in Africa after the war and had received an OBE for his services. Back in 1939 he was a member of the Polish Resistance, but was arrested by the Germans and forced on penalty of death to work in the hospitals at Auschwitz. During cross-examination by Gardiner, Dering had to admit that several sterilisation operations had been performed on perfectly healthy men. Also, the discovery of the hospital registers cast doubt on his claim that all patients were adequately anaesthetised. The defence produced witnesses to establish that doctors had refused to perform operations at Auschwitz with no threat to their lives; and that Dering had struck one patient and called her a 'damned Jewess' when she complained of the pain.

Ultimately, the jury had to find for the plaintiff, as Uris had exaggerated the number of experimental operations performed, but they showed their disgust for Dering's actions by awarding him the sum of one halfpenny, the lowest coin of the realm. Six years later Uris produced his novel, *QBVII*, which refers to courtroom Queen's Bench Number Seven, where the story's fictional trial is held. The trial in question is based on Uris's libel case.

The novel opens with the story of Adam Kelno's life after leaving post-war Eastern Europe. The British Foreign Office attempts to deport him from England for war crimes, but after serving in the Far East and subsequently receiving a knighthood, Kelno is able to bury himself in a working-class medical practice in London. It is then he is confronted with a book by Abraham Cady entitled *The Holocaust*, which mentions him in connection with supposed war crimes committed in Poland.

Uris then explores Abraham Cady's background, from his upbringing as Morris Cadyzynski in Russia, to his subsequent emigration to America where he anglicises his name. Following his service in the Second World War, he finds success as a novelist. He re-embraces his Jewish origins, which leads him to research and publish the book in question.

The last two-thirds of the novel focus on the trial of Abraham Cady for libel against Sir Adam Kelno. The case is an accurate portrayal of Uris's own experience. Despite suggestions of an ambiguous war record, the reader is not confronted with the truth of Adam Kelno's anti-Semiticism until the last pages of the book. The meeting of these two diverse characters, brought together in an Old Bailey courtroom, makes for an engrossing conclusion to a fascinating and entertaining novel.

FACTIONAL WORKS:
Leon Uris, *QB VII* (New York: Doubleday, 1970).

FURTHER READING:
Muriel Box, *Rebel Advocate: a Biography of Gerald Gardiner* (London: Victor Gollancz, 1983).

MARIA VERE GOOLD FRANCE 1907

Maria was already twice widowed (under mysterious circumstances) when she married an Irishman named Vere Goold. Although he was in line for a baronetcy, he was penniless, and the couple lived off the generosity of relatives. They ended up in Monte Carlo, where Maria styled herself Lady Vere

Goold. There they tried to gamble their way to wealth, but failed miserably. They subsequently made the acquaintance of a rich Swedish widow, Emma Levin, who loaned Maria forty pounds. After this had been gambled away, Mme. Levin demanded repayment. Maria invited the widow to their poor dwellings, Villa Menesimy. While the drunken 'lord' kept her occupied, Maria crept up behind Mme. Levin, smashed her skull in with a poker, then cut her throat. The couple dismembered the body and placed it in a trunk.

The Vere Goolds left Monte Carlo, taking the trunk with them. At Marseilles, they deposited it with a luggage clerk, with instructions to dispatch it to Charing Cross, London. However, the clerk was concerned about the smell emanating from the trunk and called the police. The Vere Goolds were called to the scene. Maria attempted to bribe the clerk, but he refused and the trunk was opened. When its horrifying contents were revealed, Maria and her husband were placed under arrest.

The couple stood trial in Monte Carlo. Maria claimed that while she and her husband were with Mme. Levin at Villa Menesimy, a stranger had burst in and stabbed the widow to death. They had hidden the body to avoid suspicion. The jury found them guilty; Maria was sentenced to death, her husband to life imprisonment. Maria's sentence was subsequently commuted, and she died of typhoid in a Cayenne prison. 'Lord' Vere Goold committed suicide shortly after.

In Marie Belloc Lowndes's novel, *The Chink and the Armour* (1912), Sylvia Bailey, a rich young widow, makes the acquaintance of Madame Wachner and her husband Fritz in the village of Lacville outside Paris. Lacville is a quiet place, its only attraction a casino. There Sylvia and her Polish friend, Anna Wolsky, also meet Paul, Comte de Virieu. Paul falls in love with Sylvia, but is unable to commit himself because of his obsessive gambling. Anna agrees to meet the Wachners at their villa and disappears later that day. Although the Wachners claim she never arrived, their maid contradicts the story. Sylvia becomes suspicious when she learns that a previous acquaintance of the Wachners died in a boating accident with Fritz at Aix-les-Bains. She too is invited to tea at the couple's home, where a trunk waits in an empty room . . .

FACTIONAL WORKS:
Marie Belloc Lowndes, *The Chink in the Armour* (London: Methuen, [1912]).

FURTHER READING:
George Dilnot, *Rogue's March* (London: Geoffrey Bles, 1934).

DON VICENTE SPAIN 1836

Don Vicente was originally a priest at a convent in Aragon. Following the Spanish Revolution of 1820, he moved to Barcelona and set up as a book-seller. He had a passion for rare books and kept the choicest items of his stock for his own collection. Then, in the neighbourhood a series of murders were committed, all with two common factors: the victims were all book collectors and their money remained untouched. One victim was found in the charred remains of his house, and for a time his death was thought to be misadventure. Then it was recalled that the man had outbid Don Vicente for a rare tome at an auction shortly before his death.

Police pursued the connection between books and the murders, and ended up at the house of Don Vicente. There they found the volume which should have been destroyed in the fire at the dead man's house. Faced with such incriminating evidence, the former priest confessed to the murders, his sole motive his consuming passion for books. At his subsequent trial, his defence tried to prove that the confession had been falsified, but Don Vicente was found guilty and executed. Apparently, the only time during his trail when he displayed any emotion was when he discovered that the stolen work was not unique—there was another copy at the Louvre in Paris!

The year of the Don's execution, Gustave Flaubert wrote a version of the story entitled 'Bibliomanie'. It was the fourteen-year-old author's first published work, appearing in the journal *Le Colibri* in 1837. The story later appeared in English translation in 1929, entitled 'Bibliomania'. Although Flaubert's version adapted the facts slightly, he added a twist at the end that would not have been out of place in the original case. This short narrative of overpowering greed and mania shows the promise of its young author.

FACTIONAL WORKS:

Gustave Flaubert, *Bibliomania* (Evanston, Ill.: Northwestern University Library, 1929). First published in French as *Bibliomanie*, 1837.

FURTHER READING:

Andrew Lang, *The Library* (London: Macmillan & Co., 1881).

FRANÇOIS-EUGÉNE VIDOCQ FRANCE 1775–1857

Like the British criminals Dick Turpin and Jack Sheppard, Vidocq's life story has been overshadowed by his legend until the two are inseparable. Vidocq himself added to his legend with his colourful and exaggerated *Mémoires*, published in 1828. He was born in Arras in 1775, joined the army and saw battle at an early age, supposedly fighting at Valmy and Jemappes. He often found himself in prison for petty crimes, but his persistence in escaping led to even longer sentences. In 1809, he volunteered to help the police as an informer.

With his penchant for disguise and his quick wits, he was so successful as an informer that he was offered the job of *chef de la Sûreté*. In his new role, he employed many ex-convicts and built up an effective spy system within the French underworld. His success was also his downfall, as he made enemies of powerful political figures. His opponents' intrigues eventually persuaded him to resign in 1827. He set up a paper-mill, but it soon foundered, and he was urged by Louis-Philipe's government to take up his old post once more. However, a second scandal led to his dismissal in 1832. Vidocq lived until the age of eighty-two, long enough to see Napoleon III take over the throne of France.

Vidocq was famous enough to have attracted the attention of the English press in the 1820s. His reputation came to the attention of dramatist Douglas Jerrold, who made him the subject of his 1829 play, *Vidocq, the French Police Spy*. Within the fictional framework of a robbery at a wealthy farmer's house, Vidocq dons the disguises of a German peasant, a beggar and a monk, to apprehend the gang responsible. His wife also helps in the investigation. It transpires that the farmer's son and his daughter's lover are members of the gang. Although Tom Taylor's *Ticket-of-Leave Man* (1863) is often cited as the first English drama to have a detective as its hero, Jerrold's play surely takes credit for that innovation.

The French novelist, Honoré de Balzac had the good fortune to meet Vidocq in 1834, at a dinner where the public executioner, Sanson, was also present. Balzac was fascinated by crime and the criminal mind, and Vidocq appears as Vautrin (and by a number of other aliases) in Balzac's *Comédie Humaine* series.

Vautrin is introduced in the 1835 novel *Le Pere Goriot* (*Old Goriot*), one of an assortment of lodgers at the Pension Vauquer; among the others is Old Goriot of the title, and Eugene de Rastignac, the main protagonist. De Rastignac has his eye on Victorine, another lodger who is shortly to come into some money. Vautrin proposes to help de Rastignac win the girl, in exchange for a share of the dowry. However, a plain-clothes policeman named Gondureau informs some of the lodgers that Vautrin is actually the ex-convict Jacques Collin, nicknamed Trompe-le-Mort (Dodgedeath). He had been arrested for a forgery he didn't commit. Gondureau intends to re-arrest Vautrin for another crime and asks for the assistance of the lodgers. The novel ends with Collin/Vautrin being led away to prison.

Collin makes a brief appearance at the end of Balzac's 1837 novel, *Illusions Perdues* (*Lost Illusions*), masquerading as the Spanish priest Father Carlos Herrera. Collin also appears in the sequel, *Splendeurs et Miséres des Courtisannes* (the novel was begun in 1838, posthumously published under this title in 1847 and was later translated as *A Harlot High and Low*). Collin attends the masked ball that opens the novel, where he is reunited with Eugene de Rastignac. In this story he also rescues a girl who attempts suicide, and again helps a young man to a profitable marriage. At the end of the novel, Collin offers his services to the police, and the reader learns that he went on to serve as the head of the Sûreté for fifteen years before retiring.

Collin's final appearance in a Balzac novel is at the end of *La Cousine Bette* (1847). One of the principal characters, the lawyer Victor Hulot, has to consult the head of the Sûreté and we learn that Collin has returned to his alias of Vautrin. Sadly, the character's career ends there, although there is some indication that Balzac had intended to include Collin in a later novel, but died before he could start it. However, Balzac did produce a play called *Vautrin* in which the convict finally played the leading role.

Vidocq was to reappear in fiction. In 1895, Dick Donovan produced another of his crime biography novels, *Eugéne Vidocq: Soldier, Spy Detective*. The bulk of the book follows his various encounters with the law, in most of which he is a victim of circumstance. He is captured, only to escape and be captured again. Unfortunately, the novel is no better than a poor magazine serial, with a number of anti-climaxes and repetitions.

A more successful attempt is Vincent McConnor's *I Am Vidocq* (1985). The novel is set in the year 1823, when Vidocq the police chief is confronted with several complex cases. A jeweller and a Spanish courtisan have both been murdered for the Tessier diamonds in their possession. Also, Le Diable Noir (The Black Devil) and his gang are looting the chateaux of France. McConnor dedicates his novel to the memory of Honoré de Balzac, and it is a worthy testament to Vidocq's career in fiction.

FACTIONAL WORKS:

Douglas Jerrold, *Vidocq, The French Police Spy* (London: J. Duncombe, [1829]).

Donovan, Dick. *Eugene Vidocq: Soldier, Spy, Detective* (London: Hutchinson & Co., [1895]).

Honoré de Balzac, *Old Goriot* (London: J. M. Dent & Sons, 1907). First published in French as *Le Pére Goriot*, 1835.

Honoré de Balzac, *Cousin Bette* (London: Hamish Hamilton, 1948). First published in French as *La Cousinne Bette*, 1847.

Honoré de Balzac, *A Harlot High and Low* (Harmondsworth, Penguin, 1970). First published in French as *Splendeurs et Miséres des Courtisannes*, 1839-47.

Honoré de Balzac, *Lost Illusions* (Harmondsworth: Penguin, 1971). First published in French as *Illusions Perdues*, 1837.

Vincent McConnor, *I Am Vidocq* (New York: Dodd Mead & Co., 1985).

FURTHER READING:

Rayner Heppenstall, *French Crime in the Romantic Age* (London: Hamish Hamilton, 1970).

MARY VOCE GB 1802

Mary Voce was the wife of a bricklayer and the mother of their two children. However, her independent behaviour caused her husband to leave her. In desperation or anger, she poisoned their youngest child. She was arrested and tried for murder. The trial at the Nottingham assizes took place on a Friday and she was sentenced to be hanged the following Monday morning.

Despite Mary's reputation and unrepentant attitude at her trial, two Methodist women spent the weekend in her cell, trying to bring her last-minute comfort. By Monday morning, they had converted the nineteen-year-old girl and she went to her death a transformed woman 'with a triumphant and heavenly smile on her countenance'. One of the Methodists was Elizabeth Evans, who told the story to her niece, Mary Ann Evans, who would later write under the name of George Eliot.

Fifty-seven years after the event, the story was reconstructed in the novel, *Adam Bede*. Hetty Sorel, the vain niece of Mr Poyser, leaves her illegitimate child under a bush because its crying disturbs her. She returns to find the baby dead and is arrested. Because of her refusal to answer questions at her trial, Hetty is sentenced to death. She is visited in the condemned cell by her friend, Dinah Morris, a Methodist preacher, who extracts a confession from her. Unlike Mary Voce, Hetty's death sentence is commuted at the last minute and she is transported for life.

FACTIONAL WORKS:
George Eliot, *Adam Bede* (Edinburgh: Blackwood, 1859).

FURTHER READING:
John Purkis, *A Preface to George Eliot* (London: Longmans, 1985).

WILHELM VOIGHT GERMANY 1906

Voight was a cobbler by trade, but had a history of petty crime and had served long prison sentences. In 1906, he was living with his sister in Potsdam and working as a shoe-machine operator. At the age of fifty-seven, Voight had lived through several decades of German military expansion and knew the deference shown to a high-ranking military officer. When he saw a uniform of a Captain of the Guards in a second-hand shop, he bought it with half his monthly wages. He wore it for one day and as expected, he was saluted by troops and fawned upon by civilians. He decided to put a plan into action.

Dressed in the uniform, he entered the Plotzensee area of Berlin and commandeered nine soldiers and one corporal. He then brought them to the nearby town of Köpenick, where he placed the burgomaster and town treasurer under arrest and sent the local police into the square to quell any disturbances that might arise. He returned to the treasurer's office and instructed the staff to bag all the loose money, over four thousand marks, claiming there was a discrepancy in the funds. He left Köpenick, with his troops still guarding the officials, and returned to Berlin. He hid the uniform in a shed in his sister's garden.

When the deceit was discovered, a reward of two thousand marks was offered for information leading to the arrest of the impostor. The left-wing press played up the story at the expense of the Prussian military. Voight was eventually captured with most of the money and the uniform still in his possession. At his trial in December 1906, he claimed that he had intended to steal only a passport at Köpenick, so that he could flee from poverty and his criminal record.

He was sentenced to four years imprisonment, but released in twenty months (it was rumoured on the orders of the Kaiser himself). After milking his notoriety on the music hall circuit in Germany, he left for America with his cherished passport, but returned to Europe just before the First World War. He died in Luxembourg in 1922.

German playwright Carl Zuckmayer's 1931 comedy, *Der Hauptmann von Köpenick* (translated as *The Captain of Köpenick*), was produced and published during the rise of an even more oppressive militarism than in Voight's day. Zuckmayer was a converted Jew, and used the story of Voight to ridicule the anti-Semitic forces gaining strength. The play opens as Voight is imprisoned for attempting to steal a work permit to gain respectability. While Voight languishes in prison, the playwright follows the progress of a captain's uniform, as it descends the social scale until it ends up in the second-hand shop. To emphasise the uniform's importance, we see the captain caught in a barroom brawl without this indication of his position. He is subsequently forced to resign his commission.

Voight is released from prison and buys the uniform from the second-hand shop. He decides to use it to steal a passport. The historical events unfold much as they did twenty-five years before, as Voight, unable to find his passport, steals the town's funds instead. The comedy ends with the erstwhile 'Captain' surrendering on condition that he receive a passport on his release from prison.

FACTIONAL WORKS:

Carl Zuckmayer, *The Captain of Kopenick* (London: Geoffrey Bles, 1932). First published in German as *Der Hauptmann von Kopenick*, 1931. (P)

FURTHER READING:

Stuart Gordon, *The Book of Hoaxes* (London: Headline, 1995).

THOMAS GRIFFITHS WAINEWRIGHT GB 1837

Thomas Griffiths Wainewright had a literary background. After the death of his father, he was raised by his grandfather, the editor of *The Monthly Review*. To support himself, Wainewright became a writer and artist and was soon recognised as a notable art critic. He moved in literary circles, numbering among his acquaintances Charles Lamb, William Hazlitt and Thomas de Quincey. Despite his success, Wainewright's finances could not keep pace with his lavish lifestyle. In 1829, his grandfather died under suspicious circumstances; he suffered a fit shortly after Wainewright had bought a quantity of strychnine. The grandson inherited the old man's fortune, but soon spent what was left after his creditors had taken their due.

Soon after, his mother-in-law and her two daughters moved in with Wainewright and his wife. The matriarch died in 1830, but Wainewright gained nothing from her death. However, he had insured his sister-in-law, Helen Abercrombie, for £18,000. When Helen died shortly afterwards, the insurance company refused to pay out. Wainewright sued but lost the case and fled to France. On his return to England, he was recognised and arrested for forgery. He was found guilty and transported to Australia. Later, he did admit to the murder of his sister-in-law (allegedly because he disliked her thick ankles), a crime for which he was never tried. He died in 1852.

It was his old friend, Edward Bulwer Lytton, who first saw the possibilities of using Wainewright as a character. In *Lucretia* (1846), there are not one but two poisoners: Lucretia Lavering and Gabriel Varney. Varney is the son of a French confidence-trickster, Olivier Dalibard. The novel opens as Dalibard takes his son to see his mother executed on the guillotine. Dalibard, whose knowledge of poisons has been handed down from the Borgias, corrupts both Varney and Lucretia, the wayward niece of an English knight. Dalibard marries Lucretia, who eventually poisons him and later poisons her second husband as well.

Meanwhile, Varney has insured his uncle for £6,000 and then poisoned him. However, he has to commit forgery to finally obtain the money. With the help of his stepmother, Varney then insures and poisons Helen Mainwaring, Lucretia's niece. A mysterious crossing-sweeper named Beck, threatens to denounce them, but is first killed by Lucretia. When Beck is revealed to be her long-lost son from her second marriage, Lucretia descends into madness. Varney is arrested for his forgeries and is transported.

Lucretia was the last of Bulwer Lytton's crime novels based on factual cases and shows a marked decline from his previous works in plotting and characterisation. The most powerful scene, the execution of Varney's mother, occurs within the first few pages. Fascinating as the trio of Dalibard, Varney and Lucretia are, the novel then descends into melodrama. The reviewer for the *Times* was particularly scathing, calling the book 'a disgrace to the author, a shame to us all'. However, Bulwer Lytton had taken the unusual step of applying to Wainewright's insurance company for the documents of the case—and even more surprisingly, he was sent them. In 1853 he revised the novel, so that Helen survives the attempt on her life.

In the Memorabilia book which he kept between 1855 and 1865, Charles Dickens had written the following outline for a story: 'Devoted to the Destruction of a man. Revenge built up from love. The secretary in the Wainewright case, who had fallen in love (or supposed he had) with the murdered girl'. In 1859, when the *New York Ledger* offered Dickens a thousand pounds for a story, he resurrected the Wainewright idea and produced 'Hunted Down'. It was serialised in *The Ledger* in August to September of that year, and appeared in Dickens's own magazine, *All the Year Round* in August 1860. It was published in pamphlet form in 1870, appended by facts of the Wainwright affair to acknowledge its basis in fact.

Dickens had seen Wainewright in 1837 when he was touring Newgate Prison with actor William Macready and writer John Forster. In Dickens's version, Wainewright is Julius Slinkton. Slinkton is suspected by an actuary named Meltham of insuring his niece and then murdering her. Meltham had been in love with the dead girl and is determined to avenge her murder.

He disguises himself as Beckwith, a dissolute alcoholic, and traps Slinkton into insuring him, in the hope that he will attempt another murder. When Slinkton falls for the plan, Meltham denounces him to the insurance investigator, Mr Sampson. Slinkton takes his own life. Although Meltham's revenge is complete, he dies a broken-hearted man.

The most authentic fictional version of Wainewright's life and times appeared in 1932. Ladbroke Black's *Prince of Poisoners* is well-researched, droll and entertaining. When the novel opens, the egotistical, psychopathic Wainewright is twenty-five. In debt, he flees London and travels to Mortlake, where he lodges with Mrs Abercromby. He falls for her daughter, Frances Ward, and marries her. However, debt forces him onto the charity of his uncle, who gives him free lodgings at Linden House. Wainewright responds by poisoning the old man and inheriting his property. Thus he embarks on his murderous career, moving from debt to wealth with the assistance of his bottle of strychnine.

The novel is full of narrow escapes from bailiffs and creditors, as Wainewright juggles his funds (and his murderous activities) while avoiding detection. Having achieved the 'artistic destruction' of Helen Abercromby, he turns his attention to Madeleine, his other sister-in-law. However, the Pelican insurance company discovers a forged note from Wainewright, and he flees to Belgium before he can be caught. He attempts to persuade Frances to follow, but she has finally become suspicious of her husband and refuses. While in Belgium, Wainewright stays with Paston, an old colleague. He persuades his friend to take out an insurance policy with the Pelican company and then poisons him.

Paston's daughter receives the insurance money, but before Wainewright can make overtures to her, he senses he is being followed and escapes to Brittany. There, a lawyer for the Pelican company finds him living comfortably at a chateau. He is arrested in Paris for some local offence and is sentenced to hard labour. On his release, Pelican persuade him to return to England (ostensibly to settle his claim with them) and he is once more imprisoned. Although the company have discovered his diary which recounts his murderous career, they are content with a prosecution for forgery. Wainewright is transported to Australia. There, he attempts to poison the fellow-servants who begrudge him his privileges. Assigned to a chain-gang at Port Arthur, he resorts to drugs to relieve his boredom and finally dies in an opium-induced trance.

Australian novelist Hal Porter created another convincing fictional Wainewright in his 1961 novel, *The Tilted Cross*. The novel covers the final months of Judas Griffin Vaneleigh, who has been transported for forgery, although poisoning has been his true method of sustaining wealth. He is contrasted with Queely Sheill, a man of strong Christian values who shows sympathy for Vaneleigh's fall in circumstances. At the house of Sir Sydney Knight, the two are joined in a struggle between good and evil, in which Sheill's innate honesty leave him open to exploitation and misunderstanding.

Sheill is arrested for a crime he has not committed and dies from gangrene after a failed attempt at escape. The novel closes as Vaneleigh too succumbs to illness; both good and evil reduced to the same end.

FACTIONAL WORKS:
Edward Bulwer Lytton, *Lucretia* (London: Saunders & Otley, 1846).
Charles Dickens, *Hunted Down* (London: John Camden Hotton, 1870).
Ladbroke Black, *The Prince of Poisoners* (London: Ivor Nicholson & Watson, 1932).
Hal Porter, *The Tilted Cross* (London: Faber & Faber, 1961).

FURTHER READING:
Charles Norman: *The Genteel Murderer* (New York: Macmillan & Co., 1956).

ISOBEL WALKER GB 1737

Isobel was the daughter of a labourer in the parish of Irongray, near Dumfries. When her father died, she was brought up by her honest and religious sister Helen. Isobel was seduced a local man named Waugh. When she discovered she was pregnant, she cut herself off from her sister and hid away from society to bear the child. Unfortunately, in August 1736, the baby died.

At that time in Scotland, there was a law intended to check the number of undisclosed infanticides. By this law, any woman bearing a child in secrecy would be assumed guilty of murder in the event of the child's death. Isobel was arrested. Her sisters prevailed upon Helen to say that she was aware of the child's birth and that it had died of natural causes. However, Helen's strong faith would not allow her to commit perjury, and she found herself the principal witness for the prosecution. Isobel was found guilty and sentenced to death.

Fortunately, the laws of Scotland recommended a stay of six weeks from the pronouncement of sentence to the day of execution. Helen promptly persuaded a local lawyer to draw up a petition explaining the peculiar circumstances of her sister's case. She then borrowed some money and set off for London on foot to present her petition to the Duke of Argyle. When she finally reached London, Argyle was so struck by her story (and her own amazing feat) that he shortly obtained a pardon for Isobel from the king. Helen returned to Scotland in time to save her sister from the gallows.

Sir Walter Scott was informed of this fascinating story by Mrs Helen Goldie, who had met Helen shortly before her death in 1791. Scott included the story of Helen and Isobel in his dense historical novel, *The Heart of Midlothian* (1818) which also focuses on the Porteous riots of 1736. These disturbances had been caused after John Porteous, captain of the Edinburgh City Guard, fired on an unruly crowd. He was tried for murder and then reprieved (coincidentally, it was once again the Duke of Argyle who had obtained the pardon). A mob stormed the Tolbooth, the Edinburgh prison known sardonically as 'the Heart of Midlothian', and killed Porteous.

In Scott's novel, the instigator of the riots is George Robertson, Effie Dean's seducer. Effie has been found guilty of the murder of her infant son and is also being held in the Tolbooth. Robertson is really a dissolute member of the noble Staunton family. Before he met Effie, he had also seduced and abandoned Madge Wildfire. Wildfire becomes mad with grief when her child by Staunton dies. It transpires that Effie's son has survived and has been sold to a band of robbers by Meg Murdockson, the mother of Madge.

The riot gives Effie an opportunity to escape, but she refuses to do so, relying on her innocence and her religious beliefs to save her. Her sister Jeannie sets off on her marathon walk to London, hindered by Meg Murdockson and her criminal associates. Meg wants Effie to hang in revenge for Staunton's abandonment of Madge and her subsequent descent into insanity. Eventually, Jeannie delivers her plea to the Duke of Argyle and Effie is released. She marries Staunton and they discover their child's whereabouts. When Staunton attempts to rescue him, the child unintentionally kills his errant father. In the meantime, Jeannie has used her new-found influence with Argyle to arrange her own marriage to the Presbyterian minister, Reuben Butler.

As with most of Scott's work, *The Heart of Midlothian* attracted many dramatists keen to adapt the novel for the stage. Daniel Terry produced a 'musical drama' which appeared in 1819 at the Theatre Royal in Covent Garden, London. Its three acts concentrate on the trials, presided over by the Earl of Oakdale, George Robertson's father. Oakdale investigates the riots and learns of his son's involvement. When he turns to Effie Dean's murder charge, Jeannie pleads for mercy and discovers in the nick of time that Effie's child has been saved by Madge Wildfire. George promises to mend his ways and the Earl blesses his son's union with Effie.

G. D. Pitt's play, *The Whistler; or, the Fate of the Lily of St. Leonards* (staged and published in 1833), concentrates principally on Effie and George's son, brought up by robbers and known as the Whistler. He saves a woman from drowning and after hearing her story, realises she is his mother; meanwhile, she has also recognised her son. When the chief of the robbers is killed, the Whistler kills the man who has committed the crime, as he has come to regard the chief as his real father. When he learns the man he has killed is in fact his natural father, who had come to rescue him, the Whistler shoots himself and plunges from a cliff. This sort of high-blown spectacle was expected by audiences of Victorian melodrama.

Captain Michael Rafter's 'opera', *The Heart of Midlothian*, was based not on Scott's novel, but on an adaptation by Eugéne Scribe and Eugéne de Planard entitled *La Prison d'Edinburg*, which took striking liberties with the original work. Jeannie's journey to London is not included, nor are the Porteous riots. Instead, Effie is raised by the Duchess of Arundel and George is the son of the Duke of Argyle. George is sent to Edinburgh to stop a gang of smugglers. Effie is arrested for murder, as in the original, but in Rafter's climax, the errant Madge returns the baby to Effie in a basket she lowers from her Tolbooth cell, while the prison goes up in flames.

However, it was T. H. Lacy's version that contained the most convoluted genesis of the now-familiar plot. The title page of his published text, *The Heart of Midlothian; or, the Sisters of St. Leonards* (1863) describes the play as 'adapted from Sir Walter Scott's admired novel, with Introductions from T. Dibdin's Play, W. Murray's Alteration of the same, Eugéne Scribe's Opera, and Dion Boucicault's Amalgamation of the above, Colin Hazlewood's Adjustment and Readjustment, J.B. Blackstone's Appropriation, and other equally Original Versions, together with a very small amount of new Matter by Thomas Hailes Lacy'. Most of those works mentioned in the title were either straightforward versions of Scott's novel or, as in the case of Boucicault's work, an unpublished text. Lacy's adaptation is a serious melodrama, following Scott's tale closely, diverging only at the conclusion of Effie's trial, when Jeannie's arrival coincides with not only the king's pardon but also George's appearance with the missing child.

FACTIONAL WORKS:
Sir Walter Scott, *The Heart of Midlothian* (Edinburgh: for A. Constable, 1818).
Daniel Terry, *The Heart of Midlothian* (London: W. Stockdale, 1819). (P)
G. D. Pitt, *The Whistler; or, The Fate of the Lily of St. Leonards* (London: J. Duncombe, [1833]). (P)
Capt. Michael Rafter, *The Heart of Midlothian* (London: C. Jeffery's, [1849]). (P)
T. H. Lacy, *The Heart of Mid-Lothian* (London: T. H. Lacy, [1863]). (P)

FURTHER READING:
W. S. Crockett, *The Scott Originals* (London: T. W. Foulis, 1912).

WILLIAM H. WALLACE CASE GB 1931

Of the twentieth-century English cases covered in this survey, the two most popular for crime faction writers have been those of Crippen and William H. Wallace. Unlike the Crippen case, the murder of Julia Wallace remains officially unsolved and has therefore attracted many speculative solutions.

On 19th January 1931, a message was taken for insurance agent William H. Wallace at his chess club. The caller, a Mr Qualtrough, had asked that Wallace visit him at 25 Menlove Gardens East in Liverpool to discuss a policy. When Wallace arrived at the club shortly after, the message was passed to him.

The following evening, Wallace went in search of Menlove Gardens East, asking several people for directions in the course of his two-hour journey. The address did not seem to exist. On his return home, he found his wife's body; her head had been smashed in with a poker. Four pounds was missing from Wallace's cash box. The police who were called to the house were struck by Wallace's calm demeanour. It appeared that the house had not been broken into; either Mrs Wallace had admitted the intruder or the killer had a key. Already there were several black marks against Wallace.

In April 1931, Wallace stood trial for his wife's murder. The prosecution case claimed that Wallace had fabricated an alibi for himself with the telephone call and the search for a non-existent address. They suggested that Wallace had bludgeoned his wife to death prior to setting out on his appointment. A mackintosh found under the body, according to the prosecution, had been used by Wallace to protect himself from bloodstains.

The defence argued that the estimated time of death given by the pathologist clashed with evidence given by the milk-boy. If the latter was right about the time Mrs Wallace had paid him, Wallace had only twenty minutes to commit the crime, a very narrow margin for a prepared murder. Also, the killing had been a particularly brutal one; Wallace was a frail fifty-two-year-old. Despite a cautious and favourable summing-up by the judge, the jury found Wallace guilty of murder. The case was then referred to the Court of Appeal, where the verdict was overturned on the grounds that it was not supported by the evidence. Wallace, a free man, returned to work, but malicious rumour continued to pursue him, and he died in 1933.

Recent opinion holds that the killer was Richard Parry, a colleague of Wallace's known to Julia. On the night of the crime, Parry's car was taken to a garage where bloodstains and a bloody glove were discovered. Parry claimed to have been with his girlfriend that night, and police did not pursue investigations with him, convinced that they had their murderer in Wallace.

The first fictional work based on the Wallace case appeared the year after his death. *The Jury Disagrees* by George Goodchild and Bechofer Roberts presents the story of John Hamilton Tanner, a travelling salesman for a wireless company. Tanner is called out by a Mr Clayton to repair a broken radio; the same night, his wife is battered to death. Tanner is tried for the murder. When the jury withdraw to reach a verdict, each of the twelve jurors investigates a different part of the evidence. Much of this evidence duplicates that in the Wallace case: a telephone call to a club, a mackintosh found at the scene of the crime, a discrepancy over time of murder. Tanner does find Mr Clayton, but it transpires that he left no message. After the jury return their verdict, one of their number finds a vital clue that leads to the real murderer.

Winifred Duke's 1935 novel, *Skin for Skin*, returns a guilty verdict against the Wallace character, here called William Bruce. Duke leaves no doubt that the Liverpool insurance salesman planned and committed the murder of his wife. As with the Wallace trial, his lack of emotion tells against him but he is eventually freed because of insufficient evidence to convict. As in her previous novel, *Bastard Verdict* (see entry on 'Harold Greenwood Case'), Duke is as fascinated by Bruce's ultimate ostracisation as she is by the crime for which he was accused.

Detective novelist John Rhode was obviously fascinated by the Wallace case, which formed the basis of two of his Dr Priestley novels. In *Vegetable Duck* (1944) the suspected poisoner Fransham follows a telephone appointment to a non-existent address on the day of his wife's murder. Even closer to the original story is his 1948 novel, *The Telephone Call*, in which the central characters are William and Julia Ridgewell. Most of the Wallace details are here: phone call to chess club, non-existent caller and address, bludgeoning of victim, raincoat under body. Although the local police suspect Ridgewell, they call in Scotland Yard's Detective Superintendent Jimmy Waghorn. Waghorn's friend Priestley suggests that the answer to Julia Ridgewell's death might be found in her life prior to her marriage; it is from the actions of her fictional friends and relations that the eventual motive of the real murderer is discovered.

In 1950 Douglas G. Browne set his detective, Harvey Tuke, on the Wallace trail. *Death in Perpetuity* introduces Tuke, an employee of the Department of Public Prosecutions, to Walter Eustiss and his niece Harriet Audrey at a party. Eustiss had been found guilty of his wife's murder years ago, in circumstances duplicating the Wallace trial, although the verdict had later been overturned on appeal.

After the party, Eustiss is knocked unconscious by a mystery assailant and Tuke, investigating the attack, finds himself re-opening the original case. Another woman is bludgeoned to death and the murderer himself is killed, before the solution is provided. The complex motive for Browne's tale, relying on distant history, is at odds with the apparently simple motive of theft suggested for the Wallace case.

Marten Cumberland transfers events from Liverpool to Paris in his Saturnin Dax novel, *One Foot in the Grave* (1952), in which the guilty verdict against Wallace, here called Thollon, is once again overturned. Unlike most of the factional treatments of the Wallace case, Cumberland presents his novel as an inverted detective story, where the murderer is known from the beginning. The interest lies in watching Saturnin Dax follow the clues that lead him to the culprit.

In Edna Sherry's 1961 novel, *Call the Witness*, the principal feature of an alibi through a telephone appointment is employed in an entirely different set of circumstances. Sherry's ultimate solution couldn't possibly have applied to the Wallace mystery. Leslie Egan's *Borrowed Alibi* (1962) finds the basic premise of the Wallace case transferred to contemporary America. When a young insurance salesman is arrested for the murder of his wife, police detective Vic Varrallo and his colleague Sergeant O'Connor recognise the similarities between this and the 1931 British case. They search for a killer who has borrowed details from the original, but the solution is original to Egan's story.

Hilary Waugh's *Prisoner's Plea* also moves the case to America. Fred C. Fellows, the Chief of Police in Stockport, Connecticut, receives a letter from Ernest Sellers, who is on Death Row for his wife's murder. Sellers persuades Fellows to re-investigate his case. The final conclusions are based strongly on suggestions put forward by the prosecution at Wallace's trial.

In 1968, Angus Hall's novel, *Qualtrough*, adds a fictional continuation to the original trial. Adam Arthur Crosse is a journalist searching for an address in order to conduct an interview. Unsuccessful in his search, he returns home to find his wife murdered. He is accused of the crime but is eventually acquitted. After the trial, Crosse is visited by a man named Qualtrough who claims to be the mysterious interviewee. Apart from the title character's name, Hall also includes a number of direct quotes from the 1931 trial. His novel is an intriguing study of a psychopathic personality.

John Hutton's *29 Herriott Street* (1979) begins with the execution of Wilfred Rimner for his wife's murder. Forty years on, a reporter investigating the facts concludes that Rimner was innocent, and constructs his own theory (one that the author, in acknowledging his source, says 'is not intended as a solution' to the original).

The most faithful Wallace treatment was published in 1978. Nine years after producing a factual investigation of the case, *The Killing of Julia Wallace*, Jonathan Goodman produced a fictional account in his novel, *The Last Sentence*. A criminologist, who is also the narrator, is studying the killing of James Willis, who had confessed to the murder of his wife in 1948. His conviction was subsequently overturned by the Court of Appeal. In tracking down the facts of his murder, the narrator finds himself re-investigating the older case as well. Goodman skilfully blends the facts of the Wallace case with his modern fictional crime. A humorous touch is that Goodman's fictional criminologist is the author of a book called *The Killing of Julia Willis*!

FACTIONAL WORKS:

George Goodchild and Bechofer Roberts, *The Jury Disagrees* (London: Hodder & Stoughton, 1934). (P)
Winifred Duke, *Skin for Skin* (London: Victor Gollancz, 1935).
John Rhode, *Vegetable Duck* (London: Collins, 1944).
John Rhode, *The Telephone Call* (London: Geoffrey Bles, 1948). US title: *Shadow of an Alibi*.
Douglas G. Browne, *Death in Perpetuity* (London: Macdonald, 1950).
Marten Cumberland, *One Foot in the Grave* (London: Hurst & Blackett, [1952]).
Edna Sherry, *Call the Witness* (New York: Dodd Mead, [1961]).
Leslie Egan, *Borrowed Alibi* (New York: Harper & Row, 1962).
Hilary Waugh, *Prisoner's Plea* (New York: Doubleday, 1963).
Angus Hall, *Qualtrough* (London: Jenkins, 1968).
Jonathan Goodman, *The Last Sentence* (London: Hutchinson & Co., 1978).
John Hutton, *29 Herriot Street* (London: Bodley Head, 1979).

FURTHER READING:

Roger Wilkes, *Wallace: The Final Verdict* (London: Bodley Head, 1984).

CHARLES WALTON MURDER GB 1945

Charles Walton, a hedge-cutter, lived with his niece in Lower Quinton, Warwickshire. On Valentine's Day 1945, he left home at nine o'clock in the morning. When he had still not returned by six that evening, his niece persuaded two neighbours to help her look for him. His body was discovered on the slopes of Meon Hill; it was pinned to the ground by his own pitchfork. His throat had been cut by his slash-hook and a sign of the cross had been carved on his chest.

The local police called in Scotland Yard for assistance and Detective Superintendent Robert Fabian was sent to Lower Quinton. He was met with silence in the local villages, although there were vague mumblings about witchcraft and the evil eye. In fact, a similar murder had been committed in nearby Long Compton eighty years before; the victim had been suspected of witchcraft. Fabian organised aerial photographs of the village and called for mine detectors to search for Walton's missing watch, in the hopes that it might bear fingerprints. These efforts brought no results and the case remains officially unsolved.

It is appropriate that a case redolent of black magic and witchcraft should form the basis for a horror thriller rather than a straightforward detective novel. Jack Gerson's *The Evil Thereof* (1991) finds Eric Braden, a reporter on a tabloid paper, assigned to a series of articles on unsolved murders. He decides to write on a crime committed twelve years earlier in Warwickshire, in which Joshua Gideon was found pinned to a tree with a pitchfork.

When Braden returns to the scene of the crime, he is met with apathy and even threats from the villagers of Lower Calderon. An interview with the Scotland Yard detective who had investigated the case, and suffered a nervous breakdown as a result, puts Braden on the track of a close-knit community dabbling in black magic. Gerson uses the Walton case as an effective basis for a contemporary but mundane horror tale.

FACTIONAL WORKS:
Jack Gerson, *The Evil Thereof* (London: Piatkus, 1991).

FURTHER READING:
Bernard Taylor and Stephen Knight, *Perfect Murder* (London: Grafton, 1987).

JOHN SELBY WATSON GB 1872

The son of poor parents, Watson was educated with the assistance of his grandfather and gained a place at Trinity College, Dublin. He was ordained in 1839 and became a curate in Somerset. In 1844 he moved to London to accept the post of headmaster at Stockwell Grammar School. This enabled him to marry Anne Armstrong, his fiancé of twenty years, who until then he had been unable to support. By this time, Reverend Watson had acquired a significant reputation as a classical scholar, but his writings and his position as headmaster did not bring in a great deal of money.

For twenty-six years, Watson combined school administration with translations of the classics and theological studies. Despite his efforts, the number of pupils declined, and in 1870 the board of governors dismissed him without a pension. At sixty-six, with no position or financial security, he fell into a depression. Colleagues noticed his distracted manner and black moods.

On 8th October 1871, the Reverend announced to the family maid that his wife had gone away for a while. Two days later, Watson was found unconscious, having attempted suicide with prussic acid. A note explained that he had killed his wife 'in a fit of rage to which she provoked me'. Anne Watson's body was discovered in a bedroom; she had been bludgeoned to death with a pistol butt. Watson was revived and charged with murder.

Tried at the Old Bailey in January of the following year, his defence was temporary insanity. He was found guilty with a recommendation to mercy. The sentence of death was commuted to life imprisonment. Watson lived the rest of his life in Parkhurst Prison, where he died in 1884.

Beryl Bainbridge's 1984 novel, *Watson's Apology*, is a well-researched, often blackly humorous account of the events leading up to the murder. The reader is presented with a series of letters (including those from Watson himself), court records and newspaper reports, which Bainbridge declares as authentic, if 'edited here and there to fit the needs of the narrative'. The story recounts a marriage soured and stifled by convention, suspicion and eventual disappointment. Bainbridge provides a convincing reconstruction of Mrs Watson's last hours, and the circumstances that drove the meek teacher to commit such a vicious act. The final chapter covers Watson's last lonely years in prison as he reflects on the actions that led him to his incarceration, and provide a fitting and moving epilogue to a sympathetic portrayal of a man pushed to his limit.

FACTIONAL WORKS:
Beryl Bainbridge, *Watson's Apology* (London: Duckworth, 1984).

FURTHER READING:
Richard S. Lambert, *When Justice Faltered* (London: Methuen, 1935).

KATE WEBSTER GB 1879

Webster, who already had a string of convictions for robbery, was thirty years old when she became housekeeper to Mrs Julia Thomas of Richmond in Surrey. The brash Irishwoman and the strong-willed widow were a mismatch from the start. On 2nd March 1879, during a violent quarrel, Webster struck her employer with an axe. She then proceeded to dismember the corpse. Parts of the body were boiled down, packaged and disposed of around Richmond. Webster sold Mrs Thomas's jewellery and with the help of John Church, a local landlord, disposed of the furniture.

When neighbours became suspicious, Webster fled to Ireland. She was arrested in Killane, wearing her former employer's clothes. She was tried at the Old Bailey in July. By this time, parts of Mrs Thomas's body had been recovered and the prosecution were able to construct a scenario of the events of that fateful day. The former housekeeper denied the charge, accusing a number of other parties of the crime, including Church. She was found guilty and, after finally confessing to the murder, was hanged on 29th July.

In 1974, John Cashman devoted his well-researched novel, *Cook General,* to the Webster case. The narrative begins with Webster's appointment as housekeeper, and follows the story to the point of her execution. Within this framework, Cashman explores Webster's earlier criminal career and her relationship with Strong, a previous associate in crime and the father of her child. The author attempts to evoke sympathy for Webster, a difficult task, given the brutal nature of the murder. Cashman sees the event as an act of impulse, brought on by Mrs Thomas's threat to call the police when she suspects Webster of stealing.

Cashman indicates in a preface that 'no facts positively proved have been altered'. As appendices, the book includes a discussion of aspects of the case, Webster's five conflicting statements to the police (including her final confession) and a glossary of thieves' slang used in the novel.

FACTIONAL WORKS:
John Cashman, *Cook General* (New York: Harper & Row, 1974).

FURTHER READING:
Richard and Molly Whittington-Egan, *The Bedside Book of Murder* (Newton Abbot: David & Charles, 1988).

JIM WILCOX USA 1902

William Cropsey, his wife and their four daughters moved from Brooklyn, New York to Elizabeth City, North Carolina in 1898. His seventeen-year-old daughter Ella, whose nickname was Nell, soon attracted the attention of Jim Wilcox, the son of the former county sheriff. Their sporadic relationship continued until 1901 when, on the evening of 20th November, Wilcox called for Nell at her home. She went out on the balcony to speak with him. Her sister Olive (Ollie) was the last of the family to see her alive as she left the house.

When she didn't return, William Cropsey went to see Wilcox, who claimed that he had argued with Nell and had walked off. The last thing he saw, he stated, was Nell crying on the balcony. Nell's disappearance attracted local and national press coverage. A tracker was sent to assist in the hunt; his hounds took him to the pier on the Pasquotank River, which ran along the front of the Cropsey's home. A medium was employed, but had no further results.

Thirty-seven days after she vanished, Nell's body was fished out of the Pasquotank. An inquest ruled that she had been murdered by a blow to the head. Jim Wilcox was held for questioning by the police. Nell's father had to dissuade a mob from breaking into the jail and lynching Wilcox on the spot. In an atmosphere of hatred and prejudice, Jim Wilcox stood trial the following year.

His lawyer called no witnesses, not even Jim himself, relying instead on the weakness of the circumstantial evidence and on his own closing speech.

However, the jury found Wilcox guilty and he was sentenced to death. An appeal to the Supreme Court resulted in a verdict of mistrial, due to a number of public outbursts in court directed against the defendant. Wilcox was retried in another county, found guilty of second-degree murder and sentenced to thirty years imprisonment. Released in 1918, Wilcox returned to Elizabeth City, where on 4th December 1934, he put a shotgun to his head and killed himself.

In 1993, local-born country singer and novelist Bland Simpson published his 'nonfiction novel', *The Mystery of Beautiful Nell Cropsey*. Apart from an unidentified narrator, the story of Nell's death is told by three people: Jim Wilcox, Ollie Cropsey and W. O. Saunders, the latter a famous newspaper editor who began his career by covering the Wilcox trial. They each give their own version of events. The mystery of the title is evident—apart from Wilcox himself, two others involved in the case committed suicide and Saunders, who may have heard the truth from Wilcox, died in a car crash in 1940.

The mystery of Nell's death is still unsolved at the end, but Simpson captures the atmosphere of a newly-civilised American town, where a brutal death can release the savagery, hate and prejudice hidden beneath a veneer of respectability. The book is illustrated with maps and photos, and contains a bibliography and a chronology of events. Despite the description of the work as non-fiction, there is no doubt that with its suppositious conversations and emotions, this is a factional novel. As with Truman Capote's *In Cold Blood*, the boundary between fiction and fact is narrowly skirted.

FACTIONAL WORKS:
Bland Simpson, *The Mystery of Beautiful Nell Cropsey* (Chapel Hill, N.C.: University of North Carolina Press, 1993).

FURTHER READING:
John Harden, *The Devil's Tramping Ground and Other North Carolina Mystery Stories* (Chapel Hill, N.C.: University of North Carolina Press, 1949).

JONATHAN WILD GB 1725

Wild was born in 1683 in Wolverhampton. He moved to London, where in 1710, he was imprisoned for debt. On his release he ran a brothel, receiving stolen goods on the side. Later, he would act as a middleman, taking details of the stolen property that passed through his hands and offering to recover items for a price. As he was never in possession of the stolen goods himself, he was able to avoid prosecution. He even went as far as advertising his services as a receiver in the press.

By this self-publicity, Wild cunningly built a reputation for himself as an honest man. As the so-called 'Thief-Taker General', he was able to bribe members of criminal gangs to inform on each other, using his knowledge of their receivership. He perfected his middleman technique, opening a sort of lost property office at the Old Bailey itself. The authorities tried to curtail his activities via the Receiving Act of 1717, which became known as the 'Jonathan Wild Act', whereby a person returning stolen property to its owner could only accept money for doing so if he assisted in the arrest of the thief. Wild used a go-between to collect his fees.

Wild's greatest coup was capturing the famous housebreaker and escapologist, Jack Sheppard. After Sheppard's execution in 1724, however, the authorities began to plan the downfall of the thief-taker general himself. Wild was arrested for a minor misdemeanour and was kept in prison while more evidence was collected against him. Finally, he was tricked into incriminating himself. Although convicted under the 1717 Act, which should have carried a sentence of transportation, Wild was sentenced to death. After a botched attempt at suicide by drinking laudanum, the 'thief-taker' followed his many victims to Tyburn on 25th May 1725.

Apart from his role as villain in the various factional treatments of Jack Sheppard, Wild appeared in two other works, including one of the earliest novels in the crime faction genre. Henry Fielding saw Jonathan Wild—corrupt, selfish, concerned only with profit and wealth—as a reflection of the grasping politicians of his time, in particular Sir Robert Walpole. Fielding's 1743 novel, ironically entitled *The History of the Life of the Late Mr Jonathan Wild the Great*, presents a fictional life story of the thief-taker, with many veiled references to Walpole's tainted ministry.

Wild is instructed in felony by the villainous under-sheriff Mr Snap and a French gambler, the Count de la Ruse. He repays each of his tutors in kind—with dishonesty. Wild marries Snap's daughter, Letitia, his equal in greed and corruption. He then decides to hound an old schoolfriend, Heartfree, a naive jeweller with a loving wife and family. He arranges for Heartfree to be ruined and thrown into prison. In the meantime, he kidnaps Mrs Heartfree and attempts to seduce her on board a ship bound for Holland. But his abused and betrayed band of thieves, whose loot he has fenced and sold at great profits, turn on him. He is thrown into prison himself, while Heartfree is pardoned and reunited with his wife. The novel ends with the defeated thief-taker on his way to the gallows, venting his spleen on society.

In 1929, Edwin Justus Mayer used Fielding's novel as the basis for his drama, *Children of Darkness*. Mayer's play is set in Mr Snap's house, where Jonathan Wild and Count de la Ruse are just two of a varied bunch of lodgers, mainly prisoners from Newgate who pay for better accommodation than the jail can provide. The proud and corrupt Letitia Snap uses her charms to seduce all the 'guests', provoking them to jealousy and mutual hatred, although she has particular designs on the Count. He and Mr Snap attempt to steal Wild's money on the day of his execution, by giving him the false hope that he can buy a pardon. By the end of the play, Letitia has been so successful in masking her interest in the Count with contempt, that in desperation he commits suicide. She is left to look elsewhere for comfort.

FACTIONAL WORKS:
Henry Fielding, 'The History of the Life of the Late Mr Jonathan Wild the Great', in *Miscellanies, vol. 3* (London: A. Millar, 1743).
Edwin Justus Mayer, *Children of Darkness* (New York: Liveright, 1929). (**P**)

FURTHER READING:
Gerald Howson, *Thief-Taker General* (London: Hutchinson & Co., 1970).

JOHN WILLIAMS GB 1811

The gruesome nature of the Ratcliffe Highway Murders created a public panic, similar to the one caused by Jack the Ripper later in the century, in an area as infamous as nearby Whitechapel for its crime and poverty. On 7th December 1811, a servant-girl was sent by her master, a hosier named Timothy Marr, to buy oysters for the family's supper. She returned to find Marr, his wife Cecilia, their baby and apprentice John Goen, all murdered; their heads had been beaten in and their throats cut.

Twelve days later, a lodger at the nearby King's Arms woke to the sound of scuffling. When he went to investigate, he saw a mysterious figure bending over a bloody corpse. He ran back to his room and escaped through the window by knotting sheets together to form a rope. He fetched the local watchman, who discovered at the inn the bodies of the landlord Mr Williamson, his wife and their maid-servant, all horribly beaten and mutilated.

A sailor's maul, a possible murder weapon, was discovered near the bodies. The government posted the considerable sum of five hundred pounds reward for information leading to the murderer. Meanwhile, local watchmen pursued their one clue—the maul—which had the initials 'J. P.' carved on it. This led them to John Petersen, a Swedish sailor. He was able to provide an alibi for the times of the murders.

However, a fellow lodger named John Williams had been seen near the King's Arms on the night of 19th December, and had returned to his lodgings the following morning with his shirt covered in blood. Williams was arrested, interrogated and locked in Coldbath Fields Prison. Before he could stand trial, he hanged himself in his cell. The authorities were convinced of his guilt, and gave him a showy suicide's burial. With the maul lying by his side, he was carted to a crossroads near the site of the murders, where a stake was driven through his heart and his body was buried in quicklime.

The case attracted the attention of Thomas de Quincey, who wrote of it in detail in his famous essay, 'On Murder, Considered as One of the Fine Arts' (1827). However, Williams's only factional appearance seems to be in Joseph Shearing's story 'Blood and Thunder', published in the 1938 collection, *Orange Blossoms.* Shearing takes certain liberties with the facts. As in life, the murderer commits suicide to escape the law, but Shearing provides three important changes. The Williams character is accompanied, even during the murders, by a yellow dog. After one of the killings, he attempts to escape disguised as a woman. Most intriguingly, however, Shearing tries to provide a motive for Williams's first murder; it transpires that he was the lover of the hosier's wife, who had rejected him in favour of her husband.

FACTIONAL WORKS:
Joseph Shearing, 'Blood and Thunder', in *Orange Blossoms* (London: William Heinemann, 1938).

FURTHER READING:
T. A. Critchley and P. D. James, *The Maul and the Pear Tree* (London: Constable & Co., 1971).

JOHN WILLIAMS GB 1912

George McKay, 'The Hooded Man', was tried under his alias, John Williams. He was convicted of murdering a policeman during a robbery. Before he was executed, he supplied one of the most memorable quotes in criminological history.

Williams had a record of theft. In 1912, he was living in Eastbourne with Florence Seymour, who was pregnant with his child. On the evening of October 9th, a man was spotted on the portico over the door to Countess Sztaray's South Cliff Avenue residence. The police were called, and Inspector Arthur Walls confronted the man and asked him to give himself up. Two shots rang out and Walls fell to the ground, dead. The intruder ran off into the night.

The following day a friend of Williams's named Edgar Power went to the police. He knew that Williams had murdered Walls, after discovering that Williams and Florence had hidden the gun. He volunteered to help the police trap the murderer and travelled with them to London, where Williams was arrested. Williams was returned to Eastbourne, his head covered with a hood, hence his nickname. The police instructed Power to tell Florence to hide the gun, and pounced as Power and Florence were searching for the weapon on the beach.

Williams stood trial at Lewes, defended by Patrick Hastings. Although the gun was a common make and could not be linked to the scene of crime, the accused was convicted on strong circumstantial evidence. Meanwhile, Florence had given birth to a son and brought the child to the condemned cell the day before her lover's execution. Williams placed a morsel of bread in his son's hand, saying, 'Now nobody can ever say that your father has never given you anything.'

Poet and novelist Cecil Day-Lewis read Patrick Hastings's own account of the trial, and was fascinated by the Judas-like character of Edgar Power. In his novel, *A Tangled Web* (1956), written under his pseudonym, Nicholas Blake, Day-Lewis gives particular emphasis to the psychology of the three principal characters. Daisy Bland is infatuated with the wastrel, Hugo

Chesterman, and in turn is loved by Hugo's friend, John Jacques (Jacko), a doctor and back-street abortionist.

Jacko's jealousy leads him to betray Hugo in the hopes of winning Daisy when his rival is out of the way. Day-Lewis draws an intricate picture of a close-knit trio who bring about their own destruction: Daisy by falling for the dubious Hugo, Hugo by his love for Daisy which leads him to his careless final robbery, and Jacko by his Iago-like intrigues. The monocled lawyer, Sir Jervaise, is a close fictional approximation of Sir Patrick Hastings, one of the last great advocates of the English bar.

FACTIONAL WORKS:
Nicholas Blake, *A Tangled Web* (London: Collins, 1956). US title: *Death and Daisy Bland*.

FURTHER READING:
Sir Patrick Hastings, *Cases in Court* (London: William Heinemann, 1947).

JOHN WAYNE WILSON USA 1973

John Wayne Wilson was a twenty-three-year old married bisexual with a long history of psychiatric treatment, who had been diagnosed as schizophrenic with suicidal and homicidal tendencies. Roseann Quinn was a twenty-nine-year-old teacher of deaf children who lived alone in New York. Although she was from a strict Catholic background, she and a group of female friends frequented the city's singles bars. It was at one of these bars, on New Year's Day 1973, that she met Wilson.

That evening, Roseann and Wilson went back to her apartment. There, either after or during sex, he stabbed and strangled her. By the time Roseann's body was discovered a few days later, Wilson had left New York, having first confessed the murder to his wife and his boyfriend. He was traced to his brother's apartment in Indianapolis, where he was arrested. During a police interview, he claimed that after sex, Roseann had turned on him and ordered him out of her apartment. However, he had told his wife and boyfriend that Roseann had berated him for his impotence. Five months later, while still awaiting trial, Wilson hanged himself in his cell with a sheet.

Novelist Judith Rossner read the news reports of the case and was fascinated by Roseann Quinn and the double life she led. Her 1975 novel, *Looking For Mr Goodbar*, reconstructs the Wilson case with the emphasis on the character of his victim. Teresa 'Terry' Dunn is a repressed Catholic girl who teaches deaf children by day and haunts the singles bars of New York by night. She is vainly seeking a lasting relationship through a series of one-night stands with a variety of men.

The novel recounts her youth, her strict upbringing and, most traumatically, an operation to straighten a deformed spine, which leaves her feeling self-conscious and afraid of commitment. Rossner gives several reasons for

Terry's craving for frequently sadistic sex: a lack of parental affection, the desertion of her first lover, and the fear that she cannot have children because of her curved spine. Her search for fulfilment ends one New Year's Day when she picks up Gary Cooper White, a Vietnam vet. She is unaware that White, who has just been propositioned in a gay bar, is in crisis over his sexual identity. Terry's cavalier attitude to sex leads inexorably to the tragic conclusion.

FACTIONAL WORKS:
Judith Rossner, *Looking for Mr Goodbar* New York, Simon & Schuster, 1975).

FURTHER READING:
Lacey Fosburgh, *Closing Time* (New York: Delacorte Press, 1977). Fosburgh uses fictional names for her protagonists, but her book is factual.

FILM ADAPTATIONS:
Looking for Mr Goodbar, d. Richard Brooks. US: Paramount, 1977. Screenplay by Richard Brooks, based on the novel by Judith Rossner.

THOMAS J. WISE GB 1934

In 1934, a book was published which shocked the British book-collecting fraternity. Its staid title, *An Enquiry into the Nature of Certain Nineteenth Century Pamphlets*, concealed the revelation of literary forgery on a grand scale. Although the authors, John Carter and Graham Pollard, did not name the forger outright, their bibliographical detective work left the reader in no doubt as to his identity: Thomas J. Wise, eminent book-collector, respected bibliographer and President of the Bibliographical Society.

Carter and Pollard were concerned by some pamphlets, supposedly first editions of lesser-known works by eminent authors such as Stevenson, Ruskin, Matthew Arnold and Elizabeth Barrett Browning, that were appearing in book sales at the beginning of this century. Carter and Pollard discovered that these pamphlets were printed on paper containing esparto grass and chemical wood, materials which were not available until after the dates of publication given. The inference was obvious—they were forgeries.

The 'detectives' traced the printers, who had assumed that they were legally producing facsimile editions, and found evidence pointing towards Wise as the instigator. After their revelations, Wise tried to accuse fellow booksellers and colleagues, but more evidence accumulated against him and he was ostracised by the bibliographic community. He died in 1937, his reputation in shreds.

Julian Symons's detective novel, *Bland Beginning* (1949), hinges on a literary forgery similar to Wise's. Symons creates a fictional lesser Victorian poet, Martin Rawlings, complete with biography and extracts from his work. When the poet's granddaughter is given what appears to be a first edition of his works as an engagement present, she and her fiancé find themselves embroiled in forgery, organised crime and murder. Symons's work is in the grand style of British detective fiction, complete with amateur sleuths and a dénouement at a village cricket match. In a postscript, Symons acknowledges his debt to Carter and Pollard's detective work.

FACTIONAL WORKS:
Julian Symons, *Bland Beginning* (London: Victor Gollancz, 1949).

FURTHER READING:
John Whitehead, *This Solemn Mockery* (London: Arlington Books, 1973).

ROBERT WOOD CASE GB 1907

Phyllis Dimmock was a prostitute who lived with Bertram Shaw in Camden Town. On 12th September 1907, Shaw arrived home early in the morning to find Dimmock's body; her throat had been cut. Although the police first suspected Shaw, he had an alibi for the time of the murder. Police attention then turned to Phyllis's clients, in particular a ship's cook named Robert Roberts. Roberts denied involvement in the murder, but claimed that Phyllis had received a mysterious letter from someone called 'Bert' and also a postcard signed 'Alice', arranging a meeting and featuring a drawing of a rising sun. The Rising Sun public house was one of Phyllis's meeting places for clients.

When the postcard Roberts mentioned turned up in the Camden Town lodgings, the police published it in the press, hoping someone would recognise the handwriting. Ruby Young, an artist's model, came forward. She claimed that the writing belonged to her lover, an artist named Robert Wood. Wood had told Young that he had met Dimmock at the Rising Sun. She had expressed an interest in postcards, so he sent her one on which he had drawn the picture. Wood had asked Young to give him an alibi for the 12th of September, and Young, convinced of his innocence, had agreed.

However, when she repeated the tale to someone else, it reached the ears of a reporter, who informed the police. Wood was arrested and identified as a man who had known Dimmock for a considerable time. Wood's trial began in December 1907. He was defended by the reputable Sir Edward Marshall Hall, who cast doubts on the integrity of the prosecution's witnesses and demonstrated that the case against Wood was purely circumstantial. When Wood himself gave evidence, he impressed both the jury and the judge, who summed up in his favour. He was acquitted and walked out of court to a jubilant reception. Ruby Young, on the other hand, had to be smuggled out of court to escape the crowd's wrath. The case made legal history, as it was the first time an accused person had given evidence on their own behalf (following the passing of the Criminal Evidence Act of 1898) and had been acquitted.

John Van Druten, a writer who was fascinated by crime (see entry on

'Rattenbury and Stoner'), adapted the Wood case in his 1932 play, *Somebody Knows*, However, in his version, a verdict is never reached.

Lance Perkins is a jobbing actor-singer, lodging at Mme. Malvinetti's. Another tenant in the house is Lily, an ex-prostitute whom Lance has promised to marry. He is fascinated by Lily's previous lifestyle, and confesses to Mme. Malvinetti's son Harcourt that all men, including himself, have a dark side to their personality.

However, Mme. Malvinetti's daughter, Eunice, harbours a secret love for Lance. When it appears that Lily has returned to her old ways, the scene is set for confrontation. Lily's strangled body is discovered in her room and Lance disappears. After a few days on the run, he returns to his lodgings, hungry and tired, and is arrested. He is defended by Sir Daniel Markby, who puts him in the witness box, where he makes a good impression. He is acquitted.

In an epilogue, a friend of Sir Daniel's proposes the theory that Lily had picked up a client, brought him home, where he had murdered her. Lance Perkins had followed Lily out that night, but had picked up another prostitute and had lost his virginity to her. Van Druten ascribed the play's commercial failure to the fact that there is no solution to the crime. In his autobiography, the author states that his intention had been to 'communicate the emotions created by an unsolved murder'; the public, however, had expected a straightforward whodunit with the killer named at the end.

Two other works based on the case are Austin Stone's 1953 novel, *In The Shadow*, and Hebe Elsna's *The Gay Unfortunate* (1958). Stone characters retain their genuine names, and he provides both motive and solution. Elsna's novel, like Van Druten's play, leaves a questionable doubt over the trial verdict; the suspicion still hangs over Roderick Channing, her fictional Wood.

FACTIONAL WORKS:
John Van Druten, *Somebody Knows* (London: Victor Gollancz, 1932). (P)
Austin Stone, *In the Shadow* (London: John Gifford, 1953).
Hebe Elsna, *The Gay Unfortunate* (London: Robert Hale, [1958]).

FURTHER READING:
John Ronald, *Murderer Mistaken* (London: John Long, 1963).

JOHANN WOYZECK GERMANY 1821

A forty-one-year-old ex-soldier and barber, Woyzeck found himself homeless and without a job in the year 1821. For some time he had been in a sporadic relationship with a widow named Woost, who was five years his senior. Although marriage had been discussed, the widow enjoyed her freedom and the opportunity to entertain other men. Because of this, Woyzeck would fly into fits of jealous rage, and had once pushed the widow down a flight of stairs.

On 21st June, Woyzeck was scheduled to meet Frau Woost in a park, but she failed to arrive. He spotted her in the street shortly after and escorted her home. However, when they reached her doorstep, she turned on him and ordered him to leave. Woyzeck pulled a knife from his pocket and stabbed her seven times, leaving her to die in the street. He was apprehended shortly after by the police and readily confessed to the killing. Because of rumours that he was insane, Woyzeck was examined by Dr Johann Clarus, who subsequently published two reports on the crime. Clarus came to the conclusion that, despite certain symptoms of mental instability, Woyzeck was legally sane at the time of the murder.

At his trial, Woyzeck was sentenced to death. Again, doubts over his sanity were raised and a petition was presented on his behalf. The judge appointed Clarus to re-examine him. The doctor interviewed the condemned man on five more occasions, but reaffirmed his original conclusion. Woyzeck was executed in August 1824.

Both of Clarus's reports, as well as other contemporary pamphlets concerning the case, were held in the personal library of Dr Ernst Büchner, the father of the German dramatist, Georg Büchner. In 1836, Georg began work on a play based on the case, but after his death from typhus the following year, the work remained unfinished. It was first published in 1875 and staged thirty-eight years later. However, early editions were unreliable (the title was misread from the illegible manuscript as *Wozzeck* until 1922), and the first philologically-correct edition did not appear until 1967.

The unfinished play is a masterpiece of early realism, a close reading of Clarus's reports of the case. Like the factual Woyzeck, Büchner's murderer is paranoid, hears phantom voices and sees visions of flames in the sky. In 1835, Büchner had fled Germany because of his political activities and radical writings. He brings many of his opinions of government and society to the character of Woyzeck, who is still in the army. Woyzeck's poverty and his feelings of social persecution and exploitation are contributory factors in the killing. How much of the fragmentary nature of the play is due to fact it was never completed is open to speculation. What is unquestionable is that this fragmentation of scenes, speeches and actions adds to the realism and immediacy, and at times almost documentary style, of its presentation.

FACTIONAL WORKS:
Georg Büchner, *Woyzeck* (London: Eyre Methuen, 1979). First published in German as *Wozzeck* in *Georg Büchner's Sämtliche Werke und Handschriftlicher Nachlass*, 1879).

FURTHER READING:
Ronald Hauser, *Georg Buchner* (New York: Twayne, 1974).

FILM ADAPTATIONS:
Woyzeck, d. Werner Herzog. Germany: ZDF, 1979. Screenplay by Werner Herzog, based on the play by Georg Büchner.

CHARLES TYSON YERKES USA 1871

Yerkes was born in 1837, the son of Quaker parents. He began work as a clerk for a firm of commission brokers, opening his own brokerage business in 1859, and subsequently his own bank in 1862. By 1871 he had become a powerful financial figure in his native city of Philadelphia. However, the Chicago fire later that year brought a rush on the stock market. Yerkes was arrested for fraud, tried and sentenced to just under three years. He was pardoned after only serving seven months of his term, and he began to work his way back up the ladder of high finance.

By 1875, he was the largest stockholder of the Continental Passenger Railway Company, which he had helped to found. He established a brokerage firm in Chicago, which enabled him to gain a stranglehold on the city's transit system. However, his was an empire established by financial chicanery and political corruption. When rival companies were set up, Yerkes brought them to heel by litigation and financial dealing. He bribed politicians and if, like Governor John P. Altgeld, they refused to be bribed, he ruined their political careers.

By 1897, his stock was rocketing on the exchange. However, his methods had created powerful enemies and press and politicians alike began to campaign against him. Despite heavy bribery, his candidates for the state legislature were defeated and he became a marked man. He sold his interests and moved to England in 1900, where he was instrumental in building the London Underground. However, by then he was a spent force and was almost bankrupt when he died in 1905.

It seems paradoxical that a character like Yerkes should attract the attention and admiration of a left-wing writer such as Theodore Dreiser. In the character of Frank Cowperwood who featured in a trilogy of novels—*The Financier* (1912), *The Titan* (1914) and *The Stoic* (1947)—Dreiser shows his ambiguous attitude to one of America's leading 'robber barons'. Yerkes, indisputably the model for Cowperwood, fascinated Dreiser as an example of Darwinian principles, especially 'the survival of the fittest'. Dreiser's trilogy illustrates the influence of commerce and capitalism on Cowperwood's psyche: his remorselessness is a direct result of his striving for wealth and position.

Cowperwood reflected certain aspects of the author himself; he is a believer in Darwin, a man of influence and an incorrigible womaniser. The Darwinian theme is raised early in the first novel, *The Financier*. Young Cowperwood watches a lobster in a tank devour a squid. The incident has a profound effect on the boy, who formulates his own rule of life: 'Things lived on each other'.

Cowperwood establishes his own brokerage firm. His ambition leads him to Edward Butler, a local politician and contractor. Butler also has a daughter named Aileen, with whom Cowperwood falls in love. With Butler's connections, Cowperwood involves himself in dubious dealings with city funds. However, in the financial crisis of 1871, he is arrested and convicted of grand larceny. After a short stay in prison, he re-establishes himself, financially if not socially. He divorces his wife and marries Aileen. However, he has lost none of his ruthlessness and, at the end of the novel, is moving from Philadelphia to Chicago for the richer pickings.

The Titan picks up Cowperwood's story as he continues to prosper, acquiring financial and political power. He has neglected Aileen, falling instead for Berenice Fleming, an ex-madam's daughter half his age. When he loses his position in Chicago, he leaves for Europe with Berenice.

The Stoic, completed by Dreiser's wife after his death and published posthumously, concentrates on Cowperwood's last years, his failing powers and his eventual death. Ironically, the author's own declining literary prowess, coupled with his own death before the trilogy's conclusion, only served to heighten the autobiographical aspects of the story in the eyes of some critics.

FACTIONAL WORKS:
Theodore Dreiser, *The Financier* (New York: Harper & Brothers, 1912).
Theodore Dreiser, *The Titan* (New York: John Lane Co., 1914).
Theodore Dreiser, *The Stoic* (New York: Doubleday, 1947).

FURTHER READING:
Charles Edward Russell, *Lawless Wealth* (New York: B. W. Dodge & Co., 1908).

CRIME FACTION COLLECTIONS

Crime faction was already well-established before anyone recognised it as a genre and decided to collect the best of its short works. American crime fiction critic and bibliographer James Sandoe was the instigator in his 1948 collection, *Murder, Plain and Fanciful*. He presented a selection of writings by various authors, some fictional, others based on fact (including Lillian de la Torre's short play on Lizzie Borden). More importantly, he included the first bibliography of crime faction—a recognition that the field was wide and diverse.

De la Torre herself produced several collections of her short pastiches concerning that unlikely eighteenth-century detective, Samuel Johnson. Many of these tales had their origin in crimes of the period. In her first collection, *Dr. Sam: Johnson, Detector* (1946), four of the nine stories are factional. 'The Flying Highwayman' is based on a villain of that name who prospered around the 1790s; 'The Manifestations in Mincing Lane' is a clever exposé of the Cock Lane Ghost fraud; 'The Conveyance of Evelina Grange' concerns the abduction of the title character to the Hebrides; and 'The Great Seal of England' investigates the 1784 disappearance of the Seal. The remaining five stories, although concerning contemporaries of Johnson, involve fictional crimes.

In de la Torre's 1960 collection, *The Detections of Dr. Sam: Johnson*, there are five factional stories. Apart from a fictional plot concerning John Donellan (see entry), Johnson investigates a genuine break-in at the home of Horace Walpole in 1771, he encounters Saint-Germain the charlatan and solves the fictional theft of the actual Ireland Shakespeare forgery. The American author also uses Johnson's tirades against the Colonies in his fictional comeuppance from a factual American spy. Subsequent Johnson mysteries collected by de la Torre have been based on fictional crimes, although the best of her factional Johnson stories, 'The Disappearing Servant Wench', remains uncollected by the author (see entry on 'Elizabeth Canning').

From the 1950s, several collections of short fiction based on the Jack the Ripper murders have appeared (see entry). As for general collections, three interesting selections have been produced in the last few years. Peter Lovesey's *The Black Cabinet* (1989) was the first substantial collection of various authors' attempts to present a variety of crimes in fiction. In addition to stories by Aldous Huxley, Harlan Ellison, Anthony Boucher and Osbert Sitwell (plus Lovesey's own story concerning George Joseph Smith) cited in the previous entries, there are other works by authors such as Angela Carter, Roy Vickers and Anthony Berkeley. Some of these fall outside the scope of the present survey, as they explore subjects such as political assassination.

Stuart Coupé and Julie Ogden's 1993 collection, *Case Reopened*, featured eleven Australian crime writers covering a selection of mysteries associated with their country. It includes convincing factional treatments of the Pyjama murder case of 1934 (in which Tony Agostini was found guilty of manslaughter), the Bogle-Chandler murders of 1963, the 1935 Shark Arm mystery and the suspicious death of Australian racehorse Phar Lap in America in 1932. All eleven works are original short stories especially commissioned for this collection.

The prolific Peter Haining brought together a mixture of fictional and factual retellings of true crimes for his 1994 book, *Tales from the Rogues' Gallery*. Works featuring Cezare Borgia, Jack the Ripper, the 1895 Crenshaw murder, Gilles de Rais and John Christie are offered from authors such as F. Scott Fitzgerald, Angela Carter, Arthur Conan Doyle and Robert Bloch.

Finally, mention should be made of one novel that manages to incorporate hypothesis on six different factual murders. Anthony Berkeley's *The Poisoned Chocolates Case* (1929) concerns a box of sweets sent to Sir Eustace Pennefather at his club. As Pennefather doesn't eat chocolates, he passes them on to Graham Bendix, who gives them to his wife. After eating them, she dies from nitrobenzene poisoning. Six members of Detective Roger Sheringham's Crime Circle (itself based on the Detection Club that Berkeley founded) try to solve the crime, which has baffled the police. They base their theories on the murderous careers of famous poisoners—Marie Lefarge, Christiana Edmunds and Carlyle Harris among them. Berkeley expanded his short story, 'The Avenging Chance', to provide Sheringham's solution to the Bendix poisoning. In all, a delightful potpourri with which to end this review of the genre.

FACTIONAL WORKS:

Anthony Berkeley, *The Poisoned Chocolates Case* (London: Collins, 1929).

Lillian de la Torre, *Dr. Sam: Johnson, Detector* (New York: Knopf, 1946).

James Sandoe, ed., *Murder, Plain and Fanciful* (New York: Sheridan House, 1948).

Lillian de la Torre, *The Detections of Dr. Sam: Johnson* (New York: Doubleday, 1960).

Peter Lovesey, ed. *The Black Cabinet* (London: Xanadu, 1989).

Stuart Coupé and Julie Ogden, eds., *Case Reopened* (St. Leonard's, Australia: Allen & Unwin, 1993).

Peter Haining, ed., *Tales from the Rogues' Gallery* (London: Little, Brown & Co., 1994). (**ss**)

CRIME FACTION BIBLIOGRAPHY

Although the present book is the first detailed study of crime faction as a literary genre, there are several books and book chapters that have served as stepping-stones in my search for further details of the field. Here is a selective list of works covering crime faction in general, and faction on specific crimes and criminals in particular.

Altick, Richard D. *Victorian Studies in Scarlet*. New York: W.W. Norton, 1970. A study of Victorian murderers, with several useful introductory chapters on Victorian writers' fascination with crime, including fiction and drama based on genuine crimes.

Barzun, Jacques and Taylor, Wendell Hertig. *A Catalog of Crime*. Revised and enlarged ed. New York: Harper and Row, 1989. A general bibliographic survey of crime literature, which indicates the basis in true crime of several novels and plays.

Bleackley, Horace W., ed. *Jack Sheppard*. Edinburgh: Hodge and Co., 1933. One of the Notable British Trials series. Contains a bibliography of fiction based on the Sheppard case.

Haining, Peter. *Buried Passions*. Sudbury: Spearman, 1980. A study of the William Corder case, which reviews in depth the early fiction and drama based on the Red Barn murder.

Hollingsworth, Keith. *The Newgate Novel, 1830-1847*. Detroit: Wayne State University Press, 1963. A survey of the novels of the early nineteenth century that fall into the 'Newgate fiction' field.

Kelly, Alexander. *Jack the Ripper: a Bibliography and Review of the Literature*. London: Association of Assistant Librarians, 1973. A comprehensive bibliography of books on the Ripper case. Section 4, 'Fiction and Drama', is of particular relevance, although Kelly tends to include modern Ripper-style fiction with little connection to the Victorian original.

Sandoe, James. 'Crime Clef'. *Wilson Library Bulletin*, December 1946. An annotated bibliography of crime faction, not all published. Sandoe helpfully gives facts and sources for the lesser known crimes. The first survey of the whole genre.

Sandoe, James, ed. *Murder, Plain and Fanciful*. New York: Sheridan House, 1948. Includes a revision of Sandoe's earlier 'Crime Clef' bibliography.

Stephens, John Russell. *The Censorship of English Drama, 1824-1901*. Cambridge: Cambridge University Press, 1980. Chapter 4, 'The Opposition to Newgate Drama', gives a useful overview of the censorship facing playwrights who adapted Newgate fiction for the stage, particularly Ainsworth's *Jack Sheppard*.

Winn, Dilys, ed. *Murderess Inc*. New York: Workman Publishing Co., 1979. Mary Groff's article, 'Ladykillers', gives basic facts of cases concerning murderous women, with brief lists of novels based on each crime.